Keto Cookbook Top 500 Ketogenic Recipes

Legal Notice

KETO COOKBOOK
TOP 500
KETOGENIC RECIPES

*The Absolute Best
500 Ultra Low Carb Ketogenic Recipes
for Maximum Fat Loss*

By: Angelica Nova

Contents

18

BREAKFAST RECIPES

Spinach and Cheese Egg Muffins [FA] [GF]

Serves: 4 / Preparation time: 5 minutes / Cooking time: 15 minutes

8 pastured eggs	¼ teaspoon salt
2 tablespoons butter	½ teaspoon pepper
2 tablespoons chopped onion	1-¼ cups grated Mozzarella cheese
1-cup chopped spinach	½ cup grated cheddar cheese

- Preheat an oven to 400°F (204°C) and prepare 8 medium muffin cups. Coat with cooking spray.
- Next, preheat a skillet over medium heat and place butter in it. Wait until the butter is melted.
- Stir in chopped onion then sauté until aromatic and lightly golden brown.
- After that, add chopped spinach to the skillet and cook until the spinach is wilted but still green. Remove from heat and let it cool.
- Divide the sautéed spinach and onion into the prepared muffin cups then set aside.
- Crack the eggs and place in a bowl.
- Next, season the eggs with salt, pepper, and Mozzarella cheese. Stir until incorporated.
- Pour the egg mixture over the spinach in the aluminum muffin cups then sprinkle grated cheddar cheese on top.
- Bake the egg muffins for approximately 15-20 minutes or until the egg is firm.
- Once the egg muffins are done, remove from the oven and let them rest for a few minutes.
- Take the muffins out of the cups and arrange on a serving dish.
- Serve and enjoy.

Per Serving: Net Carbs: 3g: Calories: 385; Total Fat: 30.4g; Saturated Fat: 16.4g; Protein: 24.3g; Carbs: 3.7g; Fiber: 0.7g; Sugar: 0.4g - Fat 72% / Protein 25% / Carbs 3%

Cauliflower Almond Fritters with Lemon Creamy Sauce [FA] [GF]

Serves: 4 / Preparation time: 10 minutes / Cooking time: 15 minutes

2 cups cauliflower florets	½ teaspoon garlic powder
¼ cup diced onion	2 tablespoons butter
2 pastured eggs	Coconut oil, to fry
½ cup almond flour	3 egg yolks
½ teaspoon turmeric	2 tablespoons lemon juice
½ teaspoon salt	¼ teaspoon paprika
¼ teaspoon pepper	

- Place the cauliflower florets in a pot then pour water to cover. Bring to boil.
- Once it is boiled, reduce the heat and cook the cauliflower florets for about 5 minutes.
- Remove the pot from heat and strain the cauliflower.
- Transfer the cooked cauliflower to a food processor and pulse until becoming rice form.
- Place the cauliflower rice in a bowl then add diced onion, eggs and almond flour.
- Season the cauliflower mixture with turmeric, salt, pepper, and garlic powder then mix well.
- Shape the cauliflower mixture into 4 medium fritters then set aside.
- Melt butter in a saucepan over medium heat then place the cauliflower fritters in the saucepan.

- Cook the cauliflower florets for approximately 3 minutes each side or until both sides of the cauliflower fritters are lightly golden brown.
- In the meantime, pour hot water into a blender and let it sit for 10 minutes.
- Next, preheat the coconut oil to approximately 95°F (35°C) then set aside.
- After 10 minutes, discard the water from the blender and place egg yolks and lemon juice into the hot blender.
- Pour hot coconut oil over the egg yolks then season with paprika. Blend the sauce mixture on low until incorporated.
- Arrange the cauliflower fritters on a serving dish then drizzle the sauce on top.
- Serve and enjoy.

Per Serving: Net Carbs: 3.8g: Calories: 284; Total Fat: 26.9g; Saturated Fat: 17.6g; Protein: 7.1g; Carbs: 5.8g; Fiber: 2g; Sugar: 2g - Fat 85% / Protein 10% / Carbs 5%

Spicy Green Omelets [FA] [GF]

Serves: 4 / Preparation time: 5 minutes / Cooking time: 15 minutes

8 pastured eggs	1 teaspoon sliced shallots
½ cup diced green bell peppers	1 teaspoon chopped green chili
¼ cup cooked green peas	¼ cup diced cheddar cheese
¼ cup chopped onion	¼ cup coconut milk
2 tablespoons chopped leek	2 tablespoons extra virgin olive oil

- Crack the eggs and place in a bowl. Stir until beaten.
- Add chopped green bell pepper, cooked green peas, chopped onion, chopped leek, sliced shallots, green chili, and cheddar cheese to the bowl.
- Pour coconut milk over the eggs then mix until combined. Set aside.
- Preheat a saucepan over medium heat then pour extra virgin olive oil into the saucepan.
- Once it is hot, pour the egg mixture over the saucepan and spread evenly.
- Cook the omelet for approximately 3-5 minutes or until the eggs are firm.
- Remove the omelet from the saucepan and transfer to a serving dish.
- Serve and enjoy.

Per Serving: Net Carbs: 5.1g: Calories: 284; Total Fat: 22.4g; Saturated Fat: 8.9g; Protein: 15.2g; Carbs: 6.4g; Fiber: 1.3g; Sugar: 1.9g - Fat 71% / Protein 21% / Carbs 8%

Creamy Kale Casserole [FA] [GF]

Serves: 4 / Preparation time: 5 minutes / Cooking time: 15 minutes

2 tablespoons butter	2 cups chopped kale
¼ cup chopped onion	½ cup heavy cream
2 teaspoons minced garlic	6 pastured eggs
¼ teaspoon salt	¼ cup cherry tomatoes
¼ teaspoon pepper	½ cup grated Mozzarella cheese

- Preheat an oven to 400°F (204°C) and prepare a casserole dish. Coat with cooking spray then set aside.
- Place butter in a skillet then melt over medium heat.
- Once the butter is melted, stir in chopped onion and minced garlic then sauté until lightly golden brown and aromatic.
- Add chopped kale to the skillet then pour heavy cream over kale.

- Season the kale with salt and pepper then stir well. Remove from heat.
- Transfer the cooked creamy kale to the prepared casserole dish then spread evenly. Set aside.
- Crack the eggs then place in a bowl. Stir the eggs until beaten then pour over the creamy kale.
- Sprinkle grated Mozzarella cheese over the creamy kale then top with cherry tomatoes.
- Bake the creamy kale for 15-20 minutes or until the eggs are firm.
- Once it is done, remove from the oven and let the creamy kale casserole rest for few minutes.
- Serve and enjoy warm.

Per Serving: Net Carbs: 6.7g: Calories: 292; Total Fat: 24.2g; Saturated Fat: 13.1g; Protein: 12g; Carbs: 7.6g; Fiber: 0.9g; Sugar: 0.6g - Fat 76% / Protein 16% / Carbs 8%

Sunny Side Up in Bell Pepper Bowls [FA] [GF] [F]

Serves: 4 / Preparation time: 5 minutes / Cooking time: 15 minutes

2 bell peppers	¼ teaspoon peppers
8 pastured eggs	3 tablespoons chopped parsley
¼ teaspoon salt	¼ cup butter

- Place 2 tablespoons of butter in a saucepan over medium heat then wait until melted.
- Once the butter is melted, cut a bell pepper into 4 rings then place in the saucepan.
- Drop an egg in each bell pepper ring then sprinkle salt, pepper, and chopped parsley on top. Cook for approximately 4 minutes or until the egg is set.
- Once it is done, remove the bell peppers with sunny side up from the saucepan and arrange on a serving dish.
- Repeat with the remaining bell peppers, eggs, and seasoning then arrange them all on a serving dish.
- Serve and enjoy warm.
- If you like, you can also sprinkle paprika over the eggs.

Per Serving: Net Carbs: 6.1g; Calories: 319; Total Fat: 25.3g; Saturated Fat: 13.2g; Protein: 16.4g; Carbs: 7g; Fiber: 0.9g; Sugar: 3.1g

Fat 73% / Protein 19% / Carbs 8%

Crunchy Almond Fluffy Pancake [FA] [GF]

Serves: 4 / Preparation time: 5 minutes / Cooking time: 15 minutes

½ cup almond flour	1 teaspoon grated lemon zest
¼ cup softened cream cheese	3 tablespoons butter
4 pastured eggs	¼ cup chopped roasted almond

- Crack the eggs then place in a bowl.
- Add softened cream cheese and grated lemon zest to the eggs then stir until incorporated.
- Pour the liquid mixture over the almond flour then mix well. Set aside.
- Preheat a saucepan over medium heat then ¾ tablespoon of butter in it.
- Wait until the butter is melted then pour a quarter of the pancake batter over the saucepan.
- Sprinkle a tablespoon of chopped roasted almond over the pancake then cook until done.
- Remove the pancake from the saucepan then place on a serving dish. Repeat with the remaining batter.
- Serve and enjoy warm.
- If you like, top the pancakes with fresh strawberries or avocados.

Per Serving: Net Carbs: 2.3g; Calories: 252; Total Fat: 22.9g; Saturated Fat: 10.5g; Protein: 9.2g; Carbs: 3.5g; Fiber: 1.2g; Sugar: 0.4g - Fat 82% / Protein 14% / Carbs 4%

Tomato Zucchini Cups [GF]

Serves: 4 / Preparation time: 10 minutes / Cooking time: 30 minutes

1 medium zucchini	½ teaspoon black pepper
¼ cup diced tomatoes	¼ teaspoon oregano
4 pastured eggs	2 tablespoons red chili flakes
¼ cup heavy cream	½ cup grated cheddar cheese
¼ teaspoon salt	2 tablespoons butter

- Preheat an oven to 400°F (149°C) and prepare 8 muffin cups. Grease each muffin cups with butter then set aside.
- Peel the zucchini then cut it into long thin strips.
- Line the coated muffin cups with zucchini strips then sprinkle diced tomatoes and cheddar cheese cubes in them.
- Crack the eggs then place in a bowl.
- Add heavy cream to the egg then season with salt, black pepper, and oregano. Stir until incorporated.
- Pour the egg mixture into each muffin cups then sprinkle red chili flakes on top.
- Bake the zucchini muffins for approximately 30 minutes or until the egg is set.
- Once it is done, remove the zucchini muffins from the oven and let them cool for a few minutes.
- Take the zucchini muffins out of the cups and arrange on a serving dish.
- Serve and enjoy.

Per Serving: Net Carbs: 4.8g: Calories: 300; Total Fat: 24.2g; Saturated Fat: 13.9g; Protein: 15.9g; Carbs: 5.9g; Fiber: 1.1g; Sugar: 2.5g - Fat 73% / Protein 21% / Carbs 6%

Veggie Coconut Pizza [GF]

Serves: 4 / Preparation time: 15 minutes / Cooking time: 27 minutes

¼ cup coconut flour	1 red tomato
5 pastured eggs	1 cup chopped baby spinach
½ cup unsweetened coconut milk	¼ cup sliced onion
1-teaspoon onion powder	½ teaspoon red chili flakes
1-½ teaspoons garlic powder	¾ tablespoon extra virgin olive oil
1-½ teaspoons Italian seasoning	½ cup grated Mozzarella cheese
¼ teaspoon baking soda	

- Preheat an oven to 375°F (191°C) and line a baking sheet with parchment paper. Set aside.
- Crack 3 eggs then place in a bowl.
- Pour unsweetened coconut milk to the eggs then season with onion powder, garlic powder, Italian seasoning, and baking soda. Stir until incorporated.
- Next, pour the egg mixture over the coconut flour then using a wooden spatula mix until combined and becoming dough.
- Roll the dough into a thin rectangle form and place on the prepared baking sheet.
- Bake the pizza crust for approximately 15 minutes or until the dough is firmly set.

- Remove the pizza crust from the oven and reduce the oven temperature to 350°F (177°C).
- Brush the pizza crust with olive oil then spread the chopped baby spinach over the crust.
- Cut the red tomato into thin slices then arrange on the pizza.
- Sprinkle grated Mozzarella cheese over the pizza then top with sliced onion and red chili flakes.
- Carefully crack the remaining eggs then slowly drop on the top of the pizza.
- Return the pizza to the oven and bake for 12 minutes or until the Mozzarella cheese is melted and the eggs are firm.
- Remove the pizza from the oven and let it warm for a few minutes.
- Serve and enjoy warm.

Per Serving: Net Carbs: 6.2g: Calories: 293; Total Fat: 22.8g; Saturated Fat: 12.5g; Protein: 15.4g; Carbs: 8.1g; Fiber: 1.9g; Sugar: 3.6g - Fat 70% / Protein 22% / Carbs 8%

Stir Fry Brussels sprouts Garlic [FA] [GF]

Serves: 4 / Preparation time: 5 minutes / Cooking time: 20 minutes

2 cups Brussels sprouts	¼ teaspoon pepper
¼ lb. ground beef	2 teaspoons red chili flakes
2 tablespoons butter	¼ cup water
1-tablespoon minced garlic	4 pastured eggs
¼ teaspoon salt	½ cup grated cheddar cheese

- Trim the Brussels sprouts then cut into quarters. Set aside.
- Preheat a skillet over medium heat then place butter in it.
- Once the butter is melted, stir in minced garlic then sauté until lightly golden brown and aromatic.
- Next, add ground beef to the skillet and stir until the beef is no longer pink.
- After that, add Brussels sprouts to the skillet then pour water over the Brussels sprouts.
- Season with salt and pepper then cook until the Brussels sprouts are tender. Add more water if it is necessary.
- In the meantime, crack the eggs then place in a bowl. Stir until incorporated then set aside.
- Once the water is completely absorbed into the Brussels sprouts, drizzle beaten egg and sprinkle red chili flakes over the Brussels sprouts. Stir until the eggs are set.
- Transfer the stir-fry Brussels sprouts to a serving dish then sprinkle grated cheddar cheese on top.
- Serve and enjoy warm.

Per Serving: Net Carbs: 4.4g: Calories: 284; Total Fat: 22.1g; Saturated Fat: 10.9g; Protein: 15.8g; Carbs: 6.2g; Fiber: 1.8g; Sugar: 1.2g - Fat 70% / Protein 24% / Carbs 6%

Blueberry Almond Plates [FA] [GF]

Serves: 4 / Preparation time: 10 minutes / Cooking time: 15 minutes

1-½ cups almond flour	2 tablespoons butter
½ teaspoon baking powder	2 tablespoons egg white
1-cup fresh blueberries	½ cup sliced almonds
2 pastured eggs	¾ teaspoon cinnamon
2 tablespoon almond milk	

- Melt butter over medium heat then let it cool.

- Preheat an oven to 350°F (177°C) and line a baking tray with parchment paper. Set aside.
- Next, combine egg whites with sliced almond and cinnamon then stir well.
- Place almond flour and baking powder in a mixing bowl then pour almond milk and melted butter over the dry mixture.
- Add eggs to the mixture then mix until incorporated.
- After that, stir fresh blueberries into the mixture then mix until just combined.
- Divide the mixture into 4 balls then press until becoming approximately ½ inch thick circle.
- Arrange on the prepared baking tray and top with the almond and cinnamon mixture.
- Bake for approximately 15 minutes or lightly golden brown.
- Once it is done, remove from the oven and let them cool.
- Serve and enjoy.

Per Serving: Net Carbs: 6.7g; Calories: 253; Total Fat: 21.1g; Saturated Fat: 6.8g; Protein: 9.1g; Carbs: 10.4g; Fiber: 3.7g; Sugar: 3.9g - Fat 75% / Protein 16% / Carbs 9%

Avocado Cheesy Layers [FA] [GF]

Serves: 4 / Preparation time: 5 minutes / Cooking time: 20 minutes

½ lb. ground beef	Vegetable oil, to fry
6 pastured eggs	1-½ tablespoons heavy cream
2 tablespoons almond flour	1-tablespoon butter
2 teaspoons minced garlic	½ cup grated cheddar cheese
¼ teaspoon salt	¾ cup avocado pure
¼ teaspoon pepper	

- Combine beef with almond flour, salt, and pepper in a bowl then set aside.
- Crack two eggs then drop over the ground beef mixture. Mix until well combined.
- Shape the beef mixture into 4 patties then set aside.
- Preheat a pan over medium heat then wait until the oil is hot.
- Once the oil is hot, place the beef patties in the pan and fry for approximately 3 minutes.
- Flip the patties then fry for another 3 minutes or until both sides of the patties are lightly golden brown and the patties are completely cooked.
- Remove the fried patties from the pan and let them cool.
- Next, crack the remaining eggs and place in a bowl.
- Add heavy cream to the eggs then stir until incorporated.
- Preheat a saucepan over medium heat then place the ¼ tablespoon of butter in it.
- Once the butter is melted, pour a quarter of the egg mixture then make an omelet.
- Sprinkle grated cheese over the omelet then cook until done.
- Remove the omelet from the saucepan then repeat with the remaining egg mixture.
- To serve, place beef patties on a serving dish then put a cheesy omelet on each patty.
- Drop or spread avocado puree on top then serve.
- Enjoy immediately!

Per Serving: Net Carbs: 3.2g; Calories: 451; Total Fat: 37.5g; Saturated Fat: 14.8g; Protein: 22.8g; Carbs: 6.3g; Fiber: 3.1g; Sugar: 0.3g - Fat 75% / Protein 22% / Carbs 3%

Coconut Nutty Granola Bars with Cranberries [FA] [GF]

Serves: 4 / Preparation time: 5 minutes / Cooking time: 20 minutes

½ cup coconut flakes	½ cup chopped dried cranberries
¼ cup sliced roasted almonds	¼ teaspoon salt
2 tablespoons chopped roasted pecans	½ cup almond butter
¼ cup chopped roasted cashews	2 teaspoons olive oil
¼ cup sunflower seeds	

- Place almond butter in a microwave-safe bowl then microwave until melted. Let it cool.
- Preheat an oven to 300°F (149°C) and line a small square baking pan with parchment paper. Set aside.
- Place coconut flakes, roasted almonds, roasted pecans, roasted cashews, salt, and sunflower seeds in a food processor then process until becoming crumbles. Transfer to a mixing bowl.
- Pour melted butter and olive oil over the crumbles then mix until combined.
- Transfer the mixture to the prepared baking pan then press evenly.
- Bake the granola for approximately 20 minutes or until the top of the granola is lightly golden brown.
- Once it is done, remove the granola from the oven and let it cool for a few minutes.
- Using a very sharp knife cut the granola into bars and arrange on a serving dish.
- Serve and enjoy!

Per Serving: Net Carbs: 5.5g: Calories: 276; Total Fat: 25.7g; Saturated Fat: 5.4g; Protein: 5.3g; Carbs: 9.7g; Fiber: 4.2g; Sugar: 2.5g - Fat 84% / Protein 8% / Carbs 8%

Coconut Plain Waffle [FA] [GF] [F]

Serves: 4 / Preparation time: 5 minutes / Cooking time: 15 minutes

¾ cup coconut flour	1 pastured egg
½ teaspoon baking powder	2 tablespoons butter
½ teaspoon baking soda	¾ cup coconut milk

- Place butter in a microwave-safe bowl then microwave until melted. Let the butter cool for a few minutes.
- Next, combine coconut flour with baking powder and baking soda then stir well.
- Pour coconut milk over the dry mixture then add an egg to the mixture. Beat until incorporated.
- After that, pour melted butter into the mixture then mix well. Let the batter rest for about 5 minutes.
- Preheat a waffle maker then make the waffles according to the machine's instructions.
- Once it is done, remove the waffles from the waffle maker and arrange on a serving dish. Repeat with the remaining batter.
- Serve and enjoy warm.

Per Serving: Net Carbs: 2.7g: Calories: 184; Total Fat: 18g; Saturated Fat: 13.9g; Protein: 3g; Carbs: 4.6g; Fiber: 1.9g; Sugar: 1.7g - Fat 88% / Protein 6% / Carbs 6%

Cheesy Peanuts Balls [FA] [GF]

Serves: 4 / Preparation time: 15 minutes / Cooking time: 5 minutes

½ cup peanut butter	¼ cup butter
½ cup cream cheese	

- Place butter and peanut butter in a mixing bowl then using an electric mixer beat until fluffy.
- Add cream cheese to the softened butter then beat again until combined.

- Place the dough in the freezer for about 10 minutes until it has hardened.
- Next, using a small cookie scoop, spoon the dough and make small balls.
- Arrange the cheesy peanut balls on a tray then refrigerate for approximately 5-10 minutes.
- Once the balls are set, remove from the refrigerator and enjoy immediately.

Per Serving: Net Carbs: 5.2g: Calories: 392; Total Fat: 37.9g; Saturated Fat: 17.1g; Protein: 10.4g; Carbs: 7.1g; Fiber: 1.9g; Sugar: 3.1g - Fat 87% / Protein 8% / Carbs 5%

Broccoli and Cheese in Cups [FA] [GF]

Serves: 4 / Preparation time: 5 minutes / Cooking time: 24 minutes

1-¼ cups chopped broccoli	1-teaspoon baking powder
2-¼ cups almond flour	¼ teaspoon salt
3 pastured eggs	¼ cup diced cheddar cheese
1-cup almond milk	2 tablespoons butter

- Preheat an oven to 350°F (177°C) and prepare 8 small muffin paper cups. Set aside.
- Place butter in a microwave-safe bowl then microwave it until melted. Let it cool.
- Combine almond flour with baking powder and salt then mix well.
- In another bowl, crack the eggs then place in it. Beat for a few seconds.
- Next, pour almond milk into the eggs then stir until combined.
- Pour the liquid mixture over the dry mixture then mix well.
- Add melted butter to the mixture then continue stirring until incorporated.
- Stir in chopped broccoli to the batter then mix until just combined.
- Divide the batter into the prepared muffin cups then top with grated cheddar cheese.
- Bake the muffins for approximately 20 minutes or until the top of the muffins are lightly golden brown and a toothpick inserted to the muffins comes out clean.
- Remove the cooked muffins from the oven and let them cool.
- Arrange the muffins on a serving dish then serve warm. Enjoy!

Per Serving: Net Carbs: 5.9g; Calories: 359; Total Fat: 32.9g; Saturated Fat: 19.4g; Protein: 11.4g; Carbs: 9.3g; Fiber: 3.4g; Sugar: 2.9g - Fat 82% / Protein 11% / Carbs 7%

Beef and Cauliflower Spicy Pan [FA] [GF]

Serves: 4 / Preparation time: 5 minutes / Cooking time: 20 minutes

2 cups cauliflower florets	½ cup water
1 lb. ground beef	1-teaspoon coconut aminos
1-tablespoon butter	¾ teaspoon cumin
½ cup chopped onion	4 pastured eggs
2 teaspoons minced garlic	½ cup diced avocado
1-teaspoon salt	2 tablespoons sliced jalapeno
½ teaspoon black pepper	1-tablespoon chopped parsley

- Preheat an oven to 225°F (107°C) and prepare a disposable aluminum pan. Coat with cooking spray and set aside.
- Place cauliflower florets in a food processor then process until smooth. Set aside.
- Preheat a skillet over medium heat then place butter in it.

- Once the butter is melted, stir in chopped onion and minced garlic then sauté until wilted and aromatic.
- Add ground beef to the skillet then season with salt, pepper, coconut aminos, and cumin. Cook until the ground beef is no longer pink.
- Pour water over the ground beef then add cauliflower crumbles to the skillet.
- Stir well and cook until the water is completely absorbed into the beef and cauliflower. Remove from heat.
- Transfer the cooked beef and cauliflower to the prepared aluminum pan and spread evenly.
- Crack the egg and drop over the beef and cauliflower then top with diced avocado, sliced jalapeno, and chopped parsley.
- Bake the beef and cauliflower pan for approximately 10 to 15 minutes or until the eggs are set and the top is lightly golden brown.
- Once it is done, remove the aluminum pan from the oven and let the beef and cauliflower pan rest for a few minutes.
- Serve and enjoy.

Per Serving: Net Carbs: 4g; Calories: 380; Total Fat: 30.3g; Saturated Fat: 11.8g; Protein: 20.7g; Carbs: 6.4g; Fiber: 2.4g; Sugar: 2.3g - Fat 72% / Protein 24% / Carbs 4%

Tomato Beef Bagels [GF]

Serves: 4 / Preparation time: 5 minutes / Cooking time: 35 minutes

1 lb. ground beef	½ cup tomato puree
¾ cup diced onion	1 ½ teaspoon paprika
1-tablespoon butter	½ teaspoon salt
2 pastured eggs	¾ teaspoon pepper

- Preheat an oven to 400°F (204°C) and line a baking tray with parchment paper. Set aside.
- Next, preheat a saucepan over medium heat and place butter in it.
- Once the butter is melted, stir in diced onion and sauté until wilted and aromatic. Remove from heat and let it cool.
- When the sautéed onion is cool, add ground beef together with eggs and tomato puree then season with paprika, salt, and pepper. Mix until combined.
- Shape the beef mixture into 8 medium bagel forms then arrange on the prepared baking tray.
- Bake the beef bagels for approximately 35 minutes or until the beef bagels are completely cooked.
- Once it is done, remove the cooked beef bagels from the oven and let it warm.
- Place 4 bagels on a serving dish then put sliced tomatoes, onion, lettuce, cheese, or any kinds of burger filling, as you desired.
- Top with the remaining beef bagels then serve immediately. Enjoy!

Per Serving: Net Carbs: 4.3g; Calories: 415; Total Fat: 33.3g; Saturated Fat: 13.6g; Protein: 21.9g; Carbs: 5.7g; Fiber: 1.4g; Sugar: 2.5g - Fat 72% / Protein 24% / Carbs 4%

Stuffed Creamy Avocado [FA] [GF] [F]

Serves: 4 / Preparation time: 5 minutes / Cooking time: 20 minutes

2 ripe avocados	¼ teaspoon pepper
4 pastured eggs	2 teaspoons chopped chives
¼ teaspoon salt	

- Preheat an oven to 350°F (177°C) and prepare a baking tray.

- Cut the avocados into halves then discard the seeds. Arrange the halved avocados on the prepared baking tray.
- Crack an egg and place in a bowl.
- Take the egg yolk from the bowl then put in the avocado hole.
- Fill the avocado hole with egg white as much as possible then sprinkle salt and pepper on top. Repeat with the remaining halved avocados and eggs.
- Once it is done, bake the stuffed avocados for approximately 20 minutes or until the eggs are set.
- Remove the stuffed avocados from the oven then quickly sprinkle chopped chives on top. Let them warm for a few minutes.
- Arrange the stuffed avocados on a serving dish then serve.
- Enjoy!

Per Serving: Net Carbs: 3g: Calories: 275; Total Fat: 24.1g; Saturated Fat: 5.6g; Protein: 8g; Carbs: 9.8g; Fiber: 6.8g; Sugar: 0.5g - Fat 79% / Protein 17% / Carbs 4%

BEEF RECIPES

Zucchini Beef Casserole

Serves: 4 / Preparation time: 14 minutes / Cooking time: 38 minutes

½ cup goat cheese	½ teaspoon pepper
2 tablespoons coconut yogurt	¼ teaspoon ginger
2 eggs	¼ teaspoon turmeric
1-cup ground beef	¾ cup coconut flour
2 tablespoons extra virgin olive oil	4 tablespoons coconut oil
¼ cup chopped onion	½ cup sliced zucchini

1-cup water

- Preheat a skillet over medium heat then pour extra virgin olive oil into the skillet.
- Once the oil is hot, stir in chopped onion and sauté until lightly golden brown and aromatic.
- Add ground beef to the skillet then season with pepper, ginger, and turmeric. Stir until the beef is no longer pink.
- Pour water over the beef then bring to boil.
- Once it is boiled, reduce the heat and cook until the water is completely absorbed into the beef.
- Once it is done, remove the beef from heat and let it cool.
- Preheat an oven to 400°F (204°C) and coat a casserole dish with cooking spray. Set aside.
- Transfer the cooked beef to the prepared casserole dish then spread evenly.
- Combine goat cheese with eggs and coconut yogurt then stir until incorporated.
- Pour the cheese mixture over the beef and arrange sliced zucchini on it.
- Pour coconut oil over the coconut flour then mix until becoming crumbles.
- Sprinkle the crumbles on top then bake the casserole for approximately 35 minutes or until set.

- Once it is done, remove the casserole from the oven and let it cool.
- Serve and enjoy.

Per Serving: Net Carbs: 2.4g; Calories: 381; Total Fat: 35.2g; Saturated Fat: 17.3g
Protein: 13.3g; Carbs: 3.8g; Fiber: 1.4g; Sugar: 1.6 g - Fat 83% / Protein 14% / Carbs 3%

Tomato Beef Chili [FA] [GF]

Serves: 4 / Preparation time: 5 minutes / Cooking time: 25 minutes

¾ lb. ground beef	1-tablespoon chili powder
½ cup chopped onion	1 tablespoon Worcestershire sauce
3 tablespoons minced garlic	1-½ teaspoons cumin
1-½ cups diced tomatoes	1-½ teaspoons oregano
1-½ cups water	1-teaspoon black pepper
¼ cup chopped green chili	2 tablespoons butter

- Place diced tomatoes in a blender then pour water into it. Blend until becoming tomato juice then set aside.
- Select the "Sauté" setting on the Instant Pot then drop butter in it.
- Wait until the butter is melted then stir in minced garlic and chopped onion. Sauté until aromatic then press the "Cancel" button.
- Add ground beef to the Instant Pot then season with green chili, chili powder, Worcestershire sauce, cumin, oregano, and black pepper.
- Pour tomato juice over the beef then put the lid on the Instant Pot. Seal it properly and close the steam valve.
- Select the "Meat/Stew" setting then cook the beef for 20 minutes.
- Once it is done, naturally release the Instant Pot then open the lid.
- Transfer the cooked beef with the liquid to a serving dish then enjoy warm.

Per Serving: Net Carbs: 6.8g; Calories: 342; Total Fat: 27.5g; Saturated Fat: 12g; Protein: 15.2g; Carbs: 9.1g; Fiber: 2.3g; Sugar: 3.6g - Fat 72% / Protein 19% / Carbs 9%

Cheesy Beef Roll Black Pepper [GF]

Serves: 6 / Preparation time: 15 minutes / Cooking time: 25 minutes

1-½ lbs. rib eye steak	½ cup chopped onion
1-teaspoon paprika	¼ lb. cheddar cheese
½ teaspoon salt	2 medium carrots
½ teaspoon black pepper	2 tablespoons butter

- Cut the rib eye into large thin slices then rub with paprika, salt, and pepper. Let it rest for 10 minutes.
- Meanwhile, cut the cheddar cheese into strips then set aside.
- Next, peel the carrots then cut into strips as well. Set aside.
- After 10 minutes, arrange the sliced rib eye on a flat surface then arrange cheese strips, carrot strips, and chopped onion on the rib eye.
- Roll the rib eye then bind with strings.
- Place butter in the Instant Pot then press the "Sauté" button.
- Once the butter is melted, place the beef roll in the Instant Pot then brown for about 5 minutes.

- Remove the browned beef roll from then Instant Pot then let it sit.
- Pour water into the Instant Pot then place a trivet in it.
- Place the browned beef roll on the trivet then close and seal the Instant Pot. Close the steam valve.
- Select "Manual" setting then cook the beef roll on high for 20 minutes.
- When the Instant Pot beeps, naturally release the Instant Pot then open the lid.
- Let the beef roll rest for about 20 minutes then cut into thick slices.
- Arrange the sliced beef rolls on a serving dish then drizzle your favorite sauce over the beef rolls.
- Serve and enjoy.

Per Serving: Net Carbs: 2.6g; Calories: 434; Total Fat: 35.2g; Saturated Fat: 16.4g; Protein: 25.1g; Carbs: 3.5g; Fiber: 0.9g; Sugar: 1.6g - Fat 73% / Protein 23% / Carbs 4%

Rosemary Rib Eye Beef Steak

Serves: 2 / Preparation time: 20 minutes / Cooking time: 15 minutes

2 rib eye beefsteak

¼ cup chopped rosemary

2 teaspoons minced garlic

¼ cup butter

1-½ tablespoons balsamic vinegar

½ teaspoon salt

½ teaspoon black pepper

- Melt butter in a saucepan over low heat then add minced garlic to the saucepan. Sauté until aromatic.
- Remove from heat then season with balsamic vinegar, salt, and pepper. Let it cool.
- Add chopped rosemary to the mixture then stir well.
- Place the rib eye in a zipper-lock plastic bag then add the spice mixture to the plastic bag.
- Shake the plastic bag and make sure the rib eye is completely seasoned.
- Marinate the rib eye for at least an hour and store in the fridge to keep it fresh.
- After an hour, remove the seasoned rib eye from the fridge then thaw at room temperature.
- Preheat an Air Fryer to 400°F (204°C) and place a rack in it.
- Once the Air Fryer is preheated, place the seasoned rib eye n the rack then cook for 15 minutes.
- Once it is done, remove from the Air Fryer then transfer to a serving dish.
- Serve and enjoy.

Per Serving: Net Carbs: 2.7g; Calories: 544; Total Fat: 49.2g; Saturated Fat: 25.1g
Protein: 20.8g; Carbs: 6g; Fiber: 3.3g; Sugar: 0.1g - Fat 81% / Protein 15% / Carbs 4%

Beef Stew with Spaghetti Squash Noodle [FA] [GF]

Serves: 4 / Preparation time: 5 minutes / Cooking time: 22 minutes

1 lb. rib eye steak

2 tablespoons butter

2 teaspoons minced garlic

½ cup chopped onion

½ cup beef broth

¼ teaspoon salt

½ teaspoon black pepper

¼ cup chopped leek

1 medium spaghetti squash

2 tablespoons extra virgin olive oil

- Cut the spaghetti squash into halves then discard the seeds.
- Pour water into the Instant Pot then place a trivet in it.
- Brush the halved spaghetti squash with olive oil then place it on the trivet.
- Put the lid on and seal the Instant Pot properly.

- Select "Manual" setting on the Instant Pot then cook the spaghetti squash on high for 7 minutes.
- Once it is done, naturally release the Instant Pot then open the lid.
- Take the cooked spaghetti squash out of the Instant Pot then let it cool.
- Using a fork shred the cooked spaghetti squash then place on a serving dish. Set aside.
- Clean the Instant Pot then place butter in the inner pot of the Instant Pot.
- Stir in chopped onion and minced garlic then sauté until aromatic.
- Next, cut the rib eye steak into very small dices then add to the Instant Pot. Sauté until aromatic then press the "Cancel" button.
- Pour beef broth over the rib eye then season with salt and pepper.
- Put the lid on and seal the Instant Pot properly. Close the steam valve.
- Select "Manual" setting then cook the beef on high for 15 minutes.
- Once it is done, naturally release the Instant Pot then open the lid.
- Top the spaghetti squash noodle with cooked beef then serve immediately.
- Enjoy warm.

Per Serving: Net Carbs: 5g; Calories: 456; Total Fat: 37.9g; Saturated Fat: 14.7g; Protein: 21g; Carbs: 6.9g; Fiber: 1.9g; Sugar: 1.9g - Fat 76% / Protein 20% / Carbs 4%

Jalapeno Spicy Fried Beef

Serves: 8 / Preparation time: 15 minutes / Cooking time: 20 minutes

1 beef roast	½ cup chopped onion
2 jalapenos	1 cup sliced bell pepper
2 tablespoons coconut oil	½ cup butter
¼ teaspoon salt	1-teaspoon cayenne
½ teaspoon black pepper	1 tablespoon red chili flakes
2 tablespoons lemon juice	1-tablespoon hot sauce
3 tablespoons minced garlic	1 tablespoon dried parsley

- Cut the jalapenos into small pieces then combine with salt, black pepper, lemon juice, and minced garlic.
- Season the beef roast with the spice mixture then let it rest for a few minutes.
- Preheat an Air Fryer to 400°F (204°C).
- Once the Air Fryer is ready, place the seasoned beef roast in the Air Fryer then spray with coconut oil.
- Sprinkle chopped onion and sliced bell pepper on over the beef roast then cook for 18 minutes.
- Meanwhile, melt butter in a saucepan then remove from heat.
- Add cayenne, red chili flakes, hot sauce, and dried parsley then stir until combined.
- Once the beef roast is done, drizzle the butter sauce over the beef roast then cook for another 20 minutes.
- Transfer the cooked beef roast to a serving dish then enjoy.

Per Serving: Net Carbs: 5.7g; Calories: 444; Total Fat: 35.3g; Saturated Fat: 22.4g
Protein: 25.4g; Carbs: 7g; Fiber: 1.3g; Sugar: 2.8g - Fat 71% / Protein 23% / Carbs 6%

Sautéed Beef Pepper with Cheese and Parsley Topping

Serves: 4 / Preparation time: 8 minutes / Cooking time: 22 minutes

1 lb. beef rib eye steak	½ teaspoon pepper
2 tablespoons extra virgin olive oil	¼ cup goat cheese
¼ cup chopped onion	2 teaspoons minced parsley

½ teaspoon grated garlic   ½ teaspoon thyme

- Cut the beef rib eye steak into thin slices then set aside.
- Preheat a skillet over medium heat then pour olive oil into the skillet.
- Once the oil is hot, stir in chopped onion and sauté until aromatic.
- Next, add sliced beef to the skillet then season with pepper. Cook until done.
- Transfer the sautéed beef to a serving dish then set aside.
- Quickly combine goat cheese with minced parsley, grated garlic, and thyme then mix until incorporated and smooth.
- Serve the sautéed beef with the cheese mixture and enjoy immediately.

Per Serving: Net Carbs: 1g; Calories: 383; Total Fat: 32.5g; Saturated Fat: 11.3g
Protein: 20.9g; Carbs: 1.6g; Fiber: 0.6g; Sugar: 0.4g - Fat 76% / Protein 23% / Carbs 1%

Beans Sprout Turmeric Beef Soup [FA] [GF]

Serves: 4 / Preparation time: 5 minutes / Cooking time: 20 minutes

1 lb. rib eye steak	2 bay leaves
1 cup beans sprouts	2 lemon grasses
3 tablespoons minced garlic	2 kaffir lime leaves
½ teaspoon pepper	¼ cup chopped leek
1-teaspoon salt	1-tablespoon coconut oil
½ teaspoon turmeric	4 cups water
1-inch galangal	1 red tomato

- Preheat a skillet over medium heat then pour coconut oil into the skillet.
- Once it is hot, stir in minced garlic then sauté until wilted and aromatic.
- Next, add rib eye steak to the skillet then season with salt, pepper, turmeric, galangal, bay leaves, lemon grasses, and kaffir lime leaves.
- Pour water over the beef then bring to boil.
- Once it is boiled, reduce the heat and cook until the beef is tender. The water will reduce into half.
- When the beef is completely cooked, take it out of the skillet then place on a flat surface. Let the cooked beef cool but leave the remaining gravy on the heat over very low heat.
- Meanwhile, place bean sprouts and water in a small pan then cook until the bean sprout is wilted. Remove from heat and discard the water.
- Once the cooked beef is cool, cut into small dices or using a fork shred the beef.
- Place the cooked beef sprouts in a bowl then put shredded beef after the sprouts.
- Sprinkle chopped leek on top then pour gravy over the gravy.
- Cut the red tomato into slices then put on the top.
- Serve and enjoy warm.

Per Serving: Net Carbs: 5.4g: Calories: 366; Total Fat: 28.6g; Saturated Fat: 13g; Protein: 20.9g; Carbs: 6.2g; Fiber: 0.8g; Sugar: 1.8g - Fat 70% / Protein 24% / Carbs 6%

Slow Cook Beef Lemon with Parsley Aroma [GF]

Serves: 4 / Preparation time: 5 minutes / Cooking time: 3 hours

2 beef rib eye

1-teaspoon black pepper

2 teaspoons minced garlic

3 tablespoons lemon juice

1-cup low sodium beef broth

1 cup chopped onion

¼ cup chopped parsley

- Rub the beef rib eye with minced garlic, black pepper, and lemon juice then place in the inner pot of an Instant Pot.
- Pour beef broth over the beef rib eye then sprinkle chopped onion on top.
- Put the lid on the Instant Pot then close it properly. Let the valve open.
- Select the "Slow Cook" menu then set the time to 3 hours.
- When the Instant Pot beeps, quick release the Instant Pot then open the lid.
- Add chopped parsley to the Instant Pot then close the lid for about 5 minutes.
- Open the lid then transfer the cooked beef rib eye to a serving dish.
- Serve and enjoy.

Per Serving: Net Carbs: 3.2g; Calories: 422; Total Fat: 33.9g; Saturated Fat: 14.9g; Protein: 24.1g; Carbs: 4.2g; Fiber: 1.3g; Sugar: 1.7g - Fat 72% / Protein 23% / Carbs 5%

Savory Pecan Beef Ribs

Serves: 4 / Preparation time: 20 minutes/ Cooking time: 15 minutes

½ beef ribs

1-tablespoon lemon juice

1 egg

3 tablespoons coconut milk

1 cup roasted pecans

1-teaspoon ginger

¼ teaspoon cayenne

¼ teaspoon salt

½ teaspoon pepper

1-tablespoon extra virgin olive oil

- Splash lemon juice over the beef ribs then let it rest for a few minutes.
- Meanwhile, crack the egg then pour coconut milk into the egg. Stir until incorporated.
- Place roasted pecans in a food processor then season with ginger, cayenne, salt, and pepper. Process until becoming flour texture.
- Dip the beef ribs in the egg mixture then roll into the pecan mixture. Make sure the rib is completely coated with the pecans.
- Preheat an Air Fryer to 400°F (204°C) and put a rack in the Air Fryer.
- Once the Air Fryer is ready, place the coated beef ribs on the rack.
- Spray olive oil over the beef ribs then cook the beef ribs. Set the time to 15 minutes.
- Once it is done, remove from the Air Fryer and serve warm.
- Enjoy!

Per Serving: Net Carbs: 2.1g; Calories: 396; Total Fat: 38g; Saturated Fat: 8.9g
Protein: 12.4g; Carbs: 5.2g; Fiber: 3.1g; Sugar: 1.7g - Fat 86% / Protein 13% / Carbs 1%

Tamarind Sour Beef Soup [FA] [GF]

Serves: 6 / Preparation time: 5 minutes / Cooking time: 20 minutes

2 lbs. rib eye beefsteak

4 cups water

½ cup chopped green beans

¼ cup chopped green tomatoes

2 tablespoons red chili flakes

1-tablespoon tamarind

1-½ tablespoons sliced shallots	2 bay leaves
2 teaspoons sliced garlic	½ teaspoon salt
1-inch galangal	

- Cut the rib eye into cubes then place in the Instant Pot.
- Pour water over the beef then season with red chili flakes, tamarind, sliced shallots, sliced garlic, galangal, bay leaves, and salt.
- Add chopped green beans and green tomatoes to the Instant Pot then close the Instant Pot properly. Close the steam valve.
- Select "Manual" setting then cook the beef soup for 20 minutes.
- When the Instant Pot beeps, naturally release the Instant Pot then open the lid.
- Transfer the beef soup to a serving bowl then enjoy right away.

Per Serving: Net Carbs: 2.2g; Calories: 425; Total Fat: 33.4g; Saturated Fat: 13.3g; Protein: 27.1g; Carbs: 2.8g; Fiber: 0.6g; Sugar: 1.2g - Fat 70% / Protein 25% / Carbs 5%

Savory Beef Stew with Coconut Gravy [GF]

Serves: 4 / Preparation time: 5 minutes / Cooking time: 40 minutes

1 lb. rib eye steak	1-inch galangal
2 cloves garlic	1 lemon grass
3 shallots	2 kaffir lime leaves
½ teaspoon cumin	¼ teaspoon salt
1-teaspoon coriander	2 cups water
1 candlenut	¼ cup coconut milk
1 bay leaf	3 teaspoons coconut aminos

- Cut the rib eye steak into thin slices then set aside.
- Place garlic, shallots, cumin, coriander, and candlenut in a food processor then process until smooth.
- Preheat a skillet over medium heat then pour coconut oil into the skillet.
- Once the oil is hot, stir in the spice mixture and sauté until aromatic.
- Next, add sliced rib eye steak to the skillet then season with bay leaf, galangal, lemon grass, lime leaves, and salt.
- Pour water over the beef and bring to boil.
- Once it is boiled, reduce the heat and cook the beef until tender. The water will be completely absorbed into the beef.
- Drizzle coconut aminos and coconut milk over the beef then bring to a simmer.
- Transfer the beef stew to a serving dish then serve immediately.
- Enjoy!

Per Serving: Net Carbs: 5.5g: Calories: 446; Total Fat: 37.6g; Saturated Fat: 19.2g; Protein: 21.3g; Carbs: 6.3g; Fiber: 0.8g; Sugar: 0.7g - Fat 76% / Protein 18% / Carbs 6%

Spiced Beef White Soup [FA] [GF]

Serves: 8 / Preparation time: 5 minutes / Cooking time: 20 minutes

1 ¼ lbs. beef chuck	2 kaffir lime leaves
2 lemon grasses	1-inch galangal
2 bay leaves	1-teaspoon ginger

½ teaspoon turmeric	½ teaspoon salt
2 tablespoons sliced shallots	1 ½ cup coconut milk
2 teaspoons sliced garlic	1-½ cups water

- Cut the beef chuck into cubes then place in the Instant Pot.
- Add lemon grasses, bay leaves, kaffir lime leaves, galangal, ginger, turmeric, sliced shallots, sliced garlic, and salt to the Instant Pot then pour water and coconut milk over the beef.
- Put the lid on and seal the Instant Pot properly. Close the steam valve.
- Select "Manual" setting on the Instant Pot and cook the beef soup on high. Set the time to 20 minutes.
- Once it is done, naturally release the Instant Pot then open the lid.
- Transfer the beef soup to a serving bowl then serve immediately.
- Enjoy warm.
- If you want to slow cook the beef soup, select "Slow Cook" setting on the Instant Pot and cook for 4 hours.

Per Serving: Net Carbs: 3.6g; Calories: 434; Total Fat: 34.7g; Saturated Fat: 19g; Protein: 25.9g; Carbs: 4.7g; Fiber: 1.1g; Sugar: 1.5g - Fat 72% / Protein 24% / Carbs 4%

Cheesy Beef Empanadas

Serves: 6 / Preparation time: 30 minutes / Cooking time: 22 minute

2 cups Mozzarella cheese	¼ cup butter
1-cup cream cheese	½ cup chopped onion
1-½ cup almond flour	¼ teaspoon salt
2 eggs	½ teaspoon black pepper
2 ½ cups ground beef	½ teaspoon nutmeg

- Place butter in a microwave-safe bowl then melt the butter.
- Pour the melted butter over the beef then add chopped onion to the bowl.
- Season with salt, black pepper, and nutmeg then stir well.
- Preheat an Air Fryer to 400°F (204°C).
- Transfer the seasoned beef to the Air Fryer then cook for 10 minutes.
- Remove the beef from the Air Fryer then let it cool.
- Next, place grated Mozzarella cheese and cream cheese in a microwave-safe bowl then melt the mixture.
- Once the cheese is melted, add eggs to the bowl then stir until incorporated.
- Stir in almond flour to the cheese mixture then mix until becoming a soft dough. If the dough is too sticky, you can add more almond flour to the dough.
- Place the dough on a flat surface then roll until thin.
- Using a circle cookies mold cut the thin dough into 12.
- Put about 2 tablespoons of beef on a circle dough then fold until becoming a half-circle. Glue with water.
- Repeat with the remaining dough and beef then set aside.
- Preheat an Air Fryer to 425°F (218°C).
- Arrange the beef empanadas in the Air Fryer then cook for 12 minutes or until lightly golden brown.
- Remove from the Air Fryer then serve warm. Enjoy!

Per Serving: Net Carbs: 4.4g; Calories: 283; Total Fat: 26.8g; Saturated Fat: 15g
Protein: 8.7g; Carbs: 3.6g; Fiber: 0.8g; Sugar: 0.8g - Fat 85% / Protein 12% / Carbs 3%

Buttery Beef Crispy [FA] [GF]

Serves: 4 / Preparation time: 10 minutes / Cooking time: 25 minutes

2 lbs. rib eye steak	¼ teaspoon cumin
2 tablespoons minced garlic	1-inch galangal
4 tablespoons sliced shallots	½ teaspoon salt
1-teaspoon turmeric	3 tablespoons butter
2 tablespoons coriander	

- Place the rib eye in the Instant Pot then sprinkle minced garlic, sliced shallots, turmeric, coriander, cumin, and salt over the rib eye.
- Add galangal to the Instant Pot then pour water over the rib eye.
- Put the lid on and seal the Instant Pot properly. Close the steam valve.
- Select "Manual" setting and cook the rib eye on high for 15 minutes.
- When the beef is done, quick release the Instant Pot then open the lid.
- Take the cooked rib eye out of the Instant Pot then place on a flat surface.
- Using a fork shred the cooked beef then set aside.
- Clean the Instant Pot then place butter in it.
- Press the "Sauté" button and stir in the shredded beef. Sauté until the shredded beef is crispy and completely coated with butter.
- Once it is done, turn the Instant Pot off and transfer the beef to a serving dish.
- Serve and enjoy.

Per Serving: Net Carbs: 3.5g; Calories: 402; Total Fat: 33.8g; Saturated Fat: 15.5g; Protein: 20.7g; Carbs: 3.4g; Fiber: 0.3g; Sugar: 0.1g - Fat 75% / Protein 20% / Carbs 5%

Spicy Beef Tender with Healthy Cucumber

Serves: 4 / Preparation time: 9 minutes / Cooking time: 23 minutes

1 lb. beef rib eye	2 tablespoons red chili flakes
2 tablespoons extra virgin olive oil	1-cup water
2 teaspoons minced garlic	1 cup chopped cucumber
2 teaspoons sliced shallot	

- Cut the beef rib eye into thin slices then set aside.
- Preheat a skillet over medium heat then pour extra virgin olive oil into it.
- Stir in minced garlic and sliced shallot to the skillet then sauté until lightly golden brown and aromatic.
- Add sliced beef to the skillet then stir until just wilted.
- After that, pour water over the beef then bring to boil.
- Once it is boiled, reduce the heat and cook until the water is completely absorbed into the beef and the beef is tender.
- Next, stir in red chili flakes and chopped cucumber to the skillet then sauté and cook until wilted.
- Once it is done, remove the cooked beef from the heat and transfer to a serving dish.
- Serve and enjoy.

Per Serving: Net Carbs: 3.2g; Calories: 386; Total Fat: 32.1g; Saturated Fat: 11g
Protein: 20.7g; Carbs: 3.7g; Fiber: 0.5g; Sugar: 1.6g - Fat 75% / Protein 22% / Carbs 3%

Spiced Beef Curry Satay

Serves: 2 / Preparation time: 20 minutes / Cooking time: 15 minutes

1 flank steak

3 cloves garlic

5 shallots

2 tablespoons coriander

1-teaspoon ginger

½ teaspoon turmeric

1-teaspoon curry powder

2 tablespoons coconut aminos

1 cup roasted pecans

1 ½ cups coconut milk

2 teaspoons red chili

- Place garlic, shallots, coriander, ginger, turmeric, curry powder, and coconut aminos in a food processor. Process until smooth.
- Cut the flank steak into cubes then season with the spice mixture. Let it sit for at least 15 minutes.
- After 15 minutes, prick the beef cubes with skewers then set aside.
- Preheat an Air Fryer to 400°F (204°C).
- Once the Air Fryer is ready, arrange the beef satay in the Air Fryer then cook for 15 minutes.
- Meanwhile, place roasted pecans and red chili in a blender.
- Pour coconut milk over the roasted pecans then blend until smooth.
- Remove the cooked beef satay from the Air Fryer then arrange on a serving dish.
- Drizzle pecan sauce on top then serve.
- Enjoy immediately.

Per Serving: Net Carbs: 6.1g; Calories: 379; Total Fat: 32.9g; Saturated Fat: 15.9g
Protein: 15.1g; Carbs: 9.5g; Fiber: 3.4g; Sugar: 2.9g - Fat 78% / Protein 16% / Carbs 6%

Hot Ginger Beef Rib Soup [FA] [GF]

Serves: 8 / Preparation time: 5 minutes / Cooking time: 20 minutes

1 lb. beef ribs

3 cups water

2 teaspoons ginger

2 teaspoons minced garlic

½ teaspoon coriander powder

½ teaspoon salt

1 bay leaf

2 tablespoons cayenne pepper

1 tomato

- Chop the beef ribs and place in the Instant Pot.
- Cut the tomato into quarters then also place in the Instant Pot.
- Add the remaining ingredients—ginger, minced garlic, coriander powder, salt, bay leaf, and cayenne pepper to the Instant Pot then pour water over the beef.
- Put the lid on and seal the Instant Pot properly. Close the steam valve.
- Select "Pressure" setting on the Instant Pot and cook the beef soup on high for 20 minutes.
- Once it is done, naturally release the Instant Pot and open the lid.
- Transfer the beef rib soup to a serving dish then enjoy warm.

Per Serving: Net Carbs: 1.2g; Calories: 468; Total Fat: 37.2g; Saturated Fat: 15g; Protein: 30.2g; Carbs: 1.7g; Fiber: 0.5g; Sugar: 0.4g - Fat 71% / Protein 25% / Carbs 4%

Juicy Beef Steak Rosemary Garlic [FA] [GF] [SF]

Serves: 4 / Preparation time: 10 minutes / Cooking time: 15 minutes

1 lb. rib eye steak	2 tablespoons butter
2 tablespoons extra virgin olive oil	2 tablespoons minced garlic
¼ teaspoon salt	1-tablespoon chopped rosemary
½ teaspoon black pepper	

- Cut the rib eye steak into large medium slices then rub with salt and pepper. Set aside.
- Preheat a cast iron skillet over medium heat then pour extra virgin olive oil into the skillet.
- Place the seasoned beef in the cast iron skillet then cook for approximately 3 to 4 minutes each side or until the beef is completely cooked.
- Once the beef is done, add butter, minced garlic, and chopped rosemary to the skillet then baste the beef with the mixture.
- Coat and cook the beef for additional 30 seconds per side then remove the beef from heat.
- Place the cooked beef on a sheet of aluminum foil then quickly wrap it. Let the beefsteak rest for about 5 minutes.
- Unwrap the beefsteak then transfer to a serving dish.
- Serve and enjoy with grilled vegetables, as you desired.

Per Serving: Net Carbs: 1.6g: Calories: 431; Total Fat: 37.9g; Saturated Fat: 14.7g; Protein: 20.4g; Carbs: 2.1g; Fiber: 0.5g; Sugar: 0g - Fat 79% / Protein 20% / Carbs 1%

Marinated Flank Steak with Beef Gravy

Serves: 2 / Preparation time: 3 hours / Cooking time: 15 minutes

1 flank steak	¼ cup beef broth
¼ cup butter	2 tablespoons coconut milk
3-½ tablespoons lemon juice	3 tablespoons coconut aminos
4 tablespoons minced garlic	1-teaspoon nutmeg
½ teaspoon salt	1 scoop Stevia
½ teaspoon pepper	1-tablespoon extra virgin olive oil
1 cup chopped onion	

- Melt butter in a microwave then let it cool.
- Combine the melted butter with lemon juice, minced garlic, salt, and pepper then mix well.
- Season the flank steak with the spice mixture then marinate for at least 3 hours. Store in the refrigerator to keep it fresh.
- Preheat a saucepan over medium heat then pour olive oil into the saucepan.
- Once the oil is hot, stir in chopped onion then sauté until translucent and aromatic.
- Pour beef broth into the saucepan then season with nutmeg. Bring to boil.
- Once it is boiled, reduce the heat then add coconut milk, coconut aminos, and stevia to the saucepan. Stir until dissolved.
- Remove the sauce from heat then let it cool.
- After 3 hours, remove the seasoned flank steak from the refrigerator then thaw at room temperature.
- Preheat an Air Fryer to 400°F (204°C).
- Once the Air Fryer is ready, place the seasoned flank steak in the Air Fryer then set the time to 15 minutes.
- After 15 minutes, open the Air Fryer then drizzle the beef gravy over the flank steak.
- Cook the flank steak again and set the time to 5 minutes.
- Remove the cooked flank steak from the Air Fryer then place on a serving dish.

- Drizzle the gravy on top then enjoy right away.

Per Serving: Net Carbs: 3.5g; Calories: 432; Total Fat: 42.7g; Saturated Fat: 20.6g
Protein: 10.6g; Carbs: 4.1g; Fiber: 0.6g; Sugar: 3.2g - Fat 89% / Protein 10% / Carbs 1%

Savory Beef Loin with Coriander [FA] [GF] [SF]

Serves: 4 / Preparation time: 5 minutes / Cooking time: 15 minutes

1 lb. rib eye steak	1-teaspoon salt
1-cup beef broth	2 lemon grasses
3 teaspoons minced garlic	2 tablespoons extra virgin olive oil
2 tablespoons coriander	

- Place the rib eye steak in the Instant Pot then pour beef broth over the beef.
- Season with minced garlic, coriander, salt, and lemon grasses then stir well.
- Put the lid on and seal the Instant Pot properly. Close the steam valve.
- Select "Pressure" setting on the Instant Pot and cook the beef on high. Set the time to 15 minutes.
- When the Instant Pot beeps, naturally release the Instant Pot then open the lid.
- Take the beef out of the Instant Pot then let it cool. Use the liquid for other purposes.
- Cut the cooked beef into slices then set aside.
- Pour olive oil into the Instant Pot then stir in the sliced beef.
- Sauté the sliced beef and cook for about 5 minutes then take it out of the Instant Pot.
- Transfer to a serving dish then serve warm.

Per Serving: Net Carbs: 1.2g; Calories: 380; Total Fat: 32.2g; Saturated Fat: 11.1g; Protein: 20.9g; Carbs: 1.3g; Fiber: 0.1g; Sugar: 0g - Fat 76% / Protein 22% / Carbs 2%

Onion Beef Stew [GF]

Serves: 4 / Preparation time: 30 minutes / Cooking time: 15 minutes

1 lb. flank steak	¼ teaspoon salt
1 cup chopped onion	½ teaspoon black pepper
3 shallots	1-teaspoon sesame oil
2 cloves garlic	2 tablespoons butter
½ teaspoon turmeric	1-cup coconut milk
1-teaspoon coriander	1 cup roasted almonds
1-tablespoon coconut aminos	

- Place shallots, garlic, turmeric, coriander, salt, and pepper in a food processor then process until smooth.
- Cut the flank steak into slices then rub with coconut aminos, sesame oil, and spice mixture. Marinate the beef for at least 30 minutes or more if you have time.
- After 30 minutes, place butter in the Instant Pot then press the "Sauté" button.
- Once the butter is melted, add chopped onion and the seasoned beef to the Instant Pot then sauté until wilted and aromatic.
- Pour coconut milk over the beef then put the lid on and seal the Instant Pot properly. Close the steam valve.
- Select "Pressure" setting on the Instant Pot and cook the beef on high for 15 minutes.
- Once it is done, naturally release the Instant Pot then open the lid.

- Transfer the beef stew to a serving dish then sprinkle roasted almonds on top.
- Serve and enjoy.

Per Serving: Net Carbs: 6.8g; Calories: 451; Total Fat: 35.4g; Saturated Fat: 21.6g; Protein: 26.2g; Carbs: 10.2g; Fiber: 3.4g; Sugar: 3.6g - Fat 71% / Protein 23% / Carbs 6%

Beef Broccoli Crunchy Nugget

Serves: 4 / Preparation time: 12 minutes / Cooking time: 23 minutes

1 lb. ground beef	2 teaspoons minced garlic
3 eggs	2 cups chopped broccoli
2 tablespoons coconut flour	1 cup grated coconut
½ teaspoon pepper	

- Preheat a steamer over medium heat and line a baking pan with aluminum foil. Set aside.
- Combine ground beef with 2 eggs, coconut flour, pepper, minced garlic, and chopped broccoli in a food processor then process until smooth.
- Transfer the mixture to the prepared baking pan then spread evenly.
- Place the baking pan in the steamer then steam the nugget for approximately 20 minutes or until set.
- Once it is done, remove the baking pan from the steamer and let it cool.
- When the nugget is already cool, take it out of the baking pan then cut into thick slices.
- Crack the remaining egg then place in a bowl. Stir the egg until just incorporated.
- Dip each nugget into the egg then roll in the grated coconut.
- Refrigerate the beef nugget for at least 2 hours.
- Once you want to serve it, remove the beef nugget from the refrigerator and fry.
- Serve and enjoy.

Per Serving: Net Carbs: 5.3g; Calories: 496; Total Fat: 39.1g; Saturated Fat: 18.9g
Protein: 25.2g; Carbs: 10.9g; Fiber: 5.6g; Sugar: 2.8g - Fat 71% / Protein 25% / Carbs 4%

Beef Rib Steak with Parsley Lemon Butter

Serves: 4 / Preparation time: 30 minutes / Cooking time: 15 minutes

2 beef rib eye steak	2 cloves garlic
2 tablespoons extra virgin olive oil	¼ teaspoon grated lemon zest
¼ teaspoon salt	2 tablespoons lemon juice
½ teaspoon pepper	1-teaspoon basil
½ cup butter	¼ teaspoon cayenne
¼ cup chopped fresh parsley	

- Brush the beef rib eye steak with olive oil then sprinkle salt and pepper over the beef. Let it sit for about 30 minutes.
- Meanwhile, place butter in a bowl then pour lemon juice over the butter.
- Using a fork mix until the butter is smooth.
- Grate the garlic then add to the butter.

- Stir in chopped fresh parsley, grated lemon zest, basil, and cayenne to the butter then mix well. Store in the fridge.
- Preheat an Air Fryer to 400°F (204°C) and put a rack in the Air Fryer.
- Place the seasoned beef rib eye on the rack then set the time to 15 minutes. Cook the beef.
- Once the beef rib eye is ready, remove from the Air Fryer then place on a serving dish.
- Serve with the butter sauce.
- Enjoy right away!

Per Serving: Net Carbs: 3.5g; Calories: 432; Total Fat: 42.7g; Saturated Fat: 20.6g
Protein: 10.6g; Carbs: 4.1g; Fiber: 0.6g; Sugar: 3.2g - Fat 89% / Protein 10% / Carbs 1%

Avocado Beef Black Pepper [FA] [GF]

Serves: 4 / Preparation time: 5 minutes / Cooking time: 15 minutes

2 lbs. flank steak	¼ teaspoon salt
1-tablespoon extra virgin olive oil	1-teaspoon coconut aminos
1 cup chopped onion	2 pastured eggs
½ teaspoon black pepper	1 ripe avocado

- Crack the eggs and place in a bowl. Stir until beaten.
- Add chopped green bell pepper, cooked green peas, chopped onion, chopped leek, sliced shallots, green chili, and cheddar cheese to the bowl.
- Pour coconut milk over the eggs then mix until combined. Set aside.
- Preheat a saucepan over medium heat then pour extra virgin olive oil into the saucepan.
- Once it is hot, pour the egg mixture over the saucepan and spread evenly.
- Cook the omelet for approximately 3-5 minutes or until the eggs are firm.
- Remove the omelet from the saucepan and transfer to a serving dish.
- Serve and enjoy.

Per Serving: Net Carbs: 5.1g: Calories: 284; Total Fat: 22.4g; Saturated Fat: 8.9g; Protein: 15.2g; Carbs: 6.4g; Fiber: 1.3g; Sugar: 1.9g - Fat 71% / Protein 21% / Carbs 8%

Shredded Beef Tomato with Parsley and Oregano [GF]

Serves: 4 / Preparation time: 5 minutes / Cooking time: 20 minutes

1 lb. rib eye steak	3 teaspoons minced garlic
2 tablespoons extra virgin olive oil	1-cup tomato puree
½ teaspoon salt	2 tablespoons red chili flakes
¼ cup chopped cilantro	1-tablespoon oregano
¼ cup chopped parsley	½ teaspoon cumin

- Cut the rib eye steak into medium pieces then set aside.
- Pour olive oil into the inner pot of an Instant Pot then press "Sauté" button.
- Add the rib eye steak to the Instant Pot then cook and flip several times until brown. Press the "Cancel" button.
- Add cilantro, chopped parsley, minced garlic, tomato puree, red chili flakes, oregano, and cumin to the Instant Pot then close and seal in properly. Let the steam valve open.
- Select "Slow Cook" setting and cook the rib eye steak on low. Set the time to 4 hours.

- When the Instant Pot beeps, naturally release the Instant Pot then open the lid.
- Take the cooked rib eye steak out of the Instant Pot then place on a flat surface.
- Using a fork shred the rib eye steak then transfer to a serving dish.
- Serve and enjoy.

Per Serving: Net Carbs: 6.1g; Calories: 409; Total Fat: 32.3g; Saturated Fat: 11g; Protein: 22g; Carbs: 7.7g; Fiber: 1.6g; Sugar: 1.3g - Fat 71% / Protein 22% / Carbs 7%

Coffee-Chili Beef Ribs

Serves: 2 / Preparation time: 20 minutes / Cooking time: 12 minutes

1 rib eye	1 ¼ tablespoons coriander
¼ cup espresso coffee	¾ tablespoon oregano
¼ cup chili powder	1 ½ teaspoons ginger
2 ½ tablespoons paprika	¼ cup butter
1-½ tablespoons mustard	¼ cup heavy cream
½ teaspoon salt	¼ cup strong coffee water
¾ teaspoon black pepper	

- Combine coffee powder with chili powder, paprika, mustard, coriander, oregano, and ginger in a bowl.
- Add salt and black pepper then mix well.
- Rub the rib eye with the spice mixture then let it rest for at least 20 minutes.
- After 20 minutes, preheat an Air Fryer to 400°F (204°C) and place a rack in the Air Fryer.
- Once the Air Fryer is done, arrange the beef ribs on the rack then set the time to 8 minutes.
- After 8 minutes, open the Air Fryer. Flip the beef and cook again for another 8 minutes.
- Meanwhile, melt butter in a saucepan over low heat.
- Once the butter is melted, remove from heat and let it cool.
- Add heavy cream and coffee water to the melted butter then stir until incorporated. The sauce will be thickened.
- Remove the cooked beef ribs from the Air Fryer then place on a serving dish.
- Serve with coffee sauce then enjoy right away.

Per Serving: Net Carbs: 4g; Calories: 275; Total Fat: 21.6g; Saturated Fat: 10.9g
Protein: 14.3g; Carbs: 9.3g; Fiber: 5.3g; Sugar: 1.3g - Fat 71% / Protein 21% / Carbs 8%

Relaxing Beef Soup with Nutmeg [FA] [GF]

Serves: 4 / Preparation time: 5 minutes / Cooking time: 20 minutes

1 lb. rib eye steak	1-½ teaspoons nutmeg
4 cups water	1-½ teaspoons pepper
½ cup chopped carrots	1-teaspoon salt
2 tablespoons sliced shallots	¼ cup chopped celeries

- Cut the beef rib eye into cubes then place in the Instant Pot.
- Pour water into the Instant Pot then season the beef with sliced shallots, nutmeg, pepper, and salt. Stir well.
- Put the lid on and seal the Instant Pot properly. Close the steam valve.
- Press "Manual" menu and cook the beef on high for 20 minutes.
- Next, quick release the Instant Pot then open the lid.

- Add chopped carrots and celeries to the Instant Pot then stir well.
- Select "Sauté" menu on the Instant Pot then cook the soup for another 5 minutes or until the carrots are tender enough.
- Transfer the beef soup to a serving bowl then serve.
- Enjoy warm.

Per Serving: Net Carbs: 1.1g; Calories: 317; Total Fat: 25.1g; Saturated Fat: 10.1g; Protein: 20.2g; Carbs: 1.5g; Fiber: 0.4g; Sugar: 0.5g - Fat 71% / Protein 25% / Carbs 4%

Cheesy Melt Beef Bombs

Serves: 4 / Preparation time: 30 minutes / Cooking time: 22 minutes

1 lb. ground beef	3 egg yolks
1 cup chopped onion	1 cup grated Mozzarella cheese
¼ teaspoon salt	1-tablespoon extra virgin olive oil
½ teaspoon pepper	

- Place ground beef and chopped onion in a bowl then season with salt and pepper.
- Add egg yolks to the beef mixture then mix until combined.
- Shape the ground beef mixture into small or medium balls and fill each beef ball with grated Mozzarella cheese.
- Preheat an Air Fryer to 375°F (191°C).
- Place the beef balls in the Air Fryer then spray with olive oil.
- Set the time to 10 minutes and cook the beef balls.
- Once it is done, remove the beef balls from the Air Fryer then serve.

Per Serving: Net Carbs: 3.7g; Calories: 436; Total Fat: 36.2g; Saturated Fat: 13.5g
Protein: 22.5g; Carbs: 4.3g; Fiber: 0.7 g; Sugar: 1.3 g - Fat 74% / Protein 20% / Carbs 6%

Green Beef Ginger Chili [FA] [GF]

Serves: 6 / Preparation time: 5 minutes / Cooking time: 20 minutes

¾ lb. beef loin	2 teaspoons minced garlic
¼ cup extra virgin olive	½ cup chopped green tomatoes
1 cup chopped onion	½ cup chopped green chili
1-inch galangal	1 lemon grass
1-teaspoon ginger	1 bay leaf
3 sliced shallots	½ cup beef broth

- Pour extra virgin olive oil into the Instant Pot then press the "Sauté" button.
- Stir in chopped onion and minced garlic then sauté until aromatic. Press the "Cancel" button.
- Cut the beef loin into slices then put into the Instant Pot.
- Add galangal, ginger, sliced shallots, minced garlic, green tomatoes, green chili, lemon grass, and bay leaf.
- Pour water over the beef then stir well.
- Put the lid on and seal the Instant Pot properly. Close the steam valve.
- Select "Manual" setting and cook the beef on high for 15 minutes.
- Once it is done, naturally release the Instant Pot and open the lid.
- Transfer the cooked beef to a serving dish then enjoy warm.

Per Serving: Net Carbs: 4.7g; Calories: 241; Total Fat: 18.7g; Saturated Fat: 4.9g; Protein: 13.1g; Carbs: 5.7g; Fiber: 1g; Sugar: 2g - Fat 70% / Protein 22% / Carbs 8%

Beef Sirloin Black Peppercorns Barbecue

Serves: 2 / Preparation time: 20 minutes / Cooking time: 18 minutes

1 lb. sirloin steak	1-½ teaspoons pepper
1-tablespoon ghee	1-teaspoon chives
1-tablespoon oregano	¼ teaspoon cayenne
½ tablespoon smoked paprika	¼ cup butter
2 tablespoons minced garlic	1-tablespoon apple cider vinegar
¾ tablespoon coriander	¾ cup water
1-½ tablespoons black peppercorns	2 cups tomato puree
¼ teaspoon salt	1-teaspoon mustard

- Prepare a grinder then place oregano, smoked paprika, minced garlic, coriander, black peppercorns, salt, pepper, chives, and cayenne in it. Grind until smooth.
- Rub the sirloin steak with the spice mixture then let it rest for 30 minutes.
- Meanwhile, place tomato puree in a pot then pour water into it. Bring to boil.
- Once it is boiled, reduce the heat then season with mustard and apple cider vinegar.
- Remove the sauce from heat then quickly put butter into it. Stir vigorously until the butter is melted. Set the barbecue sauce aside.
- Preheat an Air Fryer to 400°F (204°C).
- Add ghee to the preheated Air Fryer then place the seasoned sirloin in the Air Fryer.
- Set the time to 15 minutes then cook the sirloin.
- After 15 minutes, open the Air Fryer drawer then drizzle the barbecue sauce over the cooked sirloin steak.
- Serve and enjoy.

Per Serving: Net Carbs: 5.5g; Calories: 499; Total Fat: 40g; Saturated Fat: 23.9g
Protein: 27.2g; Carbs: 8g; Fiber: 2.5g; Sugar: 2.5g - Fat 72% / Protein 20% / Carbs 8%

Beef Meatballs in Red Sauce [FA] [GF]

Serves: 6 / Preparation time: 10 minutes / Cooking time: 25 minutes

1-½ lbs. rib eye steak	2 teaspoons minced garlic
2 tablespoons almond flour	3 teaspoons sliced shallots
2 eggs	¼ cup red chili flakes
2 tablespoons butter	½ cup Greek yogurt

- Cut the rib eye steak into cubes then place in a food processor.
- Add almond flour and eggs to the food processor then process until smooth and combined.
- Shape the beef mixture into medium balls then set aside.
- Pour water into the Instant Pot then place a trivet in it.
- Arrange the meatballs on the trivet then put the lid on and seal the Instant Pot properly. Close the steam valve.
- Select "Steam" setting on the Instant Pot and cook the meatballs for 10 minutes.
- When the Instant Pot beeps, quick release it then open the lid.

- Take the cooked meatballs out of the Instant Pot then place on a serving dish.
- Clean the Instant Pot then place butter in it. Select "Sauté" menu.
- Once the butter is melted, stir in minced garlic and sliced shallots then sauté until wilted and aromatic.
- Pour yogurt and add red chili to the sauce then bring to a simmer. Stir well.
- Once it is done, turn the Instant Pot off and drizzle then red sauce over the meatballs.
- Serve and enjoy warm.

Per Serving: Net Carbs: 2.5g; Calories: 387; Total Fat: 30.9g; Saturated Fat: 13.1g; Protein: 13.1g; Carbs: 2.6g; Fiber: 0.1g; Sugar: 1.8g - Fat 72% / Protein 24% / Carbs 4%

Simply Beef Stew with Broccoli [FA] [GF]

Serves: 4 / Preparation time: 5 minutes / Cooking time: 25 minutes

1 lb. rib eye steak	½ cup water
2 cups broccoli florets	2 tablespoons coconut aminos
2 teaspoons minced garlic	2 tablespoons butter
1-teaspoon ginger	

- Cut the rib eye steak into slices then set aside.
- Place butter in the inner pot of the Instant Pot then press the "Sauté" button.
- Stir in minced garlic then sauté until aromatic.
- Next, add sliced beef to the Instant Pot then sauté until wilted and no longer pink. Press the "Cancel" button.
- After that, pour water into the Instant Pot then season with ginger and coconut aminos.
- Put the lid on and seal the Instant Pot properly. Close the steam valve.
- Select "Manual" setting and cook the rib eye on high. Set the time to 15 minutes.
- When the Instant Pot beeps, quick release the Instant Pot then open the lid.
- Add broccoli florets to the Instant Pot then press the "Sauté" button. Bring to a simmer.
- Stir the broccoli and once it is done, turn the Instant Pot off and transfer the beef stew to a serving dish.
- Serve and enjoy warm.

Per Serving: Net Carbs: 4g; Calories: 388; Total Fat: 31g; Saturated Fat: 13.7g; Protein: 21.5g; Carbs: 5.3g; Fiber: 1.3g; Sugar: 0.8g - Fat 72% / Protein 22% / Carbs 6%

Beef Black Pepper in Bags

Serves: 8 / Preparation time: 10 minutes / Cooking time: 25 minutes

1 lb. ground beef	¼ cup coconut milk
5 tablespoons extra virgin olive oil	2 teaspoons red chili flakes
¼ cup chopped onion	¾ cup coconut flour
1-teaspoon black pepper	2 egg yolks
½ teaspoon cumin	3 tablespoons cold water
2 tablespoons coconut aminos	

- Place ground beef, black pepper, cumin, red chili flakes, and coconut aminos in a bowl.
- Pour coconut milk over the beef then mix well. Set aside.
- Preheat an Air Fryer to 375°F (191°C) and spray a tablespoon of extra virgin olive in the Air Fryer.

- Pour a tablespoon of olive oil in the Air Fryer then stir in chopped onion in it. Cook the onion for about 3 minutes.
- Next, add the ground beef mixture then cook for about 15 minutes. Remove from the Air Fryer then let it cool.
- Meanwhile, combine coconut flour with egg yolks, 3 tablespoons of olive oil and water then mix until becoming dough.
- Place the dough on a flat surface then roll until thin.
- Cut the thin dough into medium squares then put 2 tablespoons of chicken on each square.
- Fold the square and shape into a bag. Bind with a string then set aside. Repeat with the remaining beef and squares.
- Preheat an Air Fryer to 400°F (204°C).
- Brush each beef bag with the remaining virgin olive oil then arrange in the Air Fryer.
- Cook the Beef bags for 10 minutes then remove from the Air Fryer.
- Arrange on a serving dish then serve and enjoy warm.

Per Serving: Net Carbs: 1.9g; Calories: 280; Total Fat: 22.1g; Saturated Fat: 7g
Protein: 17.4g; Carbs: 2.8g; Fiber: 0.9g; Sugar: 0.6g - Fat 71% / Protein 25% / Carbs 4%

Brown Butter Pork Ribs [FA] [GF]

Serves: 8 / Preparation time: 5 minutes / Cooking time: 20 minutes

2 lbs. baby back ribs	2 tablespoons minced garlic
½ cup coconut aminos	¼ cup chopped onion
1-cup chicken broth	¼ cup butter
2 tablespoons ginger	

- Select the "Sauté" menu on the Instant Pot then place butter into it.
- Wait until the butter is melted then stir in minced garlic and chopped onion.
- Next, add baby back ribs to the Instant Pot then sauté until brown. Press the "Cancel" button.
- Add ginger to the Instant Pot then drizzle coconut aminos over the baby back ribs.
- Pour chicken broth into the Instant Pot then put the lid on it.
- Seal the Instant Pot properly and close the steam valve.
- Select "Pressure" menu on the Instant Pot and cook the pork for 20 minutes.
- Once it is done, naturally release the Instant Pot then open the lid.
- Transfer the cooked baby back ribs to a serving dish then serve.
- Enjoy!

Per Serving: Net Carbs: 4.8g; Calories: 400; Total Fat: 33g; Saturated Fat: 13.7g; Protein: 19g; Carbs: 5.1g; Fiber: 0.3g; Sugar: 0.3g - Fat 74% / Protein 19% / Carbs 7%

Warm Oxtail Soup with Nutmeg and Cloves

Serves: 4 / Preparation time: 3 minutes / Cooking time: 44 minutes

1-¼ lbs. beef rib eye	5 cups water
2 tablespoons sliced shallots	½ cup sliced carrots
¾ teaspoon nutmeg	½ cup cauliflower florets
3 cloves	¼ cup chopped leek
¾ teaspoon pepper	2 tablespoons celeries

- Cut the beef into medium pieces then place in a pot.

- Pour water into a pot then bring t boil.

- Once it is boiled, reduce the heat and season the beef with sliced shallots, nutmeg, clove, and pepper. Cook for approximately 30 minutes or until the beef is tender.

- Next, add sliced carrots, leek, and cauliflower florets to the pot then stir well. Cook until the vegetables are wilted but not too soft.

- When the soup is done, remove from heat and transfer to a serving bowl.

- Sprinkle chopped celeries on top and serve warm.

- Enjoy immediately.

Per Serving: Net Carbs: 3.5g; Calories: 409; Total Fat: 31.6g; Saturated Fat: 12.6g
Protein: 25.7g; Carbs: 4.7g; Fiber: 1.2g; Sugar: 1.5g - Fat 70% / Protein 27% / Carbs 3%

Salty Fried Beef with Red Chili Garlic Sambal [GF]

Serves: 4 / Preparation time: 5 minutes / Cooking time: 40 minutes

1 lb. rib eye steak	1 lemon grass
2 tablespoons minced garlic	4 cups water
1-teaspoon coriander	Coconut oil, to fry
1-teaspoon salt	½ cup red cayenne
1-teaspoon ground candlenut	1 clove garlic

- Cut the rib eye steak into medium slices then place in a skillet.

- Season with minced garlic, coriander, salt, candlenut, and lemon grass then pour water over the beef. Bring to boil.

- Once it is boiled, reduce the heat and cook until the beef is tender. The water will be completely absorbed into the beef.

- Remove the cooked beef from the skillet and strain the water. Set aside.

- Preheat a frying pan over medium heat then pour coconut oil into the frying pan.

- Once it is hot, put the beef into the frying pan and fry until both sides of the beef are lightly golden brown.

- Transfer the fried beef to a serving dish then set aside.

- Next, place red cayenne and garlic on a mortar then season with a pinch of salt. Mash until smooth.

- Drizzle a teaspoon of coconut oil over the red sambal then stir well.

- Serve the fried beef with red sambal and enjoy warm.

Per Serving: Net Carbs: 4.1g: Calories: 477; Total Fat: 41.7g; Saturated Fat: 22.1g; Protein: 21.6g; Carbs: 6g; Fiber: 1.9g; Sugar: 0.8g - Fat 79% / Protein 18% / Carbs 3%

Avocado Flank Steak with Cilantro

Serves: 2 / Preparation time: 20 minutes / Cooking time: 12 minutes

1 flank steak	1 cup chopped fresh cilantro
½ teaspoon salt	1-½ tablespoons oregano
½ teaspoon pepper	1 teaspoon minced garlic
2 ripe avocados	2 tablespoons butter

1-tablespoon lemon juice   ½ teaspoon red chili flakes

- Season the flank steak with salt and pepper then let it sit for about 20 minutes.
- Place butter in a microwave-safe bowl then melt the butter. Let it cool.
- Meanwhile, place fresh cilantro in a food processor then season with oregano, minced garlic, and chili flakes.
- Drizzle lemon juice over the cilantro then process until smooth.
- Cut the avocados into halves then discard the seeds.
- Scoop out the avocado flesh then place in a bowl. Using a tablespoon mash the avocados.
- Add cilantro mixture to the mashed avocado then drizzle melted butter on top. Mix until combined then set aside.
- Preheat an Air Fryer to 400°F (204°C) and put a rack in the Air Fryer.
- Once the Air Fryer is ready, place the seasoned flank steak on the rack the cook for 6 minutes.
- After 6 minutes, flip the flank steak and cook again for another 6 minutes.
- Once it is done, remove from the Air Fryer then place on a serving dish.
- Drizzle the cilantro and avocado mixture on top then serve.
- Enjoy!

Per Serving: Net Carbs: 5.2g; Calories: 616; Total Fat: 55.6g; Saturated Fat: 17.7g
Protein: 16.1g; Carbs: 20.1g; Fiber: 14.9g; Sugar: 1.4g - Fat 81% / Protein 10% / Carbs 9%

Spiced Pulled Pork [FA] [GF] [SF]

Serves: 4 / Preparation time: 54 minutes / Cooking time: 18 minutes

1 lb. pork butt   ½ teaspoon salt

2 tablespoons extra virgin olive oil   2 lemon grasses

1 ½ tablespoons coriander   ¼ cup water

2 teaspoons turmeric

- Rub the pork butt with olive oil, minced garlic, coriander, turmeric, and salt then place in the Instant Pot.
- Pour water over the pork butt then add lemon grasses on the pork butt.
- Put the lid on then seal the Instant Pot properly. Close the steam valve.
- Select the "Pressure" menu and set the time to 18 minutes. Cook the pork butt.
- Once the Instant Pot beeps, naturally release the Instant Pot then open the lid.
- Using a fork shred the cooked pork then transfer to a serving dish.
- Serve and enjoy warm.

Per Serving: Net Carbs: 1.1g; Calories: 318; Total Fat: 27.1g; Saturated Fat: 9g; Protein: 18.1g; Carbs: 1.3g; Fiber: 0.2g; Sugar: 0g - Fat 77% / Protein 22% / Carbs 1%

Almond Beef Salads [FA] [GF]

Serves: 4 / Preparation time: 15 minutes / Cooking time: 10 minutes

½ lb. rib eye steak   ¼ cup chopped onion

¼ cup coconut aminos   2 tablespoons cilantro

1-tablespoon sesame oil   ½ cup shredded zucchini

1-tablespoon extra virgin olive oil   ¼ cup shredded carrots

1 cup chopped lettuce   ¼ cup roasted almonds

1-tablespoon sesame seeds

- Cut the rib eye into thin slices then set aside.
- Rub the chicken with coconut aminos and sesame oil then let it sit for 15 minutes.
- After 5 minutes, place the marinated rib eye in the inner pot of an Instant Pot then close and seal the Instant Pot properly.
- Select "Manual" setting and cook the rib eye on high. Set the time to 10 minutes.
- Once the Instant Pot beeps, naturally release the Instant Pot then open the lid.
- Transfer the cooked rib eye to a serving dish.
- To serve, place lettuce, onion, cilantro, zucchini, and carrots in a salad bowl.
- Drizzle olive oil over the vegetables then toss to combine.
- Top the salads with the cooked rib eye then sprinkle chopped roasted almonds and sesame seeds over the rib eye.
- Serve and enjoy!

Per Serving: Net Carbs: 5.5g; Calories: 315; Total Fat: 25.5g; Saturated Fat: 7g; Protein: 14g; Carbs: 7.1g; Fiber: 1.6g; Sugar: 1.3g - Fat 73% / Protein 20% / Carbs 7%

Beef Cordon Bleu and Tomato Butter Sauce

Serves: 8 / Preparation time: 20 minutes / Cooking time: 18 minutes

1 lb. beef tenderloin	½ lb. Mozzarella cheese
½ teaspoon salt	¼ cup butter
½ teaspoon pepper	3 teaspoons minced garlic
4 slices smoked beef	2 cups cherry tomatoes
2 cups almond flour	¼ teaspoon thyme
½ cup grated coconut	¼ teaspoon oregano
1 egg	¼ teaspoon cayenne
¼ cup coconut milk	½ cup beef broth

- Cut the beef into 8 thin slices then season with salt and pepper.
- Place a slice of beef on a flat surface then put a slice of smoked beef on the beef.
- Add a tablespoon of grated Mozzarella cheese after smoked beef then roll it tightly.
- Prick the beef cordon bleu with a toothpick then repeat with the remaining sliced beef.
- Crack the egg then place in a bowl. Pour coconut milk into the egg then using a fork stir until incorporated.
- In another bowl, combine almond flour with grated coconut then mix well.
- Dip the beef cordon bleu in the egg mixture then roll it in the flour mixture.
- Preheat an Air Fryer to 400°F (204°C) and place a rack in it.
- Once the Air Fryer is ready, place the coated beef cordon bleu on the rack then set the time to 18 minutes.
- Meanwhile, preheat a saucepan over medium heat then spray with olive oil.
- Stir in minced garlic then sauté until aromatic.
- Pour beef broth into the saucepan then add cherry tomatoes to the saucepan. Bring to boil.
- Once it is boiled, reduce the heat then season with thyme, oregano, and cayenne. Cook until the tomatoes are wilted.
- Remove the cooked beef cordon bleu from the Air Fryer place on a serving dish.
- Drizzle tomato butter sauce on over the beef then serve.
- Enjoy right away.

Per Serving: Net Carbs: 3.5g; Calories: 361; Total Fat: 28.1g; Saturated Fat: 14.8g
Protein: 23g; Carbs: 5.5g; Fiber: 2g; Sugar: 2.3g - Fat 70% / Protein 25% / Carbs 5%

Mushroom Pork Chops Black Pepper [FA] [GF]

Serves: 4 / Preparation time: 5 minutes / Cooking time: 24 minutes

1 ½ lbs. boneless pork shoulder

1 cup chopped mushrooms

1-teaspoon black pepper

2 teaspoons minced garlic

¼ cup chopped onion

1 tablespoon avocado oil

2 tablespoons butter

½ cup coconut milk

¼ teaspoon salt

- Rub the boneless pork shoulder with minced garlic and black pepper then set aside.
- Pour avocado oil into the inner pot of an Instant Pot then select the "Sauté" button.
- Once the oil is hot, brown the pork shoulder for about 2-3 minutes per side. Remove the browned pork shoulder from the Instant Pot then set aside.
- Wipe and clean the inner pot of the Instant pot then sprinkle chopped onion and mushroom in the bottom of the pot.
- Add the browned pork shoulder to the Instant Pot then drop butter over the pork shoulder.
- Pour coconut milk into the Instant Pot then sprinkle salt over the pork.
- Put the lid on the Instant Pot then seal it properly. Close the steam valve.
- Select the "Manual" menu then cook the pork shoulder for 25 minutes.
- Once it is done, naturally release the Instant Pot then open the lid.
- Transfer the cooked pork shoulder to a serving dish then serve.

Per Serving: Net Carbs: 2.6g; Calories: 327; Total Fat: 27.8g; Saturated Fat: 14.3g; Protein: 15.8g; Carbs: 3.9g; Fiber: 1.3g; Sugar: 1.6g - Fat 77% / Protein 20% / Carbs 3%

Buttery Beef Loin and Cheese Sauce

Serves: 3 / Preparation time: 10 minutes / Cooking time: 15 minutes

1 lb. beef loin

1-tablespoon butter

1-tablespoon minced garlic

½ teaspoon salt

½ teaspoon dried parsley

¼ teaspoon thyme

½ cup sour cream

¾ cup cream cheese

2 tablespoons grated cheddar cheese

¼ teaspoon pepper

¼ teaspoon nutmeg

- Place butter in a microwave-safe bowl then melt the butter.
- Combine with minced garlic, salt, dried parsley, and thyme then mix well.
- Cut the beef loin into slices then brush with the butter mixture.
- Preheat an Air Fryer to 400°F (204°C).
- Once the Air Fryer is ready, place the seasoned beef loin in the Air Fryer and set the time to 15 minutes. Cook the beef loin.
- Meanwhile, place cream cheese in a mixing bowl then using an electric mixer beat until smooth and fluffy.
- Add sour cream and grated cheese then season with pepper and nutmeg. Beat again until fluffy then store in the fridge.

- Once the beef loin is done, remove from the Air Fryer then place on a serving dish.
- Serve and enjoy with cheese sauce.

Per Serving: Net Carbs: 5.4g; Calories: 441; Total Fat: 39.4g; Saturated Fat: 23.4g
Protein: 15.7g; Carbs: 5.6g; Fiber: 0.2g; Sugar: 2.7g - Fat 80% / Protein 14% / Carbs 6%

Beef Patties Barbecue [FA] [GF]

Serves: 4 / Preparation time: 5 minutes / Cooking time: 20 minutes

1-½ lbs. rib eye steak	½ cup tomato puree
1 egg	1-tablespoon mustard
1-½ teaspoons coriander	1 teaspoon Worcestershire sauce
2 tablespoons butter	½ teaspoon salt
½ cup chopped onion	½ teaspoon black pepper
2 teaspoons minced garlic	½ teaspoon cumin

- Cut the rib eyes steak into cubes then place in a food processor.
- Add coriander and egg then process until smooth.
- Shape the beef mixture into medium patties then set aside.
- Pour water into the Instant Pot then place a trivet in it.
- Arrange the patties on the trivet then close and seal the Instant Pot properly.
- Select "Manual" setting and cook the patties for 10 minutes.
- Once it is done, quickly release the Instant Pot then open the lid.
- Remove the beef patties from the Instant Pot then set aside.
- Clean the Instant Pot then place butter in it. Press the "Sauté" button.
- Once the butter is melted, stir in chopped onion and minced garlic then sauté until aromatic.
- Pour tomato puree into the Instant Pot then season with mustard, Worcestershire sauce, salt, black pepper, and cumin then bring to a simmer.
- Add beef patties to the Instant Pot then cook for about 3 minutes.
- After that, turn the Instant Pot off then arrange the beef patties on a serving dish.
- Drizzle the sauce over the beef patties then serve.
- Enjoy immediately.

Per Serving: Net Carbs: 4.8g; Calories: 490; Total Fat: 39.1g; Saturated Fat: 16.5g; Protein: 28g; Carbs: 6.2g; Fiber: 1.4g; Sugar: 2.7g - Fat 72% / Protein 23% / Carbs 5%

Appetizing Crispy Ribs Soup [GF]

Serves: 4 / Preparation time: 5 minutes / Cooking time: 50 minutes

2 lbs. beef ribs	1-teaspoon pepper
5 cups water	½ teaspoon nutmeg
1 cup almond flour	2 cloves
Coconut oil, to fry	¼ cup chopped leek
1-teaspoon salt	¼ cup chopped celeries

- Cut the beef ribs into medium pieces then place in a pot.
- Pour water over the beef ribs then bring to boil.
- Once it is boiled, add salt to the pot then reduce the heat. Cook until the beef ribs are tender.

- Take the cooked beef ribs out of the pot and place on a plate.
- Leave the beef broth in the pot over very low heat to keep it warm and season with pepper, nutmeg, cloves, and chopped leek.
- Combine almond flour with ¼ cup of beef broth then stir until incorporated.
- Dip the cooked beef ribs in the almond flour mixture and set aside.
- Next, preheat a frying pan over medium heat then pour coconut oil into the pan.
- Once the oil is hot, put the coated beef ribs in the oil and fry until both sides are lightly golden.
- Remove the fried beef ribs from the frying pan and strain the excessive oil.
- Arrange the fried beef ribs on a serving dish and serve with the seasoned beef broth.
- Sprinkle chopped celeries on top and enjoy warm!

Per Serving: Net Carbs: 2.1g: Calories: 513; Total Fat: 45.2g; Saturated Fat: 23.4g; Protein: 24.2g; Carbs: 3.6g; Fiber: 1.5g; Sugar: 0.7g - Fat 79% / Protein 19% / Carbs 2%

Delicious Beef Stew with Herbs [FA] [GF]

Serves: 6 / Preparation time: 5 minutes / Cooking time: 20 minutes

1 lb. flank steak	½ cup red chili
½ cup coconut milk	1-teaspoon ginger
1-cup water	1-inch galangal
2 lemon grasses	1 nutmeg
2 kaffir lime leaves	1-teaspoon coriander
5 shallots	1-teaspoon turmeric
2 cloves garlic	½ teaspoon salt

- Place shallots, garlic, red chili, ginger, nutmeg, coriander, turmeric, and salt in a food processor. Process until smooth.
- Cut the beef into slices then rub with the spice mixture.
- Place the seasoned beef in the Instant Pot then pour water over the beef.
- Add lemon grasses and kaffir lime leaves to the Instant Pot then seal it properly. Close the steam valve.
- Select "Pressure" setting and cook the beef on high. Set the time to 15 minutes.
- When the Instant Pot beeps, quick release the Instant Pot then open the lid.
- Pour coconut milk into the Instant Pot then stir well.
- Press "Sauté" button then cook the beef stew for another 5 minutes.
- Once it is done, transfer the beef stew to a serving dish.
- Serve and enjoy.

Per Serving: Net Carbs: 5.6g; Calories: 280; Total Fat: 21.8g; Saturated Fat: 11.1g; Protein: 14.5g; Carbs: 7.1g; Fiber: 1.5g; Sugar: 2.1g - Fat 70% / Protein 21% / Carbs 9%

Corned Beef Mozzarella

Serves: 4 / Preparation time: 15 minutes / Cooking time: 15 minutes

2 cups ground beef	2 eggs
½ cup chopped onion	1 cup grated Mozzarella cheese
2 teaspoons minced garlic	

- Preheat an Air Fryer to 375°F (191°C).

- Place ground beef in a bowl then add chopped onion and minced garlic.
- Crack the eggs then drop on the beef. Mix until combined.
- Shape the beef mixture into small fritter then arrange in the Air Fryer.
- Cook the beef fritters and set the time to 10 minutes.
- After 10 minutes, flip the beef fritters then sprinkle grated Mozzarella cheese on top.
- Cook again for 5 minutes then remove from the Air Fryer.
- Serve and enjoy warm.

Per Serving: Net Carbs: 1.9g; Calories: 389; Total Fat: 31.5g; Saturated Fat: 12.4g
Protein: 23g; Carbs: 2.2g; Fiber: 0.3g; Sugar: 0.8g - Fat 72% / Protein 24% / Carbs 4%

Spicy Beef Fritters Mushrooms [FA] [GF]

Serves: 4 / Preparation time: 10 minutes / Cooking time: 15 minutes

1 lb. rib eye steak	1-tablespoon coconut flour
½ cup diced mushrooms	2 tablespoons chopped cayenne pepper
¼ cup grated coconut	¼ teaspoon salt
3 pastured eggs	½ teaspoon pepper
3 tablespoons minced garlic	Coconut oil, to fry

- Cut the rib eye into cubes then place in a food processor. Process until smooth
- Transfer the smooth beef to a bowl then combine with diced mushrooms and grated coconut.
- Add eggs and coconut flour to the bowl then season with minced garlic, cayenne pepper, salt, and pepper. Mix well.
- Shape the beef mixture into 8 fritters then set aside.
- Next, preheat a saucepan over medium heat then pour coconut oil into it.
- Once it is hot, carefully place the beef fritters in the saucepan then cook for approximately 3 minutes.
- After that, flip the fritters and cook again for another 3 minutes or until both sides of the beef fritters are lightly golden brown and the fritters are cooked through.
- Once it is done, remove the beef fritters from the saucepan and transfer to a serving dish.
- Serve and enjoy with sautéed vegetables, as you desired.

Per Serving: Net Carbs: 4.8g: Calories: 442; Total Fat: 34.9g; Saturated Fat: 14.9g; Protein: 24.2g; Carbs: 7.4g; Fiber: 2.6g; Sugar: 1g - Fat 71% / Protein 25% / Carbs 4%

Beef and Cheese in Cabbage Bowl [FA] [GF]

Serves: 4 / Preparation time: 10 minutes / Cooking time: 15 minutes

1-½ lbs. rib eye steak	½ cup cilantro
1- cup water	2 tablespoons chopped mint leaves
2 tablespoons minced garlic	4 large cabbages
¼ cup lemon juice	½ cup grated cheddar cheese

- Cut the rib eye steak into small dices then place in the inner pot of an Instant Pot.
- Pour water over the diced rib eye then add minced garlic, lemon juice, and cilantro. Stir well.
- Put the lid on and seal the Instant Pot properly. Close the steam valve.
- Select "Manual" setting and cook the rib eye on high for 15 minutes.
- Once it is done, naturally release the Instant Pot then open the lid.

- Add chopped mint leaves to the Instant Pot then stir well.
- To serve, place the cabbages on a flat surface then fill each cabbage with the cooked beef.
- Sprinkle grated cheddar cheese on top then serve.
- Enjoy immediately

Per Serving: Net Carbs: 2.9g; Calories: 387; Total Fat: 29.9g; Saturated Fat: 13.1g; Protein: 24.5g; Carbs: 4.1g; Fiber: 1.2g; Sugar: 1.5g - Fat 70% / Protein 25% / Carbs 5%

Minty Beef Balls with Lemon Yogurt Dip

Serves: 8 / Preparation time: 10 minutes / Cooking time: 20 minutes

1 lb. ground beef	1 tablespoon chopped parsley
¼ teaspoon salt	1 egg
¼ teaspoon pepper	½ cup grated coconut
¾ teaspoon cumin	¾ cup Greek yogurt
¾ teaspoon coriander	¼ cup sour cream
¾ teaspoon cayenne pepper	2 tablespoons lemon juice
2 teaspoons minced garlic	½ teaspoon grated lemon zest
1 tablespoon chopped mint leaves	

- Combine ground beef with cumin, coriander, cayenne pepper, minced garlic, chopped mint leaves, and chopped parsley in a bowl.
- Season with salt and pepper then mix well.
- Shape the beef mixture into small balls then set aside.
- Crack the eggs then stir until incorporated.
- Dip the balls in the beaten egg then roll in the grated coconut.
- Preheat an Air Fryer to 375°F (191°C).
- Arrange the balls in the preheated Air Fryer then cook for 7 minutes.
- While waiting for the beef balls, place Greek yogurt, sour cream, lemon juice, and lemon zest in a mixing bowl.
- Using an electric mixer beat the mixture until smooth and fluffy. Store in the refrigerator.
- Once the beef balls are done remove from the Air Fryer then place on a serving dish.
- Drizzle lemon yogurt over the beef balls then serve.
- Enjoy!

Per Serving: Net Carbs: 2.2g; Calories: 230; Total Fat: 18.2g; Saturated Fat: 8.4g
Protein: 13.1g; Carbs: 2.9g; Fiber: 0.7g; Sugar: 1.4g - Fat 71% / Protein 23% / Carbs 6%

Pecan Beef Tender with Thick Gravy [FA] [GF]

Serves: 6 / Preparation time: 10 minutes / Cooking time: 15 minutes

1-½ lbs. flank steak	2 bay leaves
2 tablespoons roasted pecans	3 cloves
2 cups coconut milk	1-teaspoon cinnamon
1-cup water	1-teaspoon tamarind
2 lemon grasses	2 shallots
1-teaspoon turmeric	3 cloves garlic
2 kaffir lime leaves	¼ cup red chili flakes

1-teaspoon ginger

1 nutmeg

¼ teaspoon cumin

1-teaspoon coriander

½ teaspoon salt

½ teaspoon pepper

- Place roasted pecans together with shallots, garlic, red chili flakes, ginger, nutmeg, cumin, coriander, salt, and pepper in a blender then blend until smooth.
- Pour 2 tablespoons of coconut milk into the Instant Pot then press "Sauté" button.
- Add the spice mixture to the Instant Pot then sauté until aromatic. Press the "Cancel" button.
- Cut the flank steak into cubes then put in the Instant Pot.
- Pour water and coconut milk over the beef then season with lemon grasses, turmeric, kaffir lime leaves, bay leaves, cloves, and cinnamon. Stir well.
- Put the lid on and seal the Instant Pot properly. Close the steam valve.
- Select "Pressure" setting on the Instant Pot and cook the beef on high. Set the time to 15 minutes.
- Once the Instant Pot beeps naturally release it and open the lid.
- Transfer the cooked beef and the gravy to a serving bowl and serve.
- Enjoy warm.

Per Serving: Net Carbs: 5.9g; Calories: 430; Total Fat: 33.3g; Saturated Fat: 16.5g; Protein: 25.8g; Carbs: 9.3g; Fiber: 3.4g; Sugar: 3g - Fat 70% / Protein 24% / Carbs 6%

Beef Schnitzel with Lemon Ricotta Cheese

Serves: 4 / Preparation time: 20 minutes/ Cooking time: 15 minutes

½ lb. flank steak

½ teaspoon salt

½ teaspoon pepper

2 eggs

2 cups almond flour

½ lb. ricotta cheese

2 tablespoons butter

½ teaspoon grated lemon zest

3 tablespoons lemon juice

1 teaspoon minced garlic

- Place ricotta cheese and butter in a mixing bowl then add grated lemon zest, lemon juice, and minced garlic. Using an electric mixer beat the cheese mixture until smooth and fluffy.
- Transfer the cheese dip to a container and store in a fridge.
- Cut the beef into thin slices then set aside.
- Crack the eggs then season with salt and pepper. Stir until incorporated.
- Dip the sliced beef into the egg mixture then roll in the almond flour. Make sure the beef is completely coated with almond flour.
- Preheat an Air Fryer to 400°F (204°C) and place a rack in the Air Fryer.
- Once the Air Fryer is ready, place the coated beef on the rack then cook for 6 minutes.
- After 6 minutes, flip the beef and cook again for another 6 minutes.
- Once the beef schnitzel is ready, serve with lemon ricotta cheese.
- Enjoy!

Per Serving: Net Carbs: 4.1g; Calories: 417; Total Fat: 33.4g; Saturated Fat: 15.7g
Protein: 24.6g; Carbs: 5.8g; Fiber: 1.7g; Sugar: 1.1g - Fat 72% / Protein 26% / Carbs 2%

Beef Meatballs in Light Soup [FA] [GF] [SF]

Serves: 4 / Preparation time: 10 minutes / Cooking time: 15 minutes

1-½ lbs. rib eye steak

1-tablespoon tapioca flour

½ cup ice cubes

2 tablespoons minced garlic

3 cups water

½ teaspoon pepper

1-teaspoon salt

1 handful collard green

2 tablespoons fried shallots

- Cut the rib eye steak into cubes then place in a food processor.
- Add ice cubes, tapioca flour, and minced garlic to the food processor then process until smooth.
- Shape the beef mixture into small balls forms then set aside.
- Pour water into a pot then bring to boil.
- Once it is boiled, season the water with salt and pepper then stir well.
- Put the beef balls into the hot water and cook until the beef balls are floating.
- Once it is done, stir in collard green and cook until just wilted.
- Transfer the beef balls soup to a serving bowl then sprinkle fried shallots on top.
- Serve and enjoy immediately.

Per Serving: Net Carbs: 3.4g: Calories: 501; Total Fat: 38.8g; Saturated Fat: 15.4g; Protein: 32.4g; Carbs: 4.3g; Fiber: 0.9g; Sugar: 0g - Fat 70% / Protein 27% / Carbs 3%

Gingery Sautéed Beef with Cauliflower [FA] [GF]

Serves: 4 / Preparation time: 10 minutes / Cooking time: 15 minutes

1 lb. rib eye steak

3 tablespoons coconut oil

3 tablespoons coconut aminos

1-tablespoon minced garlic

1-teaspoon ginger

½ teaspoon salt

1-cup cauliflower florets

½ tablespoon sesame seeds

- Cut the rib eye steak into thin slices then rub with coconut aminos, minced garlic, ginger, and salt. Let the beef rest for 10 minutes.
- After 10 minutes, preheat a skillet over medium heat then pour coconut oil into the skillet.
- Once the oil is hot, add the seasoned beef to the skillet then sauté until brown and cooked through.
- Transfer the cooked beef to a serving dish then set aside.
- Stir in cauliflower florets then sauté with the remaining liquid in the skillet.
- Sprinkle the cooked cauliflower over the cooked beef then top with sesame seeds.
- Serve and enjoy.

Per Serving: Net Carbs: 2.2g: Calories: 418; Total Fat: 35.8g; Saturated Fat: 18.9g; Protein: 20.9g; Carbs: 3.1g; Fiber: 0.9g; Sugar: 0.6g - Fat 77% / Protein 21% / Carbs 2%

Rib Eye Turmeric with Lemon Mint Sauce

Serves: 3 / Preparation time: 15 minutes / Cooking time: 15 minutes

1 lb. rib eye steak

1-tablespoon butter

1 teaspoon minced garlic

¾ teaspoon oregano

¼ teaspoon turmeric

¼ cup lemon juice

½ cup mint leaves

¼ cup chopped parsley

1-teaspoon shallot

¼ cup extra virgin olive oil

¼ teaspoon salt

¼ teaspoon pepper

½ teaspoon red chili flakes

- Melt butter then combine with minced garlic, oregano, and turmeric. Mix well.
- Rub the rib eye with the turmeric mixture then let it sit for about 15 minutes.
- Meanwhile, place mint leaves, parsley, shallots, and red chili flakes in a food processor then season with salt and pepper.
- Drizzle lemon juice and olive oil over the herbs then process until smooth and incorporated.
- Transfer the sauce to a container with a lid then store in the fridge.
- Next, preheat an Air Fryer to 400°F (204°C) and place a rack in the Air Fryer.
- Wait until the Air Fryer is ready then place the seasoned rib eye on the rack.
- Set the time for 15 minutes then cook the rib eye.
- Once the rib eye is done, remove from the Air Fryer and transfer to a serving dish.
- Drizzle lemon minty sauce over the rib eye then serve.
- Enjoy!

Per Serving: Net Carbs: 1.5g; Calories: 403; Total Fat: 37.7g; Saturated Fat: 11.7g
Protein: 14.4g; Carbs: 3.1g; Fiber: 1.6g; Sugar: 0.5g - Fat 84% / Protein 14% / Carbs 2%

Coconut Steamed Beef [FA] [GF]

Serves: 4 / Preparation time: 5 minutes / Cooking time: 25 minutes

1 lb. rib eye steak	3 shallots
1-cup coconut milk	2 tablespoons red chili flakes
2 cloves garlic	½ cup chopped tomatoes

- ut the rib eye into cubes then place in a disposable aluminum pan. Set aside.
- Place garlic, shallots, and red chilies in a blender then pour coconut milk over the spices. Blend until incorporated.
- Pour the coconut milk mixture over the beef then sprinkle chopped tomatoes on top.
- Pour water into the Instant Pot then place a trivet in it.
- Place the disposable aluminum pan with beef in it on the trivet then put the lid on and seal the Instant Pot properly. Close the steam valve.
- Select "Steam" setting on the Instant Pot and cook the rib eye steak for 25 minutes.
- Once it is done, naturally release the Instant Pot then open the lid.
- Take then disposable aluminum pan out of the Instant Pot and transfer the cooked rib eye together with the gravy to a serving bowl.
- Serve and enjoy.

Per Serving: Net Carbs: 5.9g; Calories: 469; Total Fat: 39.5g; Saturated Fat: 22.7g; Protein: 22.3g; Carbs: 7.9g; Fiber: 2g; Sugar: 3.8g - Fat 76% / Protein 20% / Carbs 4%

Spinach Cheesy Beef Roll [GF]

Serves: 4 / Preparation time: 10 minutes / Cooking time: 30 minutes

2 lbs. rib eye steak	1 cup grated Mozzarella
½ teaspoon salt	2 pastured eggs
½ teaspoon pepper	1 cup almond flour
2 handfuls spinach	Coconut oil, to fry

- Cut the rib eye steak into large thin slices then rub with salt and pepper. Let it rest for a few minutes.
- Next, preheat a steamer and steam the spinach until just wilted. Remove from the steamer and let it cool.

- Next, arrange the beef on a flat surface then layer with steamed spinach.
- Sprinkle grated Mozzarella cheese over the spinach then roll the beef tightly.
- Wrap the beef roll with aluminum foil then tightly bundle it.
- Preheat the steamer again and place the wrapped beef roll in the steamer. Steam for approximately 20 minutes then remove from heat.
- Once the beef roll is cool, unwrap it and cut into thick slices.
- Crack the eggs and place in a bowl. Stir until incorporated.
- One by one, dip the sliced beef roll in the beaten egg then roll into the almond flour. Set aside and repeat with the remaining sliced beef rolls.
- After that, preheat a skillet over medium heat then pour olive oil into it.
- Once the oil is hot, put the coated sliced beef rolls in the skillet and fry for approximately 3 minutes.
- Flip the sliced beef rolls and fry for another 3 minutes.
- When both sides of the sliced beef rolls are lightly golden brown, remove from the coconut oil and strain the excessive oil.
- Serve and enjoy!

Per Serving: Net Carbs: 4g: Calories: 562; Total Fat: 46.3g; Saturated Fat: 23.6g; Protein: 31.4g; Carbs: 8.6g; Fiber: 4.6g; Sugar: 1g - Fat 74% / Protein 23% / Carbs 3%

Original Beef Steak [FA] [GF] [SF]

Serves: 4 / Preparation time: 5 minutes / Cooking time: 12 minutes

1 lb. rib eye steak	A pinch of salt
¼ cup butter	¼ teaspoon black pepper
3 teaspoons minced garlic	

- Rub the rib eye steak with minced garlic, salt, and pepper then place in the inner pot of an Instant Pot.
- Baste the rib eye with butter then close and seal the Instant Pot.
- Select "Manual " setting then cook the rib eye on high. Set the time to 12 minutes.
- Once the Instant Pot beeps, quick release the Instant Pot and open the lid.
- Take the rib eye out of the Instant Pot then place on a serving dish.
- Drizzle with your favorite sauce then enjoy!

Per Serving: Net Carbs: 0.7g; Calories: 415; Total Fat: 36.5g; Saturated Fat: 17.3g; Protein: 20.3g; Carbs: 0.8g; Fiber: 0.1g; Sugar: 0g - Fat 79% / Protein 20% / Carbs 1%

Fried Flank Steak with Hot Sauce

Serves: 2 / Preparation time: 10 minutes / Cooking time: 12 minutes

1 flank steak	1-¼ cups roasted pecans
½ teaspoon salt	1-tablespoon cayenne
2 tablespoons coriander	1-tablespoon red chili flakes
¼ cup minced garlic	1-½ cups beef broth
1-teaspoon coconut oil	2 tablespoons coconut aminos

- Place roasted pecans in a blender then pour beef broth to the blender.
- Add cayenne, red chili, and coconut aminos then blend until smooth. Set aside.
- Combine salt with coriander, salt, and minced garlic. Mix well.

- Cut the flank steak into thin slices then rub with the spice mixture.
- Preheat an Air Fryer to 400°F (204°C).
- Once the Air Fryer is ready, place the seasoned beef in the Air Fryer then spray with coconut oil. Cook the beef for 6 minutes.
- After 6 minutes, open the Air Fryer then stir the beef. Cook again for another 6 minutes.
- Serve the fried flank steak with pecans sauce.

Per Serving: Net Carbs: 6.1g; Calories: 428; Total Fat: 34.5g; Saturated Fat: 5.4g
Protein: 23g; Carbs: 10.2g; Fiber: 4.1g; Sugar: 2.3g - Fat 73% / Protein 21% / Carbs 6%

Comforting Slow Cooked Beef with Cabbage [GF]

Serves: 4 / Preparation time: 5 minutes / Cooking time: 4 hours

1-½ lbs. rib eye steak	¼ teaspoon salt
1 cup chopped onion	½ teaspoon black pepper
2 teaspoons minced garlic	½ teaspoon thyme
1 cup chopped cabbage	1- cup water

- Cut the rib eye into slices then place in the inner pot of an Instant Pot.
- Alternately, sprinkle chopped onion; minced garlic, chopped cabbage, salt, black pepper, and thyme then pour water into the Instant Pot.
- Put the lid on and seal then Instant Pot properly. Let the steam valve open.
- Select "Slow Cook" setting on the Instant Pot and cook the rib eye on low. Set the time to 4 hours.
- Once the Instant Pot beeps naturally release the Instant Pot and open the lid.
- Transfer the cooked rib eye to a serving dish then serve.
- Enjoy warm.

Per Serving: Net Carbs: 2.2g; Calories: 323; Total Fat: 25.1g; Saturated Fat: 10g; Protein: 20.5g; Carbs: 3.1g; Fiber: 0.9g; Sugar: 1.3g - Fat 70% / Protein 25% / Carbs 5%

Beef Meat Loaf [FA] [GF]

Serves: 6 / Preparation time: 10 minutes / Cooking time: 15 minutes

1-½ lbs. rib eye steak	½ teaspoon salt
¾ cup coconut milk	½ teaspoon mustard
1 egg	½ teaspoon pepper
½ cup almond flour	2 teaspoons minced garlic

- Cut the rib eye into cubes then place in a food processor.
- Pour coconut milk over the beef then add egg and almond flour to the food processor.
- Season the rib eye with salt, mustard, pepper, and minced garlic then process until smooth.
- Shape the mixture into a loaf then wrap with aluminum foil. Let the top open.
- Pour water into the Instant Pot then place a trivet in it.
- Place the wrapped meatloaf on the trivet then close and seal the Instant Pot. Close the steam valve.
- Select "Manual" setting then cook the meatloaf on high for 15 minutes.
- Once it is done, naturally release the Instant Pot then open the lid.
- Remove the wrapped meatloaf from the Instant Pot then let it rest for at least 15 minutes.
- After 15 minutes, unwrap the meatloaf then cut into slices.
- Serve and enjoy with roasted vegetables.

Per Serving: Net Carbs: 1.8g; Calories: 406; Total Fat: 34.1g; Saturated Fat: 16.7g; Protein: 22.3g; Carbs: 2.8g; Fiber: 1g; Sugar: 1.2g - Fat 76% / Protein 22% / Carbs 2%

Spicy Beef Coconut [GF]

Serves: 6 / Preparation time: 15 minutes / Cooking time: 4 hours

¾ lb. flap steak	½ teaspoon chili powder
2 cups grated young coconut	3 tablespoons red chili
1-cup coconut water	2 bay leaves
7 shallots	2 kaffir lime leaves
5 cloves minced garlic	2 inches galangal
2 teaspoons coriander	¼ cup coconut oil
½ teaspoon salt	

- Cut the beef into cubes then set aside.
- Place shallots, minced garlic, coriander, salt, chili powder, and red chili in a food processor then process until smooth.
- Transfer the spice mixture to the grated coconut then mix until combined. Set aside.
- Pour coconut oil into an Instant Pot then press the "Sauté" button.
- Add beef cubes to the Instant Pot then sauté until wilted and aromatic.
- Next, add the seasoned grated coconut to the Instant Pot then stir until the grated coconut is a bit dry.
- After that, pour coconut water to the Instant Pot then stir well.
- Select "Slow Cook" setting then cook the beef on low and set the time for 4 hours.
- Once the Instant Pot beeps, quick release the Instant Pot then stir well.
- Transfer the beef coconut to a serving dish then serve.

Per Serving: Net Carbs: 6.3g; Calories: 278; Total Fat: 22.3g; Saturated Fat: 17.1g; Protein: 12.7g; Carbs: 9.7g; Fiber: 3.4g; Sugar: 3.3g - Fat 72% / Protein 20% / Carbs 8%

Beef Meatloaf Tomato

Serves: 8 / Preparation time: 10 minutes / Cooking time: 20 minutes

2 cups ground beef	¾ teaspoon pepper
1 egg	1-cup cheddar cheese cubes
½ cup tomato puree	¼ cup chopped onion
½ teaspoon salt	3 tablespoons minced garlic

- Crack the eggs then place in a bowl.
- Season with salt, pepper, and minced garlic then whisk until incorporated.
- Pour the egg mixture into the ground beef then mix well.
- Add cheese cubes and chopped onion to the mixture then mix until combined.
- Transfer the beef mixture to a silicon loaf pan then spread evenly.
- Drizzle tomato puree on top then set aside.
- Preheat an Air Fryer to 350°F (177°C).
- Place the silicon loaf pan on the Air Fryer rack then cook the meatloaf for 20 minutes.
- Once it is done, remove from the Air Fryer then let it cool.

- Cut the beef meatloaf into slices then serve.
- Enjoy!

Per Serving: Net Carbs: 2.6g; Calories: 242; Total Fat: 19.3g; Saturated Fat: 8.7g
Protein: 13.7g; Carbs: 3.1g; Fiber: 0.5g; Sugar: 1g - Fat 71% / Protein 23% / Carbs 6%

Tasty Beef Curry in Onion Gravy [FA] [GF]

Serves: 6 / Preparation time: 5 minutes / Cooking time: 20 minutes

1-½ lbs. rib eye steak	1-cup coconut milk
2 cups chopped onion	½ teaspoon salt
2 teaspoons curry powder	2 tablespoons red chili
3 teaspoons minced garlic	1-tablespoon extra virgin olive oil
½ teaspoon ginger	

- Place onion in a food processor together with curry powder, minced garlic, ginger, and chili to the food processor.
- Pour olive oil into the inner pot of an Instant Pot then press the "Sauté" button.
- Add the onion mixture to the Instant Pot then sauté until aromatic. Press the "Cancel" button.
- After that, cut the rib eye steak into slices then place in the Instant Pot.
- Pour coconut milk over the rib eye then close and seal the Instant Pot properly. Close the steam valve.
- Select "Manual" setting on the Instant Pot and cook the rib eye for 20 minutes.
- Once it is done, naturally release the Instant Pot and open the lid.
- Transfer the beef curry to a serving dish then serve.
- Enjoy warm.

Per Serving: Net Carbs: 5.2g; Calories: 488; Total Fat: 37.3g; Saturated Fat: 18.9g; Protein: 21.8g; Carbs: 7.4g; Fiber: 2.2g; Sugar: 3.1g - Fat 75% / Protein 20% / Carbs 5%

PORK RECIPES

Spicy Pork with Kale Garlic

Serves: 4 / Preparation time: 16 minutes / Cooking time: 19 minutes

1 lb. pork shoulder	2 kaffir lime leaves
¼ lb. pork rind	1 bay leaf
5 teaspoons minced garlic	2 cups water
2 shallots	½ cup coconut milk
¼ cup red chilies	2 cups chopped kale
2 lemon grasses	2 tablespoons extra virgin olive oil

- Place red chilies in a pan then pour water to cover. Bring to boil.
- Once it is boiled, reduce the heat and cook until the red chilies are wilted.
- Remove the red chilies from heat and strain the water.
- Transfer the red chilies to a food processor then add 3 teaspoons minced garlic and shallots then process until smooth. Set aside.
- Cut the pork shoulder and pork rind into cubes then place in a skillet.

- Add the spice mixture to the skillet then pour water over the pork.
- Season the pork with lemon grasses, kaffir lime leaves, and bay leaf then bring to boil.
- Once it is boiled, reduce the heat and cook the pork until tender. The gravy will be reduced into half.
- In the meantime, preheat another skillet and pour extra virgin olive oil into it.
- Stir in minced garlic to the skillet then sauté until aromatic and wilted.
- Next, add chopped kale to the skillet then sauté until wilted.
- Remove the sautéed kale from heat then set aside.
- When the pork is tender, pour coconut milk over the pork then bring to a simmer.
- Transfer the cooked pork to a serving dish then serve with sautéed kale.
- Enjoy warm.

Per Serving: Net Carbs: 7g; Calories: 454; Total Fat: 37.5g; Saturated Fat: 15.5g
Protein: 21.7g; Carbs: 8.3g; Fiber: 1.3g; Sugar: 1g - Fat 74% / Protein 20% / Carbs 6%

Cheesy Pork Casserole [FA] [GF]

Serves: 4 / Preparation time: 10 minutes / Cooking time: 20 minutes

1 lb. pork butt	½ cup water
¼ cup butter	4 eggs
½ cup chopped onion	1 cup grated Mozzarella cheese
¼ teaspoon salt	2 tablespoons chopped leek
½ teaspoon pepper	

- Cut the pork butt into small cubes then set aside.
- Place butter in the Instant Pot then press the "Sauté" button.
- Stir in chopped onion then sauté until translucent and aromatic.
- Add pork butt to the Instant Pot then season with salt and pepper.
- Pour water over the pork then stir well.
- Put the lid on and seal the Instant Pot properly. Close the steam valve.
- Select "Pressure" setting and cook the pork for 15 minutes.
- Once the Instant Pot beeps, quick release the Instant Pot and open the lid.
- Remove the pork from the Instant Pot then transfer to a spring-form pan.
- Crack the eggs then beat until incorporated.
- Pour the egg over the pork then sprinkle grated Mozzarella cheese and chopped leek on top.
- Pour water into the Instant Pot then place a trivet in it.
- Place the spring-form on the trivet then close and seal the Instant Pot.
- Select "Manual" setting and cook the casserole for 5 minutes.
- Once it is done, naturally release the Instant Pot then open the lid.
- Take the casserole out of the Instant Pot then serve.
- Enjoy!

Per Serving: Net Carbs: 2.5g; Calories: 445; Total Fat: 37.2g; Saturated Fat: 17.4g; Protein: 25.9g; Carbs: 2.5g; Fiber: 0.4g; Sugar: 1.1g - Fat 75% / Protein 23% / Carbs 2%

Pork Shoulder with Zucchini Salads

Serves: 2 / Preparation time: 12 minutes / Cooking time: 50 minutes

½ pork shoulder	3 tablespoons extra virgin olive oil

2 teaspoons salt

1-cup sliced zucchini

¼ cup chopped onion

½ cup diced bell pepper

1-tablespoon chopped basil

1-tablespoon sesame oil

1 tablespoon lemon juice

- Score the pork shoulder on several places then rub it with salt and olive oil. Repeat for three times.
- Preheat an Air Fryer to 300°F (148°C).
- Place the seasoned pork shoulder in the Air Fryer then cook for 30 minutes.
- After 30 minutes, increase the temperature to 400°F (204°C) and cook again for 20 minutes.
- Meanwhile, place sliced zucchinis, chopped onion, diced bell pepper, and chopped basil in a salad bowl.
- Drizzle sesame oil and lemon juice over the salads then toss to combine. Store in the refrigerator.
- Once the pork shoulder is done, remove from the Air Fryer and let it sit for about 10 minutes.
- Cut into slices then arrange on a serving dish.
- Serve with zucchini salads.

Per Serving: Net Carbs: 4.3g; Calories: 372; Total Fat: 35.1g; Saturated Fat: 6.6g
Protein: 11.2g; Carbs: 5.7g; Fiber: 1.4g; Sugar: 3.3g - Fat 85% / Protein 12% / Carbs 3%

Spiced Pork Shoulder with Goat Cheese and Tender Veggies

Serves: 4 / Preparation time: 9 minutes / Cooking time: 19 minutes

1 lb. pork shoulder

2 tablespoons extra virgin olive oil

¾ teaspoon pepper

1-½ teaspoons thyme

¼ teaspoon grated lemon zest

¼ cup goat cheese

2 tablespoons almond butter

1 cup chopped green beans

½ cup sliced carrots

¼ cup chicken broth

1 tablespoon lemon juice

- Combine goat cheese with almond butter, grated lemon zest, thyme, and ¼ teaspoon of pepper then mix until incorporated. Set aside.
- Preheat a pan over medium heat then pour extra virgin olive oil into it.
- Once the oil is hot, sprinkle the ¼ teaspoon of pepper over the pork then place them on the pan.
- Cook the pork for approximately 4 minutes then flip it.
- Continue cooking the pork until both sides are lightly golden brown and the pork is completely cooked.
- Once it is done, remove the cooked pork from the pan and place on a serving dish.
- Next, add green beans and carrots to the pan then pour chicken broth into the pan. Season the vegetables with the remaining pepper then bring to boil.
- Once it is boiled, reduce the heat and cook until the vegetables are tender.
- Remove the tender vegetables from the heat and drizzle lemon juice over the vegetables. Place the vegetables next to the cooked pork.
- Top the pork with goat cheese mixture then serve.
- Enjoy warm.

Per Serving: Net Carbs: 3.1g; Calories: 423; Total Fat: 35.1g; Saturated Fat: 9.7g
Protein: 22g; Carbs: 5.4g; Fiber: 2.3g; Sugar: 1.6g - Fat 75% / Protein 22% / Carbs 3%

Pepper Pork Tender with Lemon Sauce [FA] [GF]

Serves: 4 / Preparation time: 10 minutes / Cooking time: 25 minutes

2 lbs. pork shoulder	1-cup water
½ teaspoon salt	¼ cup butter
1 ½ teaspoons black pepper	½ cup lemon juice
2 teaspoons minced garlic	¾ cup Greek yogurt

- Rub the pork shoulder with salt, black pepper, and minced garlic then place in the Instant Pot.
- Pour water over the pork then close and seal the Instant Pot properly. Close the steam valve.
- Select "Manual" setting on the Instant Pot then cook the pork on high. Set the time to 20 minutes.
- Meanwhile, place lemon juice and Greek yogurt in a blender then blend until smooth and incorporated. Set aside.
- When the Instant Pot beeps, quick release the Instant Pot then open the lid.
- Take the tender pork out of the Instant Pot then let it sit for a while.
- Clean the Instant Pot then place butter in it.
- Return the tender pork into the Instant Pot then sauté with butter.
- Once it is done, press the "Cancel" button then transfer the pork to a serving dish.
- Top with lemon sauce then serve.
- Enjoy warm.

Per Serving: Net Carbs: 3.1g; Calories: 432; Total Fat: 35.6g; Saturated Fat: 16.1g; Protein: 23.3g; Carbs: 3.1g; Fiber: 0.4g; Sugar: 2.2g - Fat 74% / Protein 22% / Carbs 4%

Crispy Pork Belly with Minty Lettuce

Serves: 4 / Preparation time: 15 minutes / Cooking time: 45 minutes

1 lb. pork belly	¼ cup chopped mint leaves
2 teaspoons salt	1 tablespoon chopped jalapeno
½ tablespoon five spice powder	¼ cup chopped onion
1-tablespoon extra virgin olive oil	1 fresh lime
1 handful fresh lettuce	1 teaspoon avocado oil
¼ cup diced cucumber	

- Remove the hair from the pork belly then wash and clean it.
- Place the pork belly in a pot then pour water to cover. Bring to boil.
- Once it is boiled, reduce the heat and cook the pork belly for about 10 minutes.
- Remove the pork belly from heat then discard the water.
- Using a kitchen towel, pat the pork belly dry then place on a flat surface.
- Score the pork belly at several places then set aside.
- Place salt, five-spice powder, and olive oil in a bowl then stir until incorporated.
- Score the pork belly at several places then rub with the spice mixture.
- After that, using a steel skewer prick the pork belly then wrap it with aluminum foil. Leave the rind open.
- Store the pork belly in the refrigerator overnight.
- In the morning, remove the pork belly from the refrigerator then thaw at room temperature. Unwrap the pork belly.
- Preheat an Air Fryer to 325°F (163°C) and place the pork belly in the Air Fryer with the rind up.
- Set the time to 20 minutes and cook the pork belly.
- After 20 minutes, increase the temperature of the Air Fryer to 350°F (177°C) and cook the pork belly for 25 minutes.

- Once it is done, remove the pork belly from the Air Fryer and let it sit for about 10 minutes.
- In the meantime, chop the fresh lettuce and place in a salad bowl.
- Add sliced cucumber, chopped onion, chopped jalapeno, and chopped mint leaves to the salad bowl.
- Cut the lime into halves then drizzle the juice over the vegetables.
- Drizzle avocado oil over the salads then toss to combine.
- Cut the crispy pork belly into slices and serve with minty lettuce salads.
- Enjoy!

Per Serving: Net Carbs: 2.3g; Calories: 347; Total Fat: 33.8g; Saturated Fat: 11.5g
Protein: 6.4g; Carbs: 4.5g; Fiber: 2.2g; Sugar: 1.2g - Fat 88% / Protein 7% / Carbs 5%

Pork Coconut Curry in Lettuce Blanket

Serves: 4 / Preparation time: 16 minutes / Cooking time: 21 minutes

¾ lb. boneless pork shoulder	½ teaspoon turmeric
2 tablespoons extra virgin olive oil	1-teaspoon pepper
2 teaspoons minced garlic	2 cups water
2 teaspoons sliced shallot	½ cup coconut milk
1-teaspoon curry powder	1 handful of fresh lettuce

- Cut the boneless pork shoulder into small dices then set aside.
- Preheat a skillet over medium heat then pour extra virgin olive oil into the skillet.
- Once t is hot, stir in minced garlic and sliced shallot to the skillet and sauté until wilted and aromatic.
- Add diced pork to the skillet then cook until the pork is just wilted.
- Season the pork with curry powder, turmeric, and pepper then pour water over the pork bring to boil.
- Once it is boiled, reduce the heat and cook until the pork is tender and the water is completely absorbed into the pork.
- Next, drizzle coconut milk over the pork and bring to a simmer.
- Occasionally stir the pork and cook until there is no more liquid in the skillet.
- Remove the pork from heat and let it cool.
- Take a large lettuce and place on a flat surface.
- Put about 2 tablespoons of cooked pork on the lettuce then wrap it tightly. Place on a serving dish.
- Repeat with the remaining lettuce and pork then serve.
- Enjoy!

Per Serving: Net Carbs: 2.9g; Calories: 369; Total Fat: 31.5g; Saturated Fat: 13.4g
Protein: 16.2g; Carbs: 5.2g; Fiber: 2.1g; Sugar: 2g - Fat 77% / Protein 20% / Carbs 3%

Savory Pork in Cheesy Cream [FA] [GF]

Serves: 4 / Preparation time: 5 minutes / Cooking time: 20 minutes

1 lb. pork shoulder	½ cup water
½ teaspoon salt	¼ cup cream cheese
½ teaspoon pepper	¼ cup cheddar cheese cubes
3 tablespoons butter	2 tablespoons chopped parsley

- Cut the pork shoulder into thin slices then set aside.
- Preheat a skillet over medium heat then place butter in it.
- Once the butter is melted, stir in pork shoulder then sauté until wilted.
- Reduce the heat and cook the pork until done.
- Remove the cooked pork from the skillet and place on a plate. Leave the remaining butter in the skillet.
- Next, pour water into the same skillet together with cream cheese.
- Add cheddar cheese cubes to the skillet then cook until the cheese is melted.
- Return the pork to the skillet and bring to a simmer.
- Transfer the pork together with the cheesy gravy to a serving dish then serve.
- Enjoy!

Per Serving: Net Carbs: 0.7g: Calories: 452; Total Fat: 39.5g; Saturated Fat: 18.4g; Protein: 22.3g; Carbs: 0.8 g; Fiber: 0.1g; Sugar: 0.1g - Fat 79% / Protein 20% / Carbs 1%

Pork Chili Stew [FA] [GF]

Serves: 4 / Preparation time: 5 minutes / Cooking time: 20 minutes

1-lb. pork shoulder	¼ teaspoon salt
2 tablespoons extra virgin olive oil	3 tablespoons chili powder
½ cup chopped onion	1-teaspoon paprika
2 teaspoons minced garlic	1-teaspoon oregano
½ cup chopped bell pepper	¼ cup chopped red chili
2 tablespoons tomato puree	1-cup chicken broth

- Cut the pork shoulder into slices then set aside.
- Pour olive oil into an Instant Pot then press the "Sauté" button.
- Stir in minced garlic and chopped onion then sauté until aromatic.
- After that, add pork shoulder to the Instant Pot then sauté until wilted. Press the "Cancel" button.
- Add the remaining ingredients to the Instant Pot then close and seal the Instant Pot. Close the steam valve.
- Select "Manual" setting on the Instant Pot and cook the baby back ribs on high for 20 minutes.
- Once it is done, naturally release the Instant Pot and open the lid.
- Transfer the pork stew to a serving dish then serve right away.

Per Serving: Net Carbs: 5.5g; Calories: 403; Total Fat: 31.6g; Saturated Fat: 9.3g; Protein: 21.8g; Carbs: 9.1g; Fiber: 3.6g; Sugar: 3.3 g - Fat 71% / Protein 22% / Carbs 7%

Tasty Pork Chops Jalapeno

Serves: 1 / Preparation time: 15 minutes / Cooking time: 20 minutes

1-pork chops	2 tablespoons extra virgin olive oil
1 egg	2 chopped jalapenos
¾ teaspoon salt	2 tablespoons chopped scallions
½ teaspoon pepper	

- Crack the egg then place in a bowl.
- Season the egg with salt and pepper then stir until incorporated.

- Cut the pork chop into slices then dip into the egg mixture. Coat thoroughly.
- Cover the bowl with plastic wrap then marinate the pork chops for 10 minutes.
- Preheat an Air Fryer to 350°F (177°C) and coat then Air Fryer with aluminum foil.
- Place the pork chops in the Air Fryer and set the time to 12 minutes.
- Don't forget to spray the pork chop with olive oil before cooking.
- After 12 minutes, increase the temperature of the Air Fryer to 400°F (204°C) and cook the pork chop for 6 minutes.
- Next, open the drawer then sprinkle jalapenos and scallions over the pork chops.
- Cook for 2 minutes then remove from the Air Fryer.
- Transfer the cooked pork chops to a serving dish then enjoy.

Per Serving: Net Carbs: 2.7g; Calories: 308; Total Fat: 25.1g; Saturated Fat: 5.9g
Protein: 18.8g; Carbs: 4.1g; Fiber: 1.4g; Sugar: 1.6g - Fat 73% / Protein 24% / Carbs 3%

Stuffed Pork Black Pepper Jalapeno with Carrots

Serves: 4 / Preparation time: 14 minutes / Cooking time: 18 minutes

½ lb. green jalapenos	2 tablespoons grated carrots
¾ lb. ground pork	½ teaspoon black pepper
½ cup goat cheese	2 eggs
2 tablespoons diced onion	2 tablespoons extra virgin olive oil

- Cut the green jalapenos into halves lengthwise then remove the seeds. Set aside.
- Crack the eggs then place the eggs in a bowl.
- Pour extra virgin olive oil into the eggs then season with black pepper. Stir until incorporated.
- Combine ground pork with goat cheese, diced onion, and grated carrot in a bowl then pour the egg mixture over the pork. Mix well.
- Preheat a steamer over medium heat then wait until it is ready.
- Fill each halved jalapeno with the pork mixture then arrange in the steamer.
- Steam the filled jalapenos for approximately 20 minutes or until set.
- Once it is done, remove the stuffed jalapenos from the steamer and arrange on a serving dish.
- If you like, you can bake the steamed jalapenos until lightly golden brown.
- Serve and enjoy warm.

Per Serving: Net Carbs: 5.1g; Calories: 343; Total Fat: 27.2g; Saturated Fat: 8.2g
Protein: 17.8g; Carbs: 5.4g; Fiber: 0.3g; Sugar: 0.6g - Fat 71% / Protein 23% / Carbs 6%

Almond Butter Crispy Pork Ribs [FA] [GF]

Serves: 4 / Preparation time: 4 minutes / Cooking time: 24 minutes

2 lbs. baby back ribs	½ teaspoon salt
2 tablespoons minced garlic	1-cup water
2 tablespoons coriander	1 cup almond flour
1-lemon grass	3 tablespoons butter

- Place the baby back ribs in the Instant Pot then sprinkle minced garlic, turmeric, coriander, and salt over the baby back ribs
- Add lemon grass to the Instant Pot then pour water over the baby back ribs.
- Put the lid on and seal the Instant Pot properly. Close the steam valve.
- Select "Manual" setting and cook the baby back rib on high for 14 minutes.
- When the baby back ribs are done, quick release the Instant Pot then open the lid.
- Take the cooked baby back ribs out of the Instant Pot then place on a flat surface.
- Cut the cooked baby back ribs into medium pieces then roll in the almond flour. Make sure that all sides of the baby back ribs are completely coated with almond flour.
- Clean the Instant Pot then place butter in it.
- Press "Sauté" button and stir in the coated baby back ribs. Sauté until the ribs are crispy and completely coated with butter.
- Once it is done, turn the Instant Pot off and arrange the baby back ribs on a serving dish.
- Serve and enjoy.

Per Serving: Net Carbs: 2.1g; Calories: 444; Total Fat: 39.2g; Saturated Fat: 15.7g; Protein: 19.9g; Carbs: 3.2g; Fiber: 0.3g; Sugar: 0.3g - Fat 79% / Protein 18% / Carbs 3%

Salty Pork Satay Tender [GF]

Serves: 4 / Preparation time: 2 hours / Cooking time: 20 minutes

1 lb. pork shoulder	1-½ teaspoons salt
4 tablespoons minced garlic	3 tablespoons extra virgin olive oil
1-½ teaspoons ginger	Papaya leaves, to wrap
1-½ teaspoons pepper	

- Cut the pork shoulder into medium cubes then place in a bowl.
- Rub the pork with minced garlic, ginger, pepper, and salt then wrap with papaya leaves. Let it rest for 2 hours.
- After 2 hours, preheat a grill over medium heat and wait until it reaches the desired temperature.
- Unwrap the pork and using skewers prick the pork.
- Once the grill is ready, grill the pork satay until cooked. Flip, rotate and baste with extra virgin olive oil for several times.
- Arrange the pork satay on a serving dish then serve.
- Enjoy warm.

Per Serving: Net Carbs: 3g: Calories: 437; Total Fat: 34.9g; Saturated Fat: 10.4g; Protein: 27g; Carbs: 3.4g; Fiber: 0.4g; Sugar: 0.1g - Fat 72% / Protein 26% / Carbs 2%

Lemon Pork Oregano [FA] [GF]

Serves: 4 / Preparation time: 5 minutes / Cooking time: 20 minutes

1 lb. pork butt	2 tablespoons butter
2 teaspoons oregano	1-½ cups low sodium chicken broth
1-teaspoon basil	3 tablespoons lemon juice
2 tablespoons minced garlic	½ cup heavy cream

- Cut the pork butt into slices then set aside.
- Place butter in the inner pot of an Instant Pot then press the "Sauté" button.
- Add sliced pork butt and minced garlic to the Instant Pot then sauté until aromatic and the pork is brown.

- Next, pour chicken broth into the Instant Pot then add basil to the pot.
- Put the lid on then seal the Instant Pot properly. Close the steam valve.
- Select "Manual" setting on the Instant Pot then cook the chicken on high for 15 minutes.
- Once it is done, quick release the Instant Pot then open the lid.
- Take the cooked pork out of the Instant Pot and arrange on a serving dish. Leave the liquid in the Instant Pot.
- Pour lemon juice and heavy cream into the Instant Pot then stir well.
- Drizzle the liquid over the cooked pork then serve.
- Enjoy immediately.

Per Serving: Net Carbs: 2.3g; Calories: 370; Total Fat: 31.5g; Saturated Fat: 15.2g; Protein: 19.3g; Carbs: 2.8g; Fiber: 0.5g; Sugar: 0.3g - Fat 77% / Protein 21% / Carbs 2%

Baby Back Ribs Tender

Serves: 2 / Preparation time: 5 minutes / Cooking time: 30 minutes

2 baby back ribs	¾ teaspoon pepper
½ teaspoon salt	2 teaspoons red chili flakes
3 teaspoons grated garlic	1-tablespoon extra virgin olive oil
¾ teaspoon ginger	

- Combine salt, grated garlic, ginger, pepper, and red chili flakes in a bowl then mix well.
- Rub the baby back ribs with the spice mixture then set aside.
- Preheat an Air Fryer to 350°F (177°C).
- Place the seasoned baby back ribs and set the time to 30 minutes. Cook the baby back ribs.
- Once it is done, remove from the Air Fryer then transfer to a serving dish.
- Serve and enjoy immediately.

Per Serving: Net Carbs: 5.2g; Calories: 409; Total Fat: 34.3g; Saturated Fat: 11g
Protein: 19.3g; Carbs: 6.3g; Fiber: 1.1g; Sugar: 2.5g - Fat 75% / Protein 18% / Carbs 7%

Grilled Lemon Pork with Cilantro Topping [GF]

Serves: 4 / Preparation time: 20 minutes / Cooking time: 15 minutes

1 ½ lbs. pork shoulder	1-teaspoon salt
¼ cup lemon juice	1-tablespoon diced jalapeno pepper
¾ teaspoon cumin	¼ cup chopped cilantro
½ teaspoon chili powder	

- Brush the pork shoulder with 2 tablespoons of lemon juice then rub with cumin, chili powder, and salt.
- Wrap the seasoned pork shoulder with plastic wrap then let it rest for 15 minutes.
- In the meantime, preheat the grill over medium heat and wait until it is ready.
- Once the grill is ready, unwrap the seasoned pork shoulder and grill for approximately 7 minutes per side or until the internal temperature of the pork shoulder has reached 145°F (63°C).
- When the grilled pork is done, remove from the grill and transfer to a serving dish.
- Combine the remaining lemon juice with diced jalapeno and chopped cilantro then mix well.
- Top the grilled pork with the cilantro topping then serve.
- Enjoy immediately.

Per Serving: Net Carbs: 0.5g: Calories: 442; Total Fat: 34.8g; Saturated Fat: 12.1g; Protein: 28.8g; Carbs: 0.8g; Fiber: 0.3g; Sugar: 0.4g - Fat 71% / Protein 28% / Carbs 1%

Pork Balls in Spicy Coconut [FA] [GF]

Serves: 4 / Preparation time: 10 minutes / Cooking time: 25 minutes

1-½ lbs. pork shoulder	3 teaspoons sliced shallots
2 tablespoons almond flour	¼ cup red chili flakes
2 eggs	¼ cup chopped cayenne pepper
2 tablespoons extra virgin olive oil	2 cups coconut milk
2 teaspoons minced garlic	

- Cut the pork shoulder into cubes then place in a food processor.
- Add almond flour and eggs to the food processor then process until smooth and combined.
- Shape the pork mixture into medium balls then set aside.
- Pour water into the Instant Pot then place a trivet in it.
- Arrange the pork balls on the trivet then put the lid on and seal the Instant Pot properly. Close the steam valve.
- Select "Steam" setting on the Instant Pot and cook the pork balls for 10 minutes.
- When the Instant Pot beeps, quick release it then open the lid.
- Take the cooked pork balls out of the Instant Pot then place on a serving dish.
- Clean the Instant Pot then place butter in it. Select "Sauté" menu.
- Once the butter is melted, stir in minced garlic and sliced shallots then sauté until wilted and aromatic.
- Pour coconut milk into the Instant Pot then add red chilies and cayenne pepper to the gravy. Bring to a simmer.
- Add pork balls to the Instant Pot then cook for about 5 minutes.
- Transfer the pork balls and the gravy to a serving dish and serve.
- Enjoy right away.

Per Serving: Net Carbs: 4.7g; Calories: 455; Total Fat: 41.3g; Saturated Fat: 23.5g; Protein: 17g; Carbs: 7.5g; Fiber: 2.8g; Sugar: 3.3g - Fat 82% / Protein 15% / Carbs 3%

Pork Balls with Cheese Sauce [GF]

Serves: 8 / Preparation time: 15 minutes / Cooking time: 25 minutes

1-½ lbs. pork butt	½ teaspoon pepper
¾ cup coconut milk	2 teaspoons minced garlic
1 egg	1-cup heavy cream
½ cup almond flour	¼ cup cream cheese
½ teaspoon salt	2 tablespoons butter
½ teaspoon mustard	2 tablespoons grated Parmesan cheese

- Cut the pork butt into cubes then place in a food processor.
- Pour coconut milk over the pork then add egg and almond flour to the food processor.
- Season the pork with salt, mustard, pepper, and minced garlic then process until smooth.
- Shape the mixture into medium balls then set aside.
- Pour water into the Instant Pot then place a trivet in it.

- Arrange the pork balls on the trivet then close and seal the Instant Pot. Close the steam valve.
- Select "Manual" setting then cook the meatloaf on high for 25 minutes.
- Once it is done, naturally release the Instant Pot then open the lid.
- Remove the pork balls from the Instant Pot then arrange on a serving dish.
- Clean the Instant Pot then place butter in it.
- Press the "Sauté" button then cook until the butter is melted. Press the "Cancel" button.
- Quickly add heavy cream into the Instant Pot together with cream cheese and grated Parmesan cheese then stir well.
- Pour the cheese sauce over the pork balls then serve.
- Enjoy immediately.

Per Serving: Net Carbs: 1.8g; Calories: 325; Total Fat: 28.3g; Saturated Fat: 14.3g; Protein: 16.7g; Carbs: 2.2g; Fiber: 0.6g; Sugar: 0.7g - Fat 78% / Protein 21% / Carbs 1%

Super Spicy Yellow Pork [FA] [GF]

Serves: 6 / Preparation time: 5 minutes / Cooking time: 20 minutes

1 ½ lbs. pork shoulder	2 lemon grasses
4 cloves garlic	3 kaffir lime leaves
3 shallots	2 bay leaves
2-teaspoon turmeric	1-inch galangal
¼ cup cayenne pepper	1 ¼ cups coconut milk
1-teaspoon ginger	1-½ cups fresh basil

- Place garlic, shallots, turmeric, cayenne pepper, and ginger in a blender.
- Pour coconut milk into the blender then blend until smooth.
- Next, cut the pork shoulder, pork butt, and pork rind into small pieces then place in the Instant Pot.
- Pour spice mixture over the pork then add lemon grasses, lime leaves, bay leaves, and galangal.
- Put the lid on the Instant Pot and seal it properly. Close the steam valve.
- Select the "Pressure" setting then cook the pork for 20 minutes.
- Once it is done, quick release the Instant Pot then open the lid.
- Add fresh basil to the Instant Pot then stir until wilted.
- Transfer the cooked pork with the liquid to a serving dish then enjoy warm.

Per Serving: Net Carbs: 6.8g; Calories: 397; Total Fat: 32.7g; Saturated Fat: 18.7g; Protein: 20g; Carbs: 9.2g; Fiber: 2.4g; Sugar: 2.1g - Fat 74% / Protein 20% / Carbs 6%

Pork Loaf with Black Pepper Tomato Sauce [FA] [GF]

Serves: 4 / Preparation time: 5 minutes / Cooking time: 20 minutes

1-½ lbs. pork butt	½ cup tomato puree
1 egg	1-tablespoon mustard
1-½ teaspoons coriander	1 teaspoon Worcestershire sauce
2 tablespoons butter	½ teaspoon salt
½ cup chopped onion	½ teaspoon black pepper
2 teaspoons minced garlic	½ teaspoon cumin

- Cut the pork butt into cubes then place in a food processor.

- Add coriander and egg then process until smooth.
- Shape the pork mixture into a loaf then wrap with aluminum foil.
- Pour water into the Instant Pot then place a trivet in it.
- Place the pork loaf on the trivet then close and seal the Instant Pot properly.
- Select "Manual" setting and cook the loaf for 15 minutes.
- Once it is done, quickly release the Instant Pot then open the lid.
- Remove the pork loaf from the Instant Pot then let it cool for a few minutes then unwrap and cut it into thick slices.
- In the meantime, clean the Instant Pot then place butter in it. Press the "Sauté" button.
- Once the butter is melted, stir in chopped onion and minced garlic then sauté until aromatic.
- Pour tomato puree into the Instant Pot then season with mustard, Worcestershire sauce, salt, black pepper, and cumin then bring to a simmer.
- Add the sliced pork loaf to the Instant Pot then cook for about 3 minutes.
- After that, turn the Instant Pot off then arrange the sliced pork loaf on a serving dish.
- Drizzle the sauce over the pork loaf then serve.
- Enjoy immediately.

Per Serving: Net Carbs: 4.8g; Calories: 480; Total Fat: 37.8g; Saturated Fat: 16g; Protein: 30g; Carbs: 6.2g; Fiber: 1.4g; Sugar: 2.7g - Fat 71% / Protein 25% / Carbs 4%

Crispy Coated Pork with Cheese

Serves: 2 / Preparation time: 15 minutes / Cooking time: 20 minutes

1 pork chop	2 tablespoons Parmesan cheese
2 tablespoons extra virgin olive oil	2 teaspoons smoked paprika
1 egg	½ teaspoon pepper
½ cup coconut flour	½ teaspoon salt
½ cup grated coconut	

- Combine coconut flour with grated coconut and Parmesan cheese then mix well.
- Season with smoked paprika, salt, and pepper then set aside.
- Crack the egg then stir until incorporated.
- Cut the pork chop into thin slices then place in a bowl.
- Take a slice of pork chop then dip in the egg.
- Next, roll the pork in the coconut flour mixture then set aside. Repeat with the remaining pork chop.
- Preheat an Air Fryer to 400°F (204°C) and place a rack in the Air Fryer.
- Arrange the coated pork chops on the rack then cook for 7 minutes.
- After 7 minutes, flip the pork chops and cook again for another 7 minutes.
- Once it is done, remove from the Air Fryer then place on a serving dish.
- Serve and enjoy.

Per Serving: Net Carbs: 4g; Calories: 390; Total Fat: 32.9g; Saturated Fat: 14.4g
Protein: 19.6g; Carbs: 8g; Fiber: 4g; Sugar: 1.9g - Fat 76% / Protein 20% / Carbs 4%

Paprika and Cayenne Pulled Pork Butt with Roasted Asparagus

Serves: 4 / Preparation time: 2 hours / Cooking time: 2 hours 34 minutes

1 lb. pork butt	2 teaspoons paprika
2 teaspoons cayenne pepper	2-½ teaspoons pepper

2 tablespoons mustard

1 bunch asparagus spears

2-½ tablespoons extra virgin olive oil

½ teaspoon minced garlic

1 tablespoon lemon juice

- Rub the pork butt with cayenne pepper, paprika, pepper, and mustard then marinate for at least 2 hours or more. Store in the fridge to keep it fresh.
- After 2 hours, remove the pork butt from the fridge and thaw at room temperature.
- Preheat an oven to 350°F (177°C) and line a baking tray with aluminum foil.
- Once the oven is ready, place the marinated pork butt on the prepared baking tray and cover with aluminum foil.
- Bake the pork butt for approximately 2 hours or until tender then remove from the oven. Let it rest for a few minutes.
- In the meantime, cut and trim the asparagus then toss with extra virgin olive oil, minced garlic, and lemon juice.
- Line a baking tray with aluminum foil then spread the seasoned asparagus on it.
- Bake the asparagus for about 20 hours or until tender.
- Once it is done, remove the asparagus from the oven and let it rest.
- Slowly unwrap the pork butt then using a fork shred the cooked pork.
- Place the pulled pork on a serving dish then serve with roasted asparagus.
- Serve and enjoy.

Per Serving: Net Carbs: 2.6g; Calories: 353; Total Fat: 29g; Saturated Fat: 9.2g
Protein: 20.4g; Carbs: 4.9g; Fiber: 2.3g; Sugar: 1.1g - Fat 74% / Protein 23% / Carbs 3%

Slow Cooked Crispy Shredded Pork [GF]

Serves: 4 / Preparation time: 5 minutes / Cooking time: 4 hours

2 lbs. pork shoulder

½ tablespoon extra virgin olive oil

½ tablespoon oregano

¼ teaspoon cumin

2 teaspoons paprika

½ teaspoon salt

½ cup chopped onion

3 teaspoons minced garlic

2 tablespoons chopped jalapeno

½ cup diced tomatoes

2 tablespoons lemon juice

2 tablespoons butter

1 ½ teaspoons black pepper

- Place pork shoulder in a slow cooker then drizzle extra virgin olive oil and lemon juice over the pork.
- Next, sprinkle oregano, cumin, paprika, salt, black pepper, chopped onion, minced garlic, chopped jalapeno, and diced tomatoes on top then cover the slow cooker with a lid.
- Cook the pork on high and set the time to 4 hours.
- Once it is done, remove the cooked pork from the slow cooker and let it cool.
- Using a fork shred the cooked pork and set aside.
- After that, preheat a saucepan over medium heat then place butter in it.
- Once the butter is melted, stir in shredded pork and sauté until crispy.
- Transfer the crispy shredded pork to a serving dish then serve.

- Enjoy warm.

Per Serving: Net Carbs: 3.2g: Calories: 379; Total Fat: 30.9g; Saturated Fat: 12g; Protein: 20g; Carbs: 4.8g; Fiber: 1.6g; Sugar: 1.6g -Fat 73% / Protein 24% / Carbs 3%

Pork and Mushroom Cabbage Roll with Cheese [FA] [GF]

Serves: 4 / Preparation time: 10 minutes / Cooking time: 15 minutes

1-lb. pork butt	1- cup water
½ cup mushroom	½ teaspoon salt
2 tablespoons butter	½ teaspoon pepper
¼ cup chopped onion	8 large cabbages
2 tablespoons coconut aminos	½ lb. grated cheddar cheese

- Cut pork butt and mushroom into small dices then place in the inner pot of an Instant Pot. Set aside.
- Place butter in an Instant Pot then press the "Sauté" button.
- Stir in chopped onion then sauté until aromatic and translucent.
- After that, add diced pork and mushroom to the Instant Pot then pour water into the Instant Pot.
- Season with salt, pepper, and coconut aminos then stir well.
- Place a trivet in the Instant Pot then place cabbages on it.
- Put the lid on and seal the Instant Pot properly. Close the steam valve.
- Select "Manual" setting and cook the pork on high for 15 minutes.
- Once it is done, naturally release the Instant Pot then open the lid.
- Take the cabbage out of the Instant Pot then let it cool.
- To serve, take a cabbage on a flat surface then put 2 tablespoons of cooked pork and mushroom.
- Add grated cheese on top then roll the cabbage. Repeat with the remaining cabbage and pork.
- Arrange the cabbage rolls on a serving dish then serve.
- Enjoy right away.

Per Serving: Net Carbs: 4.6g; Calories: 389; Total Fat: 30.6g; Saturated Fat: 14.7g; Protein: 22.8g; Carbs: 6.6g; Fiber: 2g; Sugar: 2.6g - Fat 71% / Protein 23% / Carbs 6%

Original Pork Chop Tender

Serves: 2 / Preparation time: 15 minutes / Cooking time: 45 minutes

1 pork chop	2 tablespoons mustard
1 tablespoon Worcestershire sauce	2 tablespoons lemon juice
2 tablespoons extra virgin olive oil	

- Combine Worcestershire sauce with olive oil, mustard, and lemon juice then stir until incorporated.
- Cut the pork chop into slices then place in zipper-lock plastic bag.
- Pour the spice mixture over the pork chop then shake until the pork chop slices are completely coated with seasoning.
- Marinate the pork chop for at least 2 hours or overnight.
- Preheat an Air Fryer to 350°F (177°C) and set the time to 6 minutes.
- Place the seasoned pork chop in the Air Fryer and cook it.
- After 6 minutes, increase the temperature to 375°F (191°C).
- Open the drawer then flip the pork chop.
- Cook the pork chop again and set the time to 5 minutes.
- At last, increase the temperature to 400°F (204°C) and cook the chop for 2 minutes.

- Once it is done, remove from the Air Fryer then transfer to a serving dish.
- Serve and enjoy.

Per Serving: Net Carbs: 4g; Calories: 372; Total Fat: 34.3g; Saturated Fat: 7g
Protein: 11.9g; Carbs: 5.7g; Fiber: 1.7g; Sugar: 2.6g - Fat 83% / Protein 13% / Carbs 4%

Garlic Pork with Mayo and Tomato Salsa [FA] [GF]

Serves: 4 / Preparation time: 10 minutes / Cooking time: 20 minutes

1 lb. baby back ribs	1-cup mayonnaise
3 tablespoons minced garlic	½ cup diced red tomato
1-teaspoon black pepper	1 teaspoon chopped jalapeno
½ teaspoon salt	2 tablespoons lemon juice
½ cup water	1 teaspoon chopped celeries
2 tablespoons butter	

- Cut the baby back ribs into medium pieces then rub with minced garlic, salt, and black pepper.
- Place the seasoned baby back ribs in the Instant Pot then pour water over the baby back ribs.
- Put the lid on and seal the Instant Pot properly. Close the steam valve.
- Select "Pressure" setting on the Instant Pot and cook the baby back ribs on high. Set the time to 15 minutes.
- Meanwhile, combine the diced red tomatoes with chopped jalapeno then pour lemon juice on top. Toss to combine then store in the fridge.
- Once the Instant Pot beeps, quick release the Instant Pot and open the lid.
- Take the cooked baby back ribs out of the Instant Pot then place on a flat surface.
- Clean the Instant Pot then place butter in it.
- Select "Sauté" setting on the Instant Pot then stir in the cooked baby back ribs. Sauté until crispy. Press the "Cancel" button.
- Place the cooked baby back ribs on a serving dish then drizzle mayonnaise over the baby back ribs.
- Top with tomato salsa and chopped celeries then serve.
- Enjoy right away.

Per Serving: Net Carbs: 6.6g; Calories: 293; Total Fat: 27.6g; Saturated Fat: 8.6g; Protein: 5.7g; Carbs: 7.2g; Fiber: 0.6g; Sugar: 2.8g - Fat 85% / Protein 8% / Carbs 7%

Spiced Pork Ribs Onion with Avocado Salsa [FA] [GF]

Serves: 4 / Preparation time: 5 minutes / Cooking time: 4 hours

1-½ lbs. baby back ribs	½ teaspoon thyme
1 cup chopped onion	1- cup chicken broth
2 teaspoons minced garlic	1-½ cups chopped green tomatoes
¼ teaspoon salt	1-teaspoon chopped green chili
½ teaspoon black pepper	1 ripe avocado

- Cut the baby back ribs into medium pieces then place in the inner pot of an Instant Pot.
- Alternately, sprinkle chopped onion; minced garlic, salt, black pepper, and thyme then pour water into the Instant Pot.
- Put the lid on and seal then Instant Pot properly. Let the steam valve open.

- Select "Manual" setting on the Instant Pot and cook the baby back ribs on high. Set the time to 20 minutes.
- Meanwhile, cut the avocado into halves then scoop the avocado flesh out.
- Place the avocado in a blender then add green tomato and green chili. Blend until smooth.
- Once the Instant Pot beeps naturally release the Instant Pot and open the lid.
- Transfer the cooked baby back ribs to a serving dish then top with avocado salsa.
- Serve and enjoy right away.

Per Serving: Net Carbs: 2.6g; Calories: 308; Total Fat: 25.4g; Saturated Fat: 8.6g; Protein: 15g; Carbs: 4.9g; Fiber: 2.3g; Sugar: 1.5g - Fat 74% / Protein 20% / Carbs 6%

Cheesy Almond Pork Pizza [GF]

Serves: 4 / Preparation time: 20 minutes / Cooking time: 30 minutes

½ cup almond flour	2 tablespoons coconut aminos
3 tablespoons cream cheese	½ teaspoon salt
1 pastured egg	½ teaspoon pepper
¾ lb. pork shoulder	1-cup water
1-tablespoon butter	¼ cup chopped onion
2 teaspoons minced garlic	½ cup grated Mozzarella cheese

- Cut the pork shoulder into cubes then place in a food processor. Set aside.
- Preheat a skillet over medium heat then pour butter into it.
- Once the butter is melted, stir in minced garlic then sauté until aromatic and lightly golden brown.
- Add ground pork to the skillet then season with salt, pepper, and coconut aminos.
- Pour water over the ground pork then cook until the water is completely absorbed into the pork.
- Remove the cooked pork from heat and let it cool.
- Next, preheat an oven to 400°F (204°C) and line a pizza pan with parchment paper. Set aside.
- Combine almond flour with cream cheese and egg then mix until becoming dough.
- Roll the pizza dough until thin then place in the prepared pizza pan.
- Bake the pizza dough for approximately 10 minutes or until the pizza dough is lightly golden. Remove from oven.
- Spread the cooked ground pork over the almond pizza dough then sprinkle chopped onion and Mozzarella cheese on top.
- Bake the pizza for about 8 to 10 minutes or until the Mozzarella cheese is melted.
- Remove the pizza from the oven and transfer to a serving dish.
- Cut the pizza into wedges then serve.
- Enjoy warm.

Per Serving: Net Carbs: 3.2g: Calories: 330; Total Fat: 26.3g; Saturated Fat: 10.3g; Protein: 18.3g; Carbs: 4.1g; Fiber: 0.6g; Sugar: 0.5g - Fat 72% / Protein 24% / Carbs 4%

Eggplant Pork Coconut Soup [FA] [GF]

Serves: 4 / Preparation time: 5 minutes / Cooking time: 20 minutes

1 lb. pork shoulder	2 teaspoons sliced shallots
2 teaspoons minced garlic	½ teaspoon salt

¼ teaspoon pepper

3 tablespoons red chili flakes

1-teaspoon chili powder

1 bay leaf

2 cups chicken broth

½ cup coconut milk

½ cup chopped carrots

½ cup chopped cabbage

1 cup chopped eggplant

- Cut the pork shoulder into medium pieces then place in the Instant Pot.
- Pour chicken broth over the pork then season with sliced shallots, minced garlic, salt, pepper, red chili flakes, chili powder, and bay leaf.
- Put the lid on and seal the Instant Pot properly. Close the steam valve.
- Select "Manual" setting on the Instant Pot then cook the pork on high for 15 minutes.
- When the Instant Pot beeps, quick release the Instant Pot then open the lid.
- After that, pour coconut milk into the Instant Pot then add chopped carrots, cabbage, and eggplant. Stir well.
- Select "Sauté" setting on the Instant Pot then cook the pork soup uncover for 5 minutes.
- Once it is done, turn the Instant Pot off and transfer the pork soup to a serving bowl.
- Serve and enjoy.

Per Serving: Net Carbs: 6.7g; Calories: 443; Total Fat: 34.7g; Saturated Fat: 17.7g; Protein: 23.7g; Carbs: 9.7g; Fiber: 3g; Sugar: 5g - Fat 70% / Protein 21% / Carbs 9%

Pork Roulade with Pecan Sauce [GF]

Serves: 8 / Preparation time: 15 minutes / Cooking time: 30 minutes

1-½ lbs. pork butt

½ teaspoon salt

½ teaspoon black pepper

½ teaspoon nutmeg

½ teaspoon cinnamon

1 lb. bacon

1-tablespoon extra virgin olive oil

½ cup roasted pecans

3 tablespoons coconut aminos

½ cup chicken broth

- Cut the pork butt into large thin slices then rub with nutmeg, cinnamon, salt, and pepper. Let it rest for 10 minutes.
- After 10 minutes, arrange the sliced pork butt on a flat surface then arrange bacon on it.
- Roll the rib eye then bind with strings.
- Brush the pork roll with olive oil then set aside.
- Pour water into the Instant Pot then place a trivet in it.
- Place the pork roll on the trivet then close and seal the Instant Pot. Close the steam valve.
- Select "Manual" setting then cook the beef roll on high for 30 minutes.
- Meanwhile, place roasted pecans in a blender then pour chicken broth over the pecans.
- Add coconut aminos into the blender then blend until smooth. Set aside.
- When the Instant Pot beeps, naturally release the Instant Pot then open the lid.
- Let the pork roll rest for about 15 minutes then cut it into thick slices.
- Arrange the pork rolls on a serving dish then drizzle pecan sauce on top.
- Serve and enjoy.

Per Serving: Net Carbs: 1.3g; Calories: 556; Total Fat: 46.1g; Saturated Fat: 13g; Protein: 31.7g; Carbs: 3.8g; Fiber: 1.5g; Sugar: 0.7g - Fat 75% / Protein 23% / Carbs 2%

Parmesan Pork Garlic [FA] [GF]

Serves: 8 / Preparation time: 10 minutes / Cooking time: 20 minutes

1 lb. pork shoulder

2 tablespoons extra virgin olive oil

3 tablespoons minced garlic

½ cup chicken broth

1-cup heavy cream

¼ cup cream cheese

¼ cup water

½ cup grated Parmesan cheese

¼ teaspoon pepper

- Cut the pork shoulder into thick slices then set aside.
- Pour olive oil into the Instant Pot then select the "Sauté" setting.
- Stir in minced garlic then sauté until aromatic.
- Next, add pork shoulder to the Instant Pot then sauté until the pork is wilted. Press the "Cancel" button.
- Pour chicken broth over the pork then close and seal the Instant Pot properly. Close the steam valve.
- Select "Pressure" setting on the Instant Pot and cook the pork shoulder on high. Set the time to 15 minutes.
- When the Instant Pot beeps, quick release the Instant Pot then open the lid.
- Transfer the cooked pork to a serving dish.
- After that, clean the Instant Pot then add heavy cream, cream cheese, water, and Parmesan cheese to the Instant Pot.
- Select "Sauté" setting then bring the sauce to a simmer.
- Press the "Cancel" button then drizzle the sauce over the pork.
- Sprinkle pepper on top and serve.
- Enjoy warm.

Per Serving: Net Carbs: 2.7g; Calories: 349; Total Fat: 29.2g; Saturated Fat: 13.6g; Protein: 19.9g; Carbs: 2.8g; Fiber: 0.1g; Sugar: 0.1g - Fat 75% / Protein 23% / Carbs 2%

Healthy Spiced Pork Chops

Serves: 4 / Preparation time: 15 minutes / Cooking time: 5 minutes

4 pork chops

2 teaspoons extra virgin olive oil

1-teaspoon salt

3 teaspoons minced garlic

1-teaspoon onion powder

½ teaspoon thyme

½ teaspoon cumin

1-teaspoon black pepper

- Peel the fresh shrimps then discard the head. Set aside.
- Season the egg white with salt and paprika then whisk to combine.
- Place roasted pecans in a food processor then season with pepper. Process until smooth and becoming flour.
- Roll the shrimps in the almond flour then dip in the seasoned egg white.
- Next, roll again the shrimps in the pecans mixture then set aside. Repeat with the remaining shrimps and flour.
- Preheat an Air Fryer to 400°F (204°C).
- Arrange the coated shrimps in the Air Fryer then spray with cooking spray.
- Cook the shrimps for 5 minutes then arrange on a serving dish.
- Combine Greek yogurt with chili sauce then mix until incorporated.
- Drizzle the chili yogurt mixture over the shrimps then serve.
- Enjoy right away.

Per Serving: Net Carbs: 1.4g; Calories: 284; Total Fat: 22.3g; Saturated Fat: 7.8g
Protein: 18.3g; Carbs: 1.6g; Fiber: 0.2g; Sugar: 0.2g - Fat 71% / Protein 26% / Carbs 3%

Almond Pork Schnitzel with Paprika Mayo Sauce [FA] [GF]

Serves: 4 / Preparation time: 10 minutes / Cooking time: 15 minutes

1 lb. pork shoulder	1 ½ tablespoons extra virgin olive oil
2 pastured eggs	1-¼ tablespoons mustard
2 teaspoons minced garlic	¾ teaspoon paprika
½ teaspoon salt	¾ teaspoon black pepper
¾ cup almond flour	Coconut oil, to fry
3 tablespoons mayonnaise	

- Cut the pork shoulder into large thin slices then rub with minced garlic and salt.
- Next, crack the eggs and place in a bowl. Beat until incorporated.
- Dip the seasoned pork shoulder in the egg mixture and make sure that the pork shoulder is completely coated with almond flour.
- Preheat a skillet over medium heat then pour coconut oil into it.
- Once the oil is hot, put the coated pork in the skillet and fry for about 4 minutes.
- Flip the pork schnitzel and fry for another 4 minutes or until both sides of the schnitzel are lightly golden brown.
- While frying the pork schnitzel, prepare the sauce.
- Combine mayonnaise, extra virgin olive oil, mustard, paprika, and black pepper in a bowl. Stir until incorporated.
- Once the schnitzel is done, remove from the skillet and transfer to a serving dish.
- Drizzle mayo sauce over the schnitzel then serve.
- Enjoy warm!

Per Serving: Net Carbs: 4.9g: Calories: 460; Total Fat: 37.7g; Saturated Fat: 10.3g; Protein: 24.1g; Carbs: 6.2g; Fiber: 1.3g; Sugar: 1.1g - Fat 74% / Protein 22% / Carbs 4%

Lemon Pork with Barbecue Sauce [GF]

Serves: 4 / Preparation time: 10 minutes / Cooking time: 40 minutes

1 ½ lbs. pork shoulder	¼ cup apple cider vinegar
½ teaspoon salt	½ cup water
1-teaspoon pepper	½ cup tomato puree
2 tablespoons extra virgin olive oil	¾ teaspoon garlic powder
¼ cup fresh thyme	¾ teaspoon onion powder
½ cup sliced lemons	¾ teaspoons mustard
2 tablespoons butter	½ teaspoon liquid smoke

- Preheat an oven to 350°F (177°C) and prepare a baking tray. Set aside.
- Drizzle extra virgin olive oil over the pork shoulder then rub with salt and pepper.
- Place the seasoned pork in a sheet of aluminum foil then arrange lemon slices on top.
- Sprinkle fresh thyme over the pork shoulder then wrap with aluminum foil.

- Place the wrapped pork on the prepared baking tray and bake for approximately 40 minutes or until the internal temperature has reached 145°F (63°C).
- In the meantime, place the remaining ingredients in a saucepan then bring to a simmer. Cook until the butter is melted.
- Once the sauce is done, remove from heat and let it cool.
- Once the baked pork is done, remove from the oven and let it rest for a few minutes.
- Unwrap the baked pork and transfer to a serving dish.
- Drizzle barbecue sauce on top then serve.
- Enjoy!

Per Serving: Net Carbs: 6.2g: Calories: 444; Total Fat: 36.3g; Saturated Fat: 12.8g; Protein: 20.8g; Carbs: 8.8g; Fiber: 2.6g; Sugar: 1.1g - Fat 73% / Protein 21% / Carbs 6%

Cheese and Apple Buttery Pork Roll [FA] [GF]

Serves: 4 / Preparation time: 10 minutes / Cooking time: 15 minutes

1 lb. pork shoulder	½ cup cream cheese
¼ teaspoon salt	1 fresh apple
½ teaspoon pepper	2 tablespoons butter

- Cut the apple into sticks then set aside.
- Cut the pork shoulder into large thin slices then rub with salt and pepper.
- Arrange the sliced pork shoulder on a flat surface then baste cream cheese over the pork.
- Arrange the apple sticks on the pork then roll and bind it tightly.
- Pour water into an Instant Pot then place a trivet in it.
- Brush the pork roll with butter then place on the trivet.
- Put the lid on and seal the Instant Pot properly. Close the steam valve.
- Select the "Pressure" setting on the Instant Pot and cook the pork roll on high. Set the time to 20 minutes.
- Once the Instant Pot beeps, naturally release the Instant Pot then open the lid.
- Take then pork roll out of the Instant Pot then place on a flat surface. Let it sit for about 5 minutes.
- Cut the pork roll into thick slices then arrange on a serving dish.
- Serve and enjoy.

Per Serving: Net Carbs: 5.3g; Calories: 504; Total Fat: 40.1g; Saturated Fat: 18.9g; Protein: 28.7g; Carbs: 6.4g; Fiber: 1.3g; Sugar: 4.1g - Fat 72% / Protein 23% / Carbs 5%

Spicy Baked Pulled Pork [GF]

Serves: 4 / Preparation time: 3 hours / Cooking time: 3 hours

1 ½ lbs. pork butt	1-tablespoon black pepper
½ cup salt	¼ cup mustard
4 cups water	3 teaspoons liquid smoke
1-½ teaspoons cayenne pepper	2 tablespoons butter
2 ½ teaspoons paprika	

- Pour water into a container with a lid then add salt to the water. Stir until the salt is dissolved.
- Put pork butt into the brine then soak for at least 3 hours.
- In the meantime, combine cayenne pepper with paprika, black pepper, mustard, and liquid smoke in a bowl then mix well.

- After 3 hours, remove the pork butt from the brine then wash and rinse it. Pat it dry.
- Rub the pork butt with the spice mixture then wrap with aluminum foil. Set aside.
- Preheat an oven to 350°F (177°C) and prepare a baking tray.
- Once the oven has reached the desired temperature, place the wrapped pork butt on the prepared baking tray and bake for approximately 3 hours or until the internal temperature has reached 190°F (88°C).
- Remove the baked pork from the oven and let it rest for approximately 3o minutes.
- Unwrap the baked pork and place on a flat surface.
- Using a fork shred the baked pork and serve.
- Enjoy!

Per Serving: Net Carbs: 3g: Calories: 485; Total Fat: 38.9g; Saturated Fat: 15.9g; Protein: 30g; Carbs: 5.5g; Fiber: 2.5g; Sugar: 0.9g - Fat 72% / Protein 25% / Carbs 3%

Pork Veggie Blanket [FA] [GF]

Serves: 4 / Preparation time: 5 minutes / Cooking time: 20 minutes

½ lb. pork butt

¼ lb. pork rinds

¼ cup chicken broth

1-tablespoon butter

1-tablespoon extra virgin olive oil

8 sheets large lettuce

¼ cup chopped onion

¼ cup shredded zucchini

¼ cup carrots

½ cup scrambled egg

¼ cup roasted pecans

- Cut the pork butt into thin slices and the pork rind into cubes then place in the Instant Pot.
- Add butter to the Instant Pot then press the "Sauté" button.
- Sauté the pork until wilted then pour chicken broth over the pork. Press the "Cancel" button.
- Next, put the lid on and seal the Instant Pot properly. Close the steam valve.
- Select "Manual" setting and cook the pork on high. Set the time to 20 minutes.
- In the meantime, combine chopped onion, shredded zucchini, and carrots in a bowl then drizzle olive oil over the veggie. Toss to combine then set aside.
- Once the Instant Pot beeps, naturally release the Instant Pot then open the lid.
- Transfer the cooked pork to a serving dish.
- To serve, place 2 lettuces on a flat surface then add veggie mixture on it.
- Add pork, scrambled egg, and roasted pecans over the veggie then roll the lettuces.
- Place the lettuce roll on a serving dish then repeat with the remaining lettuce and filling.
- Serve and enjoy immediately.

Per Serving: Net Carbs: 3.4g; Calories: 599; Total Fat: 50.7g; Saturated Fat: 13.1g; Protein:33.4g; Carbs: 6.7g; Fiber: 3.3g; Sugar: 2.3g - Fat 76% / Protein 22% / Carbs 2%

Pork Roast with Thai Walnuts Sauce

Serves: 2 / Preparation time: 10 minutes / Cooking time: 20 minutes

1 pork roast

½ teaspoon salt

1-tablespoon extra virgin olive oil

½ teaspoon pepper

1-teaspoon thyme

1-teaspoon rosemary

6 cloves garlic

½ cup butter

3 tablespoons roasted walnuts

3 tablespoons low sodium chicken broth

2 tablespoons lemon juice

½ teaspoon ginger

2 tablespoons minced garlic

- Place butter in a mixing bowl then add roasted walnuts, ginger, and minced garlic.
- Pour chicken broth and lemon juice into the mixing bowl then using an electric mixer beat until smooth.
- Transfer the butter mixture to a container with a lid then store in a refrigerator overnight.
- Preheat an Air Fryer to 350°F (177°C) and put garlic in the Air Fryer.
- Brush the pork roast with olive oil then place in the Air Fryer after the garlic.
- Sprinkle salt, pepper, thyme, and rosemary then cook for 30 minutes.
- Once it is done, remove from the Air Fryer then place on a serving dish.
- Serve with walnut sauce.

Per Serving: Net Carbs: 2.4g; Calories: 325; Total Fat: 32.6g; Saturated Fat: 16.4g
Protein: 6.7g; Carbs: 3.2g; Fiber: 0.8g; Sugar: 0.3g - Fat 90% / Protein 8% / Carbs 2%

Stir Fry Pork with Roasted Cashews [FA] [GF]

Serves: 4 / Preparation time: 5 minutes / Cooking time: 15 minutes

1 lb. pork shoulder

2 pastured eggs

½ cup chopped onion

½ cup diced bell pepper

¼ cup roasted cashews

1-teaspoon ginger

3 teaspoons minced garlic

½ teaspoon chili powder

2 tablespoons coconut aminos

½ teaspoon salt

2 tablespoons extra virgin olive oil

- Cut the pork shoulder into thin slices then set aside.
- Next, crack the eggs then place in a bowl. Stir until beaten.
- Preheat a skillet over medium heat then pour a tablespoon of olive oil into the skillet.
- Once the oil is hot, stir in beaten eggs and stir until becoming crumbles.
- Remove the egg from the skillet and set aside.
- Pour the remaining oil to the skillet then stir in chopped onion, minced garlic, and sliced pork shoulder. Sauté until wilted and cooked through.
- After that, add the egg to the skillet together with bell pepper and season with ginger, chili powder, coconut aminos, and salt. Stir well.
- Once it is done, transfer the cooked pork to a serving dish and sprinkle roasted cashews on top.
- Serve and enjoy.

Per Serving: Net Carbs: 6.5g: Calories: 453; Total Fat: 36.4g; Saturated Fat: 10.5g; Protein: 23.8g; Carbs: 7.5g; Fiber: 1g; Sugar: 1.9g - Fat 72% / Protein 22% / Carbs 6%

Sour and Spicy Steamed Pork [FA] [GF]

Serves: 8 / Preparation time: 10 minutes / Cooking time: 20 minutes

2 lb. baby back ribs

2 tablespoons sliced shallots

2 tablespoons sliced garlic

1-teaspoon ginger

2 bay leaves

1-inch galangal

1 cup chopped green tomatoes	2 cups coconut milk
¼ cup red chili flakes	½ teaspoon salt

- Cut the baby back ribs into small pieces then place in a disposable aluminum pan.
- Sprinkle sliced shallots, sliced garlic, galangal, bay leaves, ginger, red chili flakes, and green tomatoes over the chicken.
- Add salt to the coconut milk then stir until dissolved.
- Pour the coconut into each aluminum foil cup then set aside.
- Pour water into an Instant Pot then place a trivet in it.
- Place the disposable aluminum pan on the trivet then close and seal the Instant Pot properly. Close the steam valve.
- Turn the Instant Pot on then select "Pressure" menu and cook the baby back ribs for 20 minutes.
- Once it is done, turn the Instant Pot off and naturally release it.
- Open the lid and take the aluminum foil cups with cooked pork out of the Instant Pot.
- Transfer the cooked pork to a serving dish.
- Serve and enjoy.

Per Serving: Net Carbs: 4.2g; Calories: 390; Total Fat: 34.7g; Saturated Fat: 20.2g; Protein: 15.4g; Carbs: 6g; Fiber: 1.8g; Sugar: 2.8g - Fat 80% / Protein 16% / Carbs 4%

Hot Pork in Coconut Gravy [FA] [GF]

Serves: 4 / Preparation time: 5 minutes / Cooking time: 20 minutes

1 ½ lbs. pork butt	2 teaspoons minced garlic
1-cup coconut milk	2 teaspoons sliced shallots
1-cup water	½ teaspoon salt
2 tablespoons extra virgin olive oil	1 lemon grass
2 tablespoons curry paste	1 bay leaf
½ teaspoon turmeric	¼ cup red chili flakes

- Cut the pork butt into medium cubes then set aside.
- Next, pour olive oil into the Instant Pot then select "Sauté" setting on the Instant Pot.
- Stir in minced garlic and sliced shallots then sauté until aromatic.
- After that, add the pork butt to the Instant Pot then sauté until wilted. Press the "Cancel" button.
- Pour coconut milk and water over the pork then season with curry paste, turmeric, and salt. Stir well.
- Add lemon grass and bay leaf to the pot then sprinkle red chili flakes on top.
- Put the lid on then seal the Instant Pot properly. Close the steam valve.
- Select the "Pressure" setting on the Instant Pot and cook the pork for 20 minutes.
- Once it is done, quick release the Instant Pot and open the lid.
- Transfer the pork to a serving bowl then pour the liquid over the pork. Enjoy!

Per Serving: Net Carbs: 5.9g; Calories: 388; Total Fat: 34.7g; Saturated Fat: 18g; Protein: 14.2g; Carbs: 7.4g; Fiber: 1.5g; Sugar: 2.6g - Fat 80% / Protein 15% / Carbs 5%

Pork Butt Onion Barbecue

Serves: 2 / Preparation time: 12 minutes / Cooking time: 18 minutes

½ lb. pork butt	1-tablespoon extra virgin olive oil

½ teaspoon salt	1-teaspoon cayenne pepper
½ teaspoon pepper	½ teaspoon garlic powder
½ cup chopped onion	½ teaspoon onion powder
2 tablespoons tomato sauce	2-½ tablespoons Worcestershire sauce
½ teaspoon cider vinegar	½ teaspoon mustard
½ teaspoon chili powder	1 tablespoon Stevia

- Combine tomato sauce with cider vinegar, chili powder, cayenne pepper, garlic powder, onion powder, Worcestershire sauce, mustard, and Stevia in a bowl then stir until incorporated. Set aside.
- Preheat an Air Fryer to 350°F (177°C).
- Spray the pork but with olive oil then season with salt and pepper.
- Place the seasoned pork in the Air Fryer then sprinkle chopped onion on top.
- Cook the pork butt and set the time to 6 minutes.
- After 6 minutes, open the drawer and flip the pork.
- Drizzle the sauce over the pork butt then cook again for 6 minutes.
- Once it is done, remove from the Air Fryer and transfer to a serving dish.
- Serve and enjoy.

Per Serving: Net Carbs: 6.8g; Calories: 459; Total Fat: 38.1g; Saturated Fat: 10.1g
Protein: 20.6g; Carbs: 9.2g; Fiber: 2.4g; Sugar: 3.7g - Fat 75% / Protein 20.6% / Carbs 9.2%

Buttery Pork Chops Garlic [FA] [GF] [SF]

Serves: 4 / Preparation time: 5 minutes / Cooking time: 20 minutes

1 lb. pork chops	A pinch of salt
¼ cup butter	¼ teaspoon black pepper
3 teaspoons minced garlic	

- Rub the pork chops with minced garlic, salt, and pepper then place in the inner pot of an Instant Pot.
- Baste the pork chops with butter then close and seal the Instant Pot.
- Select "Manual " setting and cook the pork chops on high. Set the time to 20 minutes.
- Once the Instant Pot beeps, quick release the Instant Pot and open the lid.
- Take the cooked pork chops out of the Instant Pot then place on a serving dish.
- Serve and enjoy!

Per Serving: Net Carbs: 0.7g; Calories: 468; Total Fat: 39.7g; Saturated Fat: 17.9g; Protein: 25.7g; Carbs: 0.8g; Fiber: 0.1g; Sugar: 0g - Fat 76% / Protein 22% / Carbs 2%

Spicy Glazed Pork Loaf

Serves: 8 / Preparation time: 10 minutes / Cooking time: 20 minutes

1-½ cups ground pork	½ teaspoon cayenne
½ cup diced pork rinds	¼ cup butter
½ teaspoon paprika	½ cup tomato puree
½ teaspoon pepper	½ teaspoon chili powder
2 teaspoons minced garlic	2 tablespoons coconut aminos
½ cup chopped onion	½ teaspoon Worcestershire sauce
½ teaspoon cumin	1 teaspoon lemon juice

- Combine ground pork and pork rinds in a bowl then season with paprika, pepper, minced garlic, cumin, cayenne, and chopped onion. Mix well.
- Transfer the pork mixture to a silicone loaf pan then spread evenly. Set aside.
- Next, melt the butter in a microwave then set aside.
- Combine the melted butter with tomato puree, chili powder, coconut aminos, Worcestershire sauce, and lemon juice. Stir until incorporated.
- Drizzle the glaze mixture over the pork loaf then set aside.
- Preheat an Air Fryer to 350°F (177°C).
- Once the Air Fryer is preheated, place the silicon loaf pan on the Air Fryer's rack then cook for 20 minutes.
- Remove from the Air Fryer then let it cool.
- Cut the pork loaf into slices then serve.

Per Serving: Net Carbs: 4.7g; Calories: 255; Total Fat: 20.1g; Saturated Fat: 10.4g
Protein: 13g; Carbs: 6g; Fiber: 1.3g; Sugar: 2.4g - Fat 71% / Protein 20% / Carbs 9%

Turmeric Pork Tender with Basils Aroma [FA] [GF]

Serves: 4 / Preparation time: 5 minutes / Cooking time: 20 minutes

1 lb. pork shoulder	2 lemon grasses
2 cloves garlic	2 kaffir lime leaves
2 shallots	2 cups fresh basils
1-½ teaspoons turmeric	3 cups water
¼ cup cayenne	½ teaspoon salt
1-inch galangal	2 tablespoons extra virgin olive oil
2 bay leaves	

- Cut the pork shoulder into small dices then set aside.
- Place garlic, shallots, turmeric, and cayenne in a food processor then process until smooth.
- Preheat a skillet over medium heat then pour extra virgin olive oil into the skillet.
- Once the oil is hot, stir in the spice mixture and sauté until wilted and aromatic.
- Add diced pork shoulder to the skillet then season with salt, galangal, bay leaves, lemon grasses, and lime leaves. Stir well.
- Pour water over the pork then bring to boil.
- Once it is boiled, reduce the heat and sprinkle fresh basils on top. Cook until the pork is tender.
- Transfer the cooked pork together with the gravy to a serving dish then serve.
- Enjoy!

Per Serving: Net Carbs: 5.6g: Calories: 386; Total Fat: 31.1g; Saturated Fat: 9.2g; Protein: 20.4g; Carbs: 7.5g; Fiber: 1.9g; Sugar: 0.7g - Fat 73% / Protein 21% / Carbs 6%

Pork Veggie Stew with Sesame Seeds [FA] [GF]

Serves: 4 / Preparation time: 5 minutes / Cooking time: 20 minutes

1 lb. pork butt	½ cup water
½ cup chopped carrots	2 tablespoons coconut aminos
½ cup chopped green collard	2 tablespoons butter
2 teaspoons minced garlic	1-tablespoon sesame seeds
1-teaspoon ginger	

- Cut the pork butt into slices then set aside.
- Place butter in the inner pot of the Instant Pot then press the "Sauté" button.
- Stir in minced garlic then sauté until aromatic.
- Next, add sliced pork to the Instant Pot then sauté until wilted and no longer pink. Press the "Cancel" button.
- After that, pour water into the Instant Pot then season with ginger and coconut aminos.
- Put the lid on and seal the Instant Pot properly. Close the steam valve.
- Select "Manual" setting and cook the pork on high. Set the time to 15 minutes.
- When the Instant Pot beeps, quick release the Instant Pot then open the lid.
- Add carrots and chopped collard to the Instant Pot then press the "Sauté" button. Bring to a simmer.
- Stir the vegetables until wilted then turn the Instant Pot off.
- Transfer the pork stew to a serving dish then sprinkle sesame seeds on top.
- Serve and enjoy right away.

Per Serving: Net Carbs: 5.9g; Calories: 341; Total Fat: 26.9g; Saturated Fat: 11.8g; Protein: 19.2g; Carbs: 5.9g; Fiber: 1.8g; Sugar: 1.1g - Fat 71% / Protein 23% / Carbs 6%

Pork Stew with Greens [FA] [GF]

Serves: 4 / Preparation time: 5 minutes / Cooking time: 18 minutes

1 lb. pork shoulder

½ cup chopped onion

1-tablespoon extra virgin olive oil

¼ cup chopped celery stalk

2 cups green collard

1-cup chicken broth

¾ teaspoon salt

½ teaspoon pepper

½ teaspoon nutmeg

- Turn the Instant Pot on then pour olive oil into the inner pot of the Instant Pot.
- Press the "Sauté" button on the Instant Pot then wait until the oil is hot.
- Stir in chopped onion and sauté until translucent and aromatic.
- Next, cut pork shoulder into small pieces then add to the Instant Pot. Sauté until the pork is no longer pink then press the "Cancel" button.
- Pour chicken broth into the Instant Pot then season with salt, pepper, and nutmeg. Stir well.
- Put the lid on and seal the Instant Pot properly. Close the steam valve.
- Press "Manual" button on the Instant Pot and cook the pork on high. Set the time to 15 minutes.
- Once the Instant Pot beeps, quick release the Instant Pot and open the lid.
- Add chopped green collard and celery stalk to the Instant Pot then stir well.
- Press the "Sauté" button and cook the stew uncover for 3 minutes. Press the "Cancel" button.
- Transfer the pork stew to a serving bowl then serve.
- Enjoy warm!

Per Serving: Net Carbs: 2.6g; Calories: 383; Total Fat: 30.5g; Saturated Fat: 9.2g; Protein: 21.5g; Carbs: 5.1g; Fiber: 2.5g; Sugar: 1.4g - Fat 72% / Protein 22% / Carbs 6%

Tomato Pork Butt with Creamy Garlic Sauce [FA] [GF]

Serves: 4 / Preparation time: 5 minutes / Cooking time: 20 minutes

1 lb. pork butt

1-cup low sodium chicken broth

¼ cup chopped tomatoes

¾ teaspoon basil

¾ teaspoon oregano

1-tablespoon butter

2 tablespoons minced garlic

1-cup heavy cream

- Pour chicken broth into the Instant Pot then add chopped tomatoes to the pot.
- Season the liquid with basil and oregano then stir until combined.
- Add the pork butt to the Instant Pot then put the lid on. Seal the Instant Pot properly and close the steam valve.
- Select "Pressure" setting on the Instant Pot and cook the pork on high for 15 minutes.
- Once the pork is done, quickly release the Instant Pot then open the lid.
- Take the cooked pork out of the Instant Pot and place on a flat surface. Pour the liquid into another bowl.
- Place butter in the Instant Pot then select the "Sauté" setting.
- Stir in minced garlic then sauté until aromatic and lightly golden.
- Pour the liquid into the Instant Pot then bring to a simmer for about 5 minutes. Press the "Cancel" button.
- Next, pour heavy cream into the Instant Pot then mix well.
- After that, using a fork shred the pork into pieces. Return it back to the Instant Pot.
- Stir until the pork is completely coated with liquid then transfer to a serving dish.
- Serve and enjoy immediately.

Per Serving: Net Carbs: 3.1g; Calories: 394; Total Fat: 34.1g; Saturated Fat: 16.7g; Protein: 19.6g; Carbs: 3.1g; Fiber: 0.4g; Sugar: 0.4g - Fat 78% / Protein 20% / Carbs 2%

RED MEAT RECIPES

Coconut Creamy Goat Fritters with Sautéed Eggplant

Serves: 4 / Preparation time: 19 minutes / Cooking time: 14 minutes

1 lb. ground goat meat

½ cup chopped leek

2 teaspoons minced garlic

1 egg

4 tablespoons extra virgin olive oil

½ teaspoon pepper

1 cup cubed eggplant

¼ cup coconut milk

½ tablespoon coconut flour

1 tablespoons lemon

- Season the ground goat meat with minced garlic and pepper then combine with egg. Mix well.
- Add chopped leek to the meat and mix until just combined.
- Shape the meat mixture into medium fritters then set aside.
- Next, preheat a saucepan over medium heat then pour extra virgin olive oil into it.
- Once the oil is hot, put the fritters on the saucepan. Don't be too close.
- Cook the fritters for approximately 3 minutes each side or until the fritters are lightly golden brown and cooked through.
- Remove the fritters from the pan and arrange on a serving dish.
- After that, put the cubed eggplant into the pan and sauté with the remaining olive oil until just wilted.
- Remove the eggplant from heat and place next to the fritters.
- Keep the saucepan over medium heat then pour the coconut flour and coconut mixture into the saucepan. Bring to a simmer.

- Once it is done, remove from heat and add lemon to the sauce.
- Drizzle the coconut sauce over the fritters and eggplants then serve.
- Enjoy!

Per Serving: Net Carbs: 3.8g; Calories: 513; Total Fat: 46g; Saturated Fat: 17.8g
Protein: 21.5g; Carbs: 5.5g; Fiber: 1.7g; Sugar: 1.8g - Fat 81% / Protein 16% / Carbs 3%

Spiced Lamb Satay

Serves: 3/ Preparation time: 10 minutes / Cooking time: 40 minutes

2 boneless lamb shoulders	¼ teaspoon cumin
½ teaspoon salt	2 kaffir lime leaves
½ teaspoon pepper	2 lemon grasses
1-teaspoon ginger	1-tablespoon extra virgin olive oil
½ teaspoon nutmeg	

- Place salt, pepper, ginger, nutmeg, and cumin in a bowl then mix well.
- Cut the lamb shoulder into medium cubes then rub with the spice mixture.
- Marinate the lamb cubes for 10 minutes then prick using steel skewers.
- Preheat an Air Fryer to 400°F (204°C) and arrange the lamb satay in the Air Fryer.
- Spray the lamb satay with olive oil then put lime leaves and lemon grasses on top.
- Cook the lamb satay and set the time to 8 minutes.
- Once it is done, remove from the Air Fryer and enjoy with any kind of low carb sauce, as you desired.

Per Serving: Net Carbs: 3.4g; Calories: 249; Total Fat: 20.2g; Saturated Fat: 6.1g
Protein: 12.9g; Carbs: 3.7g; Fiber: 0.3g; Sugar: 0.1g - Fat 73% / Protein 21% / Carbs 6%

Spicy Turmeric Goat Satay

Serves: 4 / Preparation time: 9 minutes / Cooking time: 29 minutes

1 lb. ground goat meat	1-teaspoon turmeric
½ cup diced onion	2 teaspoons red chili flakes
2 teaspoons grated garlic	1 egg

- Preheat a steamer over medium heat and wait until it is ready.
- Season the ground goat meat with diced onion, grated garlic, turmeric, and red chili flakes then mix well.
- Crack the egg then add to the seasoned goat meat mixture then mix until combined.
- Take half of a handful of the mixture then mold the meat mixture around a wooden skewer. Repeat with the remaining goat meat.
- Arrange the satay in the steamer and steam for approximately 20 minutes or until set.
- Once the satay is done, remove from the steamer and let it rest for a few minutes.
- Next, preheat a grill over medium heat and once it is done, arrange the satay on the grill and grill for about 3 minutes each side or until both sides of the satay are lightly golden brown.
- Arrange the grilled satay on a serving dish then serve.
- Enjoy warm.

Per Serving: Net Carbs: 3.4g; Calories: 355; Total Fat: 28.3g; Saturated Fat: 12.4g
Protein: 21.1g; Carbs: 4.2g; Fiber: 0.8g; Sugar: 1.9g - Fat 77% / Protein 19% / Carbs 4%

Sautéed Lamb Black Pepper in Coconut Flour Envelope [GF]

Serves: 4 / Preparation time: 5 minutes / Cooking time: 35 minutes

½ lb. lamb loin	½ cup chopped leek
2 tablespoons butter	½ cup coconut flour
½ cup chopped onion	½ cup coconut milk
¼ teaspoon salt	1 pastured egg
½ teaspoon black pepper	Coconut oil, to fry

1 cup water

- Cut the lamb loin into very small dices then set aside.
- Preheat a skillet over medium heat then place butter in it.
- Once the butter is melted, stir in chopped onion then sauté until lightly golden brown and aromatic.
- Next, stir in lamb loin and sauté until wilted.
- Season the lamb with salt and black pepper then pour water over the lamb. Bring to boil.
- Once it is boiled, reduce the heat and cook until the lamb is tender. The water will completely be absorbed into the lamb.
- Remove the cooked lamb from heat and let it cool.
- Combine coconut flour with coconut milk and egg then stir until incorporated.
- Preheat a saucepan and make thin omelets with the coconut flour mixture.
- Take an omelet and place on a flat surface.
- Combine sautéed lamb with chopped leek then put 2 tablespoons of the mixture on the omelet. Fold like an envelope then set aside. Repeat with the remaining omelets and lamb filling.
- After that, preheat a frying pan over medium heat and pour coconut oil into the pan.
- Once it is hot, put the lamb envelopes and fry for 3 minutes.
- Slowly flip the lamb envelopes and fry for another 3 minutes or until both sides of the lamb envelopes are lightly golden brown.
- Remove the fried lamb envelopes from the frying pan and strain the excessive oil.
- Serve and enjoy warm.

Per Serving: Net Carbs: 4.1g: Calories: 436; Total Fat: 41g; Saturated Fat: 27.9g; Protein: 12.4g; Carbs: 6g; Fiber: 1.9g; Sugar: 2.2g - Fat 85% / Protein 11% / Carbs 4%

Lamb Chop Garlic and Avocado Mayo

Serves: 2 / Preparation time: 10 minutes / Cooking time: 12 minutes

2 lamb chops	2 ripe avocados
2 teaspoons minced garlic	½ cup mayonnaise
¾ tablespoon oregano	2 tablespoons cilantro
¼ teaspoon salt	1 tablespoon lemon juice
½ teaspoon black pepper	

- Season the lamb chops with minced garlic, oregano, salt, and black pepper. Let them rest for about 5 minutes.
- Preheat an Air Fryer to 400°F (204°C) and place a rack in it.
- Once the Air Fryer is ready, place the seasoned lamb chops on the rack then cook for 12 minutes.
- Meanwhile, cut the avocados into halves then discard the seeds.

- Scoop out the avocado flesh then place in a blender.
- Add cilantro, mayonnaise, and lemon juice to the blender then blend until smooth and creamy.
- Once the lamb chops are done, remove from the Air Fryer and transfer to a serving dish.
- Serve and enjoy with the Avocado Mayonnaise.

Per Serving: Net Carbs: 2.8g; Calories: 398; Total Fat: 35.6g; Saturated Fat: 10.1g
Protein: 11.7g; Carbs: 10g; Fiber: 7.2g; Sugar: 0.7g - Fat 81% / Protein 11% / Carbs 8%

Lamb Meatballs with Cucumber Avocado-Creamy Sauce

Serves: 4 / Preparation time: 20 minutes / Cooking time: 34 minutes

1 lb. ground lamb	½ teaspoon cumin
½ cup diced onion	½ teaspoon pepper
2 teaspoons minced garlic	1 ripe avocado
½ teaspoon grated lemon zest	1 medium cucumber
½ teaspoon oregano	1 tablespoon lemon juice
½ teaspoon coriander	¼ cup Greek yogurt

- Preheat an oven 350°F (177°C) and line a baking tray with aluminum foil.
- Season ground lamb with onion, minced garlic, grated lemon zest, oregano, coriander, cumin, and pepper then mix well.
- Shape the mixture onto medium balls forms then arrange on the prepared baking tray.
- Bake the lamb balls for approximately 25 minutes or until set.
- Meanwhile, cut the avocado into halves then discard the seed.
- Scoop out the avocado flesh then place in a food processor.
- Next, peel the cucumber and discard the seeds.
- Cut the cucumber into cubes then add to the food processor.
- Pour lemon juice and yogurt to the food processor then process until smooth and creamy.
- Once the lamb balls are done, remove from the oven and transfer to a serving dish.
- Drizzle cucumber avocado sauce on top and serve immediately.
- Enjoy!

Per Serving: Net Carbs: 5.7g; Calories: 455; Total Fat: 37.2g; Saturated Fat: 14.3g
Protein: 22.3g; Carbs: 10g; Fiber: 4.3g; Sugar: 2.7g - Fat 74% / Protein 21% / Carbs 5%

Garlic Buttery Lamb Chop [FA] [GF]

Serves: 4 / Preparation time: 5 minutes / Cooking time: 20 minutes

1-½ lbs. lamb chops	3 tablespoons minced garlic
2 tablespoons extra virgin olive oil	¾ teaspoon garlic powder
½ teaspoon salt	¼ cup chopped parsley
½ teaspoon pepper	2 tablespoons lemon juice
½ cup butter	

- Combine butter with minced garlic, garlic powder, chopped parsley, and lemon juice then using a hand mixer mix until smooth. Store in the fridge.
- Cut the lamb chops into several thick slices then rub with salt and pepper. Set aside.
- Preheat a grill over medium heat then wait until it reaches the desired temperature.
- Once the grill is ready, grill the lamb chops until cooked through. Don't forget to flip and rotate the lamb chops. Brush with extra virgin olive oil during the process.
- Remove the cooked lamb from the grill and transfer to a serving dish.
- Serve with butter and parsley mixture. Enjoy warm.

Per Serving: Net Carbs: 2.7g: Calories: 497; Total Fat: 44.6g; Saturated Fat: 19.4g; Protein: 18.9g; Carbs: 3.1g; Fiber: 0.4g; Sugar: 0.4g - Fat 81% / Protein 17% / Carbs 2%

Juicy Lamb Chop Rosemary

Serves: 1/ Preparation time: 10 minutes / Cooking time: 18 minutes

1 lamb chop	½ teaspoon black pepper
½ handful fresh rosemary	10 cloves garlic
½ teaspoon salt	2 tablespoons extra virgin olive oil

- Place the lamb chop in a bowl then season with salt and black pepper.
- Drizzle olive oil over the lamb chop then stir well.
- Place a rack in the Air Fryer then transfer the seasoned lamb to the rack.
- Sprinkle garlic over the lamb chop then add fresh rosemary on top.
- Preheat an Air Fryer to 400°F (204°C) and set the time to 15 minutes. Cook the lamb chops.
- Once it is done, transfer to a serving dish then serve.

Per Serving: Net Carbs: 5g; Calories: 307; Total Fat: 27.3g; Saturated Fat: 7.6g
Protein: 10.6g; Carbs: 5.8g; Fiber: 0.8g; Sugar: 0.2g - Fat 80% / Protein 14% / Carbs 6%

Slow Cooked Mint Lamb Leg with Green Beans [GF]

Serves: 4 / Preparation time: 5 minutes / Cooking time: 6 hours

1-½ lbs. boneless lamb leg	2 cups chopped green beans
¼ cup butter	½ teaspoon salt
4 tablespoons minced garlic	¼ teaspoon pepper
¼ cup chopped mint leaves	

- Cut the boneless lamb leg into medium cubes then place in a slow cooker.
- Drop butter at several places over the lamb leg then sprinkle minced garlic, mint leaves, salt, and pepper.
- Cover the slow cooker with the lid and cook the lamb leg for 4 hours.
- After 4 hours, open the slow cooker and add chopped green beans.
- Cook for another 2 hours until the green beans are tender but crispy and the lamb is juicy.
- Serve and enjoy.

Per Serving: Net Carbs: 4.8g: Calories: 394; Total Fat: 30.7g; Saturated Fat: 15.3g; Protein: 21.9g; Carbs: 7.3g; Fiber: 2.5g; Sugar: 0.9g - Fat 70% / Protein 25% / Carbs 5%

Minty Goat Roll with Roasted Broccoli and Carrots

Serves: 4 / Preparation time: 12 minutes / Cooking time: 38 minutes

¾ lb. goat meat

½ cup extra virgin olive oil

1-teaspoon pepper

½ cup chopped mint leaves

1-teaspoon thyme

¼ cup chopped parsley

1-teaspoon sage

1 tablespoon lemon juice

1-teaspoon rosemary

1-cup broccoli florets

3 teaspoons minced garlic

1 cup chopped carrots

½ teaspoon grated lemon zest

½ cup diced onion

- Preheat an oven to 350°F (177°C) and prepare a disposable aluminum pan. Set aside.
- Combine ¼ cup of olive oil with pepper, thyme, sage, rosemary, minced garlic, and grated lemon zest then stir until incorporated.
- Cut the goat meat into thin slices then rub with the spice mixture. Let it rest for a few minutes.
- Next, combine chopped mint leaves with parsley then pour the remaining olive oil and lemon juice over the greens. Mix well.
- Arrange the sliced meat on a flat surface then put the mint leaves mixture on top.
- Roll the goat meat and tightly bind with string.
- Spread broccoli florets, chopped carrots, and diced onion in the prepared aluminum pan then place the rolled goat meat on it.
- Place the aluminum pan in the oven and bake for approximately 40 minutes or until the goat meat is tender and cooked through.
- Once it is done, remove the aluminum pan from the oven let it rest for a few minutes.
- Take the rolled goat meat out of the aluminum pan and place on a flat surface.
- Cut the rolled goat meat into thick slices and arrange on a serving dish.
- Top with the roasted vegetables then serve.
- Enjoy!

Per Serving: Net Carbs: 5.4g; Calories: 337; Total Fat: 27.3g; Saturated Fat: 4.2g
Protein: 17.6g; Carbs: 8.4g; Fiber: 3g; Sugar: 2.5g - Fat 72% / Protein 22% / Carbs 6%

Lamb Curry in Wrap

Serves: 8 / Preparation time: 20 minutes / Cooking time: 25 minutes

1 lb. lamb loin

1-teaspoon black pepper

1-tablespoon extra virgin olive oil

½ teaspoon salt

1 cup chopped onion

¼ cup coconut milk

2 tablespoons sliced shallots

1-cup coconut flour

1 cup chopped leek

3 egg yolks

1-teaspoon curry powder

2 cups water

½ teaspoon turmeric

- Place the lamb loin a food processor then process until smooth.
- Place the ground lamb in a bowl then add chopped onion, sliced shallots, and chopped leek to the bowl.
- Season with curry powder, turmeric, salt, and pepper then pour a ½ tablespoon of olive oil and coconut milk to the bowl. Mix well.
- Preheat an Air Fryer to 400°F (204°C).

- Transfer the lamb mixture to the Air Fryer then cook for 15 minutes.
- Meanwhile, combine coconut flour with egg yolks and water then stir until smooth and incorporated.
- Using a saucepan make 8 thin omelets then set aside.
- Once the lamb is done, remove from the Air Fryer then place in a bowl.
- Take a sheet of coconut flour omelet then place on a flat surface.
- Drop 2 tablespoons of cooked lamb on the omelets then fold until becoming a tight roll. Repeat with the remaining lamb and coconut flour omelet.
- Preheat the Air Fryer again to 375°F (191°C).
- Arrange the lamb rolls in the Air Fryer then spray with the remaining olive oil.
- Cook the lamb rolls for 10 minutes then remove from the Air Fryer. If you like the lamb rolls to be more golden brown, cook the lamb rolls for another 5 minutes.
- Serve and enjoy.

Per Serving: Net Carbs: 3.9g; Calories: 276; Total Fat: 21.8g; Saturated Fat: 9.6g
Protein: 13.8g; Carbs: 5.4g; Fiber: 1.5g; Sugar: 1.5g - Fat 71% / Protein 23% / Carbs 2%

Hot Lamb Cabbage Stew with Curry Coconut Gravy [FA] [GF]

Serves: 4 / Preparation time: 5 minutes / Cooking time: 15 minutes

1 lb. lamb loin	2 cups water
2 tablespoons extra virgin olive oil	½ teaspoon salt
2 teaspoons sliced shallots	½ teaspoon pepper
¾ teaspoon curry powder	½ cup coconut milk
2 tablespoons chopped cayenne	1-teaspoon coconut aminos

- Cut the lamb loin into thin slices then set aside.
- Preheat a skillet over medium heat then pour extra virgin olive oil into the skillet.
- Once the oil is hot, stir in sliced shallots, chopped cayenne, and curry powder then sauté until aromatic.
- Add lamb loin to the skillet then season with salt and pepper. Sauté until wilted.
- Next, pour water over the lamb loin and bring to boil.
- Once it is boiled, reduce the heat and cook until the lamb loin is tender. The water will reduce into the half.
- After that, drizzle coconut milk and coconut aminos over the lamb and stir well.
- Add chopped cabbage to the skillet then bring to a simmer.
- Transfer the lamb stew to a serving bowl then serve.
- Enjoy warm.

Per Serving: Net Carbs: 2.9g: Calories: 461; Total Fat: 40.7 g; Saturated Fat: 18.4g; Protein: 20.3g; Carbs: 4.9g; Fiber: 2g; Sugar: 1.8g - Fat 79% / Protein 19% / Carbs 2%

Cheesy Moist Lamb Fritters

Serves: 1/ Preparation time: 10 minutes / Cooking time: 18 minutes

1 boneless lamb loin	2 tablespoons chopped coriander
1-teaspoon ginger	2 tablespoons chopped onion
2 teaspoons minced garlic	2 tablespoons chopped mint leaves
½ teaspoon garam masala	1 tablespoon lemon juice
½ teaspoon chili powder	1-teaspoon nutmeg

| 2 egg yolks | ½ teaspoon salt |
| ¼ cup grated cheddar cheese | 2 tablespoons heavy cream |

- Cut the lamb loin into cubes then place in a food processor. Process until smooth.
- Transfer the smooth lamb to a bowl then season with ginger, minced garlic, salt, garam masala, chili powder, coriander, and nutmeg.
- Add egg yolks, chopped onion, cheddar cheese, and mint leaves to the bowl then pour lemon juice and heavy cream into the bowl.
- Using a spatula mix the ingredients until combined.
- Shape the mixture into medium fritters then arrange in the Air Fryer.
- Preheat an Air Fryer to 400°F (204°C) and cook the fritters for 6 minutes.
- Once it is done, arrange on a serving dish then enjoy warm.

Per Serving: Net Carbs: 4.1g; Calories: 379; Total Fat: 33.6g; Saturated Fat: 14.5g
Protein: 14.5g; Carbs: 5.4g; Fiber: 1.3g; Sugar: 1.2g - Fat 80% / Protein 15% / Carbs 5%

Gingery Baked Goat Curry with Cauliflower

Serves: 4 / Preparation time: 12 minutes / Cooking time: 44 minutes

¾ lb. goat meat	1 cup chopped onion
4 tablespoons extra virgin olive oil	2 cups cauliflower florets
1-teaspoon ginger	½ teaspoon pepper
½ teaspoon cumin	¾ cup coconut milk
1-teaspoon cilantro	1-tablespoon curry
¾ teaspoon turmeric	

- Preheat an oven to 350°F (177°C) and prepare a disposable aluminum pan. Set aside.
- Place ginger, cumin, cilantro, and turmeric in a bowl then pour olive oil over the spices. Stir until incorporated.
- Cut the goat meat into cubes then rub with the olive oil mixture.
- Place the seasoned goat meat in the prepared aluminum pan then sprinkle chopped onion over the goat meat.
- Bake the goat meat for approximately 30 minutes or until tender.
- In the meantime, combine coconut milk, curry, and pepper in a saucepan then bring to a simmer. Remove from heat.
- After 30 minutes, take the aluminum pan out of the oven and sprinkle cauliflower florets over the goat meat.
- Drizzle coconut sauce on top then cover the aluminum pan with aluminum foil.
- Return the aluminum pan to the oven and bake for about 15 minutes.
- Once it is done, remove the aluminum pan from the oven and let it rest for a few minutes.
- Discard the cover then transfer the cooked goat meat to a serving dish together with the cauliflower.
- Serve and enjoy.

Per Serving: Net Carbs: 6g; Calories: 339; Total Fat: 26.9g; Saturated Fat: 12.1g
Protein: 18.4g; Carbs: 9.6g; Fiber: 3.6g; Sugar: 4g - Fat 71% / Protein 22% / Carbs 7%

Creamy Almond Lamb Leg Soup [GF]

Serves: 4 / Preparation time: 5 minutes / Cooking time: 45 minutes

1 lb. lamb leg	2 tablespoons chopped shallots
4 cups water	½ teaspoon pepper
1 cup unsweetened almond milk	2 cloves
2 tablespoons extra virgin olive oil	½ teaspoon cinnamon
1-teaspoon ginger	¼ cup chopped leek
1-teaspoon salt	2 tablespoons ground almond
2 teaspoons minced garlic	

- Chop the lamb leg then set aside.
- Preheat a skillet over medium heat then pour extra virgin olive oil into the skillet.
- Once the oil is hot, stir in minced garlic and chopped shallots then sauté until aromatic and lightly golden brown.
- Add chopped lamb to the skillet then sauté until wilted.
- Next, pour water over the lamb then bring to boil. Season the lamb with ginger, salt, pepper, cloves, and cinnamon.
- Once it is boiled, reduce the heat and cook until the lamb is tender.
- After that, add chopped leek and almond milk into the soup then bring to a simmer.
- Transfer the lamb soup to a serving bowl then sprinkle ground almond on top.
- Serve and enjoy.

Per Serving: Net Carbs: 3.2g: Calories: 403; Total Fat: 33.7g; Saturated Fat: 11.3g; Protein: 21.3g; Carbs: 4.6g; Fiber: 1.4g; Sugar: 0.4g - Fat 75% / Protein 22% / Carbs 3%

Crunchy Crusted Pecan Of Goat

Serves: 4 / Preparation time: 9 minutes / Cooking time: 44 minutes

1 lb. goat leg	½ teaspoon grated lemon zest
½ teaspoon pepper	1-cup ground pecans
3 tablespoons extra virgin olive oil	1-tablespoon mustard
½ cup chopped onion	

- Preheat an oven to 400°F (204°C) and line a baking tray with aluminum foil.
- Score the goat leg at several places then sprinkle pepper over the goat leg.
- Wait until the oven is ready then oven the goat leg for approximately 10 minutes.
- In the meantime, preheat a saucepan over medium heat then pour extra virgin olive oil into it.
- Once the oil is hot, stir in chopped onion and sauté until wilted and aromatic.
- After that, add ground pecans and grated lemon zest to the saucepan then stir well.
- Take the goat leg from the oven and coat with mustard.
- Top the goat leg with the pecan mixture then return to the oven and bake for approximately 35 minutes or until the goat leg is tender.
- Once it is done, remove the cooked goat leg from the oven and transfer to a serving dish.
- Serve and enjoy.

Per Serving: Net Carbs: 2.4g; Calories: 460; Total Fat: 40.1g; Saturated Fat: 11.9g
Protein: 21.5g; Carbs: 3.8g; Fiber: 1.4g; Sugar: 0.8g - Fat 78% / Protein 20% / Carbs 2%

Spicy Cumin Lamb Shoulder

Serves: 6 / Preparation time: 52 minutes / Cooking time: 15 minutes

1 lb. lamb shoulder	2 tablespoons sliced scallions
2 tablespoons cumin	½ cup chopped cilantro
1-teaspoon cayenne	2 egg yolks
2 tablespoons red chili flakes	1 ½ teaspoon onion powder
2 tablespoons extra virgin olive oil	2 teaspoons chili pepper
1-tablespoon coconut aminos	1-teaspoon tomato puree
1-½ tablespoons minced garlic	½ cup butter
1-teaspoon salt	¼ teaspoon pepper

- Place cumin, cayenne, red chili flakes, and minced garlic in a zipper-lock plastic bag then season with salt.
- Pour olive oil and coconut aminos to the plastic bag then mix until combined.
- Add the lamb shoulder to the plastic bag then shake until the lamb shoulder is completely coated with the spice mixture.
- Marinate the lamb chops for at least an hour and store in the fridge to keep it fresh.
- Meanwhile, melt butter in a saucepan over medium heat.
- Once the butter is melted, stir in onion powder, chili pepper, tomato puree, and pepper then mix well.
- Add egg yolks to the butter then quickly stir until incorporated.
- Remove the sauce from heat then let it rest.
- After an hour, remove the lamb shoulder from the fridge. Thaw at room temperature.
- Preheat an Air Fryer to 400°F (204°C).
- Take the seasoned lamb shoulder out of the plastic bag then transfer to Air Fryer.
- Cook the lamb chops then set the time to 15 minutes.
- Once it is done, remove the cooked lamb chops from the Air Fryer then drizzle butter sauce over the lamb chops.
- Top with cilantro and sliced scallions then serve.
- Enjoy!

Per Serving: Net Carbs: 2.9g; Calories: 354; Total Fat: 29.6g; Saturated Fat: 13.5g
Protein: 20.1g; Carbs: 3.5g; Fiber: 0.6g; Sugar: 0.7g - Fat 75% / Protein 23% / Carbs 2%

Spicy Lamb Curry Rolls

Serves: 2 / Preparation time: 10 minutes / Cooking time: 15 minutes

½ lb. boneless lamb loin	1-teaspoon curry powder
2 tablespoons butter	1 teaspoon red chili flakes
½ cup chopped onion	½ teaspoon cayenne
2 teaspoons minced garlic	½ cup coconut milk
¼ teaspoon salt	½ lb. steamed cabbage
¼ teaspoon pepper	2 tablespoons extra virgin olive oil
½ teaspoon turmeric	

- Cut the lamb loin into small dices then set aside.
- Preheat a skillet over medium heat then melt butter in it.

- Stir in minced garlic and chopped onion then sauté until aromatic.
- Add diced lamb then season with salt, pepper, turmeric, curry powder, and red chili flakes then pour coconut milk over the lamb.
- Cook until the liquid is absorbed into the lamb then remove from heat.
- Lay a sheet of steamed cabbage then put 2 tablespoons of lamb curry on it.
- Wrap the lamb with cabbage and roll it tightly. Repeat with the remaining cabbage and lamb.
- Preheat an Air Fryer to 375°F (191°C) and place a rack in it.
- Wait until the Air Fryer reaches the desired temperature then arrange the cabbage roll on the rack.
- Cook the cabbage rolls and set the time to 15 minutes.
- Once the cabbage rolls are done, remove from the Air Fryer then arrange on a serving dish.
- Serve and enjoy warm.

Per Serving: Net Carbs: 5.5g; Calories: 370; Total Fat: 33.2g; Saturated Fat: 16.5g
Protein: 11.6g; Carbs: 8.4g; Fiber: 2.9g; Sugar: 4.1g - Fat 81% / Protein 13% / Carbs 6%

Grilled Lamb Shoulder with Creamy Mint Sauce

Serves: 4 / Preparation time: 2 hours / Cooking time: 22 minutes

1 lb. lamb shoulder	3 tablespoons chopped fresh dill
4 tablespoons extra virgin olive oil	¼ cup chopped fresh mint leaves
½ teaspoon oregano	1 tablespoon lemon juice
2 tablespoons wine	¼ cup coconut cream
1-teaspoon rosemary	

- Rub the lamb shoulder with olive oil, oregano, wine, and rosemary then marinate for at least 2 hours. Store in the fridge to keep it fresh.
- In the meantime, place fresh dill, mint leaves, lemon juice and coconut cream in a food processor then process until smooth.
- Transfer the creamy sauce to a container with a lid and store in the refrigerator.
- After 2 hours, take the lamb shoulder out of the fridge and thaw at room temperature.
- Preheat a grill over medium heat then arrange the marinated lamb shoulder on it.
- Grill the lamb for approximately 10 minutes each side or until the lamb is completely cooked.
- Once it is done, remove the grilled lamb shoulder from the grill and place on a serving dish.
- Top with creamy mint sauce then serve immediately.
- Enjoy warm.

Per Serving: Net Carbs: 1.9g; Calories: 342; Total Fat: 26.8g; Saturated Fat: 8.3g
Protein: 23.1g; Carbs: 3.2g; Fiber: 1.3g; Sugar: 0.7g - Fat 70% / Protein 28% / Carbs 2%

Lamb and Cauliflower Fried Curry Rice [FA] [GF]

Serves: 4 / Preparation time: 5 minutes / Cooking time: 20 minutes

¾ lb. lamb loin	2 pastured eggs
2 tablespoons butter	3 cups cauliflower florets
2 teaspoons sliced shallots	2 tablespoons chopped leek
¾ teaspoon curry powder	

- Preheat a steamer over medium heat then steam the cauliflower florets until half tender.
- Transfer the steamed cauliflower to a food processor then process until smooth.
- Next, cut the lamb loin into very thin slices then set aside.
- Preheat a skillet over medium heat then place butter in it.
- Once the butter is melted, stir in sliced lamb and sauté until wilted and tender.
- After that, stir in sliced shallots then sauté until aromatic and lightly golden brown.
- Add cauliflower rice to the skillet together with curry powder then stir until the cauliflower rice is completely seasoned.
- Crack the eggs then beat until incorporated.
- Drizzle the egg mixture over the cauliflower rice then sprinkle chopped leek on top.
- Quickly stir the cauliflower rice and lamb until combined.
- Transfer the lamb cauliflower fried rice to a serving dish and serve.
- Enjoy warm.

Per Serving: Net Carbs: 3.3g: Calories: 349; Total Fat: 27.6g; Saturated Fat: 12.7g; Protein: 18.9g; Carbs: 5.4g; Fiber: 2.1g; Sugar: 1.9g - Fat 71% / Protein 25% / Carbs 4%

Macadamia Nutty Lamb Ribs

Serves: 4 / Preparation time: 10 minutes / Cooking time: 40 minutes

1 lb. lamb ribs	½ cup roasted macadamia nuts
2 teaspoons minced garlic	½ cup roasted almonds
1-tablespoon extra virgin olive oil	1-tablespoon chopped rosemary
½ teaspoon salt	1 egg
½ teaspoon pepper	

- Add minced garlic to the olive oil then stir until combined.
- Brush the lamb ribs with the olive oil mixture then season with salt and pepper. Let it sit for a few minutes.
- Meanwhile, place roasted macadamia and almonds in a food processor then add chopped rosemary to the food processor. Process until becoming flour then transfer to a bowl.
- In another bowl, crack the egg then stir until incorporated.
- Preheat an Air Fryer to 225°F (107°C) and place a rack in it.
- Dip the seasoned lamb ribs in the egg then coat with the nut mixture. Make sure that all sides of the lamb ribs are completely coated with the nut mixture.
- Once the Air Fryer reaches the desired temperature, place the coated lamb ribs on the rack and set the time to 25 minutes. Cook the Lamb ribs.
- After 25 minutes, increase the temperature to 400°F (204°C) and cook the lamb ribs for 5 minutes.
- Once it is done, remove the cooked lamb ribs from the Air Fryer then quickly wrap with aluminum foil. Let it sit for 10 minutes.
- Unwrap the cooked lamb ribs then place on a serving dish.
- Serve and enjoy!

Per Serving: Net Carbs: 3.7g; Calories: 455; Total Fat: 41.2g; Saturated Fat: 7.1g
Protein: 18.2g; Carbs: 8.3g; Fiber: 4.6g; Sugar: 2g - Fat 81% / Protein 16% / Carbs 3%

Stir Fry Ground Lamb with Crispy Cabbage [FA] [GF]

Serves: 4 / Preparation time: 5 minutes / Cooking time: 20 minutes

1 lb. ground lamb	2 teaspoons minced garlic
2 tablespoons butter	2 cups sliced cabbage
¼ cup chopped bell pepper	1 ½ cups tomato puree
½ cup chopped onion	¼ teaspoon salt

- Preheat a skillet over medium heat then place butter in it.
- Once the butter is melted, stir in chopped onion and minced garlic then sauté until wilted and aromatic.
- After that, add ground lamb to the skillet and cook until wilted.
- Stir in the remaining ingredients to the skillet then cover for about 5 minutes.
- Once it is done, remove from heat and transfer to a serving dish.
- Serve and enjoy.

Per Serving: Net Carbs: 6.4g: Calories: 411; Total Fat: 32.8g; Saturated Fat: 15.7g; Protein: 21g; Carbs: 8.3g; Fiber: 1.9g; Sugar: 2.1g - Fat 72% / Protein 22% / Carbs 6%

Oven Baked Lamb Ribs Macadamia with Tomato Salsa

Serves: 4 / Preparation time: 16 minutes / Cooking time: 21 minutes

¾ lb. lamb ribs	½ teaspoon pepper
½ cup macadamia	1-cup cherry tomatoes
1 teaspoon minced garlic	1-tablespoon macadamia oil
½ cup fresh parsley	1-tablespoon balsamic vinegar
4 tablespoons extra virgin olive oil	

- Preheat an oven to 400°F (204°C) and line a baking tray with aluminum foil. Set aside.
- Cut the lamb ribs into medium pieces then set aside.
- Place the macadamia in a food processor then add minced garlic, fresh parsley, olive oil, and pepper to the food processor. Process until smooth.
- Coat the lamb ribs with the macadamia mixture then arrange on the prepared baking tray.
- Place the coated lamb ribs in the oven and bake for approximately 25 minutes or until the lamb is completely cooked.
- In the meantime, cut the cherry tomatoes into halves then place in a disposable aluminum cup.
- Drizzle macadamia oil over the tomatoes then toss to combine. Set aside.
- Once the lamb is done, remove from the oven and arrange on a serving dish.
- Next, place the tomatoes in the oven and bake for approximately 5 minutes.
- Remove the tomatoes from the oven and drizzle balsamic vinegar over the tomatoes. Stir well.
- Top the baked lamb with tomato salsa then serve.
- Enjoy warm.

Per Serving: Net Carbs: 3.1g; Calories: 486; Total Fat: 44.2g; Saturated Fat: 8.2g
Protein: 19.9g; Carbs: 6.1g; Fiber: 3g; Sugar: 2.4g - Fat 82% / Protein 15% / Carbs 3%

Per Serving: Net Carbs: 3.2g; Calories: 456; Total Fat: 35.9g; Saturated Fat: 9.6g; Protein: 27.9g; Carbs: 4.3g; Fiber: 1.1g; Sugar: 2.2g - Fat 71% / Protein 25% / Carbs 4%

Savory Lamb Garlic with Walnut Green Pesto

Serves: 4 / Preparation time: 11 minutes / Cooking time: 17 minutes

1-½ lbs. lamb chops

3 teaspoons minced garlic

½ teaspoon pepper

3 cups fresh basil

½ cup roasted walnuts

½ cup extra virgin olive oil

1 tablespoon lemon juice

- Preheat an oven to 400°F (204°C) and line a baking tray with aluminum foil.

- In the meantime, rub the lamb chops with minced garlic and pepper then set aside.

- Preheat a saucepan over medium heat then pour about a tablespoon of olive oil into the saucepan.

- Once the oil is hot, place the lamb chops in the saucepan then sauté until seared.

- After that, transfer the lamb chops to the prepared baking tray then place in the oven.

- Bake the lamb chop for 15 minutes or until it is completely cooked.

- Meanwhile, place fresh basil, roasted walnuts, lemon juice, and extra virgin olive to the food processor then process until smooth and creamy.

- When the lamb is done, remove from the oven and transfer to a serving dish.

- Top the lamb with basil and walnut mixture then serve.

- Enjoy!

Per Serving: Net Carbs: 1.5g; Calories: 491; Total Fat: 43.6g; Saturated Fat: 7.2g
Protein: 26.5g; Carbs: 3g; Fiber: 1.5g; Sugar: 0.3g - Fat 80% / Protein 19% / Carbs 1%

Tasty Lamb Chop in Cheesy Creamy Gravy [FA] [GF]

Serves: 4 / Preparation time: 5 minutes / Cooking time: 20 minutes

1 lb. lamb loin

2 tablespoons butter

½ cup chopped onion

1-cup water

1 cup almond milk

1-tablespoon almond flour

¼ teaspoon salt

¼ teaspoon pepper

¼ teaspoon nutmeg

¼ teaspoon oregano

1 tablespoon lemon juice

- Cut the lamb loin into very thin slices then set aside.

- Preheat a skillet over medium heat then place butter in it.

- Once the butter is melted, stir in chopped onion and sauté until wilted and aromatic.

- Add sliced lamb loin to the skillet then cook until wilted and no longer pink.

- Pour water over the lamb then cook until the lamb is tender.

- Season the lamb with salt; pepper, nutmeg, and oregano then stir well.

- Combine almond milk with almond flour then stir well.

- Pour the almond mixture over the lamb then bring to a simmer. Remove from heat.

- Transfer the lamb and creamy gravy to a serving dish then drizzle lemon juice on top.
- Serve and enjoy.

Per Serving: Net Carbs: 3.2g: Calories: 439; Total Fat: 39.9g; Saturated Fat: 24.7g; Protein: 16g; Carbs: 5g; Fiber: 1.8g; Sugar: 2.8g - Fat 80% / Protein 17% / Carbs 3%

Easy Lamb Ribs with Minty Yogurt

Serves: 1/ Preparation time: 10 minutes / Cooking time: 18 minutes

1 lb. lamb ribs

½ teaspoon salt

½ teaspoon pepper

2 tablespoons mustard

1 teaspoon chopped rosemary

1 cup Greek yogurt

¼ cup chopped mint leaves

- Brush mustard over the lamb ribs then sprinkle salt, pepper, and rosemary over the lamb.
- Preheat an Air Fryer to 350°F (177°C).
- Once the Air Fryer is ready, place the lamb ribs in the Air Fryer and set the time to 18 minutes.
- In the meantime, combine yogurt with chopped mint leaves then stir well. Set aside.
- Once the lamb ribs are done, remove from the Air Fryer and transfer to a serving dish.
- Serve with minty yogurt then enjoy!
- This lamb ribs will be great to be enjoyed with roasted vegetables.

Per Serving: Net Carbs: 2g; Calories: 163; Total Fat: 15.3g; Saturated Fat: 2.7g
Protein: 4.3g; Carbs: 4.4g; Fiber: 2.4g; Sugar: 1g - Fat 85% / Protein 11% / Carbs 6%

Lamb Sirloin Steak with Parsley Sauce

Serves: 8 / Preparation time: 35 minutes / Cooking time: 15 minutes

1 lb. lamb sirloin

½ cup chopped onion

3 teaspoons ginger

4 teaspoons minced garlic

1-½ teaspoons fennel

1-½ teaspoons cinnamon

¾ teaspoon cardamom

2-½ teaspoons cayenne

¾ teaspoon salt

1-cup butter

¼ cup chopped scallions

3 teaspoons minced garlic

¼ cup chopped parsley

¾ teaspoon chives

1 ½ teaspoons horseradish

1-¼ teaspoons thyme

¾ teaspoon paprika

¼ teaspoon pepper

- Place chopped onion, ginger, garlic, fennel, cinnamon, cardamom, cayenne, and salt in a food processor. Process until smooth.
- Cut the lamb sirloin into thin slices then rub with the spice mixture. Marinate the lamb sirloin for at least 30 minutes.
- After 30 minutes, preheat an Air Fryer to 400°F (204°C).
- Place the seasoned sliced lamb in the Air Fryer then cook for 15 minutes.
- Meanwhile, melt butter in a saucepan then stir in minced garlic to the saucepan. Sauté until aromatic.
- Add scallions, parsley, chives, horseradish, thyme, paprika, and pepper then stir until thickened.
- Remove the sauce from heat then let it cool.

- Once the lamb is done, remove from the Air Fryer then place on a serving dish.
- Drizzle parsley sauce on top then serve.
- Enjoy with roasted vegetables or any kinds of side dish, as you desired.

Per Serving: Net Carbs: 2.1g; Calories: 358; Total Fat: 37.1g; Saturated Fat: 22.8g
Protein: 5.1g; Carbs: 3g; Fiber: 0.9g; Sugar: 0.6g - Fat 93% / Protein 4% / Carbs 3%

Baked Lamb Ribs Rosemary

Serves: 4 / Preparation time: 9 minutes / Cooking time: 19 minutes

1-lb. lamb leg	¼ cup chopped rosemary
3 tablespoons minced garlic	½ tablespoon pepper
3 tablespoons extra virgin olive oil	

- Preheat an oven to 375°F (190°C) and line a baking tray with aluminum foil.
- Rub the lamb leg with minced garlic and olive oil then sprinkle pepper over the lamb leg.
- Place the seasoned lamb leg on the prepared baking tray and sprinkle chopped rosemary over the lamb leg.
- Once the oven is ready, place the baking tray in the oven and bake the lamb leg for approximately 20 minutes or until the lamb leg is tender and cooked through.
- When the baked lamb leg is done, take it out from the oven and arrange on a serving dish
- Serve and enjoy warm.

Per Serving: Net Carbs: 3g; Calories: 413; Total Fat: 35.1g; Saturated Fat: 11.8g
Protein: 20.7g; Carbs: 4.9g; Fiber: 1.9g; Sugar: 0.1g - Fat 76% / Protein 21% / Carbs 3%

POULTRY RECIPES

Grilled Chicken Satay with Spicy Cashew Sauces

Serves: 4 / Preparation time: 4 minutes / Cooking time: 19 minutes

1-¼ lbs. boneless chicken thighs	¼ cup water
½ teaspoon pepper	2 tablespoons coconut aminos
3 tablespoons extra virgin olive oil	1 teaspoon minced garlic
¼ cup roasted cashews	1 kaffir lime leaf
2 tablespoons red chili flakes	

- Cut the boneless chicken thighs into cubes then season with pepper. Let the chicken rest
- Place roasted cashews in a blender then add red chili flakes and minced garlic to the blender.
- Pour water into over the cashews then blend until smooth.
- Transfer the cashew mixture to a saucepan then add kaffir lime leaf to it. Bring to a simmer.
- Once it is done, remove the cashew sauce from heat then drizzle coconut aminos over the sauce. Stir well then let it cool.
- Next, preheat a grill over medium heat then wait until it is ready.
- In the meantime, using a wooden skewer prick the chicken cubes then brush with extra virgin olive oil.

- Once the grill is ready, place the chicken satay on it and grill until done. Don't forget to flip the chicken satay and make sure that both sides of the chicken satay are completely cooked.
- Arrange the cooked chicken satay on a serving dish then drizzle cashew sauce on top.
- Serve and enjoy warm.

Per Serving: Net Carbs: 4.3g; Calories: 451; Total Fat: 33.2g; Saturated Fat: 8.8g
Protein: 32.1g; Carbs: 5g; Fiber: 0.7g; Sugar: 1.7g - Fat 73% / Protein 23% / Carbs 4%

Chicken Veggie Soup [FA] [GF]

Serves: 4 / Preparation time: 5 minutes / Cooking time: 20 minutes

¾ lb. chicken wings

1 cup chopped chicken skin

1 cup chopped mushroom

½ cup chopped onion

1-tablespoon extra virgin olive oil

½ cup chopped carrots

¼ cup chopped celery stalk

2 ½ cups chicken broth

¾ teaspoon salt

½ teaspoon pepper

½ teaspoon nutmeg

- Turn the Instant Pot on then pour olive oil into the inner pot of the Instant Pot.
- Press the "Sauté" button on the Instant Pot then wait until the oil is hot.
- Stir in chopped onion and sauté until translucent and aromatic.
- Next, cut the chicken wings and chicken skin into small pieces then add to the Instant Pot. Sauté until the chicken is no longer pink then press the "Cancel" button.
- Add mushroom and carrots to the Instant Pot then pour chicken broth into the Instant Pot.
- Season with salt, pepper, and nutmeg then stir well.
- Put the lid on and seal the Instant Pot properly. Close the steam valve.
- Press "Soup" button on the Instant Pot and cook the chicken soup on high. It will take about 10 minutes.
- Once the Instant Pot beeps, quick release the Instant Pot and open the lid.
- Add chopped celery stalk to the Instant Pot then stir well.
- Transfer the chicken soup to a serving bowl then serve.
- Enjoy warm!

Chicken and Cheese Delicious Balls [FA]

Serves: 4 / Preparation time: 15 minutes / Cooking time: 10 minutes

¾ lb. boneless chicken thighs

2 pastured eggs

¼ cup mayonnaise

¼ cup coconut flour

¾ cup grated Mozzarella cheese

1-teaspoon dill

½ teaspoon pepper

¼ teaspoon salt

Coconut oil, to fry

- Cut the boneless chicken thighs into pieces then place in a food processor.
- Add eggs, mayonnaise, and coconut flour to the food processor then season the chicken with dill, pepper, and salt. Process until smooth.
- Shape the chicken mixture into medium balls and fill each ball with grated mozzarella.
- Preheat a frying pan over medium heat and pour coconut oil into the frying pan.

- Once the oil is hot, put the chicken balls into the frying pan and fry the balls until cooked and lightly golden brown.
- Remove the chicken balls from the frying pan and strain the excessive oil.
- Arrange the chicken balls on a serving dish then serve.
- Enjoy immediately.

Per Serving: Net Carbs: 5.1g: Calories: 490; Total Fat: 40.8g; Saturated Fat: 21.3g; Protein: 25.4g; Carbs: 5.5g; Fiber: 0.4g; Sugar: 1.3g - Fat 75% / Protein 21% / Carbs 4%

Coconut Creamy Chicken Cheese

Serves: 4 / Preparation time: 12 minutes / Cooking time: 14 minutes

¾ lb. boneless chicken thighs	1 ½ teaspoons Italian seasoning
2-½ tablespoons extra virgin olive oil	½ cup grated Parmesan cheese
¼ cup coconut milk	1 ½ cup chopped spinach
¾ cup chicken broth	½ cup halved cherry tomatoes
2 teaspoons minced garlic	

- Cut the boneless chicken thighs into medium pieces then set aside.
- Preheat a skillet over medium heat then pour extra virgin olive oil into it.
- Once the oil is hot, stir in minced garlic then sauté until lightly golden and aromatic.
- Next, add the boneless chicken thighs to the skillet then stir until wilted.
- Pour chicken broth over the chicken then bring to boil.
- Once it is boiled, reduce the heat and cook until the chicken is completely done.
- Pour coconut milk over the chicken and season the chicken with Italian seasoning.
- Once it is done, add chopped spinach and cherry tomatoes to the skillet. Stir until just wilted.
- Transfer the cooked chicken together with the gravy and vegetables to a serving dish then quickly sprinkle grated Parmesan cheese on top. Stir well.
- Serve and enjoy warm.

Per Serving: Net Carbs: 3.5g; Calories: 432; Total Fat: 42.7g; Saturated Fat: 20.6g
Protein: 10.6g; Carbs: 4.1g; Fiber: 0.6g; Sugar: 3.2g - Fat 72% / Protein 25% / Carbs 3%

Garlic Chicken Balls

Serves: 4 / Preparation time: 15 minutes / Cooking time: 18 minutes

½ lb. boneless chicken thighs	½ teaspoon salt
½ cup chopped mushroom	1-¼ cups roasted pecans
1-teaspoon minced garlic	1-teaspoon extra virgin olive oil
1-teaspoon pepper	

- Cut the boneless chicken into cubes then place in a food processor.
- Add roasted pecans to the food processor then season with minced garlic, pepper, and salt. Process until smooth.
- Cut the mushrooms into very small dices then add to the chicken mixture.

- Using your hand mix the chicken with diced mushrooms then shape into small balls. Set aside.
- Preheat an Air Fryer to 375°F (191°C).
- Brush the balls with extra virgin olive oil then arrange the chicken balls in the Air Fryer.
- Cook the chicken balls for 18 minutes then arrange on a serving dish.
- Serve and enjoy.

Per Serving: Net Carbs: 2.1g; Calories: 525; Total Fat: 46.8g; Saturated Fat: 7.7g
Protein: 23.7g; Carbs: 5.7g; Fiber: 3.6g; Sugar: 1.6g - Fat 80% / Protein 18% / Carbs 2%

Chicken Wings Barbecue [FA] [GF]

Serves: 4 / Preparation time: 5 minutes / Cooking time: 20 minutes

1 lb. chicken wings	½ teaspoon garlic powder
½ cup coconut oil	¼ teaspoon onion powder
¼ cup tomato puree	¼ teaspoon salt
2 tablespoons apple cider vinegar	¼ teaspoon chili powder
1-½ teaspoons Worcestershire sauce	¼ teaspoon cayenne
½ teaspoon hickory smoke	½ cup water
½ teaspoon smoked paprika	

- Preheat a skillet over medium heat then pour coconut oil into the skillet.
- Once it is hot, put the chicken wings into the skillet and fry until both sides are lightly golden brown and the chicken wings are cooked.
- In the meantime, place tomato puree, apple cider vinegar, Worcestershire sauce, hickory smoke, smoked paprika; salt, chili powder, and cayenne in a saucepan then pour water over the ingredients. Stir well and bring to a simmer.
- Remove the barbecue sauce from heat and let it cool.
- Once the fried chicken wings are done, take them out of the skillet and strain the excessive oil.
- Place the fried chicken wings on a serving dish then drizzle barbecue sauce on top.
- Serve and enjoy immediately.

Per Serving: Net Carbs: 3.5g: Calories: 504; Total Fat: 45.4g; Saturated Fat: 28.6g; Protein: 21.4g; Carbs: 4g; Fiber: 0.5g; Sugar: 2.6g - Fat 81% / Protein 16% / Carbs 3%

Turkey Breast with Strawberry Glaze

Serves: 4 / Preparation time: 30 minutes / Cooking time: 37 minutes

2 lbs. turkey breast	2 tablespoons chopped shallots
1-teaspoon salt	2 tablespoons lemon juice
¾ teaspoon black pepper	1-tablespoon coconut flour
1-tablespoon olive oil	¼ cup chicken broth
1-cup fresh strawberries	½ cup butter

- Season the turkey breast with salt and black pepper.
- Preheat an Air Fryer to 375°F (191°C).
- Place the turkey in the Air Fryer then cook for 15 minutes.
- While waiting for the turkey, pour chicken broth into a saucepan then add shallots and lemon juice. Bring to boil.

- Once it is boiled, stir in coconut flour then stir until incorporated and smooth.
- Add butter to the saucepan then cook until the butter is melted. Remove from heat then set aside.
- After 15 minutes of cooking time, open the Air Fryer then flip the turkey. Cook the turkey for another 15 minutes.
- Meanwhile, place the fresh strawberries in a food processor. Process until smooth.
- Drizzle the strawberry over the turkey then cook again for 7 minutes.
- Remove the turkey from heat then serve with the sauce.
- Enjoy!

Per Serving: Net Carbs: 6.4g; Calories: 344; Total Fat: 28.3g; Saturated Fat: 15.5g
Protein: 15.7g; Carbs: 7.8g; Fiber: 1.4g; Sugar: 5g - Fat 74% / Protein 18% / Carbs 8%

Tomato Chicken Stew with Baby Spinach

Serves: 4 / Preparation time: 9 minutes / Cooking time: 41 minutes

1 lb. chopped boneless chicken thighs	½ cup halved cherry tomatoes
3 tablespoons extra virgin olive oil	1-cup water
2 tablespoons minced garlic	½ cup coconut milk
½ teaspoon oregano	1 cup chopped baby spinach
½ teaspoon pepper	

- Preheat a skillet over medium heat then pour extra virgin olive oil into it.
- Once it is hot, stir in minced garlic then sauté until lightly golden and aromatic.
- Next, add chopped boneless chicken thighs to the skillet and sauté until the chicken is no longer pink.
- Season the chicken with oregano and pepper then pour water over the chicken. Bring to boil.
- Once it is boiled, reduce the heat and cook until the chicken is tender and the water is completely absorbed into the chicken.
- Pour coconut milk into the skillet and add halved cherry tomatoes to the stew. Bring to a simmer.
- Once it is done, add chopped baby spinach to the skillet and stir well.
- Remove the chicken stew from heat and transfer to a serving dish.
- Serve and enjoy warm.

Per Serving: Net Carbs: 2.8g; Calories: 410; Total Fat: 34.8g; Saturated Fat: 12.9g
Protein: 21.3g; Carbs: 4g; Fiber: 1.2g; Sugar: 1.1g - Fat 76% / Protein 21% / Carbs 3%

Savory Chicken Turmeric [FA] [GF]

Serves: 4 / Preparation time: 5 minutes / Cooking time: 20 minutes

1 lb. chicken thighs	2 bay leaves
3 cloves garlic	2 lemon grasses
3 shallots	3 kaffir lime leaves
1 candlenut	1-teaspoon salt
1-tablespoon extra virgin olive oil	½ teaspoon pepper
1-teaspoon turmeric	2 cups water
1-inch galangal	½ cup coconut milk

- Place garlic, shallots, candlenuts, and turmeric in a food processor then process until smooth.
- Preheat a skillet over medium heat then pour extra virgin olive into the skillet.
- Once the oil is hot, stir in spice mixture and sauté until aromatic.
- Add chicken thighs to the skillet then sauté until the chicken is completely seasoned.
- Pour water over the chicken then add galangal, bay leaves, lemon grasses, kaffir lime leaves, salt, and pepper. Bring to boil.
- Once it is boiled, reduce the heat and cook until the chicken is tender.
- Pour coconut milk into the skillet then stir well and bring to a simmer.
- Transfer the chicken together with the turmeric gravy to a serving bowl.
- Serve and enjoy. If you like, sprinkle fried shallots on top as a garnish.

Per Serving: Net Carbs: 6.6g: Calories: 404; Total Fat: 31.5g; Saturated Fat: 12.1g; Protein: 22.4g; Carbs: 8.6g; Fiber: 1.3g; Sugar: 1.3g - Fat 70% / Protein 23% / Carbs 7%

Chicken Pumpkin Stew [FA] [GF]

Serves: 8 / Preparation time: 5 minutes / Cooking time: 15 minutes

1-½ lbs. chicken thighs	2 cups coconut milk
3 cups pumpkin cubes	½ cup water
2 tablespoons butter	½ teaspoon salt
½ cup chopped onion	1-tablespoon lemon juice
3 teaspoons minced garlic	½ cup chopped cilantro
1-teaspoon ginger	¾ cup grated Cheddar cheese
2 teaspoons curry powder	

- Place butter in the inner pot of an Instant Pot then press the "Sauté" button.
- Once the butter is melted, stir in chopped onion, minced garlic, and chicken thighs then sauté until wilted and aromatic. Press the "Cancel" button.
- Pour coconut milk and water over the chicken then season with ginger, curry powder, salt, and lemon juice. Stir well.
- Put the lid on and seal the Instant Pot properly then close the steam valve.
- Select "Manual" setting and cook the chicken on high. Set the time to 10 minutes.
- When the Instant Pot beeps, quickly release it and open the lid.
- After that, add pumpkin cubes, chopped cilantro and grated Cheddar cheese to the Instant Pot then stir well.
- Press "Sauté" button again and cook until the Cheddar cheese is completely melted. It will take around 5 minutes.
- Once it is done, press the "Cancel" button then transfer the chicken and pumpkin stew to a serving dish.
- Serve and enjoy.

Per Serving: Net Carbs: 5.8g; Calories: 405; Total Fat: 33.6g; Saturated Fat: 20.5g; Protein: 19.8g; Carbs: 7.8g; Fiber: 2g; Sugar: 3g - Fat 75% / Protein 20% / Carbs 5%

Savory Chicken Turmeric with Creamy Coconut Lemon Sauce

Serves: 4 / Preparation time: 11 minutes / Cooking time: 31 minutes

1 lb. boneless chicken thighs	2 tablespoons extra virgin olive oil

2 teaspoons minced garlic
½ teaspoon turmeric
1 lemon grass
2 tablespoons coconut oil

2 tablespoons lemon juice
¾ cup chicken broth
¼ cup coconut milk
1-tablespoon coconut flour

¼ cup chopped onion

- Cut the boneless chicken thighs into cubes then set aside.
- Preheat a skillet over medium heat then pour extra virgin olive oil into the skillet.
- Once the oil is hot, stir in minced garlic and sauté until lightly golden brown and aromatic.
- Add chicken cubes to the skillet then season with turmeric and lemon grass.
- Pour ½ cup chicken broth over the chicken cubes then bring to boil.
- Once it is boiled, reduced the heat and cook until the liquid is completely absorbed into the chicken.
- In the meantime, preheat a saucepan over medium heat then pour coconut oil into the pan.
- Stir in chopped onion then sauté until wilted and lightly golden brown.
- After that, reduce the heat and pour coconut milk into the saucepan.
- Combine chicken broth with coconut flour then stir well.
- Next, pour the chicken broth mixture to the saucepan then stir until incorporated. Bring to a simmer.
- Once it is done, remove the sauce from heat and drizzle lemon juice over the sauce. Stir well and set aside.
- Go back to the chicken and when it is done, remove the chicken from heat and transfer to a serving dish.
- Drizzle the lemon sauce over the chicken then serve.
- You can also serve the lemon sauce in a separated bowl.
- Enjoy warm!

Per Serving: Net Carbs: 2.8g; Calories: 420; Total Fat: 35.1g; Saturated Fat: 15.6g
Protein: 21.4g; Carbs: 4.7g; Fiber: 1.9g; Sugar: 1.3g - Fat 75% / Protein 22% / Carbs 3%

Spicy Chicken Curry [FA] [GF]

Serves: 4 / Preparation time: 5 minutes / Cooking time: 20 minutes

2 lbs. boneless chicken thighs

½ teaspoon salt

1-cup coconut milk

1 lemon grass

1-cup water

1 bay leaf

2 tablespoons curry paste

1 tablespoon red chili flakes

½ teaspoon turmeric

½ cup chopped cabbage

2 teaspoons minced garlic

½ cup cubed cucumber

2 teaspoons sliced shallots

- Cut the boneless chicken thighs into medium cubes then place in the Instant Pot.
- Pour coconut milk and water over the chicken then season with curry paste, turmeric, minced garlic, sliced shallots, and salt. Stir well.
- Add lemon grass and bay leaf to the pot then sprinkle red chili flakes on top.
- Put the lid on then seal the Instant Pot properly. Close the steam valve.
- Select the "Pressure" setting on the Instant Pot and cook the chicken for 8 minutes.
- Once it is done, quick release the Instant Pot and open the lid.
- Take the chicken out of the Instant Pot then place on a serving dish.
- After that, select the "Sauté" menu on the Instant Pot then cook the liquid for about 5 minutes.

- Add chopped cabbage to the Instant Pot then stir until wilted.
- Pour the liquid together with the cabbage over the chicken then sprinkle cubed cucumber on top.
- Serve and enjoy warm.

Per Serving: Net Carbs: 6.8g; Calories: 383; Total Fat: 31.6g; Saturated Fat: 16.4g; Protein: 17.3g; Carbs: 8.7g; Fiber: 1.9g; Sugar: 3.1g - Fat 74% / Protein 20% / Carbs 6%

Chicken and Cheese Roll with Almond Sauce

Serves: 6 / Preparation time: 60 minutes / Cooking time: 12 minutes

1 lb. boneless chicken breast	2 eggs
3 tablespoons extra virgin olive oil	1 cup almond flour
3 tablespoons lemon juice	½ cup butter
3 teaspoons minced garlic	¼ cup almond milk
1-teaspoon oregano	1-teaspoon ginger
½ teaspoon black pepper	½ cup roasted almonds
½ lb. Mozzarella cheese	

- Pour olive oil and lemon juice in a bowl then add minced garlic, oregano, and black pepper to the bowl. Mix well.
- Cut the boneless chicken breast into slices then rub with the spice mixture. Let them sit for about an hour.
- Meanwhile, cut the Mozzarella cheese into sticks then set aside.
- Place roasted almonds in a food processor then process until becoming flour. Set aside.
- After an hour, take a slice of chicken breast then put a Mozzarella stick on it.
- Roll the chicken then prick with a toothpick. Repeat with the remaining chicken and Mozzarella cheese.
- Next, crack the eggs then place in a bowl. Stir until incorporated.
- Preheat an Air Fryer to 375°F (191°C) and place a rack in it.
- Dip a chicken roll in the egg then roll in the almond flour. Do the same with the remaining chicken rolls.
- Arrange the coated chicken rolls on the rack in the Air Fryer then set the time to 6 minutes.
- After 6 minutes, open the Air Fryer then flip the chicken rolls. Continue cooking for another 6 minutes.
- Meanwhile, place butter in a mixing bowl then add floured roasted almonds and ginger to the bowl.
- Pour almond milk into the bowl then using an electric mixer beat until incorporated and fluffy. Set aside.
- Once the chicken rolls are ready, remove from the Air Fryer and place on a serving dish.
- Serve with almond sauce. Enjoy!

Per Serving: Net Carbs: 3g; Calories: 453; Total Fat: 40.4g; Saturated Fat: 17.6g
Protein: 20.5g; Carbs: 5.1g; Fiber: 2.1g; Sugar: 1.6g - Fat 81% / Protein 18% / Carbs 1%

Chicken Avocado Creamy Salad

Serves: 4 / Preparation time: 11 minutes / Cooking time: 29 minutes

1 lb. boneless chicken thighs	1 ripe avocado
½ cup almond milk	2 tablespoons chopped celeries
1-teaspoon oregano	2 tablespoons cilantro
2 tablespoons lemon juice	¼ cup diced onion
3 tablespoons extra virgin olive oil	¼ teaspoon pepper

- Add oregano to the almond milk then stir well.
- Cut the boneless chicken thighs into slices then rub with almond milk mixture. Let it rest for approximately 10 minutes.

- In the meantime, preheat an oven to 250°F (121°C) and line a baking tray with aluminum foil.
- Once the oven is ready, spread the seasoned chicken on the prepared baking tray and bake for approximately 20 minutes or until the chicken is done.
- While waiting for the chicken, cut the avocado into halves then remove the seed.
- Peel the avocado then cut into cubes.
- Place the avocado cubes in a salad bowl then drizzle lemon juice and extra virgin olive oil over the avocado.
- Add chopped celeries, cilantro, onion, and pepper to the salad bowl then toss to combine.
- Once the chicken is done, remove from the oven and transfer to a serving dish.
- Top the chicken with avocado salad then serve immediately.
- Enjoy right away.

Per Serving: Net Carbs: 2.8g; Calories: 448; Total Fat: 40.3g; Saturated Fat: 13.7g
Protein: 16.9g; Carbs: 7.3g; Fiber: 4.5g; Sugar: 1.8g - Fat 81% / Protein 16% / Carbs 3%

Red Hot Wrapped Steamed Chicken [FA] [GF]

Serves: 4 / Preparation time: 5 minutes / Cooking time: 20 minutes

¾ lb. chicken thighs	2 tablespoons red chilies
½ lb. chicken skin	½ cup cayenne
2 cloves garlic	¼ teaspoon salt
3 shallots	1 bay leaf
¼ teaspoon turmeric	½ cup diced tomatoes

- Cut the chicken thighs and chicken skin into medium pieces then place in a bowl.
- Place garlic, shallots, turmeric, red chilies, cayenne, and salt in a food processor then process until smooth.
- Rub the chicken with the spice mixture then add diced tomatoes to the chicken. Toss to combine.
- Place the seasoned chicken on a sheet of aluminum foil then put bay leaf on it.
- Tightly wrap the chicken and place in a disposable aluminum pan.
- Preheat a steamer over medium heat and steam the chicken for approximately 20 minutes.
- Once it is done, remove the steamed chicken from the steamer and let it cool for about 10 minutes.
- Unwrap the steamed chicken and transfer to a serving dish.
- Serve and enjoy.

Per Serving: Net Carbs: 6.2g: Calories: 492; Total Fat: 38.6g; Saturated Fat: 10.8g; Protein: 27.9g; Carbs: 9.8g; Fiber: 3.6g; Sugar: 2.2g - Fat 71% / Protein 24% / Carbs 5%

Refreshing Buttery Chicken Wings [FA] [GF]

Serves: 4 / Preparation time: 5 minutes / Cooking time: 10 minutes

1 ½ chicken wings	4 tablespoons coconut aminos
½ cup butter	½ teaspoon pepper
1 cup chopped onion	¼ teaspoon salt
2 teaspoons minced garlic	½ cup water

3 tablespoons lemon juice

- Place butter in the inner pot of an Instant Pot then press the "Sauté" button.
- Once the butter is melted, stir in chopped onion then sauté until aromatic.
- Add chicken wings to the Instant Pot then drizzle coconut aminos over the chicken.
- Sprinkle salt and pepper over on the chicken then pour water into the Instant Pot.
- Put the lid on and seal the Instant Pot properly. Close the steam valve.
- Select "Pressure" menu on the Instant Pot then cook the chicken on high for 10 minutes.
- Once it is done, quick release the Instant Pot then open the lid.
- Splash lemon juice over the chicken then stir well.
- Transfer the chicken to a serving dish then serve.
- Enjoy immediately.

Per Serving: Net Carbs: 6.3g; Calories: 544; Total Fat: 43.2g; Saturated Fat: 18.1g; Protein: 30.9g; Carbs: 7.3g; Fiber: 1g; Sugar: 1.5g - Fat 71% / Protein 23% / Carbs 6%

Crispy Chicken with Cheese Sauce

Serves: 4 / Preparation time: 9 minutes / Cooking time: 41 minutes

1 lb. boneless chicken thigh	½ cup extra virgin olive oil, to fry
½ teaspoon black pepper	1 cup almond yogurt
1 cup almond flour	1 cup grated cheddar cheese
1 egg	2 teaspoons mustard

- Cut the boneless chicken thigh into slices then set aside.
- Crack the egg then place in a bowl.
- Season the egg with black pepper then stir until incorporated.
- Dip the sliced chicken in the beaten egg then roll in the almond flour. Make sure that the chicken is completely coated with almond flour.
- Preheat a frying pan over medium heat then pour olive oil into the pan.
- Once the oil is hot, put the chicken in the frying pan and fry until both sides of the chicken are lightly golden brown and the chicken is completely cooked.
- Remove the fried chicken from the frying pan and let it rest for a few minutes to discard the excessive oil. Place the crispy chicken on a serving dish.
- In the meantime, place almond yogurt, grated cheddar cheese, and mustard in a saucepan then bring to a simmer over very low heat.
- Stir the sauce until incorporated then remove from heat.
- Drizzle the cheese sauce over the chicken then serve.
- Enjoy warm!

Per Serving: Net Carbs: 4.5g; Calories: 439; Total Fat: 42.2g; Saturated Fat: 10.7g
Protein: 12.7g; Carbs: 5.6g; Fiber: 1.1g; Sugar: 3.4g - Fat 87% / Protein 9% / Carbs 4%

Turkey Cilantro Creamy Butter

Serves: 4 / Preparation time: 30 minutes / Cooking time: 20 minutes

1 lb. turkey breast	½ cup cilantro

| 1 teaspoon minced garlic | ¼ cup chicken broth |
| 2 tablespoons lemon juice |
¾ teaspoon cumin	2 tablespoons lemon juice
¼ teaspoon salt	½ cup butter
½ teaspoon pepper	½ teaspoon garlic powder
2 tablespoons extra virgin olive oil	¼ cup grated Parmesan cheese

- Cut the turkey breast into slices then set aside.
- Combine cilantro with minced garlic, cumin, salt, and pepper then pour olive oil, chicken broth, and lemon juice into the mixing bowl. Stir until incorporated.
- Rub the turkey breast with the spice mixture then let it sit for about 30 minutes. Store in the fridge to keep it fresh.
- Meanwhile, combine butter with garlic powder and Parmesan cheese then using an electric mixer mix until combined and fluffy. Set aside.
- After 30 minutes of seasoning process, take the turkey out of the fridge.
- Preheat an Air Fryer to 350°F (177°C) and place a rack in the Air Fryer.
- Place the seasoned turkey on the rack then cook for 20 minutes.
- Open the Air Fryer then flip the turkey. Cook the turkey again for another 20 minutes.
- Once it is done, remove the turkey from the Air Fryer then place on a serving dish.
- Serve and enjoy with creamy butter.

Per Serving: Net Carbs: 3.9g; Calories: 402; Total Fat: 36.3g; Saturated Fat: 19.7g
Protein: 16.8g; Carbs: 4.1g; Fiber: 0.2g; Sugar: 0.4g - Fat 81% / Protein 17% / Carbs 2%

Salty Grilled Chicken Wings [FA] [GF] [SF]

Serves: 4 / Preparation time: 5 minutes / Cooking time: 25 minutes

1 lb. chicken wings	1-cup water
1-teaspoon salt	2 lemon grasses
3 teaspoons minced garlic	¼ cup butter

- Rub the chicken wings with salt and minced garlic then place in a skillet.
- Pour water over the chicken then put lemon grasses on it. Bring to boil.
- Once it is boiled, reduce the heat and cook until the chicken is tender.
- Once it is done, remove the chicken from heat and discard the liquid.
- Next, preheat a grill over medium heat then place the chicken wings directly on the grid.
- Baste the chicken wings with butter as many as possible and grill the chicken until brown. Don't forget to flip and rotate the chicken wings.
- Once it is done, remove the grilled chicken wings from the grill and arrange on a serving dish.
- Serve and enjoy warm.

Per Serving: Net Carbs: 1.3g: Calories: 357; Total Fat: 29.5g; Saturated Fat: 12.3g; Protein: 21.3g; Carbs: 1.3g; Fiber: 0g; Sugar: 0g - Fat 74% / Protein 25% / Carbs 1%

Broken Fried Duck with Green Chili Topping and Fried Cabbage

Serves: 4 / Preparation time: 14 minutes / Cooking time: 34 minutes

| 1 ½ lbs. bone-in duck thighs | 4 tablespoons minced garlic |
| 3 tablespoons lemon juice | 1-teaspoon ginger |

2 lemon grasses

1 bay leaf

2 cups water

2 cups chopped cabbage

½ cup extra virgin olive oil, to fry

2 tablespoons chopped green chili

- Rub the duck with lemon juice then let it rest for approximately 10 minutes.
- After 10 minutes, place the duck in a skillet then season with 3 tablespoons of minced garlic, ginger, lemon grasses, and bay leaf.
- Pour water over the duck then bring to boil.
- Once it is boiled, reduce the heat and cook until the water is completely absorbed into the duck.
- Once it is done, remove the duck from heat and set aside.
- Preheat a frying pan over medium heat and pour olive oil into the pan.
- Once the oil is hot, put the cooked duck in the frying pan and fry until both sides of the duck are lightly golden brown.
- Remove the fried duck from the frying pan and discard the excessive oil.
- Place the fried duck on a mortar then press until broken.
- Arrange the fried duck on a serving dish then set aside.
- Next, quickly fry the chopped cabbage then place next to the fried duck.
- After that, place green chili, the remaining minced garlic, and a teaspoon of olive oil in a food processor then process until smooth.
- Top the duck with green chili mixture then serve.
- Enjoy immediately.

Per Serving: Net Carbs: 5.4g; Calories: 436; Total Fat: 39g; Saturated Fat: 18.2g
Protein: 16.8g; Carbs: 6.6g; Fiber: 1.2g; Sugar: 1.7g - Fat 81% / Protein 14% / Carbs 5%

Fried Chicken Steak with Mushroom Puree

Serves: 4 / Preparation time: 30 minutes / Cooking time: 25 minutes

1 lb. boneless chicken thighs

½ cup almond flour

¼ cup sunflower seeds

¼ teaspoon thyme

½ teaspoon pepper

1-cup water

1-teaspoon olive oil

3 tablespoons butter

½ cup chopped onion

2 teaspoons minced garlic

1 cup chopped mushroom

1 ½ cup homemade chicken broth

¼ teaspoon salt

- Melt butter in a saucepan then stir in chopped onion and mushroom to the saucepan. Sauté until wilted and aromatic.
- Remove from heat then let it cool.
- Once the sautéed mushrooms and onions are cool, transfer to a blender then pour chicken broth into the blender.
- Season with salt then blend until smooth.
- Return the mushroom mixture to the saucepan then bring to a simmer.
- Cook until the sauce is thickened then let it cool.
- Place sunflower seeds in a food processor then process until becoming flour.
- Transfer the sunflower flour to a bowl then combine with almond flour.
- Season with thyme and pepper then mix well.
- Cut the boneless chicken into slices then roll in the almond and sunflower flour mixture.

- Dip the chicken slices in the water and return back to the flour mixture.
- Roll the chicken again until the chicken is completely coated with flour.
- Preheat an Air Fryer to 375°F (191°C) and place a rack in it.
- Once the Air Fryer is ready, arrange the chicken on the rack then cook for 6 minutes.
- Open the drawer then flip the chicken. Cook for another 6 minutes.
- Remove the chicken from the Air Fryer then place on a serving dish.
- Serve with mushroom puree then enjoy!

Per Serving: Net Carbs: 2.8g; Calories: 346; Total Fat: 27.6g; Saturated Fat: 9.9g
Protein: 19.8g; Carbs: 5.2g; Fiber: 2.4g; Sugar: 1.6g - Fat 71% / Protein 23% / Carbs 6%

Yellow Turmeric Shredded Chicken [FA] [GF] [SF] [F]

Serves: 4 / Preparation time: 5 minutes / Cooking time: 20 minutes

1 lb. boneless chicken thigh	2 lemon grasses
¼ cup ghee	½ teaspoon salt
2 teaspoons turmeric	

- Place the boneless chicken thigh in the inner pot of an Instant Pot.
- Add ghee and lemon grasses then sprinkle salt and turmeric over the chicken.
- Put the lid on then seal the Instant Pot properly. Close the steam valve.
- Select the "Pressure" menu and set the time to 20 minutes. Cook the chicken.
- Once the Instant Pot beeps, naturally release the Instant Pot then open the lid.
- Using a fork shred the cooked chicken then transfer to a serving dish.
- Serve and enjoy warm.

Per Serving: Net Carbs: 1.1g; Calories: 358; Total Fat: 29.9g; Saturated Fat: 13g; Protein: 20.2g; Carbs: 1.3g; Fiber: 0.2g; Sugar: 0g - Fat 75% / Protein 23% / Carbs 2%

Tomato Chili Chicken Tender with Fresh Basils

Serves: 4 / Preparation time: 14 minutes / Cooking time: 31 minutes

1-¼ lbs. boneless chicken thighs	¼ cup diced red tomatoes
2 tablespoons minced garlic	2 tablespoons red chili flakes
2 lemon grasses	3 tablespoons extra virgin olive oil
2 cups water	½ cup fresh basils

- Cut the boneless chicken thighs into medium cubes then place in a skillet.
- Season the chicken with minced garlic and lemon grasses then pour water over the chicken. Bring to boil.
- Once it is boiled, reduce the heat and cook until the water is completely absorbed into the chicken.
- Remove the cooked chicken from heat then set aside.
- Next, preheat a saucepan over medium heat then pour olive oil into it.
- Once the oil is hot, stir in the chicken and cook until lightly brown.
- Add red tomatoes, red chili flakes, and fresh basils to the saucepan then stir until wilted and the chicken is completely seasoned.

- Transfer the chicken to a serving dish then serve.
- Enjoy!

Per Serving: Net Carbs: 3.9g; Calories: 410; Total Fat: 31.9g; Saturated Fat: 7.8g
Protein: 25.9g; Carbs: 4.5g; Fiber: 0.6g; Sugar: 1.5g - Fat 70% / Protein 26% / Carbs 4%

Cheesy Chicken with Ranch Seasoning [FA] [GF]

Serves: 4 / Preparation time: 4 minutes / Cooking time: 14 minutes

2 lbs. boneless chicken thighs	3 tablespoons minced garlic
¾ cup cream cheese	½ teaspoon salt
½ cup tarragon	1-teaspoon black pepper
½ cup chopped parsley	½ cup grated cheddar cheese
½ cup dill	1-cup water

- Place tarragon in a bowl then add chopped parsley, dill, minced garlic, salt, and black pepper to the bowl. Mix until combined then set aside.
- Pour water into the Instant Pot then add chicken in it.
- Cut the cream cheese into cubes then sprinkle over the chicken.
- Add the seasoning mixture to the Instant Pot then close and seal the Instant Pot properly. Close the steam valve.
- Select "Pressure" setting on the Instant Pot and cook the chicken on high for 10 minutes.
- When the Instant Pot beeps, quick release the Instant Pot then open the lid.
- Take the chicken out of the Instant Pot then using a fork shred the cooked chicken. Return the shredded chicken to the Instant Pot.
- Add grated cheddar cheese to the Instant Pot then close the lid. You don't need to turn the Instant Pot on. The remaining heat is enough to melt the cheese. Let it sit for 4 minutes.
- After 5 minutes, open the lid and stir well.
- Transfer the cooked chicken to a serving dish together with the liquid then serve.
- Enjoy!

Per Serving: Net Carbs: 6.9g; Calories: 474; Total Fat: 38.3g; Saturated Fat: 19.6g; Protein: 25.3g; Carbs: 8.4g; Fiber: 1.5g; Sugar: 0.3g - Fat 73% / Protein 21% / Carbs 6%

Lasagna Cheesy Chicken Layers [GF]

Serves: 4 / Preparation time: 10 minutes / Cooking time: 30 minutes

½ lb. boneless chicken thighs	½ teaspoon salt
¼ lb. chicken skin	½ teaspoon pepper
4 pastured eggs	½ cup tomato puree
2 tablespoons butter	½ cup grated Mozzarella cheese
½ cup diced onion	

- Cut the boneless chicken thighs and chicken skin into medium pieces then place in a food processor.
- Process the boneless chicken thighs and skin until smooth then set aside.
- Crack 2 eggs then place in a bowl.
- Season the egg with salt and pepper then set aside.
- Next, preheat a saucepan over medium heat then place butter in it.
- Once the butter is melted, stir in chopped onion and sauté until lightly golden brown and aromatic. Remove from heat and let it cool.

- In the meantime, crack the remaining eggs then place in a bowl. Stir until incorporated.
- Preheat a saucepan over medium heat and make 2 thin omelets in it. Set aside.
- After that, preheat an oven to 300°F (149°C) and prepare a medium round baking pan. Line with aluminum foil or parchment paper.
- Combine the ground chicken with sautéed onion and egg mixture then mix well.
- Divide the chicken mixture into 2 and place one part in the prepared baking pan. Spread evenly.
- Drizzle half of tomato puree over the chicken then place an omelet on it.
- Repeat with the remaining chicken mixture, tomato puree, and omelets.
- Sprinkle Mozzarella cheese on top then bake the chicken for approximately 25 minutes. The Mozzarella will be melted and lightly golden brown.
- Once it is done, remove the chicken lasagna from the oven and let it cool for a few minutes.
- Transfer the chicken lasagna to a serving dish then serve warm.
- Enjoy!

Per Serving: Net Carbs: 4.7g: Calories: 474; Total Fat: 36.9g; Saturated Fat: 14.7g; Protein: 28.5g; Carbs: 5.6g; Fiber: 0.9g; Sugar: 2.4g - Fat 70% / Protein 26% / Carbs 4%

Spicy Duck with Steamed Green Collard

Serves: 4 / Preparation time: 16 minutes / Cooking time: 41 minutes

1 ½ lbs. bone-in duck thighs	3 tablespoons red chili flakes
2 tablespoons extra virgin olive oil	1 kaffir lime leaf
2 tablespoons minced garlic	2 cups water
2 teaspoons sliced shallots	½ cup coconut milk
1-teaspoon turmeric	1 cup chopped collard green

- Preheat a steamer over medium heat then steam the collard green until just tender.
- Remove the steamed collard green from heat then set aside.
- Preheat a skillet over medium heat then pour olive oil into it.
- Once the oil is hot, stir in minced garlic and sliced shallots then sauté until wilted and aromatic.
- Next, add the duck to the skillet and season with turmeric, red chili flakes, and kaffir lime leaves.
- After that, pour water over the duck then bring to boil.
- Once it is boiled, reduce the heat and cook until the duck is tender and cooked through.
- Pour coconut milk into the skillet then bring to a simmer. Occasionally stir the gravy until incorporated.
- When it is done, remove the cooked duck and the gravy to a serving bowl serve with steamed collard green.
- Enjoy!

Per Serving: Net Carbs: 6.7g; Calories: 353; Total Fat: 28.2g; Saturated Fat: 12g
Protein: 17.9g; Carbs: 8.9g; Fiber: 2.2g; Sugar: 3.1g - Fat 72% / Protein 20% / Carbs 8%

Chicken Cilantro with Green Butter

Serves: 8 / Preparation time: 60 minutes / Cooking time: 18 minutes

8 chicken drumsticks	2 tablespoons minced garlic
1-cup fresh cilantro	2 teaspoons ginger
1 jalapeno	2-½ tablespoons extra virgin olive oil

1-½ cup butter

1 ¾ teaspoons salt

½ teaspoon coriander

½ teaspoon pepper

¼ cup lemon juice

- Chop ½ cup fresh cilantro and jalapeno then place in a bowl.
- Add minced garlic, ginger, 1 ½ teaspoon salt, olive oil, and 2 tablespoons lemon juice to the bowl. Mix well.
- Rub the chicken drumsticks with the cilantro mixture then marinate for at least an hour to overnight. Store in the fridge to keep them fresh.
- After an hour, remove the seasoned drumsticks from the fridge then thaw at room temperature.
- Preheat an Air Fryer to 400°F (204°C).
- Place the chicken drumsticks in the Air Fryer then cook for 18 minutes.
- Meanwhile, place butter and the remaining fresh cilantro in a bowl.
- Season with the remaining salt, coriander, and pepper then pour lemon juice into the bowl.
- Using an immersion blender blend the mixture until smooth and incorporated and smooth. Set aside.
- Once the chicken drumsticks are done, remove from the Air Fryer then place on a serving dish.
- Serve with the green cilantro butter then enjoy immediately.

Per Serving: Net Carbs: 1.1g; Calories: 399; Total Fat: 37.1g; Saturated Fat: 18.2g
Protein: 16.3g; Carbs: 1.4g; Fiber: 0.3g; Sugar: 0.3g - Fat 84% / Protein 15% / Carbs 1%

Sticky Chicken with Spicy Sauce

Serves: 4 / Preparation time: 12 minutes / Cooking time: 29 minutes

1-½ lbs. boneless chicken thighs

2 tablespoons lemon juice

4 tablespoons extra virgin olive oil

½ cup chopped onion

2 tablespoons diced green chili

1-tablespoon chili powder

1-tablespoon sweet paprika

1-teaspoon cumin

½ teaspoon oregano

3 tablespoons tomato puree

- Preheat an oven to 250°F (121°C) and line a baking tray with aluminum foil. Set aside.
- Cut the boneless chicken thighs into slices then rub with 2 tablespoons of extra virgin olive oil and lemon juice.
- Spread the chicken on the prepared baking tray then set aside.
- Next, preheat a saucepan over medium heat then pour the remaining olive oil into it.
- Once the oil is hot, stir in chopped onion and sauté until aromatic and lightly golden brown.
- After that, add tomato puree into the saucepan then season with diced green chili, chili powder, sweet paprika, cumin, and oregano. Stir well.
- Drizzle the sauce over the chicken then cover with aluminum foil.
- Place the baking tray in the preheated oven and bake the chicken for approximately 30 minutes or until the chicken is cooked through.
- Once it is done, remove the cooked chicken from the oven and let it rest for a few minutes.
- Unwrap the cooked chicken and transfer to a serving dish.
- Drizzle the remaining liquid over the chicken then serve.
- Enjoy warm.

Per Serving: Net Carbs: 3.2g; Calories: 386; Total Fat: 31.7g; Saturated Fat: 7.1g
Protein: 21g; Carbs: 5.2g; Fiber: 2g; Sugar: 1.8g - Fat 74% / Protein 23% / Carbs 3%

Chicken Oregano with Creamy Lemon Sauce [FA] [GF] [SF]

Serves: 4 / Preparation time: 5 minutes / Cooking time: 20 minutes

1 lb. chicken thighs	2 tablespoons butter
2 teaspoons oregano	1-½ cups low sodium chicken broth
1-teaspoon basil	3 tablespoons lemon juice
2 teaspoons red chili flakes	½ cup heavy cream
2 tablespoons minced garlic	

- Brush the chicken thighs with butter then place in the inner pot of an Instant Pot.
- Sprinkle oregano, basil, red chili flakes, and minced garlic over the chicken thighs then pour chicken broth into the Instant Pot.
- Put the lid on then seal the Instant Pot properly. Close the steam valve.
- Select "Manual" setting on the Instant Pot then cook the chicken on high for 10 minutes.
- Once it is done, quick release the Instant Pot then open the lid.
- Take the cooked chicken thighs out of the Instant Pot and arrange on a serving dish.
- Next, select the "Sauté" setting on the Instant Pot then stir the remaining liquid for about 5 minutes.
- Pour lemon juice and heavy cream into the Instant Pot then stir well.
- Drizzle the liquid over the cooked chicken thighs then serve.
- Enjoy immediately.

Per Serving: Net Carbs: 3.3g; Calories: 364; Total Fat: 28.6g; Saturated Fat: 12.2g; Protein: 21.8g; Carbs: 4g; Fiber: 0.7g; Sugar: 4g - Fat 75% / Protein 23% / Carbs 2%

Chicken Steak with Mushroom Sauce [FA] [GF]

Serves: 4 / Preparation time: 5 minutes / Cooking time: 20 minutes

2 lbs. boneless chicken thighs	5 tablespoons butter
½ teaspoon salt	½ cup chopped mushrooms
½ teaspoon black pepper	2 teaspoons minced garlic
¾ cup almond yogurt	¼ teaspoon thyme

- Rub the boneless chicken thighs with salt and pepper then set aside.
- Preheat a saucepan over medium heat then place 4 tablespoons of butter in it.
- Once the butter is melted, put seasoned chicken thighs in the saucepan and cook until tender. Occasionally flip and rotate the chicken.
- Remove the cooked chicken thighs from the saucepan then place on a hot plate. Set aside.
- Next, preheat a saucepan over medium heat then place the remaining butter in it.
- Once the butter is melted, stir in minced garlic then sauté until lightly golden brown and aromatic.
- Add chopped mushrooms to the saucepan then season with thyme. Stir well and remove from heat.
- Pour almond yogurt over the sautéed mushrooms then stir well.
- Drizzle the mushroom sauce over the chicken thighs then serve immediately.
- Enjoy warm.

Per Serving: Net Carbs: 2.9g: Calories: 513; Total Fat: 41.1g; Saturated Fat: 16.7g; Protein: 31.1g; Carbs: 3.4g; Fiber: 0.5g; Sugar: 1.4g - Fat 72% / Protein 25% / Carbs 3%

Garlicky Chicken Asparagus

Serves: 4 / Preparation time: 11 minutes / Cooking time: 39 minutes

1-½ lbs. boneless chicken thighs	¾ teaspoon oregano
3 tablespoons extra virgin olive oil	½ teaspoon black pepper
2 tablespoons lemon juice	½ lb. chopped asparagus
3 tablespoons minced garlic	1 fresh lemon

- Preheat an oven to 250°F (121°C) and line a baking tray with parchment paper.
- Next, cut the boneless chicken thighs into medium cubes then set aside.
- Combine extra virgin olive oil with lemon juice, minced garlic, oregano, and black pepper then mix well.
- Rub the boneless chicken thighs with the spice mixture then spread on the prepared baking tray.
- Sprinkle asparagus over the chicken then arrange sliced lemon on top.
- Bake the chicken for approximately 25 minutes or until the chicken is cooked through.
- Once it is done, remove the cooked chicken from the oven and transfer to a serving dish.
- Serve and enjoy.

Per Serving: Net Carbs: 3.5g; Calories: 470; Total Fat: 36.2g; Saturated Fat: 9.1g
Protein: 31.1g; Carbs: 4.6g; Fiber: 1.1g; Sugar: 0.9g - Fat 70% / Protein 27% / Carbs 3%

Coconut Garlic Chicken Wings

Serves: 4 / Preparation time: 20 minutes / Cooking time: 12 minutes

1 lb. chicken wings	2 tablespoons coconut milk
2 tablespoons lemon juice	½ cup grated cheddar cheese
1 egg	3 tablespoons sour cream
¾ teaspoon paprika	½ cup Greek yogurt
2 tablespoons minced garlic	6 tablespoons mayonnaise
¼ teaspoon salt	1-½ tablespoons chopped parsley
½ teaspoon pepper	

- Drizzle lemon juice over the chicken wings then let them rest for about 5 minutes.
- Next, crack the egg then place in a bowl.
- Season with paprika, minced garlic, salt, and pepper then pour coconut milk into the egg. Stir until incorporated.
- Dip the chicken wing in the egg mixture and let then rest for a few minutes until the liquid is absorbed into the chicken wings.
- Meanwhile, place grated cheese, sour cream, Greek yogurt, mayonnaise, and chopped parsley in a mixing bowl.
- Using an electric mixer beat until smooth and fluffy.
- Transfer the sauce to a container then store in the fridge.
- Preheat an Air Fryer to 400°F (204°C) and place a rack in it.

- Once the Air Fryer is ready, place the seasoned chicken wings on the rack then set the time to 12 minutes. Cook the chicken wings.
- After 12 minutes, remove the chicken from the Air Fryer then arrange on a serving dish.
- Serve and enjoy warm.

Per Serving: Net Carbs: 5.1g; Calories: 634; Total Fat: 57.1g; Saturated Fat: 15g
Protein: 24.3g; Carbs: 5.6g; Fiber: 0.5g; Sugar: 3g - Fat 81% / Protein 15% / Carbs 4%

Marinated Chicken Lemon Jalapeno

Serves: 4 / Preparation time: 11 minutes / Cooking time: 2 hours 19 minutes

1-½ lbs. chicken thighs	3 tablespoons chopped jalapeno
4 tablespoons extra virgin olive oil	3 tablespoons lemon juice
2 cups chopped onion	2 teaspoons thyme
2 tablespoons minced garlic	1-teaspoon cinnamon

- Combine extra virgin olive oil with lemon juice then season with onion, jalapeno, minced garlic, thyme, and cinnamon. Stir well.
- Rub the chicken thighs with the spice mixture then marinate for approximately 2 hours. Store in the fridge to keep it fresh.
- After 2 hours, remove the marinated chicken from the fridge and thaw at room temperature.
- In the meantime, preheat a grill over medium heat then wait until it is ready.
- Place the marinated chicken thighs on the grill and grill for approximately 20 minutes or until cooked through. Occasionally, brush the chicken thighs with the remaining marinade.
- Once it is done, remove the grilled chicken thighs from the grill and arrange on a serving dish.
- Serve and enjoy.

Per Serving: Net Carbs: 6g; Calories: 396; Total Fat: 31.3g; Saturated Fat: 7.1g
Protein: 21.1g; Carbs: 8g; Fiber: 2g; Sugar: 2.9g - Fat 71% / Protein 23% / Carbs 6%

Spiced Chicken Asparagus [FA] [GF]

Serves: 4 / Preparation time: 5 minutes / Cooking time: 15 minutes

¾ lb. boneless chicken thighs	1-teaspoon oregano
1-tablespoon butter	1-teaspoon thyme
½ cup chopped onion	½ teaspoon paprika
3 teaspoons minced garlic	¼ teaspoon salt
2 tablespoons lemon juice	¼ teaspoon pepper
½ cup chicken broth	2 handfuls asparagus spears

- Cut the chicken into medium cubes then set aside.
- Select "Sauté" setting on Instant Pot then place butter in it.
- After that, stir in minced garlic and chopped onion then sauté until aromatic.
- Next, add chopped chicken to the Instant Pot then stir until wilted and brown. Press the "Cancel" button.
- Pour chicken broth over the chicken then season with oregano, thyme, paprika, salt, and pepper. Stir well.
- Put the lid on and seal the Instant Pot properly. Close the steam valve.

- Select "manual" setting on the Instant Pot then cook the chicken on high. Set the time to 10 minutes.
- Meanwhile, remove the woody ends of the asparagus then cut them into diagonal slices. Set aside.
- When the Instant Pot beeps, quick release it and open the lid.
- Stir in sliced asparagus and stir well.
- Press the "Sauté" button and bring to a simmer until the asparagus is tender.
- Once it is done, press the "Cancel" button then transfer the chicken together with asparagus and gravy to a serving dish.
- Serve and enjoy.

Per Serving: Net Carbs: 2.8g; Calories: 451; Total Fat: 35.1g; Saturated Fat: 13.8g; Protein: 28.5g; Carbs: 3.8g; Fiber: 1g; Sugar: 1.3g - Fat 70% / Protein 25% / Carbs 5%

Cheesy Tomato Chicken [FA] [GF]

Serves: 4 / Preparation time: 5 minutes / Cooking time: 13 minutes

1 lb. boneless chicken thighs

1-cup low sodium chicken broth

¼ cup chopped tomatoes

¾ teaspoon basil

¾ teaspoon oregano

½ teaspoon red chili flakes

2 tablespoons minced garlic

¾ cup grated Parmesan cheese

1-cup heavy cream

- Pour chicken broth into the Instant Pot then add chopped tomatoes to the pot.
- Season the liquid with basil, oregano, minced garlic, and red chili flakes then stir until combined.
- Add the boneless chicken thighs to the Instant Pot then put the lid on. Seal the Instant Pot properly and close the steam valve.
- Select "Pressure" setting on the Instant Pot and cook the chicken on high for 8 minutes.
- Once the chicken is done, quickly release the Instant Pot then open the lid.
- Take the cooked chicken out of the Instant Pot and place on a flat surface. Leave the liquid in the Instant Pot.
- Select the "Sauté" setting on the Instant Pot and bring the liquid to a simmer for about 5 minutes.
- Stir in grated Parmesan cheese and heavy cream to the Instant Pot then mix well.
- Meanwhile, cut the cooked chicken into cubes then return it back to the Instant Pot.
- Stir until the chicken is completely coated with liquid then transfer to a serving dish.
- Serve and enjoy immediately.

Per Serving: Net Carbs: 3.4g; Calories: 376; Total Fat: 29.3g; Saturated Fat: 12.7g; Protein: 23.3g; Carbs: 3.8g; Fiber: 0.4g; Sugar: 0.7g - Fat 70% / Protein 24% / Carbs 6%

Grilled Chicken Thighs Rosemary

Serves: 4 / Preparation time: 11 minutes / Cooking time: 39 minutes

1-½ lbs. chicken thighs

3 tablespoons balsamic vinegar

3 tablespoons extra virgin olive oil

3 tablespoons minced garlic

1-½ teaspoons thyme

2 teaspoons chopped rosemary

½ teaspoon pepper

- Combine balsamic vinegar with extra virgin olive oil then season with minced garlic, thyme, pepper, and chopped rosemary.
- Rub the chicken thighs with the spice mixture then let it rest for approximately 15 minutes.

- In the meantime, preheat a grill over medium heat then wait until it is ready.

- Place the seasoned chicken thighs on the grill then grill until all sides of the chicken are golden brown and cooked through. Brush the chicken thighs with the marinade once every 5 minutes.

- Once it is done, remove the chicken from the grill and transfer to a serving dish.

- Serve and enjoy warm.

Per Serving: Net Carbs: 2.3g; Calories: 465; Total Fat: 36.2g; Saturated Fat: 9.1g
Protein: 30.5g; Carbs: 2.9g; Fiber: 0.6g; Sugar: 0.1g - Fat 70% / Protein 28% / Carbs 2%

Baked Chicken Paprika [GF]

Serves: 4 / Preparation time: 5 minutes / Cooking time: 30 minutes

1-½ lbs. chicken thighs	1-tablespoon minced garlic
¼ cup extra virgin olive oil	½ teaspoon salt
2 ½ tablespoons smoked paprika	½ teaspoon pepper
3 tablespoons lemon juice	

- Preheat an oven to 350°F (177°C) and coat a casserole dish with cooking spray.

- Cut the chicken thighs into medium pieces then place in the prepared casserole dish.

- Drizzle olive oil and lemon juice over the chicken then sprinkle smoked paprika, minced garlic, salt, and pepper.

- Rub the chicken with the seasonings then bake for 30 to 40 minutes or until the chicken thighs are lightly golden brown and cooked through.

- Once it is done, remove the baked chicken from the oven and let it cool.

- Serve and enjoy.

Per Serving: Net Carbs: 1.7g: Calories: 499; Total Fat: 40.2g; Saturated Fat: 9.7g; Protein: 30.9g; Carbs: 3.5g; Fiber: 1.8g; Sugar: 0.7g - Fat 73% / Protein 25% / Carbs 2%

Turkey Spicy Butter Sauce

Serves: 4 / Preparation time: 30 minutes / Cooking time: 25 minutes

½ lb. turkey breast	½ cup butter
2 eggs	1 tablespoon Worcestershire sauce
½ cup coconut flour	½ tablespoon lemon juice
¼ teaspoon salt	½ teaspoon cayenne
¼ teaspoon pepper	¼ teaspoon chili powder

- Crack the eggs then place in a bowl.
- Season the eggs with salt and pepper then stir until dissolved.
- Cut the turkey into slices then dip in the eggs mixture.
- Next, roll the sliced turkey in the coconut flour then set aside.
- Preheat an Air Fryer to 400°F (204°C).
- Once the Air Fryer is ready, place a rack in it then arrange the coated turkey on the rack.
- Cook the turkey for 15 minutes then remove from heat.
- Meanwhile, melt butter in a saucepan then add Worcestershire sauce, lemon juice, cayenne, and chili pepper. Stir well.
- Serve the turkey with spicy butter sauce.

- Enjoy right away.

Per Serving: Net Carbs: 3.6g; Calories: 307; Total Fat: 26.5g; Saturated Fat: 15.7g
Protein: 13g; Carbs: 4.7g; Fiber: 1.1g; Sugar: 3.1g - Fat 78% / Protein 17% / Carbs 5%

Crispy Chicken Butter [FA] [GF]

Serves: 4 / Preparation time: 5 minutes / Cooking time: 15 minutes

1 lb. chicken thighs	¼ teaspoon salt
Coconut oil, to fry	½ teaspoon pepper
½ cup chopped onion	2 tablespoons butter

- Preheat a frying pan over medium heat then pour coconut oil into it.
- Cut the chicken thighs into small pieces and once the coconut oil is hot, put the chopped chicken thighs in the oil.
- Fry the chopped chicken thighs for about 3 minutes then flip them.
- Cook for another 3 minutes or until the chicken thighs are lightly golden brown and crispy.
- Remove the fried chicken thighs from the frying pan and strain the excessive oil.
- Next, preheat a saucepan then pour 1 tablespoon of coconut oil.
- Once it is hot, stir in chopped onion and sauté until wilted and aromatic.
- After that, add fried chicken to the saucepan together with butter then season with salt and pepper. Stir until the chicken is completely coated with butter.
- Once it is done, remove the chicken from heat and transfer to a serving dish.
- Serve and enjoy warm.

Per Serving: Net Carbs: 1.1g: Calories: 532; Total Fat: 50g; Saturated Fat: 32.2g; Protein: 20.3g; Carbs: 1.5g; Fiber: 0.4g; Sugar: 0.6g - Fat 85% / Protein 14% / Carbs 1%

Refreshing Chicken Steak Tomato

Serves: 8 / Preparation time: 5 minutes / Cooking time: 15 minutes

1 lb. boneless chicken breast	½ teaspoon nutmeg
½ teaspoon salt	1 bay leaf
½ teaspoon pepper	1 ½ teaspoons paprika
1-cup butter	½ teaspoon cloves
1 cup diced tomatoes	½ teaspoon cayenne

- Preheat an Air Fryer to 375°F (191°C).
- Cut the chicken breast into thick slices then arrange in the Air Fryer.
- Sprinkle salt and pepper over the chicken then cook for 15 minutes.
- Meanwhile, melt butter over low heat then add diced tomatoes to the melted butter.
- Season with nutmeg, bay leaf, paprika, cloves, and cayenne then bring to a simmer.
- Once it is done, remove the sauce from heat then let it cool.
- When the chicken is done, remove from the Air Fryer then place on a serving dish.
- Top with tomato sauce then serve right away.

Per Serving: Net Carbs: 1.2g; Calories: 361; Total Fat: 32g; Saturated Fat: 19.5g
Protein: 18.1g; Carbs: 2g; Fiber: 0.8g; Sugar: 0.9g - Fat 80% / Protein 19% / Carbs 1%

Cheesy Chicken Zucchini in Savory Coconut Gravy

Serves: 4 / Preparation time: 11 minutes / Cooking time: 34 minutes

1 lb. boneless chicken thighs

2 tablespoons extra virgin olive oil

2 tablespoons minced garlic

½ teaspoon black pepper

1 teaspoon Italian seasoning

½ cup coconut milk

1 cup sliced zucchini

¾ cup grated cheddar cheese

¼ cup chopped parsley

- Cut the boneless chicken thighs into cubes then set aside.
- Next, preheat a skillet over medium heat then pour extra virgin olive oil into it.
- Once the oil is hot, add chicken cubes to the skillet and sauté until wilted. Cook until the chicken is done.
- Remove the cooked chicken from the skillet and place on a plate.
- Next, stir in minced garlic to the skillet then sauté until lightly golden brown and aromatic.
- After that, pour coconut milk into the skillet and season with black pepper and Italian seasoning. Bring to a simmer.
- Once it is done, put the cooked chicken and sliced zucchini to the skillet and stir until the chicken is completely coated with the seasoned coconut milk.
- Transfer the cooked chicken and the gravy to a serving dish then sprinkle grated cheddar cheese on top.
- Garnish with fresh parsley and serve.
- Enjoy immediately.

Per Serving: Net Carbs: 3.5g; Calories: 471; Total Fat: 38.6g; Saturated Fat: 16.9g
Protein: 26.7g; Carbs: 4.8g; Fiber: 1.3g; Sugar: 1.8g - Fat 74% / Protein 23% / Carbs 3%

Cinnamon Chicken Coffee [GF]

Serves: 4 / Preparation time: 20 minutes / Cooking time: 20 minutes

1 lb. chicken wings

1 cup brewed coffee

¼ teaspoon salt

2 teaspoons cayenne pepper

2 tablespoons butter

½ cup roasted almonds

1-teaspoon cinnamon

- Add salt and cayenne pepper to the brewed coffee then stir until dissolved.
- Add chicken wings to the coffee mixture then marinate the chicken wings for at least 20 minutes.
- After 20 minutes, take the chicken wings out of the coffee marinade then transfer to the Instant Pot.
- Add butter to the Instant Pot then pour half of the coffee marinade over the chicken wings.
- Put the lid on and seal the Instant Pot properly. Close the steam valve.
- Select "Manual" setting on the Instant Pot then cook the chicken wings on high for 10 minutes.
- Once the Instant Pot beeps, naturally release the Instant Pot then open the lid.
- Transfer the cooked chicken wings to a serving dish then sprinkle roasted almonds and cinnamon on top.
- Serve and enjoy.

Per Serving: Net Carbs: 1.7g; Calories: 374; Total Fat: 29.7g; Saturated Fat: 9.1g; Protein: 23.7g; Carbs: 3.7g; Fiber: 2g; Sugar: 0.8g - Fat 71% / Protein 25% / Carbs 4%

Savory Coconut Fried Chicken Wings [FA] [GF]

Serves: 4 / Preparation time: 15 minutes / Cooking time: 6 minutes

1 lb. chicken wings

1 pastured egg

2 tablespoons coconut milk

2 teaspoons minced garlic

1-½ teaspoons basil

1-½ teaspoons thyme

¼ teaspoon oregano

½ teaspoon salt

1-teaspoon black pepper

¾ teaspoon mustard

¾ teaspoon paprika

¾ teaspoon ginger

½ teaspoon turmeric

1-cup coconut flour

Coconut oil, to fry

- Rub the chicken wings with minced garlic, basil, thyme, mustard, paprika, ginger, and turmeric then let them rest for 5 minutes.
- In the meantime, crack the egg and place in a bowl.
- Pour coconut milk into the egg then stir until incorporated. Set aside.
- Combine coconut flour with salt, oregano, and black pepper then mix well.
- Dip the chicken wings into the egg mixture then roll into the coconut flour. Make sure that the chicken wings are completely coated.
- Preheat a frying pan over medium heat then pour coconut oil into the frying pan.
- Once the oil is hot, put the coated chicken wings in the frying pan and fry the chicken wings for approximately 3 minutes.
- After 3 minutes, flip the chicken wings and fry for another 3 minutes or until both sides of the chicken wings are lightly golden brown.
- Remove the fried chicken wings from the frying pan and strain the excessive oil.
- Arrange the fried chicken wings on a serving dish then serve immediately.
- Enjoy warm.

Per Serving: Net Carbs: 2.5g: Calories: 428; Total Fat: 35.4g; Saturated Fat: 19.3g; Protein: 23.6g; Carbs: 4.6g; Fiber: 2.1g; Sugar: 0.6g - Fat 74% / Protein 24% / Carbs 2%

Buttery Whole Chicken

Serves: 4 / Preparation time: 10 minutes / Cooking time: 60 minutes

1 whole chicken

½ cup butter

1-teaspoon black pepper

3 tablespoons minced garlic

- Place butter in mixing bowl then add minced garlic and black pepper.
- Using a hand mixer beat the butter until combined.
- Brush the chicken with the butter mixture and drop the remaining butter in the chicken cavity.
- Preheat an Air Fryer to 350°F (177°C).
- Place the chicken in the Air Fryer then cook for 30 minutes.
- After 30 minutes, flip the chicken and cook again for another 30 minutes.
- Once the internal temperature of the chicken has reached 165°F (74°C), remove it from the Air Fryer.
- Let the chicken rest for a few minutes then serve.
- Enjoy warm.

Per Serving: Net Carbs: 2.1g; Calories: 274; Total Fat: 27.6g; Saturated Fat: 15.9g
Protein: 5.5g; Carbs: 2.4g; Fiber: 0.3g; Sugar: 0.1g - Fat 91% / Protein 8% / Carbs 1%

Spicy Chicken Turmeric

Serves: 4 / Preparation time: 8 minutes / Cooking time: 16 minutes

¾ lb. boneless chicken thighs

2 tablespoons lemon juice

2 tablespoons extra virgin olive oil

2 cloves garlic

3 shallots

2 tablespoons red chili flakes

2 teaspoons cayenne

½ teaspoon turmeric

2 kaffir lime leaves

2 bay leaves

2 cups water

- Drizzle lemon juice over the chicken thighs then let it rest for approximately 10 minutes.
- In the meantime, place garlic, shallots, red chili flakes, and cayenne in a food processor then process until smooth.
- Next, preheat a skillet over medium heat then pour extra virgin olive oil into it.
- Once the oil is hot, stir in the spice mixture and sauté until aromatic.
- After that, add chicken to the skillet and stir until the chicken is no longer pink.
- Season the chicken with kaffir lime leaves and bay leaves then pour water over the chicken. Bring to boil.
- Once it is boiled, reduce the heat and cook until the chicken is completely seasoned and cooked through.
- Transfer the cooked chicken together with the gravy to a serving dish and serve.
- Enjoy!

Per Serving: Net Carbs: 5.5g; Calories: 268; Total Fat: 20.2g; Saturated Fat: 4.9g
Protein: 15.9g; Carbs: 6.3g; Fiber: 0.6g; Sugar: 1.5g - Fat 70% / Protein 22% / Carbs 8%

Hot Steamed Chicken in Cup [FA] [GF] [F]

Serves: 4 / Preparation time: 10 minutes / Cooking time: 10 minutes

1 lb. chicken wings

2 tablespoons sliced shallots

2 tablespoons sliced garlic

2 bay leaves

½ cup chopped green tomatoes

¼ cup red chili flakes

2 cups coconut milk

½ teaspoon salt

- Cut the chicken wings into small pieces then divide into 4 aluminum foil cups.
- Sprinkle sliced shallots, sliced garlic, red chili flakes, and green tomatoes over the chicken.
- Cut the bay leaves into halves then put each piece on each aluminum foil.
- Add salt to the coconut milk the stir until dissolved.
- Pour the coconut into each aluminum foil cup then set aside.
- Pour water into an Instant Pot then place a trivet in it.
- Arrange the aluminum cups on the trivet then close and seal the Instant Pot properly. Close the steam valve.
- Turn the Instant Pot on then select "Pressure" menu and cook the chicken for 10 minutes.
- Once it is done, turn the Instant Pot off and naturally release it.
- Open the lid and take the aluminum foil cups with cooked chicken out of the Instant Pot.
- Arrange the aluminum foil cups on a serving dish then enjoy.

Per Serving: Net Carbs: 6.2g; Calories: 474; Total Fat: 39.6g; Saturated Fat: 24.1g; Protein: 23.8g; Carbs: 8.7g; Fiber: 2.5g; Sugar: 3.9g - Fat 72% / Protein 20% / Carbs 8%

Warm Chicken Soup Gingery [FA] [GF]

Serves: 4 / Preparation time: 5 minutes / Cooking time: 25 minutes

½ lb. chicken thighs	¼ teaspoon nutmeg
½ lb. chicken skin	1-teaspoon salt
3 teaspoons minced garlic	4 cups water
1-teaspoon ginger	

- Cut the chicken thighs and chicken skin into medium pieces then place in a pot.
- Pour water into the pot then bring to boil.
- Once it is boiled, reduce the heat and season the soup with minced garlic, ginger, nutmeg, and salt.
- Cook the soup until the gravy has reduced into the half then remove from heat.
- Transfer the chicken soup to a serving bowl then serve.
- Enjoy warm!

Per Serving: Net Carbs: 1g: Calories: 387; Total Fat: 32.4g; Saturated Fat: 9.2g; Protein: 21.1g; Carbs: 1.1g; Fiber: 0.1g; Sugar: 0.1g - Fat 75% / Protein 24% / Carbs 1%

Savory Chicken Coconut with Cheese Wrap

Serves: 8 / Preparation time: 30 minutes / Cooking time: 20 minutes

2 cups grated cheddar cheese	¼ cup minced garlic
1-cup cream cheese	¼ teaspoon salt
1-½ cup coconut flour	½ teaspoon turmeric
4 egg yolks	1-teaspoon pepper
2 ½ cups ground chicken	¼ cup coconut milk
2 tablespoons butter	½ teaspoon coconut oil

- Preheat a saucepan over medium heat then add butter to the saucepan.
- Once the butter is melted, stir in minced garlic then sauté until aromatic and lightly golden brown.
- Add ground beef to the saucepan then season with salt, turmeric, and pepper.
- Pour coconut milk over the ground chicken then cook until the liquid is absorbed into the chicken.
- Remove from heat then let it cool.
- Next, place grated cheddar cheese and cream cheese in a microwave-safe bowl then melt the mixture.
- Once the cheese is melted, add egg yolks to the bowl then stir until incorporated.
- Add coconut flour to the cheese mixture then mix until becoming a soft dough.
- Roll the dough until thin then cut into 8 squares.
- Divide the chicken into 8 then put on each square. Fold them tightly like envelopes.
- Preheat an Air Fryer to 425°F (218°C).
- Arrange the chicken envelopes in the Air Fryer then cook for 10 minutes or until lightly golden brown.
- Remove from the Air Fryer then serve warm.
- Enjoy!

Per Serving: Net Carbs: 3.5g; Calories: 385; Total Fat: 30.2g; Saturated Fat: 17.9g
Protein: 24g; Carbs: 4.5g; Fiber: 1g; Sugar: 0.7g - Fat 71% / Protein 25% / Carbs 4%

Chicken Cheese Balls with Coconut Crumbles

Serves: 4 / Preparation time: 4 minutes / Cooking time: 26 minutes

1 lb. boneless chicken thigh

½ cup grated cheddar cheese

2 eggs

2 tablespoons almond flour

¼ teaspoon pepper

1 cup grated coconut

½ cup extra virgin olive oil, to fry

- Cut the boneless chicken thigh then put in a food processor. Process until smooth.
- Transfer the chicken to a mixing bowl then add almond flour to the chicken.
- Crack an egg and drop in the bowl and after that, mix the chicken with the almond flour and egg until combined.
- Shape the chicken mixture into small balls then set aside.
- Crack the remaining egg and place in a bowl.
- Season the egg with pepper then mix well.
- Next, dip each chicken ball in the egg mixture then roll in the grated coconut. Make sure that the cheese balls are completely coated with grated coconut.
- After that, preheat a frying pan over medium heat then pour olive oil into it.
- Once the oil is hot, carefully put the chicken cheese balls in the skillet and fry until all sides are lightly golden brown and crispy.
- Remove the fried chicken cheese balls from the frying pan then strain the oil.
- Arrange the cheese balls on a serving dish and serve.
- Enjoy immediately.

Per Serving: Net Carbs: 1.3g; Calories: 592; Total Fat: 53.9g; Saturated Fat: 16.7g
Protein: 25.4g; Carbs: 3.6g; Fiber: 1.9g; Sugar: 1.5g - Fat 82% / Protein 17% / Carbs 1%

Spinach Creamy Chicken [FA] [GF]

Serves: 4 / Preparation time: 10 minutes / Cooking time: 10 minutes

1-½ lbs. chicken thighs

1 cup chopped spinach

2 tablespoons butter

½ teaspoon salt

½ teaspoon pepper

½ cup cream cheese

½ cup mayonnaise

½ cup sour cream

1 cup grated Parmesan cheese

1-cup chicken broth

- Place butter in an Instant Pot then press the "Sauté" button.
- Cut the chicken thighs into pieces then add to the Instant Pot. Sauté until brown then press the "Cancel" button.
- Next, pour chicken broth over the chicken the season with salt and pepper.
- Put the lid on and seal the Instant Pot properly. Close the steam valve.
- Press "Pressure" setting on the Instant Pot and cook the chicken on high for 10 minutes.
- Once it is done, quick release the Instant Pot then open the lid.
- Add spinach, cream cheese, mayonnaise, sour cream, and grated Parmesan cheese to the Instant Pot then stir until dissolved.

- Press the "Sauté" button then bring to a simmer.
- Once it is done, transfer the chicken to a serving dish together with the spinach and gravy.
- Serve and enjoy.

Per Serving: Net Carbs: 6.6g; Calories: 434; Total Fat: 35.9g; Saturated Fat: 15.2g; Protein: 21g; Carbs: 6.8g; Fiber: 0.2g; Sugar: 1.5g - Fat 74% / Protein 20% / Carbs 6%

Cheesy Chicken Meatballs [FA] [GF]

Serves: 4 / Preparation time: 10 minutes / Cooking time: 10 minutes

1-½ lbs. boneless chicken thighs	½ teaspoon black pepper
½ cup Cheddar cheese cubes	3 teaspoons minced garlic
½ cup almond flour	¼ teaspoon oregano
2 eggs	¼ cup butter
½ teaspoon salt	

- Cut the boneless chicken thighs into cubes then place in a food processor.
- Add almond flour and eggs to the food processor then season with salt, black pepper, minced garlic, and oregano. Process until smooth.
- Next, shape the chicken mixture into medium balls and fill each ball with a cheddar cheese cube. Set aside.
- Pour water into an Instant Pot then place a trivet in it.
- Arrange the chicken balls on the trivet then drop butter over the chicken balls.
- Put the lid on and seal the Instant Pot properly. Close the steam valve.
- Select "Manual" setting on the Instant Pot then cook the chicken balls on low for 10 minutes.
- Once it is done, naturally release the Instant Pot then open the lid.
- Take the chicken balls out of the Instant Pot then arrange on a serving dish.
- Enjoy the chicken balls right away.

Per Serving: Net Carbs: 1.9g; Calories: 464; Total Fat: 38g; Saturated Fat: 16.6g; Protein: 27.9g; Carbs: 2.1g; Fiber: 0.5g; Sugar: 0.4g - Fat 74% / Protein 24% / Carbs 2%

Savory Chicken Fennel

Serves: 4 / Preparation time: 30 minutes / Cooking time: 25 minutes

1-½ lbs. chicken thighs	1-½ teaspoons smoked paprika
2 teaspoons fennel	1-teaspoon curry
1 cup chopped onion	½ teaspoon turmeric
¾ tablespoon coconut oil	½ teaspoon salt
1-½ teaspoons ginger	½ teaspoon pepper
2 ½ teaspoons minced garlic	1 ½ cups coconut milk

- Place fennel, chopped onion, and smoked paprika in a bowl.
- Season with salt, minced garlic, ginger, curry, pepper, and turmeric then pour coconut oil into the mixture. Mix well.
- Rub the chicken thighs with the spice mixture then let them sit for 30 minutes.
- After 30 minutes, preheat an Air Fryer to 375°F (191°C).
- Transfer the chicken together with the spices to the Air Fryer then cook for 15 minutes.

- After that, pour coconut milk over the chicken then stir well.
- Cook the chicken again and set the time to 10 minutes.
- Once it is done, arrange the chicken on a serving dish then pour the gravy over the chicken.
- Enjoy!

Per Serving: Net Carbs: 4.3g; Calories: 414; Total Fat: 33.7g; Saturated Fat: 19.4g
Protein: 22.5g; Carbs: 6.4g; Fiber: 2.1g; Sugar: 2.9g - Fat 73% / Protein 22% / Carbs 5%

Crispy Chicken Oregano with Coconut Coating

Serves: 4 / Preparation time: 8 minutes / Cooking time: 14 minutes

½ lb. boneless chicken thigh	¼ cup almond flour
2 eggs	1 cup grated coconut
½ teaspoon oregano	1-cup extra virgin olive oil, to fry
½ teaspoon pepper	

- Cut the chicken thigh into slices then set aside.
- Crack the eggs then place the eggs in a bowl.
- Season the eggs with pepper and oregano then stir well.
- Next, add almond flour to the seasoned eggs then mix until combined.
- Dip the sliced chicken into the egg mixture then roll in the grated coconut. Make sure that the chicken is completely coated with the grated coconut.
- Preheat a frying pan over medium heat then pour extra virgin olive oil into it.
- Put the coated chicken into the frying pan then fry until both sides are lightly golden brown and the chicken is completely cooked.
- Once it is done, remove the chicken from the frying pan strain the oil.
- Arrange on a serving dish and serve the chicken warm.
- Enjoy immediately.

Per Serving: Net Carbs: 1.5g; Calories: 464; Total Fat: 45.5g; Saturated Fat: 13.1g
Protein: 13.5g; Carbs: 3.4g; Fiber: 1.9g; Sugar: 1.4g - Fat 88% / Protein 19% / Carbs 1%

Appetizing Lemon Grass Fried Chicken [GF] [SF]

Serves: 4 / Preparation time: 5 minutes / Cooking time: 25 minutes

1 lb. chicken thighs	4 lemon grasses
1-teaspoon salt	2 bay leaves
¾ teaspoon coriander	2 cups water
½ teaspoon turmeric	Coconut oil, to fry
3 teaspoons minced garlic	

- Place chicken thighs in a skillet then season with salt, coriander, turmeric, minced garlic, lemon grasses, and bay leaves.
- Pour water over the chicken then bring to boil.
- Once it is boiled, reduce the heat and cook the chicken until tender. The water will be totally absorbed into the chicken.

- Remove the chicken from heat and let it cool.
- Next, preheat a frying pan over medium heat then pour coconut oil into the pan.
- Once the oil is hot, put the cooked chicken into the frying pan and fry for about 3 minutes.
- Flip the chicken and fry for another 3 minutes or until both sides of the chicken are lightly golden brown.
- Once it is done, remove the chicken from the frying pan and strain the excessive oil.
- Arrange on a serving dish then serve.
- Enjoy warm!

Per Serving: Net Carbs: 2.1g: Calories: 485; Total Fat: 44.3g; Saturated Fat: 28.6g; Protein: 20.3g; Carbs: 2.3g; Fiber: 0.2g; Sugar: 0g - Fat 82% / Protein 16% / Carbs 2%

Spicy Chicken Curry Samosa

Serves: 4 / Preparation time: 20 minutes / Cooking time: 20 minutes

1 lb. ground chicken	¼ teaspoon coriander
5 tablespoons extra virgin olive oil	2 teaspoons red chili flakes
¼ cup chopped onion	2 tablespoons diced tomatoes
½ teaspoon curry powder	¾ cup almond flour
¼ teaspoon turmeric	¼ cup water

- Place ground chicken, chopped onion, curry powder, turmeric, coriander, red chili flakes, and diced tomatoes in a bowl. Mix well.
- Preheat an Air Fryer to 375°F (191°C) and spray a tablespoon of extra virgin olive in the Air Fryer.
- Transfer the ground chicken mixture to the Air Fryer then cook for 10 minutes.
- Once the chicken is done, remove from the Air Fryer then transfer to a container. Let it cool.
- Meanwhile, combine almond flour with 3 tablespoons of olive oil and water then mix until becoming dough.
- Place the dough on a flat surface then roll until thin.
- Using a 3-inches circle mold cookies cut the thin dough.
- Put 2 tablespoons of chicken on circle dough then fold it. Repeat with the remaining dough and chicken.
- Preheat an Air Fryer to 400°F (204°C).
- Brush each chicken samosa with the remaining virgin olive oil then arrange in the Air Fryer.
- Cook the chicken samosas for 10 minutes then remove from the Air Fryer.
- Arrange on a serving dish then serve with homemade tomato sauce or green cayenne.
- Enjoy warm.

Per Serving: Net Carbs: 1.5g; Calories: 365; Total Fat: 30.3g; Saturated Fat: 5.6g
Protein: 23.1g; Carbs: 2.5g; Fiber: 1g; Sugar: 0.8g - Fat 75% / Protein 24% / Carbs 1%

Crispy Almond Chicken with Tomato Onion Sauce

Serves: 4 / Preparation time: 11 minutes / Cooking time: 21 minutes

¾ lb. boneless chicken thighs	1 cup chopped onion
1 egg	½ cup tomato puree
¼ cup almond flour	¼ teaspoon pepper
½ cup extra virgin olive oil, to fry	

- Cut the boneless chicken thighs into thin slices then set aside.
- Crack the egg then place in a bowl. Beat until incorporated.

- Next, dip the sliced chicken in the beaten egg then roll in the almond flour. Repeat with the remaining chicken and almond flour.
- After that, preheat a pan over medium heat then pour olive oil into it.
- Once the oil is hot, put the coated chicken into the pan then fry until both sides are lightly golden brown and the chicken is cooked through.
- Remove the cooked chicken from the pan and discard the excessive oil.
- Arrange the fried chicken on a serving dish then set aside.
- Take 2 tablespoons of oil then pour into a saucepan.
- Stir in chopped onion then sauté until lightly golden brown and aromatic.
- Next, add tomato puree to the saucepan then season with pepper. Stir well and bring to a simmer.
- Once it is done, remove the sauce from heat then drizzle the tomato sauce over the chicken.
- Serve and enjoy warm.

Per Serving: Net Carbs: 2.8g; Calories: 433; Total Fat: 40g; Saturated Fat: 7.8g
Protein: 17.2g; Carbs: 3.7g; Fiber: 0.9g; Sugar: 1.4g - Fat 83% / Protein 14% / Carbs 3%

Creamy Gravy Chicken Masala [FA] [GF]

Serves: 4 / Preparation time: 5 minutes / Cooking time: 15 minutes

1-½ lbs. boneless chicken thighs	1 cup diced tomatoes
1-cup Greek yogurt	½ cup water
1 ¾ tablespoon garam masala	1-teaspoon paprika
2 tablespoons lemon juice	½ teaspoon turmeric
1-teaspoon pepper	½ teaspoon salt
½ teaspoon ginger	½ teaspoon cayenne
2 tablespoons butter	1-cup heavy cream

- Combine Greek yogurt with 1 tablespoon of garam masala, lemon juice, pepper, and ginger then mix well.
- Cut the chicken into medium pieces then rub with the yogurt mixture.
- Place butter in the Instant Pot then select "Sauté" setting.
- Once the butter is melted, place the seasoned chicken in the Instant Pot then sauté until brown. Press the "Cancel" button.
- Next, place diced tomatoes in a blender then pour water over the tomatoes.
- Season with the remaining garam masala, paprika, turmeric, salt, and cayenne then blend until smooth and incorporated.
- Pour the tomato mixture over the chicken then put the lid on and seal the Instant Pot properly. Close the steam valve.
- Select "Manual" setting on the Instant Pot then cook the chicken on high for 10 minutes.
- Once it is done, quick release the Instant Pot then open the lid.
- Quickly add heavy cream to the Instant Pot then stir well.
- Transfer the chicken together with the gravy to a serving dish then serve.
- Enjoy warm.

Per Serving: Net Carbs: 3.8g; Calories: 429; Total Fat: 34.7g; Saturated Fat: 16.1g; Protein: 23.9g; Carbs: 4.9g; Fiber: 1.1g; Sugar: 2.5g - Fat 73% / Protein 22% / Carbs 5%

Avocado Chicken Paprika [FA] [GF]

Serves: 4 / Preparation time: 5 minutes / Cooking time: 15 minutes

1-½ lbs. boneless chicken thighs	¼ cup butter
½ teaspoon salt	½ cup chopped onion
½ teaspoon pepper	1-cup chicken broth
1 teaspoon minced garlic	2 ripe avocados
2 teaspoons paprika	1 tablespoon lemon juice

- Combine the spice—salt, pepper, minced garlic, and paprika in a bowl then mix well.
- Rub the chicken with the spice mixture then baste with butter.
- Place the seasoned chicken in the Instant Pot then sprinkle chopped onion over the chicken.
- Select "Sauté" setting on the Instant Pot then sauté the chicken for about 2 minutes.
- Brown the chicken until wilted and the onion is translucent. Press the "Cancel" button.
- Pour chicken broth over the chicken then put the lid on the Instant Pot and seal it properly.
- Select "Pressure" menu then cook the chicken for 10 minutes.
- In the meantime, cut the avocados into halves then discard the seeds.
- Cut the avocados into cubes then combine with lemon juice. Set aside.
- Once the chicken is done, quick release the Instant Pot then open the lid.
- Transfer the chicken to a serving dish then top with the avocados.
- Serve and enjoy.

Per Serving: Net Carbs: 2.7g; Calories: 435; Total Fat: 35.7g; Saturated Fat: 13.4g; Protein: 22.6g; Carbs: 6.4g; Fiber: 3.7g; Sugar: 1.1g - Fat 73% / Protein 21% / Carbs 6%

Cheesy Chicken Loaf with Broccoli and Carrot

Serves: 4 / Preparation time: 9 minutes / Cooking time: 19 minutes

1-¼ lbs. boneless chicken thighs	½ teaspoon pepper
2 eggs	½ cup chopped broccoli
3 tablespoons extra virgin olive oil	½ lb. carrots
½ cup chopped onion	1-cup cheddar cheese cubes

- Preheat a steamer and prepare a loaf pan. Coat with cooking spray and set aside.
- Peel the carrots and cut into small dices. Set aside.
- Cut the boneless chicken thigh into cubes then place in a food processor. Process until smooth then set aside.
- Next, preheat a saucepan over medium heat then pour olive oil into it.
- Once the oil is hot, stir in chopped onion and sauté until wilted and aromatic. Remove from heat.
- Combine the chicken with eggs then season with pepper.
- Add sautéed onion, chopped broccoli, carrots, and cheese cubes to the chicken mixture then mix well.
- Transfer the chicken mixture to the prepared loaf pan then spread evenly.

- Place the loaf pan in the steamer and steam the chicken loaf for approximately 20 minutes.
- Once the chicken loaf is done, remove from the steamer and let it cool for a few minutes.
- Take the chicken loaf out of the pan then let it cool for about 10 minutes.
- Cut the chicken loaf into thick slices then arrange on a serving dish.
- Serve and enjoy!

Per Serving: Net Carbs: 6.2g; Calories: 433; Total Fat: 33.8g; Saturated Fat: 11.6g
Protein: 24.4g; Carbs: 8.3g; Fiber: 2.1g; Sugar: 3.8g - Fat 70% / Protein 24% / Carbs 6%

Chicken Fritter Tomato Salsa

Serves: 4 / Preparation time: 15 minutes / Cooking time: 15 minutes

1 lb. boneless chicken breast	1-teaspoon cilantro
4-egg yolk	¼ teaspoon cumin
2 tablespoons unsweetened almond flour	¼ cup butter
½ teaspoon salt	2 tablespoons sour cream
½ teaspoon pepper	2 tablespoons mayonnaise
1-teaspoon extra virgin olive oil	2 teaspoons chili powder
½ cup diced tomatoes	2 teaspoons minced garlic
¼ cup chopped onion	

- Melt butter over low heat then let it cool.
- Cut the chicken breast into cubes then place in food processor.
- Add egg yolks and almond flour to the food processor then season with salt and pepper. Process until smooth.
- Shape the mixture into fritter forms then arrange in an Air Fryer.
- Preheat an Air Fryer to 375°F (191°C).
- Spray the chicken fritters with olive oil then cook for 15 minutes.
- Meanwhile, place diced tomatoes and chopped onion in a blender then pour melted butter, sour cream, and mayonnaise over the tomatoes.
- Season with cumin, chili powder, and minced garlic then blend until smooth and fluffy.
- Once the chicken fritters are done, remove from the Air Fryer then place on a serving dish.
- Drizzle tomato salsa on top then serve.
- Enjoy right away.

Per Serving: Net Carbs: 4.7g; Calories: 286; Total Fat: 22.4g; Saturated Fat: 10.3g
Protein: 16.9g; Carbs: 5.8g; Fiber: 1.1g; Sugar: 1.6g - Fat 71% / Protein 23% / Carbs 6%

Cauliflower Chicken Casserole [FA] [GF]

Serves: 8 / Preparation time: 5 minutes / Cooking time: 10 minutes

¾ lb. boneless chicken thighs	1-tablespoon butter
1 lb. cauliflower florets	1 cup diced cheddar cheese
½ cup heavy cream	¼ cup chopped leek
2 tablespoons lemon juice	¼ cup chopped tomatoes

¼ teaspoon salt

¼ teaspoon pepper

1-cup fresh basil

1 teaspoon minced garlic

2 tablespoons roasted pecans

¼ cup extra virgin olive oil

1 cup grated Mozzarella cheese

- Place chopped tomatoes, salt, pepper, basil, minced garlic, and roasted pecans in a blender then pour olive oil into the blender. Blend until smooth then set aside.
- Select "Sauté" setting on the Instant Pot then place butter in it.
- Next, cut the boneless chicken thighs into small dices then add to the Instant Pot. Sauté until brown. Press the "Cancel" button.
- After that, add cauliflower floret, chopped leeks, and diced cheddar cheese to the Instant Pot then stir with chicken.
- Pour heavy cream and tomato sauce over the chicken then sprinkle grated Mozzarella cheese on top.
- Put the lid on and seal the Instant Pot properly. Close the steam valve.
- Select "Manual" setting and cook the chicken casserole on high. Set the time to 8 minutes.
- Once it is done, naturally release the Instant Pot then serve.
- Enjoy!

Per Serving: Net Carbs: 2.1g; Calories: 380; Total Fat: 33g; Saturated Fat: 11.8g; Protein: 18.5g; Carbs: 3.3g; Fiber: 1.2g; Sugar: 1.2g - Fat 77% / Protein 20% / Carbs 3%

Scrumptious Chicken Satay with Curry Gravy [GF]

Serves: 4 / Preparation time: 5 minutes / Cooking time: 30 minutes

1 lb. boneless chicken thighs

¼ lb. chicken skin

3 tablespoons lemon juice

1-½ teaspoons salt

1-tablespoon extra virgin olive oil

2 teaspoons minced garlic

2 teaspoons sliced shallots

½ teaspoon curry powder

1 bay leaf

1 lemon grass

1 kaffir lime leaves

½ cup water

¼ cup coconut milk

- Cut the boneless chicken thighs and chicken skin into medium pieces then rub with lemon juice and 1 teaspoon of salt. Let it rest for about 10 minutes.
- In the meantime, preheat a skillet over medium heat then pour extra virgin olive oil into it.
- Once the oil is hot, stir in minced garlic and sliced shallots then sauté until lightly golden brown and aromatic.
- Pour water into the skillet then season with curry powder, bay leaf, lemon grass, and kaffir lime leaves. Bring to boil.
- Once it is boiled, pour coconut milk into the gravy and stir well. Bring to a simmer.
- Remove the gravy from heat and let it cool.
- Next, preheat a grill over medium heat.
- Using skewers alternately prick boneless chicken thighs and chicken skin and once the grill is ready, arrange the chicken satay directly on the grill.
- Grill the chicken for approximately 15 minutes or until the chicken satay is golden brown and completely cooked. Don't forget to flip and rotate the chicken satay.
- Once it is done, remove the chicken satay from the grill and arrange on a serving dish.

- Serve with curry gravy and enjoy warm.

Per Serving: Net Carbs: 2.6g: Calories: 474; Total Fat: 38.5g; Saturated Fat: 12.8g; Protein: 27.8g; Carbs: 3.1g; Fiber: 0.5g; Sugar: 0.8g - Fat 73% / Protein 25% / Carbs 2%

Spinach Cheesy Chicken Roll [FA] [GF]

Serves: 4 / Preparation time: 10 minutes / Cooking time: 10 minutes

1 lb. boneless chicken thighs

1 cup chopped spinach

½ cup cream cheese

½ teaspoon pepper

1-tablespoon butter

- Cut the boneless chicken into large thin slices then arrange on a flat surface.
- Spread spinach on the chicken then baste cream cheese on top.
- Sprinkle pepper over the cheese then roll the chicken and bind it tightly.
- Pour water into an Instant Pot then place a trivet in it.
- Brush the chicken roll with butter then place on the trivet.
- Put the lid on and seal the Instant Pot properly. Close the steam valve.
- Select the "Pressure" setting on the Instant Pot and cook the chicken roll on high. Set the time to 10 minutes.
- Once the Instant Pot beeps, naturally release the Instant Pot then open the lid.
- Take the chicken roll out of the Instant Pot then place on a flat surface. Let it sit for about 5 minutes.
- Cut the chicken roll into thick slices then arrange on a serving dish.
- Serve and enjoy.

Per Serving: Net Carbs: 1g; Calories: 369; Total Fat: 30g; Saturated Fat: 13.2g; Protein: 22.5g; Carbs: 1.2g; Fiber: 0.2g; Sugar: 0.1g - Fat 73% / Protein 24% / Carbs 3%

Oregano Chicken Rolls

Serves: 8 / Preparation time: 20 minutes / Cooking time: 14 minutes

½ lb. boneless chicken breast

1-teaspoon oregano

2 ½ teaspoons paprika

1-½ teaspoons minced garlic

¾ teaspoon cumin

½ teaspoon salt

½ teaspoon pepper

1-teaspoon extra virgin olive oil

1 bell pepper

1 onion

1 cup grated cheddar cheese

¼ cup butter

¼ cup Greek yogurt

1 egg yolk

2 cups roasted pecans

- Cut the chicken breast into large-thin slices.
- Rub the chicken with oregano, paprika, minced garlic, cumin, salt, and pepper. Set aside.
- Cut the bell pepper into sticks then set aside.
- Peel and chop the onion then also set aside.
- Lay a slice of chicken on a flat surface then arrange bell pepper stick, chopped onion, and grated cheddar cheese on it.
- Roll the chicken then prick with a toothpick. Repeat with the remaining chicken and filling.
- Place butter in a microwave-safe bowl then melt the butter.
- Take the melted butter out of the microwave then add egg yolk and Greek yogurt to the melted butter. Stir until incorporated then set aside.
- Next, place roasted pecans in a food processor then process until smooth and becoming flour form.

- Take a chicken roll then dip in the butter mixture.
- Roll the chicken in the pecans flour then set aside. Repeat with remaining chicken rolls.
- Preheat an Air Fryer to 375°F (191°C).
- Arrange the chicken roll in the Air Fryer then spray with olive oil.
- Cook the chicken roll for 14 minutes then transfer to a serving dish.
- Serve and enjoy.

Per Serving: Net Carbs: 4g; Calories: 393; Total Fat: 35g; Saturated Fat: 9.4g
Protein: 15.9g; Carbs: 7.5g; Fiber: 3.5g; Sugar: 2.9g - Fat 81% / Protein 16% / Carbs 3%

Avocado Chicken Salads [FA] [GF]

Serves: 4 / Preparation time: 5 minutes / Cooking time: 15 minutes

¾ lb. boneless chicken thighs	2 ripe avocados
2 tablespoons minced garlic	2 tablespoons extra virgin olive oil
½ teaspoon chili powder	1-½ teaspoons mustard
1-teaspoon salt	2 tablespoons coconut oil
¼ teaspoon pepper	

- Cut the boneless chicken thighs into small dices then set aside.
- Next, preheat a skillet over medium heat then pour coconut oil into it.
- Once the oil is hot, stir in minced garlic and sauté until wilted and aromatic.
- After that, add diced chicken to the skillet then season with salt, pepper, and chili powder. Sauté until the chicken is cooked through.
- Remove the cooked chicken from heat and transfer to a serving bowl.
- Peel the avocados and discard the seeds.
- Cut the avocados into small cubes then sprinkle over the cooked chicken.
- Drizzle extra virgin olive oil and mustard over the chicken then toss to combine.
- Serve and enjoy immediately.

Per Serving: Net Carbs: 1.7g: Calories: 323; Total Fat: 28g; Saturated Fat: 10.8g; Protein: 15.7g; Carbs: 2.6g; Fiber: 0.9g; Sugar: 0.1g - Fat 78% / Protein 20% / Carbs 2%

Hot Chicken Legs Oregano

Serves: 4 / Preparation time: 30 minutes / Cooking time: 20 minutes

4 chicken legs	½ teaspoon salt
½ cup butter	1-½ teaspoons pepper
2 tablespoons oregano	½ teaspoon thyme
¼ cup chili powder	2 teaspoons paprika
2 teaspoons minced garlic	2 tablespoons chopped parsley
1-½ tablespoons basil	

- Preheat an Air Fryer to 375°F (191°C).
- Combine oregano with chili powder, minced garlic, basil, salt, pepper, thyme, paprika, and chopped parsley then mix well.
- Brush the chicken legs with butter and sprinkle the dry spice mixture over the chicken.
- Place a rack in the Air Fryer then arrange the seasoned chicken legs on it.

- Cook the chicken legs for 30 minutes then check the tenderness. Cook for a few more minutes if it is necessary.
- Remove the cooked chicken from the Air Fryer then place on a serving dish.
- Serve and enjoy.

Per Serving: Net Carbs: 3g; Calories: 453; Total Fat: 38.8g; Saturated Fat: 18.9g
Protein: 22.8g; Carbs: 7.3g; Fiber: 4.3g; Sugar: 0.8g - Fat 77% / Protein 20% / Carbs 3%

Hot Shredded Chicken Cheese [GF]

Serves: 4 / Preparation time: 5 minutes / Cooking time: 40 minutes

¾ lb. boneless chicken thighs	1-½ tablespoons chili powder
1-½ tablespoons butter	¾ tablespoon cumin
½ cup chopped onion	¼ cup grated cheddar cheese
2 cups water	¼ teaspoon salt
¼ cup diced tomatoes	¼ teaspoon pepper

- Place the boneless chicken thighs in a pot then pour water over the chicken. Bring to boil.
- Once it is boiled, reduce the heat and cook the chicken until tender.
- Remove the chicken from heat and let it cool.
- Once the chicken is cool, place on a flat surface then using a fork shred the chicken. Set aside.
- Next, preheat a skillet over medium heat then place butter in it.
- Once the butter is melted, stir in chopped onion and sauté until wilted and aromatic.
- After that, add shredded chicken and diced tomatoes to the skillet then season with chili powder, cumin, salt, and pepper.
- Once it is done, transfer the cooked chicken to a microwave-safe serving dish and sprinkle grated Mozzarella cheese on top.
- Microwave until the Mozzarella cheese is melted then serve.
- Enjoy immediately.

Per Serving: Net Carbs: 2.7g: Calories: 398; Total Fat: 30.9g; Saturated Fat: 13.3g; Protein: 25.5g; Carbs: 3.9g; Fiber: 1.2g; Sugar: 1.3g - Fat 71% / Protein 25% / Carbs 4%

Gingery Brown Chicken Wings [FA] [GF]

Serves: 4 / Preparation time: 5 minutes / Cooking time: 12 minutes

1 lb. chicken wings	1-teaspoon minced garlic
½ cup coconut aminos	¼ cup chopped onion
½ cup water	¼ cup butter
2 tablespoons ginger	

- Select the "Sauté" menu on the Instant Pot then place butter into it.
- Wait until the butter is melted then stir in minced garlic and chopped onion.
- Next, add chicken wings to the Instant Pot then sauté until brown. Press the "Cancel" button.
- Add ginger to the Instant Pot then drizzle coconut aminos over the chicken wings.
- Pour water into the Instant Pot then put the lid on it.
- Seal the Instant Pot properly and close the steam valve.
- Select "Pressure" menu on the Instant Pot and cook the chicken for 7 minutes.

- Once it is done, naturally release the Instant Pot then open the lid.
- Transfer the cooked chicken wings to a serving dish then serve.
- Enjoy!

Per Serving: Net Carbs: 2.3g; Calories: 375; Total Fat: 29.7g; Saturated Fat: 12.3g; Protein: 21.5g; Carbs: 2.8g; Fiber: 0.5g; Sugar: 1.4g - Fat 71% / Protein 23% / Carbs 6%

Zucchini Chicken Pecans with Ginger Gravy [FA] [GF]

Serves: 4 / Preparation time: 5 minutes / Cooking time: 20 minutes

1-½ lbs. boneless chicken thighs	¼ teaspoon salt
¼ cup butter	1-teaspoon ginger
1 cup diced zucchinis	1 teaspoon red chili flakes
½ cup diced bell pepper	½ teaspoon black pepper
½ cup chopped onion	½ cup water
3 teaspoons minced garlic	¼ cup chopped roasted pecans
¾ cup coconut aminos	

- Cut the boneless chicken thighs into medium cubes then set aside.
- Place butter in the Instant Pot then press the "Sauté" button.
- Add chopped onion and minced garlic to the Instant Pot then sauté until aromatic.
- Next, add chicken cubes to the Instant Pot then stir until wilted. Press the "Cancel" button.
- After that, pour water over the chicken then season it with ginger, red chili flakes, black pepper, and salt.
- Add coconut aminos to the Instant Pot then close and seal it properly.
- Select "Manual" setting on the Instant Pot then cook the chicken on high for 15 minutes.
- Once it is done, naturally release the Instant Pot then open the lid.
- Transfer the cooked chicken to a serving dish then sprinkle chopped roasted pecans on top.
- Serve and enjoy.
- If you want to slow cook the chicken, select the "Slow Cook" setting on the Instant Pot then cook it on low for 3 hours.

Per Serving: Net Carbs: 5.6g; Calories: 435; Total Fat: 35.3g; Saturated Fat: 10.8g; Protein: 22.1g; Carbs: 7.7g; Fiber: 2.1g; Sugar: 2.2g - Fat 73% / Protein 20% / Carbs 7%

Coconut Chicken Nuggets [GF]

Serves: 4 / Preparation time: 10 minutes / Cooking time: 30 minutes

1 lb. ground chicken	½ teaspoon pepper
2 pastured eggs	2 egg whites
3 tablespoons coconut flour	1 cup grated coconut
½ teaspoon salt	½ cup coconut oil

- Preheat a steamer over medium heat then prepare a baking pan. Coat with cooking spray.
- Crack the eggs then place in a bowl.
- Season the eggs with salt and pepper then stir until incorporated. Set aside.
- Combine ground chicken with coconut flour then mix well.
- Pour egg mixture over the ground chicken then mix until combined.
- Transfer the chicken mixture in the prepared baking pan then spread evenly.

- Place the baking pan in the steamer and steam for approximately 20 minutes or until firm and the chicken is completely cooked.
- Once it is done, remove the chicken nugget from steamer and let it cool.
- Once it is cool, take the chicken nugget out of the baking pan and cut into medium thick squares.
- Dip the chicken nuggets in the egg whites then roll into the grated coconut.
- To serve, preheat a frying pan over medium heat then pour coconut oil into the pan.
- Once the oil is hot, out the chicken nuggets into the frying pan and fry until both sides of the chicken are lightly golden brown.
- Arrange the chicken nuggets on a serving dish then serve.
- Enjoy!

Per Serving: Net Carbs: 4.4g: Calories: 496; Total Fat: 38.7g; Saturated Fat: 31.2g; Protein: 31.6g; Carbs: 7.8g; Fiber: 4.4 g; Sugar: 1.8g - Fat 70% / Protein 17% / Carbs 3%

Gingery Chicken Satay

Serves: 8 / Preparation time: 30 minutes / Cooking time: 18 minutes

2 lbs. boneless chicken	1-teaspoon coriander
2 teaspoons minced garlic	2 tablespoons coconut aminos
1-teaspoon ginger	½ cup roasted cashews
2 teaspoons sliced scallions	1 ½ cups coconut milk

- Cut the chicken into cubes then rub with minced garlic, ginger, sliced scallions, and coriander. Let it sit for about 15 minutes.
- Meanwhile, place roasted cashews in a blender then pour coconut milk into the blender.
- Add coconut aminos to the blender then blend until smooth.
- Pour the cashews and coconut milk mixture over the chicken then squeeze until the chicken is completely seasoned.
- Prick the chicken with skewers then set aside.
- Preheat an Air Fryer to 375°F (191°C).
- Arrange the chicken satay in the Air Fryer then pour the liquid over the chicken satay. Cook for 18 minutes.
- Once it is done, remove the chicken satay from the Air Fryer then arrange on a serving dish.
- Drizzle the gravy over the chicken satay then serve.
- Enjoy!

Per Serving: Net Carbs: 5.6g; Calories: 400; Total Fat: 31.7g; Saturated Fat: 15.3g
Protein: 22.4g; Carbs: 6.9g; Fiber: 1.3g; Sugar: 2g - Fat 71% / Protein 22% / Carbs 7%

Almond Crispy Chicken in Sour Tomato Sauce [FA] [GF]

Serves: 4 / Preparation time: 5 minutes / Cooking time: 25 minutes

¾ lb. boneless chicken thighs	¾ cup tomato puree
1 pastured egg	¼ teaspoon salt
1 cup almond flour	¼ teaspoon nutmeg
Coconut oil, to fry	¼ teaspoon pepper
1-tablespoon butter	¼ cup water
½ cup chopped onion	

- Cut the boneless chicken thighs into medium pieces then set aside.
- Crack the egg then place in a bowl. Stir until beaten.
- Dip the chicken in the egg then roll into the almond flour. Make sure that the chicken is completely coated with almond flour.
- Preheat a frying pan over medium heat and pour coconut oil into the pan.
- Once it is hot, put the coated chicken in the frying pan then fry until the chicken is lightly golden brown.
- Remove the fried chicken from the frying pan and strain the excessive oil. Set aside.
- Preheat a saucepan over medium heat then place butter in it.
- Once the butter is melted, stir in chopped onion and sauté until lightly golden brown and aromatic.
- Next, pour tomato puree and water into the saucepan then season with salt, nutmeg, and pepper. Stir well and bring to a simmer.
- Add fried chicken to the saucepan then stir until the chicken is completely coated with tomato sauce.
- Once it is done, remove the chicken from heat and transfer to a serving dish.
- Drizzle the remaining tomato sauce over the chicken then serve.
- Enjoy!

Per Serving: Net Carbs: 5.5g: Calories: 388; Total Fat: 38.1g; Saturated Fat: 27g; Protein: 7.7g; Carbs: 7.5g; Fiber: 2g; Sugar: 3.2g - Fat 88% / Protein 6% / Carbs 6%

Wrapped Lettuce Chicken Garlic with Lemon Parsley Sauce [GF]

Serves: 4 / Preparation time: 5 minutes / Cooking time: 3 hours

1 lb. boneless chicken thighs	1 shallot
½ lb. chicken skin	1 cup chopped parsley
2 tablespoons chopped celery stalk	¼ cup mint leaves
½ cup chopped onion	¼ cup lemon juice
1 teaspoon minced garlic	¼ cup extra virgin olive oil
¾ cup chicken broth	¼ teaspoon salt
4 large fresh lettuces	¼ teaspoon pepper
½ cup shredded carrots	½ teaspoon cayenne pepper

- Cut the boneless chicken thighs and chicken skin into very small cubes then place in the inner pot of an Instant Pot.
- Sprinkle chopped celery stalk, chopped onion, and minced garlic over the chicken then pour chicken broth into the Instant Pot.
- Put the lid on and seal the Instant Pot properly. Let the steam valve open.
- Select "Slow Cook" setting and cook the chicken on low. Set the time to 3 hours.
- In the meantime, place shallot, parsley, mint leaves, lemon juice, olive oil, salt, pepper, and cayenne pepper in a blender then blend until smooth.
- Transfer the smooth sauce to a container with a lid then chill in the fridge.
- When the Instant Pot beeps, naturally release the Instant Pot and open the lid.
- Transfer the cooked chicken to a place or a container and let it cool.
- To serve, place a lettuce on a flat surface then put about 2 tablespoons of cooked chicken on it.
- Add shredded carrots on the chicken and drizzle lemon parsley sauce on top.
- Wrap the chicken tightly with lettuce and place on a serving dish. Repeat with the remaining chicken and lettuces.

- Serve and enjoy.

Per Serving: Net Carbs: 4.1g; Calories: 467; Total Fat: 36.5g; Saturated Fat: 9.6g; Protein: 27.7g; Carbs: 6g; Fiber: 1.9g; Sugar: 2.1g - Fat 70% / Protein 23% / Carbs 7%

Chicken Coconut Cream Soup [FA] [GF] [F]

Serves: 4 / Preparation time: 5 minutes / Cooking time: 20 minutes

½ lb. boneless chicken thighs	¼ cup diced carrots
1-tablespoon butter	¼ cup chopped celery
¼ cup chopped onion	1-cup water
1-teaspoon pepper	1-cup coconut milk
½ teaspoon salt	3 tablespoons coconut flour

- Place butter in the Instant Pot then press the "Sauté" button.
- Once the butter is melted, add chopped onion to the Instant Pot then sauté until aromatic. Press the "Cancel" button.
- Pour water into the Instant Pot then season with pepper and salt. Stir well.
- Next, cut the chicken into very small pieces then add to the Instant Pot together with chopped carrots and celeries.
- Put the lid on and seal the Instant Pot properly. Close the steam valve.
- Select "Soup" setting on the Instant Pot and cook the chicken soup on high. In will take for 10 minutes.
- Once it is done, quick release the Instant Pot then open the lid.
- Stir in coconut flour and coconut milk mixture over the chicken then stir well.
- Select the "Sauté" menu again then cook the soup for 5 minutes.
- Transfer the chicken soup to a serving bowl then serve.
- Enjoy warm.

Per Serving: Net Carbs: 5.6g; Calories: 457; Total Fat: 35.7g; Saturated Fat: 21g; Protein: 23.1g; Carbs: 11.2g; Fiber: 5.6g; Sugar: 3.5g - Fat 70% / Protein 21% / Carbs 9%

Red Hot Chicken in Wrap [FA] [GF]

Serves: 4 / Preparation time: 5 minutes / Cooking time: 10 minutes

½ lb. chicken wings	¼ cup cayenne
1 lb. chicken skin	1-teaspoon turmeric
5 cloves garlic	½ teaspoon salt
8 shallots	¾ cup diced tomatoes
½ cup red chilies	½ cup fresh basil

- Place garlic, shallots, turmeric, salt, red chilies, and cayenne in a food processor. Process until smooth.
- Transfer the spice mixture to a bowl then add diced tomatoes and fresh basil. Mix until combined.
- Cut the chicken wings and chicken skin into small pieces then rub with the spice mixture.
- Divide the chicken and spices into several parts then wrap each part with aluminum foil. Set aside.
- Pour water into the Instant Pot then place a trivet in it.
- Arrange the wrapped chicken on the trivet then seal the Instant Pot properly. Close the steam valve.
- Select "Pressure" menu on the Instant Pot then cook the chicken on high for 10 minutes.
- Once the Instant Pot beeps, naturally release the Instant Pot then open the lid.

- Take the chicken in wrap out of the Instant Pot then let them rest for about 5 minutes.
- Unwrap the chicken then transfer to a serving dish together with the spices.
- Serve and enjoy warm.

Per Serving: Net Carbs: 6.7g; Calories: 488; Total Fat: 39.1g; Saturated Fat: 10.9g; Protein: 25.6g; Carbs: 8g; Fiber: 1.3g; Sugar: 1.9g - Fat 72% / Protein 21% / Carbs 97%

Chicken Wings Black Pepper with Sesame Seeds

Serves: 2 / Preparation time: 10 minutes / Cooking time: 15 minutes

2 lbs. chicken wings

1-½ teaspoons salt

1-½ teaspoons black pepper

1-¼ tablespoons ginger powder

1-½ tablespoons minced garlic

1-½ tablespoons extra virgin olive oil

½ tablespoon mayonnaise

1-tablespoon sesame seeds

- Place salt, black pepper, ginger powder, and minced garlic in a bowl then mix well.
- Rub the chicken wings with the spice mixture then let them sit for about 5 minutes.
- Preheat an Air Fryer to 400°F (204°C).
- Brush the chicken wings with extra virgin olive oil then arrange in the Air Fryer.
- Cook the chicken wings for 15 minutes then arrange on a serving dish.
- Drizzle mayonnaise over the chicken wings then sprinkle sesame seeds on top.
- Serve and enjoy warm.

Per Serving: Net Carbs: 6.9g; Calories: 207; Total Fat: 16.9g; Saturated Fat: 3.2g
Protein: 7.1g; Carbs: 8g; Fiber: 1.1g; Sugar: 0.3g - Fat 73% / Protein 14% / Carbs 13%

Asparagus Chicken Thigh with Pine Nuts Green Pesto [FA] [GF]

Serves: 8 / Preparation time: 5 minutes / Cooking time: 20 minutes

1 lb. boneless chicken thighs

1 cup chopped asparagus

1-cup cherry tomatoes

½ cup chicken broth

1-cup fresh basil

½ cup toasted pine nuts

1 cup grated Parmesan cheese

½ cup extra virgin olive oil

1 teaspoon minced garlic

¼ teaspoon pepper

½ teaspoon salt

- Place the boneless chicken thighs in the Instant Pot then add asparagus and tomatoes around the chicken.
- Pour chicken broth over the chicken then close and seal the Instant Pot properly. Close the steam valve.
- Select "Manual" setting on the Instant Pot then cook the chicken on high. Set the time to 20 minutes.
- Meanwhile, place fresh basil, pine nuts, Parmesan cheese, minced garlic, pepper, and salt in a blender then pour olive oil into the blender. Blend until smooth then set aside.
- Once the Instant Pot beeps, naturally release the Instant Pot then open the lid.
- Transfer the cooked chicken to a serving dish then drizzle the pine nuts green pesto over the chicken.
- Serve and enjoy.

Per Serving: Net Carbs: 4g; Calories: 476; Total Fat: 12.8g; Saturated Fat: 12.8g; Protein: 30.2g; Carbs: 5g; Fiber: 1g; Sugar: 1.3g - Fat 74% / Protein 25% / Carbs 1%

Crispy Fried Chicken

Serves: 8 / Preparation time: 15 minutes / Cooking time: 22 minutes

1 lb. chicken thighs

1-teaspoon salt

1-teaspoon pepper

1 cup almond flour

1-cup water

2 cups roasted pecans

1-teaspoon black pepper

- Rub the chicken thighs with salt and pepper then let it sit for 5 minutes.
- Meanwhile, place roasted pecans in a food processor then process until smooth and becoming flour.
- Roll the seasoned chicken thighs in the almond flour then dip in the water.
- Combine the remaining almond flour with pecans flour then mix well.
- Remove the chicken thighs from water then roll in the pecans mixture. Using your finger squeeze the chicken thighs until all sides of the chicken thighs are completely coated with pecans mixture.
- Preheat an Air Fryer to 400°F (204°C).
- Arrange the coated chicken thighs in the Air Fryer then set the time to 22 minutes.
- Once it is done, check the doneness of the chicken thighs. If you want them to be more golden brown, give the chicken thighs an additional 5 minutes in the Air Fryer.
- Place the crispy fried chicken on a serving dish then sprinkle black pepper on top.
- Serve and enjoy hot.

Per Serving: Net Carbs: 2.2g; Calories: 455; Total Fat: 41.7g; Saturated Fat: 5.9g
Protein: 18g; Carbs: 6.3g; Fiber: 4.1g; Sugar: 1.7g - Fat 81% / Protein 16% / Carbs 3%

Spicy Coconut Steamed Chicken [FA] [GF]

Serves: 4 / Preparation time: 5 minutes / Cooking time: 20 minutes

1 lb. chicken thighs

2 teaspoons sliced garlic

1-tablespoon sliced shallots

2 tablespoons red chili flakes

1-inch galangal

2 bay leaves

¼ cup chopped green tomatoes

1-cup coconut milk

½ teaspoon salt

- Preheat a steamer over medium heat.
- Cut the chicken thighs into medium pieces then place in a disposable aluminum pan.
- Add sliced garlic, shallot, red chili flakes, bay leaves, galangal, chopped green tomatoes, and salt to the disposable aluminum pan then pour coconut milk over the chicken.
- Place the disposable aluminum pan with chicken in the steamer and steam for approximately 15-20 minutes or until the chicken is tender.
- Once it is done, remove the steamed chicken from the steamer and transfer to a serving bowl.
- Serve and enjoy.

Per Serving: Net Carbs: 5g: Calories: 454; Total Fat: 35.7g; Saturated Fat: 19g; Protein: 27.1g; Carbs: 6.9g; Fiber: 1.9g; Sugar: 3.5g - Fat 71% / Protein 25% / Carbs 4%

Delicious Chicken Tabasco with Spicy Mayo

Serves: 4 / Preparation time: 30 minutes / Cooking time: 22 minutes

1-½ lbs. chicken drumsticks

1 ½ tablespoons extra virgin olive oil

1-½ tablespoons white wine vinegar

1-tablespoon tomato paste

¼ teaspoon salt

½ teaspoon smoked paprika

1-½ tablespoons Tabasco

¾ cup mayonnaise

1-teaspoon chili powder

1 teaspoon minced garlic

- Place extra virgin olive oil, white wine vinegar, tomato paste, salt, smoked paprika, and Tabasco in a zipper-lock plastic bag. Stir to combine.
- Add chicken drumsticks to the plastic bag then shake until the chicken is completely coated with the spice mixture.
- Let the chicken sit for about 30 minutes to ensure the spice is completely absorbed into the chicken.
- After 30 minutes, preheat an Air Fryer to 375°F (191°C).
- Place the seasoned chicken drumsticks in the Air Fryer then cook for 22 minutes.
- Meanwhile, add chili powder and minced garlic to the mayonnaise. Mix until incorporated.
- Remove the cooked chicken drumsticks from the Air Fryer then place on a serving dish.
- Serve with mayonnaise garlic.

Per Serving: Net Carbs: 1.1g; Calories: 350; Total Fat: 29g; Saturated Fat: 6.3g
Protein: 21.3g; Carbs: 1.5g; Fiber: 0.4g; Sugar: 0.9g - Fat 75% / Protein 24% / Carbs 1%

Savory Stuffed Chicken Onion [FA] [GF]

Serves: 4 / Preparation time: 5 minutes / Cooking time: 25 minutes

1 medium whole chicken	2 cups chopped onion
½ cup butter	6 cloves garlic
1-teaspoon pepper	

- Brush the chicken with butter then sprinkle pepper over the chicken.
- Fill the chicken cavity with chopped onion and garlics then set aside.
- Turn the Instant Pot then select the "Sauté" menu.
- Place the chicken in the inner pot then let it brown for about 2 minutes per side.
- Next, press the "Cancel" button and remove the chicken from the Instant Pot.
- Pour water into the Instant Pot then place a trivet in it.
- Put the lid on and seal the Instant Pot properly.
- Select the "Manual" menu on the Instant Pot then cook the chicken on high for 25 minutes.
- Once the timer beeps, turn the Instant Pot off and naturally release it.
- Open the lid then transfer the cooked chicken to a serving dish. let it rest for about 5 minutes.
- Cut the chicken into slices then serve.

Per Serving: Net Carbs: 3.8g; Calories: 416; Total Fat: 32.4g; Saturated Fat: 14.7g; Protein: 21.8g; Carbs: 4.8g; Fiber: 1g; Sugar: 1.7g - Fat 71% / Protein 21% / Carbs 8%

Pepper Chicken Log with Spicy Tomato Sauce [FA] [GF]

Serves: 4 / Preparation time: 5 minutes / Cooking time: 20 minutes

1 lb. boneless chicken thighs	1-teaspoon pepper
3 tablespoons minced garlic	2 tablespoons red chili flakes
2 eggs	½ teaspoon chili powder
4 red tomatoes	1-cup water
½ teaspoon nutmeg	2 tablespoons butter
½ teaspoon salt	¼ cup chopped onion

- Cut the boneless chicken thighs into cubes then place in a food processor.
- Add minced garlic and eggs to the food processor then process until combined.

- Transfer the chicken mixture to a sheet of aluminum foil then shape into a log. Wrap the chicken log with the aluminum foil tightly then set aside.
- Pour water into the Instant Pot then place a trivet in it.
- Place the wrapped chicken log on the trivet then put the lid on and seal the Instant Pot properly. Close the steam valve.
- Select "Manual" setting and cook the chicken log on high. Set the time to 10 minutes.
- When the Instant Pot beeps, quick release the Instant Pot then open the lid.
- Take the chicken log out of the Instant Pot then let it rest for a few minutes.
- Meanwhile, cut the red tomatoes into medium pieces then place in a blender.
- Season with nutmeg, salt, pepper, red chili flakes, and chili powder then pour water into the blender. Blend until smooth then set aside.
- Unwrap the chicken log then cut into thick slices.
- Remove the trivet from the Instant Pot then clean it.
- Turn the Instant Pot on then select "Sauté" menu.
- Add butter to the Instant Pot then wait until melted.
- Stir in chopped onion then sauté until translucent and aromatic.
- Next, pour the tomato mixture into the Instant Pot then bring to a simmer. Turn the Instant Pot off.
- Arrange the chicken on a serving dish then drizzle the tomato sauce over the chicken.
- Serve and enjoy!

Per Serving: Net Carbs: 5.1g; Calories: 404; Total Fat: 31.1g; Saturated Fat: 13.1g; Protein: 24.2g; Carbs: 6.7g; Fiber: 1.6g; Sugar: 2.7g - Fat 70% / Protein 24% / Carbs 6%

Spicy Chicken in Creamy Gravy [FA] [GF]

Serves: 4 / Preparation time: 5 minutes / Cooking time: 20 minutes

1 lb. chicken thighs	1-teaspoon chili powder
2 tablespoons extra virgin olive oil	1 bay leaf
¾ cup chopped onion	1 lemon grass
2 teaspoons minced garlic	2 cups chicken broth
2 teaspoons sliced shallots	¼ cup heavy cream
½ teaspoon salt	3 tablespoons sour cream
¼ teaspoon pepper	1 tablespoon lemon juice
3 tablespoons red chili flakes	

- Turn the Instant Pot then press the "Sauté" button.
- Pour olive oil into the Instant Pot then stir in chopped onion, minced garlic, and sliced shallots. Sauté until aromatic then press the "Cancel" button.
- Add chicken thighs to the Instant Pot then season with salt, pepper, red chili flakes, chili powder, bay leaf, and lemon grass.
- Pour chicken broth over the chicken thighs then stir well.
- Put the lid on and seal the Instant Pot properly. Close the steam valve.
- Select the "Manual" menu on the Instant Pot then cook the chicken on high. Set the time to 10 minutes.
- When the Instant Pot beeps, quick release the Instant Pot then open the lid.
- Pour heavy cream and sour cream into the Instant Pot then press "Sauté". Stir well and bring to a simmer for 5 minutes.
- Once it is done, turn the Instant Pot then drizzle lemon juice over the chicken. Stir well.

- Transfer the cooked chicken to a serving dish together with the gravy.
- Serve and enjoy warm.

Per Serving: Net Carbs: 6.2g; Calories: 488; Total Fat: 38.8g; Saturated Fat: 15.4g; Protein: 23.8g; Carbs: 7.5g; Fiber: 1.3g; Sugar: 3.2g - Fat 72% / Protein 20% / Carbs 8%

SEAFOOD RECIPES

Spinach Salmon Nugget

Serves: 4 / Preparation time: 11 minutes / Cooking time: 21 minutes

½ lb. salmon fillet	1 egg
½ teaspoon pepper	1 cup chopped spinach
3 teaspoons minced garlic	½ cup extra virgin olive oil, to fry

- Preheat a steamer over medium heat then steam the spinach for a few minutes or until just wilted. Remove from the steamer.
- Cut the salmon fillet into cubes then place in a food processor then add minced garlic and pepper to the food processor. Process until smooth.
- Crack the egg and add to the salmon mixture.
- Add chopped steamed spinach to the mixture then mix until just combined.
- Preheat a steamer again then prepare a baking pan. Line the baking pan with aluminum foil.
- Place the salmon mixture in the steamer then steam for approximately 10 minutes or until set.
- Once it is done, remove from the steamer and let it cool for a few minutes.
- Take the salmon nugget out of the baking pan and cut into thick slices.
- Next, preheat a frying pan and pour extra virgin olive oil into it.
- Put the sliced salmon nugget in the frying pan and fry until both sides are lightly golden brown.
- Take the fried salmon nugget out of the frying pan and strain the excessive oil.
- Arrange the fried salmon nuggets on a serving dish and serve.
- Enjoy warm.

Per Serving: Net Carbs: 2.7g; Calories: 445; Total Fat: 37.8g; Saturated Fat: 6g
Protein: 25.2g; Carbs: 5.6g; Fiber: 2.9g; Sugar: 0.6g - Fat 76% / Protein 22% / Carbs 2%

Squid Super Black Ink [FA] [GF] [SF]

Serves: 4 / Preparation time: 5 minutes / Cooking time: 24 minutes

1 lb. fresh squids	¼ teaspoon salt
2 teaspoons minced garlic	2 kaffir lime leaves
2 teaspoons coriander	½ cup butter

- Wash and clean the squids. Do not remove the ink.
- Cut the butter into cubes then place in the Instant Pot.
- Rub the squids with minced garlic, coriander, and salt then place in the Instant Pot.

- Add kaffir lime leaves to the Instant Pot then close and seal the Instant Pot.
- Select "Manual" setting and cook the squids to 20 minutes.
- Once it is done, naturally release the Instant Pot then open the lid.
- Transfer the cooked squids to a serving dish and serve.
- Enjoy right away.

Per Serving: Net Carbs: 4.6g; Calories: 289; Total Fat: 24.2g; Saturated Fat: 14.9g; Protein: 13.6g; Carbs: 4.6g; Fiber: 0g; Sugar: 0g - Fat 75% / Protein 20% / Carbs 5%

Creamy Tomato Shrimps [FA] [GF]

Serves: 4 / Preparation time: 5 minutes / Cooking time: 24 minutes

1 lb. fresh shrimps	1-teaspoon minced garlic
¼ cup Greek yogurt	¼ cup butter
2 teaspoons cumin	2 tablespoons sliced shallots
1 ½ teaspoons paprika	1 cup diced tomatoes
2 teaspoons lemon juice	½ cup water
½ teaspoon salt	1-cup heavy cream
1-teaspoon ginger	½ teaspoon grated lime zest

- Combine Greek yogurt with cumin, paprika, lemon juice, salt, ginger, and minced garlic then stir well.
- Add fresh shrimps to the yogurt mixture then marinade for 10 minutes.
- Meanwhile, place butter in the Instant Pot then select "Sauté" setting.
- Stir in sliced shallot then sauté until lightly golden. Press the "Cancel" button.
- Add diced tomatoes, heavy cream, and grated lime zest to the Instant Pot then pour water into it. Stir well.
- After 10 minutes, add shrimps to the Instant Pot together with the marinade.
- Put the lid on and seal the Instant Pot properly. Close the steam valve.
- Select "Manual" setting on the Instant Pot then cook the shrimps for 3 minutes. Be careful not to overcook.
- Once it is done, quick release the Instant Pot then open the lid.
- Transfer the cooked shrimps together with the liquid to a serving dish then serve right away.
- Enjoy!

Per Serving: Net Carbs: 4.4g; Calories: 296; Total Fat: 24.1g; Saturated Fat: 14.5g; Protein: 16.4g; Carbs: 5.5g; Fiber: 1.1g; Sugar: 1.9g - Fat 73% / Protein 22% / Carbs 5%

Stir Fry Crab in Creamy Chili

Serves: 4 / Preparation time: 11 minutes / Cooking time: 21 minutes

4 whole crabs	¾ cup coconut milk
4 tablespoons minced garlic	2 kaffir lime leaves
¼ cup extra virgin olive oil	1-cup fresh basil
½ cup chopped onion	2 tablespoons lemon juice
2 teaspoons chopped green chili	

- Cut the crabs into halves then set aside.
- Preheat a skillet over medium heat then pour extra virgin olive oil into the skillet.

- Once the oil is hot, stir in minced garlic then sauté until wilted and aromatic.
- Add halved crabs to the skillet then stir until cooked and crispy.
- Remove the crabs from heat then place on a plate.
- Stir in chopped onion and green chili to the skillet then sauté with the remaining olive oil.
- Pour coconut milk over the onion then season with kaffir lime leaves. Bring to a simmer.
- Add fresh basils to the skillet then return the crabs to the skillet. Cook for approximately 2 minutes.
- Once it is done, remove from heat then drizzle lemon juice over the crabs.
- Transfer the crabs to a serving dish then enjoy.

Per Serving: Net Carbs: 7g; Calories: 320; Total Fat: 25.9g; Saturated Fat: 12.6g
Protein: 2g; Carbs: 8.6g; Fiber: 1.6g; Sugar: 3.3g - Fat 73% / Protein 18% / Carbs 9%

Fried Shrimps with Avocado Topping

Serves: 8 / Preparation time: 10 minutes / Cooking time: 15 minutes

2 lbs. fresh shrimps	¼ teaspoon salt
2 teaspoons extra virgin olive oil	½ teaspoon pepper
½ cup chopped onion	1 ripe avocado
2 tablespoons chopped celeries	½ cup chopped roasted pecans
2 tablespoons diced paprika	

- Preheat an Air Fryer to 400°F (204°C).
- Place chopped onion in the Air Fryer then spray with extra virgin olive oil. Cook the onion for 5 minutes.
- Next, add fresh shrimps to the Air Fryer then cook for another 5 minutes.
- After that, add chopped celeries and paprika to the Air Fryer then season with salt and pepper. Mix well.
- Let the Air Fryer at 400°F (204°) and cook the ingredients for 5 minutes.
- Once it is done, transfer the cooked shrimps and the other ingredients to a serving dish.
- Peel the ripe avocado then discard the seed. Cut into cubes.
- Sprinkle avocado cubes and chopped roasted pecans on top then serve.
- Enjoy!

Per Serving: Net Carbs: 5.4g; Calories: 248; Total Fat: 20.9g; Saturated Fat: 3g
Protein: 7.8g; Carbs: 9.9g; Fiber: 4.5g; Sugar: 4.7g - Fat 76% / Protein 13% / Carbs 11%

Super Easy Squid Stew [FA] [GF]

Serves: 4 / Preparation time: 5 minutes / Cooking time: 24 minutes

1 lb. fresh squids	3 teaspoons minced garlic
2 tablespoons extra virgin olive oil	2 cups chopped tomatoes
½ cup butter	½ cup chicken broth
½ cup chopped onion	1-teaspoon thyme

- Place butter and olive oil in the Instant Pot then press the "Sauté" button.
- Once the butter is melted, stir in fresh squids then sauté until golden brown.
- Next, stir in chopped onion and minced garlic then sauté until aromatic. Press the "Cancel" button.

- Add chopped tomatoes and thyme to the Instant Pot then pour chicken broth over the ingredients. Stir well.
- Put the lid on and seal the Instant Pot properly.
- Select "Manual" setting and cook the squids on high for 15 minutes.
- Once it is done, naturally release the Instant Pot then open the lid.
- Transfer the cooked squids to a serving dish and enjoy warm.

Per Serving: Net Carbs: 7g; Calories: 403; Total Fat: 32.1g; Saturated Fat: 16.1g; Protein: 21.4g; Carbs: 8g; Fiber: 1g; Sugar: 1.9g - Fat 84% / Protein 10% / Carbs 6%

Cheesy Shrimps and Kale [FA] [GF]

Serves: 4 / Preparation time: 3 minutes / Cooking time: 5 minutes

½ lb. fresh shrimps	¾ teaspoon dried basil
2 tablespoons butter	¼ teaspoon salt
¼ cup cream cheese	1 tablespoon grated Parmesan cheese
¼ cup water	¼ cup halved cherry tomatoes
¼ cup heavy cream	½ cup chopped kale

- Place butter in the Instant Pot then select "Sauté" setting.
- Stir in fresh shrimps then sauté until the shrimps are pink. Press the "Cancel" button.
- Add the remaining ingredients—cream cheese, water, heavy cream, dried basil, salt, Parmesan cheese, cherry tomatoes, and kale then close and seal the Instant Pot properly.
- Select "Manual" setting and cook the shrimps on low for 4 minutes.
- Once it is done, quick release the Instant Pot then open the lid.
- Stir the shrimps and the other ingredients then transfer to a serving dish.
- Serve and enjoy warm.

Per Serving: Net Carbs: 2.5g; Calories: 220; Total Fat: 17.8g; Saturated Fat: 11.3g; Protein: 13.2g; Carbs: 2.9g; Fiber: 0.4g; Sugar: 0.6g - Fat 73% / Protein 24% / Carbs 3%

Nutty Avocado Veggie Salmon Salads [FA] [GF]

Serves: 4 / Preparation time: 5 minutes / Cooking time: 15 minutes

¾ lb. salmon fillet	¼ cup mayonnaise
2 tablespoons butter	2 tablespoons lemon juice
¼ cup roasted almonds	2 tablespoons extra virgin olive oil
1 cup chopped lettuce	½ teaspoon pepper
½ cup sliced cucumber	½ teaspoon salt
¼ cup avocado cubes	

- Preheat a pan over medium heat then place butter in it.
- Once the butter is melted, place salmon fillet in the pan and cook for about 3 minutes.
- Carefully flip the salmon and cook for another 3 minutes or until the salmon is cooked through.
- Once it is done, remove from the pan and transfer to a plate.
- Using a fork shred the salmon into medium chunks then place in a salad bowl.
- Add chopped lettuce, sliced cucumber, and avocado cubes into the salad bowl then drizzle mayonnaise, lemon juice, and extra virgin olive oil mixture over the salads.

- Season the salad with salt and pepper then toss to combine.
- Sprinkle roasted almond on top then serve.
- Enjoy right away or store in the refrigerator for later usage.

Per Serving: Net Carbs: 5.9g: Calories: 488; Total Fat: 38.1g; Saturated Fat: 9.2g; Protein: 31.3g; Carbs: 6.9g; Fiber: 1g; Sugar: 1.7g - Fat 70% / Protein 25% / Carbs 5%

Tuna Balls in Garlic Tomato Gravy

Serves: 4 / Preparation time: 14 minutes / Cooking time: 23 minutes

¾ lb. tuna fillet	4 cups water
1-tablespoon coconut flour	½ teaspoon pepper
2 tablespoons chopped leek	½ cup chopped tomato
2 tablespoons extra virgin olive oil	¼ cup chopped celeries
3 teaspoons minced garlic	

- Cut the tuna fillet into cubes then place in a food processor.
- Add coconut flour into the food processor then process until smooth.
- Transfer the tuna mixture to a bowl then add chopped leek to the bowl. Mix until just combined.
- Shape the tuna mixture into small balls form then set aside.
- Pour 2 cups of water into a pot then bring to boil.
- Once the water is boiled, slowly put the small tuna balls then cook until they are floating.
- In the meantime, preheat a skillet over medium heat then pour extra virgin olive oil into the skillet.
- Once the oil is hot, stir in minced garlic then sauté until aromatic.
- Pour the remaining water into the skillet then bring to boil.
- Once it is boiled, season the gravy with pepper then add chopped tomatoes and celeries to the gravy.
- When the tuna balls are floating, take them out of the pot and transfer to the gravy. Bring to a simmer.
- Transfer to a serving bowl then serve warm.
- Enjoy immediately.

Per Serving: Net Carbs: 2.5g; Calories: 449; Total Fat: 38.6g; Saturated Fat: 1.5g
Protein: 21.9g; Carbs: 4.3g; Fiber: 1.8g; Sugar: 1.1g - Fat 77% / Protein 21% / Carbs 2%

Salmon Steak with Tomato Pepper Sauce [FA] [GF]

Serves: 4 / Preparation time: 5 minutes / Cooking time: 10 minutes

1 lb. salmon fillet	¼ cup chopped tomato
¼ cup butter	½ cup water
3 teaspoons minced garlic	1 teaspoon Worcestershire sauce
A pinch of salt	1-teaspoon paprika
¼ cup almond butter	1-teaspoon chili powder
¼ cup chopped onion	¼ teaspoon pepper

- Rub the salmon fillet with minced garlic and salt then place in the inner pot of an Instant Pot.

- Baste the salmon fillet with butter then close and seal the Instant Pot.
- Select "Manual " setting and cook the salmon on high. Set the time to 5 minutes.
- Once the Instant Pot beeps, quick release the Instant Pot and open the lid.
- Take the cooked salmon out of the Instant Pot then place on a serving dish.
- Next, place chopped tomatoes and water in a blender then blend until incorporated.
- Pour the tomato mixture to the Instant Pot then add the remaining ingredients—almond butter, chopped onion, Worcestershire sauce, paprika, chili powder, and pepper. Stir well.
- Select "Sauté" setting on the Instant Pot and cook the sauce for 5 minutes. Press the "Cancel" button.
- Drizzle the sauce over the salmon and serve right away.
- Enjoy!

Per Serving: Net Carbs: 4.7g; Calories: 394; Total Fat: 32g; Saturated Fat: 10.2g; Protein: 23g; Carbs: 6.1g; Fiber: 1.4g; Sugar: 1.8g - Fat 73% / Protein 23% / Carbs 4%

Fried Tuna Crispy

Serves: 4 / Preparation time: 15 minutes / Cooking time: 10 minutes

½ lb. tuna steak	½ teaspoon chili powder
1 tablespoon lemon juice	¼ teaspoon salt
1 egg	¼ teaspoon pepper
1 cup roasted pecans	1-teaspoon extra virgin olive oil
1-teaspoon ginger	

- Splash lemon juice over the tuna then let it rest for a few minutes.
- Next, crack the egg then place in a bowl.
- Season the egg with salt, pepper, and chili powder then stir until incorporated. Set aside.
- Place roasted pecans in a food processor then process until becoming flour texture.
- After that, add ginger to the pecans then process again until combined. Transfer the pecans mixture to a bowl.
- Dip the tuna in the egg mixture then roll in the pecan mixture.
- Return to the egg mixture then roll again in the pecan mixture. Make sure that all sides of the tuna are completely coated with pecan.
- Preheat an Air Fryer to 400°F (204°C) and place a rack in it.
- Once the Air Fryer is ready, place the coated tuna on the rack then cook for 5 minutes.
- Flip the tuna and cook again for another 5 minutes. The tuna will be lightly golden brown.
- Remove the fried tuna from the Air Fryer then place in a serving dish.
- Serve and enjoy.

Per Serving: Net Carbs: 1.7g; Calories: 313; Total Fat: 28g; Saturated Fat: 3.1g
Protein: 14.4g; Carbs: 4.6g; Fiber: 2.9g; Sugar: 1.4g - Fat 81% / Protein 18% / Carbs 1%

Mixed Tuna Soup in Green Coconut Gravy

Serves: 4 / Preparation time: 4 minutes / Cooking time: 16 minutes

½ lb. tuna fillet	½ cup fresh basil
2 tablespoons extra virgin olive oil	1 bay leaf
2 teaspoons sliced garlic	1-inch galangal
2 teaspoons sliced shallots	1-cup coconut milk
2 teaspoons green chili	1-cup water

½ cup chopped eggplant   ½ cup chopped spinach

½ cup chopped kale

- Place garlic, shallots, and green chili in the food processor then process until smooth.
- Preheat a skillet over medium heat then pour extra virgin olive into it.
- Once it is hot, stir in the spice mixture then sauté until aromatic.
- Pour water over the spice then bring to boil.
- Once it is boiled, add tuna, eggplant, kale, and spinach then season with fresh basil, bay leaf, and galangal.
- Pour coconut milk into the skillet then bring to boil.
- Once it is boiled, remove the soup from heat and transfer to a serving dish.
- Serve and enjoy warm.

Per Serving: Net Carbs: 2.4g; Calories: 302; Total Fat: 26.5g; Saturated Fat: 1.1g
Protein: 13.9g; Carbs: 3.1g; Fiber: 0.7g; Sugar: 0.5g - Fat 79% / Protein 18% / Carbs 3%

Savory Fried Fish with Red Sambal [FA] [GF]

Serves: 4 / Preparation time: 10 minutes / Cooking time: 15 minutes

1 lb. catfish	Coconut oil, to fry
3 tablespoons minced garlic	½ cup cayenne
½ teaspoon turmeric	2 shallots
1-teaspoon salt	2 slices red tomatoes
2 teaspoons coriander	

- Combine minced garlic with turmeric, salt, and coriander then mix well.
- Rub the catfish with the spice mixture then let it rest for 5 minutes.
- Next, preheat a frying pan over medium heat then pour coconut oil into it.
- Once the oil is hot, put the seasoned catfish into the frying pan and fry until cooked through and both sides of the catfish are lightly golden brown.
- Remove the fried catfish from the frying pan and strain the excessive oil. Place on a serving dish.
- After that, put cayenne, shallots, and red tomatoes into the frying pan and fry for approximately 2 minutes.
- Remove from heat and transfer to a food processor. Process until smooth.
- Serve the fried catfish with red sambal and enjoy warm.

Per Serving: Net Carbs: 6.5g: Calories: 343; Total Fat: 26.9g; Saturated Fat: 14.7g; Protein: 23.2g; Carbs: 9.8g; Fiber: 3.3g; Sugar: 1.6g - Fat 71% / Protein 21% / Carbs 8%

Gingery Tuna Cheese [FA] [GF]

Serves: 4 / Preparation time: 5 minutes / Cooking time: 10 minutes

1 lb. tuna fillet	2 teaspoons minced garlic
¼ cup coconut aminos	¼ cup chopped onion
½ cup chicken broth	¼ cup butter
1-tablespoon ginger	

- Select the "Sauté" menu on the Instant Pot then place butter into it.
- Wait until the butter is melted then stir in minced garlic and chopped onion.
- Next, add tuna fillet to the Instant Pot then sauté until brown. Press the "Cancel" button.
- Add ginger to the Instant Pot then drizzle coconut aminos over the tuna.
- Pour chicken broth into the Instant Pot then put the lid on it.
- Seal the Instant Pot properly and close the steam valve.
- Select "Manual" menu on the Instant Pot and cook the tuna for 20 minutes.
- Once it is done, naturally release the Instant Pot then open the lid.
- Transfer the cooked tuna to a serving dish then sprinkle grated cheddar cheese on top.
- Enjoy!

Per Serving: Net Carbs: 3.4g; Calories: 398; Total Fat: 34.2g; Saturated Fat: 6.9g; Protein: 18.8g; Carbs: 3.6g; Fiber: 0.2g; Sugar: 0.4g - Fat 77% / Protein 19% / Carbs 4%

Baked Calamari with Avocado Lemon Salsa

Serves: 4 / Preparation time: 12 minutes / Cooking time: 11 minutes

1 lb. fresh squid	2 tablespoons mayonnaise
1 cup almond flour	¼ teaspoon pepper
1 egg	1-teaspoon tomato puree
4 tablespoons extra virgin olive oil	1 teaspoon lemon juice
1 ripe avocado	

- Crack the egg then place in a bowl.
- Pour extra virgin olive oil into the bowl then mix until incorporated.
- Remove the squid ink and put the squid in the egg mixture. Soak for a few minutes.
- Preheat an oven to 400°F (204°C) and line a baking tray with aluminum foil.
- Once the oven is ready, take the squids out of the marinade and transfer to the almond flour.
- Shake the squids several times until the squids are completely coated with flour.
- Transfer the coated squids to the prepared baking tray and spread evenly.
- Bake the squids for approximately 10 minutes then flip all of the squids.
- Bake again for another 10 minutes or until the squids is crispy and lightly golden brown.
- Remove the squids from the oven and transfer to a serving dish.
- Cut the avocado into halves then discard the seed.
- Scoop out the avocado flesh and mash until smooth and creamy.
- Add mayonnaise, pepper, tomato puree, and lemon juice to the avocado then mix until combined.
- Serve the baked squids with avocado lemon salsa.
- Enjoy!

Per Serving: Net Carbs: 5.4g; Calories: 390; Total Fat: 30.7g; Saturated Fat: 5.2g
Protein: 21.5g; Carbs: 9.6g; Fiber: 4.2g; Sugar: 0.6g - Fat 71% / Protein 23% / Carbs 6%

Tuna Steak with Cauliflower Cheesy Sauce

Serves: 3 / Preparation time: 5 minutes / Cooking time: 8 minutes

1 lb. tuna steak

½ teaspoon salt

½ teaspoon pepper

1-tablespoon olive oil

3 tablespoons butter

2 teaspoons minced garlic

1-cup cauliflower florets

½ cup vegetable broth

¾ cup grated cheddar cheese

- Season the tuna with salt and pepper then place in a disposable aluminum pan.
- Preheat an Air Fryer to 350°F (177°C) and place a rack in it.
- Wait until the Air Fryer reaches the desired temperature then place the aluminum pan on it.
- Spray the tuna with olive oil then cook for 8 minutes.
- Meanwhile, preheat a saucepan over medium heat then melt butter in it.
- Stir in minced garlic and cauliflower florets then sauté until wilted.
- Pour vegetable broth into the saucepan and add cheese to it. Bring to a simmer.
- Remove the sauce from heat then let it cool.
- Using an immersion blender blend the sauce until smooth and creamy.
- When the tuna is done, remove from the Air Fryer then place on a serving dish.
- Serve with cauliflower cheesy sauce then enjoy right away.

Per Serving: Net Carbs: 2.1g; Calories: 344; Total Fat: 30.7g; Saturated Fat: 14.7g
Protein: 15.5g; Carbs: 3.1g; Fiber: 1g; Sugar: 1.1g - Fat 80% / Protein 18% / Carbs 2%

Baked Oyster in Spicy Sauce [FA] [GF]

Serves: 4 / Preparation time: 15 minutes / Cooking time: 10 minutes

2 lbs. oyster

¼ cup red chilies

2 tablespoons extra virgin olive oil

¼ cup butter

¼ cup chopped fresh basils

- Preheat an oven to 350°F (177°C) and line a baking tray with parchment paper.
- Spread chopped fresh basils on the baking tray then set aside.
- Place butter in a microwave-safe bowl then microwave until melted. Let it cool.
- Place red chilies in a food processor then pour olive oil into it. Process until smooth.
- Add red chili mixture to the melted butter then stir well.
- Next, rub the oyster with red chili mixture then spread on the prepared baking tray with basils.
- Bake the oyster for approximately 3 minutes or until tender.
- Once it is done, remove from the oven and transfer to a serving dish.
- Serve and enjoy warm.

Per Serving: Net Carbs: 6.7g: Calories: 277; Total Fat: 22.3g; Saturated Fat: 9.3g; Protein: 12.4g; Carbs: 7.4g; Fiber: 0.7g; Sugar: 2.3g - Fat 72% / Protein 18% / Carbs 10%

Green Spaghetti with Cheesy White Prawn Sauce

Serves: 4 / Preparation time: 4 minutes / Cooking time: 16 minutes

½ lb. fresh prawns

2 tablespoons extra virgin olive oil

¾ cup diced onion

1 cup almond milk

1 cup diced cheddar cheese

1 tablespoon almond flour

3 medium zucchinis

2 tablespoons lemon juice

¼ teaspoon pepper

- Peel the zucchinis then discard the seeds.
- Using a julienne peeler cut the zucchinis into noodles form then place in a bowl.
- Drizzle lemon juice and sprinkle pepper over the zucchinis noodles then set aside.
- Next, preheat a saucepan over medium heat then pour olive oil into it.
- Once it is hot, stir in diced onion and sauté until wilted and aromatic.
- Add prawn to the saucepan and cook for a few minutes or until the prawns turn to pink.
- Combine almond flour with almond milk then pour into the saucepan.
- Stir in cheddar cheese and cook for a few minutes or until the cheese is melted. Remove from heat.
- Drizzle the cheese prawn sauce over the zucchini noodles then mix well.
- Serve and enjoy immediately.

Per Serving: Net Carbs: 6.5g; Calories: 407; Total Fat: 31.9g; Saturated Fat: 20g
Protein: 22.5g; Carbs: 9.9g; Fiber: 3.4g; Sugar: 4.7g - Fat 71% / Protein 23% / Carbs 6%

Jalapeno Salmon Stew [FA] [GF]

Serves: 2 / Preparation time: 5 minutes / Cooking time: 5 minutes

1 lb. salmon fillet

2 tablespoons lemon juice

½ teaspoon salt

½ teaspoon pepper

2 tablespoons chopped jalapenos

2 teaspoons minced garlic

2 tablespoons extra virgin olive oil

2 tablespoons chopped parsley

1-teaspoon paprika

½ teaspoon cumin

¼ cup chicken broth

¼ cup coconut milk

- Splash lemon juice over the salmon fillet then let it sit for 5 minutes.
- Pour olive oil into the Instant Pot then press "Sauté" button.
- Stir in minced garlic to the Instant Pot then sauté until aromatic.
- Next, add salmon fillet to the Instant Pot then sauté until wilted. Press the "Cancel" button.
- Pour chicken broth and coconut milk into the Instant Pot then season with salt, pepper, chopped jalapenos, chopped parsley, paprika, and cumin. Stir well.
- Put the lid on and seal the Instant Pot properly.
- Select "Manual" setting and cook the salmon on high for 5 minutes.
- Once it is done, naturally release the Instant Pot then open the lid.
- Transfer the salmon stew to a serving dish then serve.
- Enjoy warm.

Per Serving: Net Carbs: 3.4g; Calories: 484; Total Fat: 38.4g; Saturated Fat: 11.6g; Protein: 32.2g; Carbs: 5.3g; Fiber: 1.9g; Sugar: 2.1g - Fat 71% / Protein 25% / Carbs 4%

Spicy Salmon Fritter [FA] [GF]

Serves: 4 / Preparation time: 5 minutes / Cooking time: 20 minutes

¾ lb. salmon fillet

2 tablespoons almond flour

1 egg

1-½ teaspoons coriander

¼ teaspoon salt

½ teaspoon pepper

¼ teaspoon nutmeg

2 tablespoons grated cheddar cheese

½ cup butter

- Cut the salmon fillet into cubes then place in a food processor.
- Add coriander, salt, pepper, nutmeg, cheese, and egg then process until smooth.
- Shape the salmon mixture into medium fritters then set aside.
- Drop butter at some places in the Instant Pot then arrange the salmon fritter on it.
- Put the lid on and seal the Instant Pot properly.
- Select "Manual" setting and cook the salmon fritters on high for 5 minutes.
- Once it is done, quickly release the Instant Pot then open the lid.
- Take the salmon fritters out of the Instant Pot then arrange on a serving dish.
- Serve and enjoy.

Per Serving: Net Carbs: 0.2g; Calories: 338; Total Fat: 28.1g; Saturated Fat: 12.5g; Protein: 21.8g; Carbs: 0.3g; Fiber: 0.1g; Sugar: 0.1g - Fat 75% / Protein 24% / Carbs 1%

Squid Tomato Soup with Oregano

Serves: 4 / Preparation time: 4 minutes / Cooking time: 22 minutes

¾ lb. fresh squid

2 tablespoons extra virgin olive oil

½ lb. red tomatoes

2 cups water

½ cup coconut milk

½ cup chopped onion

2 teaspoons minced garlic

1-tablespoon lemon juice

1-teaspoon oregano

2 cups chopped collard green

- Place the red tomatoes in a blender then pour water into it. Blend until smooth then set aside.
- Remove the squid ink then cut into rings. Set aside.
- Preheat a skillet over medium heat then pour extra virgin olive oil into the skillet.
- Once the oil is hot, stir in chopped onion and minced garlic then sauté until wilted and aromatic.
- Next, add squids to the skillet then sauté until just wilted.
- After that, pour the tomato mixture to the skillet then season with oregano. Bring to boil.
- Once it is boiled, stir in collard green and pour coconut milk into the skillet. Bring to a simmer.
- Once it is done, remove from heat and transfer to a serving bowl.
- Drizzle lemon juice over the soup then serve warm.
- Enjoy immediately.

Per Serving: Net Carbs: 7g; Calories: 283; Total Fat: 22.6g; Saturated Fat: 11.3g
Protein: 13.3g; Carbs: 9.8g; Fiber: 2.8g; Sugar: 3.5g - Fat 72% / Protein 18% / Carbs 10%

Salmon Croquettes with Avocado Garlic

Serves: 4 / Preparation time: 15 minutes / Cooking time: 12 minutes

½ lb. salmon fillet

2 egg yolks

¼ cup chopped celeries

1 ripe avocado

¼ cup chopped onion

1 ½ teaspoons Worcestershire sauce

½ tablespoon dill

½ cup grated cheddar cheese

2 teaspoons minced garlic

2 teaspoons mustard

1-teaspoon extra virgin olive oil

1 tablespoon lemon juice

¾ cup mayonnaise

- Cut salmon fillet into cubes then place in a food processor.
- Add egg yolks, chopped celeries, chopped onion, dill, and minced garlic then process until smooth.
- Shape the salmon mixture into several small balls forms then set aside.
- Preheat an Air Fryer to 375°F (191°C) and place a rack in it.
- Wait until the Air Fryer is ready then arrange the salmon balls on the rack.
- Spray olive oil over the salmon balls and cook. Set the time to 12 minutes.
- While waiting for the salmon balls, cut the avocado into halves then discard the seed.
- Scoop out the avocado flesh then place it in a bowl.
- Using a fork, mash the avocado until smooth then pour mayonnaise, Worcestershire sauce, and lemon juice over the avocado.
- Season with mustard then stir until combined.
- Once the salmon balls are ready, arrange on a serving dish then drizzle avocado mayo over the salmon balls.
- Sprinkle grated cheddar cheese on top then serve.
- Enjoy right away.

Per Serving: Net Carbs: 3g; Calories: 332; Total Fat: 29.8g; Saturated Fat: 6.7g
Protein: 11.7g; Carbs: 5.6g; Fiber: 2.6g; Sugar: 1.6g - Fat 81% / Protein 14% / Carbs 5%

Coconut Crab Cakes with Green Leaves

Serves: 4 / Preparation time: 11 minutes / Cooking time: 16 minutes

¼ lb. crabmeat

2 eggs

½ teaspoon pepper

1 cup chopped spinach

3 teaspoons minced garlic

¼ cup chopped leek

½ cup coconut flakes

½ cup extra virgin olive oil, to fry

- Combine crabmeat with coconut flakes, eggs, chopped spinach, and chopped leek then season with pepper and minced garlic. Mix well.
- Shape the mixture into medium fritter forms then set aside.
- Next, preheat a frying pan over medium heat then pour extra virgin olive oil into the frying pan.
- Once the oil is done, put the crab fritter into the frying pan and fry for approximately 3 minutes.
- Flip the fritters then fry for another 3 minutes or until set and both sides of the fritters are lightly golden brown.
- Remove from the frying pan and strain the excessive oil.
- Once it is done, arrange the crab cakes on a serving dish then enjoy with sautéed veggie, as you desired.

Per Serving: Net Carbs: 2.1g; Calories: 313; Total Fat: 31.3g; Saturated Fat: 7.2g
Protein: 6.9g; Carbs: 3.3g; Fiber: 1.2g; Sugar: 1g - Fat 90% / Protein 7% / Carbs 3%

Refreshing Fish Soup [FA] [GF]

Serves: 4 / Preparation time: 5 minutes / Cooking time: 15 minutes

1 lb. fish fillet

½ cup water

1-½ cups coconut milk

½ teaspoon ginger

2 teaspoons minced garlic

¼ cup chopped onion

1 kaffir lime leaves

1 lemon grass

½ teaspoon pepper

1-teaspoon salt

1 medium zucchini

- Pour water and coconut milk into a pot then season with ginger, minced garlic, chopped onion, kaffir lime leaves, lemon grass, salt, and pepper. Bring to boil.
- Once it is boiled, reduce the heat and stir in the fish fillet. Bring to a simmer.
- When the fish is done, remove from heat then transfer to a serving bowl.
- Peel the zucchini then cut into thin slices.
- Sprinkle sliced zucchini over the soup then serve.
- Enjoy warm!

Per Serving: Net Carbs: 5.2g: Calories: 444; Total Fat: 40.9g; Saturated Fat: 19g; Protein: 15.4g; Carbs: 7.5g; Fiber: 2.3g; Sugar: 3.3g - Fat 83% / Protein 12% / Carbs 5%

Roasted Carrots

Total Time: 45 minutes - Serves: 6

Ingredients:

- 16 small carrots
- 1 tbsp fresh parsley, chopped
- 1 tbsp dried basil

- 6 garlic cloves, minced
- 4 tbsp olive oil
- 1 1/2 tsp salt

Directions:

- Preheat the oven to 375 F/ 190 C.
- In a bowl, combine together oil, carrots, basil, garlic, and salt.
- Spread the carrots onto a baking tray and bake in preheated oven for 35 minutes.
- Garnish with parsley and serve.

Nutritional Value (Amount per Serving): Calories 139; Fat 9.4 g; Carbohydrates 14.2 g; Sugar 6.6 g; Protein 1.3 g; Cholesterol 0 mg;

Crunchy Coconut Crab Cakes [FA] [GF]

Serves: 4 / Preparation time: 10 minutes / Cooking time: 5 minutes

1-½ lbs. crab meat

1 egg

½ cup grated coconut

½ cup butter

½ cup chopped onion

½ teaspoon salt

½ teaspoon black pepper

- Place crabmeat, egg, and grated coconut in a food processor then process until smooth.
- Shape the crab mixture into medium patties forms then set aside.

- Place butter in the Instant Pot then press "Sauté" button.
- Once the butter is melted, stir in chopped onion and sauté until translucent and aromatic. Press the "Cancel" button.
- Season with salt and pepper then slowly add the crab cakes in the Instant Pot.
- Put the lid on and seal the Instant Pot properly.
- Select "Manual" setting then cook the crab cakes on high for 5 minutes.
- Once it is done, naturally release the Instant Pot then open the lid.
- Take the crab cake out of the Instant Pot then arrange on a serving dish.
- Drizzle the liquid over the crab cakes then serve.
- Enjoy!

Per Serving: Net Carbs: 3.9g; Calories: 362; Total Fat: 29.5g; Saturated Fat: 17.9g; Protein: 16.3g; Carbs: 5.2g; Fiber: 1.3g; Sugar: 1.3g - Fat 73% / Protein 18% / Carbs 9%

Zucchini Salmon Clear Soup

Serves: 4 / Preparation time: 6 minutes / Cooking time: 11 minutes

1 lb. salmon fillet	½ teaspoon basil
3 tablespoons extra virgin olive oil	½ teaspoon oregano
1-teaspoon minced garlic	½ teaspoon ginger
3 cups water	1 cup chopped zucchini
½ teaspoon pepper	

- Cut the salmon fillet into cubes then set aside.
- Preheat a skillet over medium heat then pour extra virgin olive oil into it.
- Once the oil is hot, put the salmon cubes into the skillet then fry for a few minutes or until the salmon is lightly golden brown.
- Remove the salmon from the skillet then set aside.
- Stir in minced garlic and sauté until aromatic.
- Next, pour water into the skillet then season with pepper, basil, oregano, and ginger. Bring to boil.
- Once it is boiled, add chopped zucchini and fried salmon to the gravy and cook for approximately 2 minutes.
- Transfer the soup to a serving bowl then serve warm.
- Enjoy immediately.

Per Serving: Net Carbs: 0.8g; Calories: 276 Total Fat: 21.6g; Saturated Fat: 3.5g
Protein: 20.3g; Carbs: 1.2 g; Fiber: 0.4g; Sugar: 0.3g - Fat 70% / Protein 29% / Carbs 1%

Sour Shredded Tuna Garlic [FA] [GF]

Serves: 6 / Preparation time: 5 minutes / Cooking time: 5 minutes

1 lb. tuna fillet	2 tablespoons butter
2 teaspoons oregano	1-½ cups low sodium chicken broth
1-teaspoon basil	3 tablespoons lemon juice
2 tablespoons minced garlic	½ cup heavy cream

- Cut the tuna into small chunks then set aside.
- Place butter in the inner pot of an Instant Pot then press the "Sauté" button.
- Add tuna and minced garlic to the Instant Pot then sauté until aromatic and the pork is brown.
- Next, pour chicken broth into the Instant Pot then add basil to the pot.
- Put the lid on then seal the Instant Pot properly. Close the steam valve.
- Select "Manual" setting on the Instant Pot then cook the chicken on high for 5 minutes.
- Once it is done, quick release the Instant Pot then open the lid.
- Take the cooked tuna out of the Instant Pot and arrange on a serving dish. Leave the liquid in the Instant Pot.
- Pour lemon juice and heavy cream into the Instant Pot then stir well.
- Drizzle the liquid over the cooked tuna then serve.
- Enjoy immediately.

Per Serving: Net Carbs: 1.6g; Calories: 351; Total Fat: 30.9g; Saturated Fat: 4.8g; Protein: 16.6g; Carbs: 1.9g; Fiber: 0.3g; Sugar: 0.2g - Fat 79% / Protein 19% / Carbs 2%

Buttered Scallops with Thyme

Serves: 2 / Preparation time: 10 minutes / Cooking time: 7 minutes

1 lb. scallops

½ tablespoon butter

½ cup chopped fresh thyme

¼ teaspoon salt

½ teaspoon pepper

- Remove the shells of the scallops then wash and rinse them.
- Season the scallops with salt and pepper then set aside.
- Drop butter on several places in a disposable aluminum pan then sprinkle thyme on it.
- Arrange the scallops on the thyme then set aside.
- Preheat an Air Fryer to 400°F (204°C) and place a rack in the Air Fryer.
- Set the time to 7 minutes then cook the scallops.
- Once the scallops are done, remove from the Air Fryer then transfer to a serving dish together with the liquid and thyme.
- Serve and enjoy.

Per Serving: Net Carbs: 4.1g; Calories: 264; Total Fat: 24.2g; Saturated Fat: 14.9g
Protein: 6.4g; Carbs: 8.7g; Fiber: 4.6g; Sugar: 0.2g - Fat 83% / Protein 10% / Carbs 7%

Tomato Creamy Tuna with Sautéed Broccoli and Cauliflower

Serves: 4 / Preparation time: 3 minutes / Cooking time: 13 minutes

½ lb. tuna fillet

3 tablespoons extra virgin olive oil

½ cup chopped onion

1-cup tomato puree

½ teaspoon pepper

½ teaspoon oregano

1-cup broccoli florets

1-cup cauliflower florets

2 tablespoons almond butter

- Preheat a skillet over medium heat then pour olive oil into it.
- Once the oil is hot, put the tuna into the skillet and fry until the tuna is lightly golden brown.
- Remove the tuna from the skillet then set aside.

- Next, stir in chopped onion and sauté until lightly golden brown and aromatic.

- After that, pour tomato puree into the skillet and season with pepper and oregano.

- Bring to a simmer then add fried tuna to the skillet. Stir well and cook for approximately 2 minutes.

- In the meantime, preheat a saucepan over medium heat then add almond butter to the saucepan.

- Stir in broccoli florets and cauliflower florets to the saucepan then sauté until aromatic. Cook until the vegetables are tender but still crunchy.

- Once everything is done, transfer the tuna to a serving dish together with the gravy and serve with sautéed broccoli and cauliflower.

- Enjoy!

Per Serving: Net Carbs: 4.4g; Calories: 392 Total Fat: 34.5g; Saturated Fat: 1.9g
Protein: 16.5g; Carbs: 7g; Fiber: 2.6g; Sugar: 2g - Fat 79% / Protein 83% / Carbs 4%

Super Black Squids Tender [FA] [GF] [SF]

Serves: 4 / Preparation time: 5 minutes / Cooking time: 15 minutes

1 lb. fresh squids	¼ teaspoon salt
1-tablespoon minced garlic	2 kaffir lime leaves
1-teaspoon coriander	½ cup butter

- Place the squids in a skillet. Do not remove the ink.
- Add minced garlic, coriander, salt, and kaffir lime leaves to the skillet then cover the skillet with the lid.
- Cook the squids over very low heat for approximately 15 minutes or until tender.
- Once it is tender, add butter to the skillet then sauté until the squids are completely coated with butter.
- Transfer to serving dish then serve.
- Enjoy warm.

Per Serving: Net Carbs: 5.5g: Calories: 309; Total Fat: 24.5g; Saturated Fat: 15g; Protein: 16.9g; Carbs: 5.5g; Fiber: 0g; Sugar: 0g - Fat 71% / Protein 22% / Carbs 7%

Spicy and Savory Prawn Garlic

Serves: 4 / Preparation time: 5 minutes / Cooking time: 5 minutes

20 fresh large prawns	¼ teaspoon salt
2 teaspoons chili powder	2 tablespoons extra virgin olive oil
2 teaspoons black pepper	1-cup mayonnaise
2 tablespoons red chili flakes	1 tablespoon lemon juice
2 tablespoons minced garlic	¼ cup chopped parsley

- Wash and clean the prawns then season with chili, black pepper, minced garlic, and salt.
- Preheat an Air Fryer to 400°F (204°C) and place a rack in the Air Fryer.
- Place the seasoned prawns on the rack then sprinkle red chili flakes on top.
- Cook the prawns and set the time to 5 minutes.
- In the meantime, combine mayonnaise with lemon juice and chopped parsley then mix well.
- Serve the fried prawns with mayonnaise.
- Enjoy!

Per Serving: Net Carbs: 4.8g; Calories: 319; Total Fat: 27.1g; Saturated Fat: 4.3g
Protein: 13g; Carbs: 6.1g; Fiber: 1.3g; Sugar: 2.4 g - Fat 76% / Protein 16% / Carbs 8%

Salmon Lemon Black Pepper with Roasted Kale Garlic

Serves: 4 / Preparation time: 6 minutes / Cooking time: 41 minutes

¾ lb. salmon fillet	2 fresh lemons
6 tablespoons extra virgin olive	3 cups chopped kale
1-teaspoon black pepper	3 teaspoons minced garlic

- Preheat an oven to 400°F (204°C) and prepare 2 disposable aluminum pans.
- Cut the lemons into thin slices then arrange a half of the salmon slices on the bottom of the prepared aluminum pan.
- Brush the salmon fillet with olive oil then place on the lemon slices in the aluminum pan.
- Sprinkle black pepper over the salmon then cover the salmon with the remaining lemon slices.
- Place the salmon in the oven and bake for approximately 30 minutes or until the salmon is opaque and cooked through.
- In the meantime, place the chopped kale in another aluminum pan then drizzle the remaining olive oil over the kale.
- Season the kale with minced garlic and toss to combine.
- Once the salmon is done, remove it from the oven and put kale in it.
- Roast the kale for approximately 7 minutes or until done.
- Remove the kale from the oven and transfer to a serving dish together with the salmon.
- Serve and enjoy.

Per Serving: Net Carbs: 5.7g; Calories: 479; Total Fat: 37.6g; Saturated Fat: 6g
Protein: 31.5g; Carbs: 7.2g; Fiber: 1.5g; Sugar: 0.8g - Fat 71% / Protein 24% / Carbs 5%

Lemon Grass Savory Fish Satay [FA] [GF]

Serves: 4 / Preparation time: 10 minutes / Cooking time: 15 minutes

1 lb. salmon fillet	1 candlenut
½ cup grated coconut	1-teaspoon cayenne
3 teaspoons minced garlic	8 lemon grasses
½ teaspoon turmeric	2 tablespoons extra virgin olive oil
½ teaspoon salt	2 tablespoons butter

- Cut salmon fillet into cubes then place in a food processor.
- Add grated coconut together with minced garlic, cayenne, candlenut, turmeric, and salt then process until smooth.
- Transfer the fish mixture to a bowl then drizzle olive oil over the fish. Mix well.
- Take a lemon grass and cover with the fish mixture, like satay. Repeat with the remaining lemon grasses and fish mixture.
- Next, preheat a steamer and steam the fish satay for 10 minutes or until set. Take them out of the steamer.

- After that, preheat a pan over medium heat then place butter in it.
- Once the butter is melted, fry the fish satay until just lightly golden brown on both sides then arrange on a serving dish.
- Serve and enjoy warm.

Per Serving: Net Carbs: 4.8g: Calories: 399; Total Fat: 32.7g; Saturated Fat: 12.8g; Protein: 21.6g; Carbs: 7.2g; Fiber: 2.4g; Sugar: 1.5g - Fat 74% / Protein 21% / Carbs 5%

Lobster Tails with Dill and Butter Sauce [FA] [GF]

Serves: 4 / Preparation time: 5 minutes / Cooking time: 10 minutes

1 lb. lobster tails	2 teaspoons minced garlic
½ teaspoon salt	2 tablespoons lemon juice
½ teaspoon pepper	1-teaspoon dill

1-cup butter

- Pour water into an Instant Pot then place a trivet in it.
- Arrange the lobster tails on the trivet then sprinkle salt and pepper over the lobster.
- Put the lid on and seal the Instant Pot properly.
- Select "Manual" setting and cook the lobster on high for 5 minutes.
- Once it is done, naturally release the Instant Pot then open the lid.
- Transfer the cooked lobster to a serving dish then set aside.
- Clean the Instant Pot then place butter in it.
- Select "Sauté" setting and stir in minced garlic. Sauté until aromatic.
- Add lemon juice and dill to the Instant Pot then stir well. Press the "Cancel" button.
- Drizzle the sauce over the lobster then serve.
- Enjoy!

Per Serving: Net Carbs: 0.8g; Calories: 514; Total Fat: 47.1g; Saturated Fat: 29.5g; Protein: 22.3g; Carbs: 1g; Fiber: 0.2g; Sugar: 0.2g - Fat 82% / Protein 17% / Carbs 1%

Fish Balls with Chives and Lemon Garlic Creamy Sauce

Serves: 4 / Preparation time: 6 minutes / Cooking time: 24 minutes

½ lb. fish fillet	1 egg
4 tablespoons extra virgin olive oil	2-tablespoon coconut flour
½ cup chopped onion	2 tablespoons lemon juice
4 teaspoons minced garlic	1 ½ cups coconut milk

½ cup chives

- Preheat a skillet over medium heat then pour 2 tablespoons of extra virgin olive oil into it.
- Once it is hot, stir in chopped onion and sauté until wilted and aromatic. Remove from heat.
- Preheat an oven to 350°F (177°C) and line a baking tray with aluminum foil. Set aside.
- Cut the fish fillet into cubes then place in a food processor.
- Add sautéed onion, ¼ cup chives, egg, and a tablespoon of coconut flour to the food processor then process until smooth.
- Shape the mixture into small balls form then arrange on the prepared baking tray.

- Place the baking tray in the oven and bake the fish balls for approximately 20 minutes or until the fish balls are set.
- In the meantime, preheat a saucepan over medium heat then pour the remaining extra virgin olive oil into it.
- Once it is hot, stir in minced garlic to the saucepan and sauté until wilted and aromatic.
- Combine the remaining coconut flour into coconut milk then stir until incorporated.
- Pour into the saucepan then bring to a simmer.
- Once it is done, remove from heat and drizzle lemon juice on top. Stir well.
- When the fish balls are done, remove from the oven and transfer to a serving dish.
- Drizzle the sauce over the fish balls then serve.
- Enjoy warm.

Per Serving: Net Carbs: 6.8g; Calories: 476; Total Fat: 37.7g; Saturated Fat: 22.4g
Protein: 25g; Carbs: 11.8g; Fiber: 5g; Sugar: 4.5g - Fat 71% / Protein 23% / Carbs 6%

Steamed Mackerel Tomato Chili [FA] [GF]

Serves: 4 / Preparation time: 5 minutes / Cooking time: 10 minutes

1 lb. fresh mackerel	¼ cup red chilies
¼ cup extra virgin olive oil	½ cup chopped red tomatoes
2 cloves garlic	1-cup fresh basil
3 shallots	

- Pour olive oil into the Instant Pot then press "Sauté" button.
- Add fresh mackerel to the Instant Pot then sauté until aromatic. Press the "Cancel" button.
- Take the mackerel out of the Instant Pot then place on a plate.
- Next, place garlic, shallots, red chilies and tomatoes in a food processor then process until smooth.
- Spread basils in a disposable aluminum pan then arrange the mackerel on it.
- Pour the spice mixture over the mackerel then set aside.
- Pour water into the Instant Pot then place a trivet in it.
- Place the aluminum pan on the trivet then close and seal the Instant Pot properly.
- Select "Manual" setting and cook the mackerel on high for 5 minutes.
- Once it is done, naturally release the Instant Pot then open the lid.
- Take the aluminum pan out of the Instant Pot then transfer to a serving dish.
- Serve and enjoy.

Per Serving: Net Carbs: 6.7g; Calories: 491; Total Fat: 41.5g; Saturated Fat: 5.6g; Protein: 22.8g; Carbs: 8.8g; Fiber: 2.1g; Sugar: 3.2g - Fat 76% / Protein 19% / Carbs 5%

Cheesy Salmon Bombs [FA] [GF]

Serves: 8 / Preparation time: 10 minutes / Cooking time: 5 minutes

1-½ lbs. salmon fillet	¼ cup cheddar cheese cubes
¾ cup coconut milk	½ cup almond flour
1 egg	½ teaspoon salt

½ teaspoon mustard

½ teaspoon pepper

2 teaspoons minced garlic

1-cup heavy cream

¼ cup cream cheese

2 tablespoons butter

1-tablespoon grated Parmesan cheese

- Cut the salmon fillet into cubes then place in a food processor.
- Pour coconut milk over the salmon then add egg and almond flour to the food processor.
- Season the salmon with salt, mustard, pepper, and minced garlic then process until smooth.
- Shape the mixture into medium balls and fill each ball with cheddar cheese cubes. Set aside.
- Pour water into the Instant Pot then place a trivet in it.
- Arrange the salmon balls on the trivet then close and seal the Instant Pot. Close the steam valve.
- Select "Manual" setting then cook the meatloaf on high for 5 minutes.
- Once it is done, naturally release the Instant Pot then open the lid.
- Remove the salmon balls from the Instant Pot then arrange on a serving dish.
- Clean the Instant Pot then place butter in it.
- Press the "Sauté" button then cook until the butter is melted. Press the "Cancel" button.
- Quickly add heavy cream into the Instant Pot together with cream cheese and grated Parmesan cheese then stir well.
- Pour the cheese sauce over the salmon balls then serve.
- Enjoy immediately.

Per Serving: Net Carbs: 2g; Calories: 352; Total Fat: 27.4g; Saturated Fat: 14.7g; Protein: 22.7g; Carbs: 2.8g; Fiber: 0.8g; Sugar: 0.9g - Fat 70% / Protein 25% / Carbs 5%

Steamed Prawn and Veggie Bags

Serves: 4 / Preparation time: 6 minutes / Cooking time: 41 minutes

2 lbs. fresh shrimps

¼ cup diced carrot

¼ cup chopped leek

½ cup diced onion

4 tablespoons extra virgin olive oil

¼ cup coconut milk

2 eggs

¼ cup grated cheddar cheese

1 cup almond flour

½ cup water

- Combine almond flour with water then add an egg into the mixture. Stir until mixture.
- Make several omelets with this mixture then set aside.
- Peel the prawns and remove the head.
- Place the prawns in the food processor then process until smooth. Set aside.
- Next, preheat a skillet over medium heat then pour 2 tablespoons of olive oil into it.
- Once it is hot, stir in chopped onion and sauté until lightly golden brown and aromatic.
- Add carrot and leek to the skillet then pour coconut milk over the veggies. Cook until the coconut milk is completely absorbed into the veggies.
- Place the smooth prawn, sautéed veggies, and the remaining eggs in a bowl then mix until combined.
- Place an omelet on a flat surface then drop a tablespoon of prawn mixture on it.
- Fold like an envelope then set aside. Repeat with the remaining omelets and prawn mixture.

- Next, preheat a saucepan over medium heat then pour the remaining olive oil into it.
- Once the oil is hot, slowly put the prawn envelopes in the saucepan and cook for approximately 2 minutes.
- Flip them and cook for another 2 minutes or until both sides are lightly golden brown.
- Remove from the saucepan and arrange on a serving dish.
- Serve and enjoy warm.

Per Serving: Net Carbs: 3.7g; Calories: 315; Total Fat: 26g; Saturated Fat: 7.8g
Protein: 16.8g; Carbs: 5.4g; Fiber: 1.7g; Sugar: 2.1g - Fat 74% / Protein 21% / Carbs 5%

Scallops with Lemon Parsley Butter

Serves: 4 / Preparation time: 60 minutes / Cooking time: 5 minutes

1 lb. scallops	1 ½ tablespoons extra virgin olive oil
1 tablespoon lemon juice	¼ cup chopped parsley
¼ teaspoon salt	½ cup butter
¼ teaspoon pepper	½ teaspoon grated lemon zest

- Wash scallops then pat them dry.
- Splash lemon juice over the scallops then season with salt and pepper.
- Marinate the scallops for an hour and store in the refrigerator to keep them fresh.
- After an hour, remove the scallops from the refrigerator then thaw at room temperature. Transfer the scallops to an aluminum pan.
- Preheat an Air Fryer to 400°F (204°C) and place a rack in it.
- Place the aluminum pan with scallops on the rack then cook for 5 minutes.
- Remove the scallops from the Air Fryer then transfer to a serving dish.
- Melt butter in a saucepan then remove from heat.
- Add chopped parsley and grated lemon zest then stir until thickened.
- Drizzle the butter over the scallops then serve.
- Enjoy right away.

Per Serving: Net Carbs: 1.8g; Calories: 307; Total Fat: 28.8g; Saturated Fat: 15.4g
Protein: 11.1g; Carbs: 2g; Fiber: 0.2g; Sugar: 0.1g - Fat 84% / Protein 14% / Carbs 2%

Shrimp in Nutty Coconut Turmeric Gravy [FA] [GF]

Serves: 4 / Preparation time: 8 minutes / Cooking time: 3 minutes

1 lb. fresh shrimps	¼ teaspoon salt
1-tablespoon extra virgin olive oil	½ teaspoon cayenne pepper
2 teaspoons minced garlic	¾ cup coconut milk
½ teaspoon turmeric	¼ cup roasted pecans

- Place roasted pecans in a blender then pour coconut milk over the pecans. Blend until incorporated then set aside.
- Pour olive oil into an Instant Pot then select "Sauté" setting.
- Stir in minced garlic to the Instant Pot then sauté until aromatic and lightly golden. Press the "Cancel" button.

- Add fresh shrimps together with turmeric, salt, and pepper then pour the coconut milk mixture over the shrimps.
- Close and seal the Instant Pot properly then select "Manual" setting. Cook the shrimps on low for 3 minutes.
- Once it is done, quick release the Instant Pot then open the lid.
- Transfer the shrimps and the gravy to a serving dish and serve.
- Enjoy!

Per Serving: Net Carbs: 3.2g; Calories: 408; Total Fat: 35.3g; Saturated Fat: 11.8 g; Protein: 21.9g; Carbs: 7.1g; Fiber: 3.8g; Sugar: 2.7g - Fat 78% / Protein 21% / Carbs 1%

Steamed Prawns with Green Basils and Light Spinach Soup

Serves: 4 / Preparation time: 6 minutes / Cooking time: 14 minutes

1 lb. fresh prawns	½ cup grated coconut
2 teaspoons minced garlic	1-cup coconut milk
¼ cup red chili flakes	2 cups chopped spinach
½ cup chopped tomatoes	2 teaspoons sliced shallots
2 lemongrasses	1-½ cups water
1-cup fresh basils	

- Season the coconut milk with red chili flakes and minced garlic then stir well. Set aside.
- Preheat a steamer over medium heat then prepare a disposable aluminum pan.
- Combine the prawn with chopped tomatoes, lemon grasses, fresh basils, and grated coconut then stir well.
- Place the mixture in the prepared aluminum pan then spread evenly.
- Pour the coconut milk over the mixture then steam for approximately 15 minutes.
- In the meantime, pour water into a pot then bring to boil.
- Once it is boiled, stir in chopped spinach and season with sliced shallots. Stir well and remove from heat.
- When the steamed prawn is done, remove from the steamer and transfer to a serving dish.
- Serve with spinach soup.
- Enjoy.

Per Serving: Net Carbs: 3.3g; Calories: 231; Total Fat: 17.8g; Saturated Fat: 15.7g
Protein: 12.6g; Carbs: 7.7g; Fiber: 3g; Sugar: 3.6g - Fat 70% / Protein 24% / Carbs 6%

Hot and Spicy Steamed Squids [FA] [GF]

Serves: 4 / Preparation time: 5 minutes / Cooking time: 15 minutes

½ lb. fresh squids	2 medium red tomatoes
1-tablespoon minced garlic	½ teaspoon turmeric
2 tablespoons chopped shallots	1 bay leaf
½ cup red chilies	½ cup butter

- Remove the squid's ink then wash and rinse the squids.
- Fill each squid with butter then arrange on a disposable aluminum pan.

- Sprinkle minced garlic; chopped shallots, red chilies, diced tomatoes, turmeric, and bay leaf over the squids then place the disposable aluminum pan in a steamer.
- Steam the squids for approximately 20 minutes or until tender.
- Once it is done, remove the disposable aluminum pan from the steamer then transfer the steamed squids together with the spices to a serving dish.
- Serve and enjoy.

Per Serving: Net Carbs: 5.4g: Calories: 319; Total Fat: 24.7g; Saturated Fat: 15g; Protein: 17.5g; Carbs: 7.1g; Fiber: 0.7g; Sugar: 1.4g - Fat 70% / Protein 22% / Carbs 8%

Roasted Salmon with Cheesy Fennel Salads

Serves: 4 / Preparation time: 5 minutes / Cooking time: 12 minutes

1 ½ lbs. salmon fillet	½ cup Greek yogurt
3 teaspoons chopped parsley	½ cup cream cheese
1-½ teaspoon thyme	2 teaspoons minced garlic
½ teaspoon salt	2 tablespoons unsweetened orange juice
1-teaspoon extra virgin olive oil	1 ½ teaspoons lemon juice
1 cup sliced fennel	1-½ tablespoons chopped dill

- Combine chopped parsley with thyme and salt then mix well.
- Brush the salmon fillet with olive oil then sprinkle the parsley mixture over the salmon.
- Preheat an Air Fryer to 375°F (191°C).
- Place the seasoned salmon fillet in the Air Fryer basket the cook for 12 minutes.
- Meanwhile, place butter, cream cheese, and Greek yogurt in a mixing bowl.
- Using a hand mixer mix the ingredients until smooth and fluffy.
- Add minced garlic, lemon juice, orange juice, chopped dill, and sliced fennel to the mixture. Mix well.
- Once the salmon is done, remove from the Air Fryer then place on a serving dish.
- Serve salmon with the cheesy fennel salads then enjoy.

Per Serving: Net Carbs: 5.3g; Calories: 495; Total Fat: 41.1g; Saturated Fat: 21.9g
Protein: 25.7g; Carbs: 6.3g; Fiber: 1g; Sugar: 1.9g - Fat 75% / Protein 21% / Carbs 4%

Sautéed Spicy Squid with Green Chili [FA] [GF]

Serves: 4 / Preparation time: 5 minutes / Cooking time: 15 minutes

1 lb. fresh squids	½ cup green chili flakes
½ cup butter	1-inch galangal
1 tablespoon sliced garlic	2 bay leaves
1 tablespoon sliced shallots	¼ teaspoon salt

- Remove the squid's ink then cut the squids into rings. Set aside.
- Place butter in a skillet over medium heat then wait until melted.
- Stir in sliced garlic and shallot then sauté until lightly golden brown and aromatic.
- Next, add green chili flakes to the skillet then stir until wilted.
- Stir in squid rings to the skillet then season with salt, galangal, and bay leaves.
- Reduce the heat into very low and cook until the squids are tender. You don't need to add water to the skillet.

- Once it is done, remove the skillet from heat and transfer the cooked squids to a serving dish.
- Serve and enjoy.

Per Serving: Net Carbs: 5.3g: Calories: 311; Total Fat: 24.6g; Saturated Fat: 15g; Protein: 17,2g; Carbs: 5.6g; Fiber: 0.3g; Sugar: 0.5g - Fat 71% / Protein 22% / Carbs 7%

Green Chili Squid Black Pepper

Serves: 4 / Preparation time: 4 minutes / Cooking time: 16 minutes

½ lb. fresh squids	¼ cup chopped green chili
3 tablespoons extra virgin olive oil	½ cup coconut milk
2 teaspoons minced garlic	1-teaspoon coconut aminos
2 teaspoons sliced shallots	1-teaspoon black pepper

- Remove the squid ink and cut the squids into rings.
- Preheat a skillet over medium heat then pour extra virgin olive oil into the skillet.
- Once the oil is hot, stir in minced garlic and sliced shallots then sauté until wilted and aromatic.
- Next, add the squid to the skillet and sauté until just wilted.
- Pour coconut milk over the squids then cook until the liquid is completely absorbed into the squids.
- Add chopped green chili, coconut aminos, and black pepper to the skillet then stir until the squids are completely seasoned and cooked through.
- Remove the squids from heat and transfer to a serving dish.
- Serve and enjoy.

Per Serving: Net Carbs: 5.4g; Calories: 235; Total Fat: 18.7g; Saturated Fat: 8.1g
Protein: 11.9g; Carbs: 6.2g; Fiber: 0.8g; Sugar: 1.1g - Fat 72% / Protein 19% / Carbs 9%

Mussels Garlic Butter with Parsley [FA] [GF]

Serves: 2 / Preparation time: 5 minutes / Cooking time: 10 minutes

½ lb. mussels	1-cup chicken broth
¼ cup butter	1-cup chopped parsley
2 teaspoons minced garlic	

- Place butter in the Instant Pot then press "Sauté" button.
- Once the butter is melted, stir in minced garlic then sauté until aromatic. Press the "Cancel" button.
- Add mussels to the Instant Pot then pour chicken broth over the mussels.
- Sprinkle chopped parsley on top then close and seal the Instant Pot properly.
- Select "Manual" setting and cook the mussels for 5 minutes.
- Once it is done naturally release the Instant Pot then open the lid.
- Transfer the cooked mussels to a serving dish and serve.
- Enjoy!

Per Serving: Net Carbs: 6.4g; Calories: 436; Total Fat: 38g; Saturated Fat: 22.6g; Protein: 17.2g; Carbs: 7.5g; Fiber: 1.1g; Sugar: 0.7g - Fat 78% / Protein 16% / Carbs 6%

Cod Coconut Fritter

Serves: 8 / Preparation time: 10 minutes / Cooking time: 12 minutes

1 lb. cod fillet	1 tablespoon chopped parsley
¼ cup grated coconut	2 teaspoons minced garlic
½ cup grated cheddar cheese	2 teaspoons paprika
2 tablespoons lemon juice	¼ cup butter
¼ teaspoon grated lemon zest	½ cup mayonnaise

- Melt butter in a microwave then let it cool.
- Cut the cod fillet into cubes then place in a food processor.
- Add grated coconut to the food processor then season with lemon juice, grated lemon zest, chopped parsley, minced garlic, and paprika. Process until smooth.
- Add melted butter to the mixture then mix well.
- Shape the cod mixture into fritters form then let them sit.
- Preheat an Air Fryer to 380°F (191).
- Arrange the cod fritter in the Air Fryer then cook for 6 minutes.
- After 6 minutes, flip the fritter then cook again for another 6 minutes.
- Once it is done, remove from the Air Fryer then serve with mayonnaise.
- Enjoy!

Per Serving: Net Carbs: 3.5g; Calories: 348; Total Fat: 27.4g; Saturated Fat: 11.4g
Protein: 19.3g; Carbs: 9.7g; Fiber: 6.2g; Sugar: 1.9g - Fat 75% / Protein 16% / Carbs %

Crispy Prawn with Almond Cheesy Sauce

Serves: 4 / Preparation time: 11 minutes / Cooking time: 16 minutes

½ lb. fresh prawns	¼ cup extra virgin olive oil, to fry
1 egg	¼ cup chopped onion
½ teaspoon pepper	¼ cup water
1 cup almond flour	½ cup grated cheese

- Peel the prawns and remove the head.
- Crack the egg then place in a bowl.
- Season the egg with pepper then stir until incorporated.
- Dip the prawns in the egg then roll into the almond flour. Set aside.
- Preheat a frying pan over medium heat then pour extra virgin olive oil into it.
- Once the oil is hot, put the prawns in the frying pan and fry until the prawns are lightly golden brown.
- Remove the fried prawns from the frying pan and strain the excessive oil. Arrange on a serving dish.
- Take about 2 tablespoons of extra virgin olive oil then pour into a saucepan. Preheat it over medium heat.
- When the oil is hot, stir in chopped onion and sauté until wilted and aromatic.
- Pour water into the saucepan then add grated cheese to the saucepan. Bring to a simmer.
- Stir in 1 tablespoon of almond flour and stir until thick.
- Drizzle the cheese sauce over the fried prawns then serve.
- Enjoy!

174

Per Serving: Net Carbs: 2.4g; Calories: 291; Total Fat: 22.8g; Saturated Fat: 5.7g
Protein: 19.4g; Carbs: 3.3g; Fiber: 0.9g; Sugar: 0.7g - Fat 71% / Protein 26% / Carbs 3%

Spicy Tuna in a Cup [FA] [GF]

Serves: 8 / Preparation time: 10 minutes / Cooking time: 10 minutes

1 lb. tuna fillet	½ cup water
¼ cup butter	¼ cup grated cheddar cheese
½ cup chopped onion	4 eggs
¼ teaspoon salt	1 cup grated Mozzarella cheese
½ teaspoon pepper	2 tablespoons chopped parsley

- Cut the tuna into small chunks then set aside.
- Place butter in the Instant Pot then press the "Sauté" button.
- Stir in chopped onion then sauté until translucent and aromatic.
- Add tuna to the Instant Pot then season with salt and pepper.
- Pour water over the tuna then stir well.
- Put the lid on and seal the Instant Pot properly. Close the steam valve.
- Select "Pressure" setting and cook the tuna on high for 5 minutes.
- Once the Instant Pot beeps, quick release the Instant Pot and open the lid.
- Remove the tuna from the Instant Pot then transfer to a disposable aluminum pan.
- Add grated cheddar cheese to the tuna then stir well.
- Crack the eggs then beat until incorporated.
- Pour the egg over the tuna then sprinkle grated Mozzarella cheese and chopped parsley on top.
- Pour water into the Instant Pot then place a trivet in it.
- Place the disposable aluminum pan on the trivet then close and seal the Instant Pot.
- Select "Manual" setting and cook the casserole for 5 minutes.
- Once it is done, naturally release the Instant Pot then open the lid.
- Take the casserole out of the Instant Pot then serve.
- Enjoy!

Per Serving: Net Carbs: 1g; Calories: 314; Total Fat: 27.2g; Saturated Fat: 5.4g; Protein: 16.6g; Carbs: 1.2g; Fiber: 0.2g; Sugar: 0.5g - Fat 78% / Protein 21% / Carbs 1%

Hot Mackerel Chili

Serves: 2 / Preparation time: 5 minutes / Cooking time: 8 minutes

2 medium mackerels	2 tablespoons red chili flakes
1-tablespoon extra virgin olive oil	¼ teaspoon salt
1 teaspoon lemon juice	1-tablespoon butter
2 teaspoons minced garlic	

- Splash lemon juice over the mackerels then let it rest for about 5 minutes.
- Rub the mackerels with minced garlic, red chili flakes, and salt then set aside.
- Preheat an Air Fryer to 350°F (177°C).
- Once the Air Fryer is ready, place the seasoned mackerels in the Air Fryer then cook for 5 minutes.
- After 5 minutes, open the drawer and flip the mackerels. Cook again for another 5 minutes.

- Remove the cooked mackerels from the Air Fryer then place on a rack.
- Quickly brush the cooked mackerels with butter then serve.
- Enjoy!

Per Serving: Net Carbs: 0.5g; Calories: 413; Total Fat: 37.1g; Saturated Fat: 9.2g
Protein: 21g; Carbs: 0.7g; Fiber: 0.2g; Sugar: 0.4g - Fat 81% / Protein 18% / Carbs 1%

Fried Crab Garlic with Zucchini Pickles

Serves: 4 / Preparation time: 11 minutes / Cooking time: 26 minutes

4 soft shell crabs

4 tablespoons minced garlic

½ cup extra virgin olive oil

1 medium zucchini

½ cup chopped onion

2 teaspoons celery seeds

1-teaspoon turmeric

1-cup apple cider vinegar

- Cut the zucchini into thin slices then place in a jar with a lid.
- Add chopped onion, celery seeds, and turmeric to the jar then pour apple cider vinegar to the jar.
- Cover the jar with the lid and shake for a few seconds. Store the pickles in the refrigerator.
- Place the crabs in the pot then pour water to cover.
- Season with minced garlic then bring to boil.
- Once it is boiled, turn the stove off and cover the pot with the lid. Let it rest for approximately 5 minutes.
- After 5 minutes, open the pot and take the crabs out of the pot.
- Preheat a frying pan over medium heat then pour extra virgin olive oil into it.
- Once it is hot, put the crabs into the frying pan then fry until crispy.
- Once it is done, remove from the frying pan and transfer to a serving dish.
- Serve with zucchini pickles.

Per Serving: Net Carbs: 5.8g; Calories: 385; Total Fat: 29.4g; Saturated Fat: 4.1g
Protein: 21.5g; Carbs: 7.1g; Fiber: 1.3g; Sugar: 1.8g - Fat 70% / Protein 24% / Carbs 6%

Soft Lemon Crab Cakes

Serves: 8 / Preparation time: 15 minutes / Cooking time: 10 minutes

1 lb. crabmeat

2-½ tablespoons lemon juice

½ cup diced bell pepper

¼ cup chopped onion

1-cup mayonnaise

1 tablespoon yellow mustard

1 ½ teaspoons black pepper

1-½ tablespoons chopped parsley

1-¼ teaspoons garlic powder

¼ teaspoon cayenne pepper

2 tablespoons extra virgin olive oil

½ cup roasted walnuts

- Place the roasted walnuts in a food processor then process until smooth.
- Add crabmeat to the food processor then season with lemon juice, yellow mustard, black pepper, garlic powder, and cayenne pepper. Process until smooth.
- Transfer the crab and walnuts mixture to a bowl then add chopped onion and diced bell pepper to the mixture.

- Pour mayonnaise over the mixture then mix well.
- Divide the mixture into 16 then roll into balls.
- Press each ball using your hands until becoming patty form. Repeat with the remaining patties.
- Preheat an Air Fryer to 375°F (191°C).
- Arrange the patties in the Air Fryer then spray with extra virgin olive oil.
- Cook the patties for 10 minutes. You may cook them in two batches.
- Once it is done, remove the cooked crab patties from the Air Fryer then serve.
- Enjoy immediately.

Per Serving: Net Carbs: 3.3g; Calories: 246; Total Fat: 20.3g; Saturated Fat: 2.7g
Protein: 10.1g; Carbs: 4.2g; Fiber: 0.9g; Sugar: 1.2g - Fat 74% / Protein 16% / Carbs 10%

Red Curry Calamari [FA] [GF]

Serves: 4 / Preparation time: 5 minutes / Cooking time: 15 minutes

¾ lb. fresh squids	2 teaspoons minced garlic
2 cups heavy cream	2 teaspoons sliced shallots
½ cup water	½ teaspoon salt
2 tablespoons extra virgin olive oil	1 lemon grass
2 tablespoons curry paste	1 bay leaf
½ teaspoon turmeric	¼ cup red chili flakes

- Cut the squids into thick slices then set aside.
- Pour olive oil into the Instant Pot then select "Sauté" setting on the Instant Pot.
- Stir in minced garlic and sliced shallots then sauté until aromatic.
- After that, add the calamari to the Instant Pot then sauté until wilted. Press the "Cancel" button.
- Pour water over the pork then season with curry paste, turmeric, and salt. Stir well.
- Add lemon grass and bay leaf to the pot then sprinkle red chili flakes on top.
- Put the lid on then seal the Instant Pot properly. Close the steam valve.
- Select the "Pressure" setting on the Instant Pot and cook the pork for 15 minutes.
- Once it is done, quick release the Instant Pot and open the lid.
- Pour heavy cream into the Instant Pot the stir well.
- Transfer the calamari to a serving bowl then pour the liquid over the calamari. Enjoy!

Per Serving: Net Carbs: 6.3g; Calories: 366; Total Fat: 31.5g; Saturated Fat: 15.1g; Protein: 14.9g; Carbs: 6.6g; Fiber: 0.3g; Sugar: 0.3g - Fat 77% / Protein 16% / Carbs 7%

Grilled Salmon Garlic with Tahini Sauce

Serves: 4 / Preparation time: 14 minutes / Cooking time: 12 minutes

1 ½ lbs. salmon	½ teaspoon black pepper
1 fresh lime	3 tablespoons tahini paste
10 cloves garlic	¼ cup water
¼ cup extra virgin olive oil	1 tablespoon lemon juice
1-teaspoon cumin	¼ teaspoon garlic powder
¾ teaspoon coriander	¾ cup chopped parsley
1 ½ teaspoons paprika	

- Cut the lime into halves then squeeze the juice over the salmon. Let the salmon rest for approximately 10 minutes.
- In the meantime, place garlic cloves in a food processor then add extra virgin olive oil, cumin, coriander, paprika, and black pepper to the food processor. Process until smooth.
- Wash and rinse the salmon then pat it dry.
- Rub the salmon with the garlic mixture then set aside.
- Next, prepare a grill and preheat it to medium heat.
- Once the grill is ready, place the seasoned salmon directly on the grill and grill for approximately 5 minutes each side.
- Once it is done, remove the grilled salmon from the grill and transfer to a serving dish.
- Place tahini paste and garlic powder in a food processor then pour water and lemon juice over the paste. Process until smooth.
- Transfer the tahini sauce to a serving bowl then add chopped parsley to the sauce. Mix well.
- Serve the grilled salmon with tahini sauce and enjoy warm.

Per Serving: Net Carbs: 5.9g; Calories: 298; Total Fat: 24.5g; Saturated Fat: 3.7g
Protein: 15.1g; Carbs: 8.4g; Fiber: 2.5g; Sugar: 0.7g - Fat 74% / Protein 18% / Carbs 8%

Coconut Crab Cakes Mayo [FA] [GF]

Serves: 4 / Preparation time: 15 minutes / Cooking time: 10 minutes

1 lb. crabmeat	1 pastured egg
2 tablespoons coconut flour	2 tablespoons mayonnaise
1 cup grated coconut	½ teaspoon mustard
2 tablespoons chopped parsley	2 tablespoons butter
½ teaspoon salt	2 tablespoons coconut oil
½ teaspoon pepper	

- Melt butter over medium heat then set aside.
- Combine crabmeat with coconut flour, grated coconut, chopped parsley, and egg then mix well.
- Season the mixture with salt, pepper, mayonnaise, and mustard then drizzle melted butter over the crabmeat mixture.
- Shape the crabmeat mixture into fritter forms then set aside.
- Next, preheat a saucepan over medium heat then pour coconut oil into it.
- Once the coconut oil is hot, arrange the crabmeat cakes in the saucepan and cook for approximately 4 minutes.
- Carefully flip the crabmeat cakes and cook for another 4 minutes or until cooked through.
- Once it is done, remove from the saucepan and transfer to a serving dish.
- Serve and enjoy.

Per Serving: Net Carbs: 6g: Calories: 310; Total Fat: 25g; Saturated Fat: 17.2g; Protein: 10.5g; Carbs: 10.5g; Fiber: 4.5g; Sugar: 2.3g - Fat 73% / Protein 21% / Carbs 6%

Spiced Cod Coconut [FA] [GF]

Serves: 4 / Preparation time: 5 minutes / Cooking time: 10 minutes

1-½ lbs. cod fillet	2 teaspoons sliced shallots
2 cups coconut milk	½ teaspoon salt
2 tablespoons extra virgin olive oil	1 lemon grass
2 tablespoons curry paste	1 bay leaf
½ teaspoon turmeric	¼ cup red chili flakes
2 teaspoons minced garlic	

- Cut the cod fillet into cubes then set aside.
- Next, pour olive oil into the Instant Pot then select "Sauté" setting on the Instant Pot.
- Stir in minced garlic and sliced shallots then sauté until aromatic.
- After that, add the cod to the Instant Pot then sauté until the cod is no longer pink. Press the "Cancel" button.
- Pour coconut milk over the cod then season with curry paste, turmeric, and salt. Stir well.
- Add lemon grass and bay leaf to the pot then sprinkle red chili flakes on top.
- Put the lid on then seal the Instant Pot properly.
- Select the "Manual" setting on the Instant Pot and cook the cod for 5 minutes.
- Once it is done, quick release the Instant Pot and open the lid.
- Transfer the cod together with the gravy to a serving bowl and serve. Enjoy!

Per Serving: Net Carbs: 5.1g; Calories: 353; Total Fat: 27.7g; Saturated Fat: 17.6g; Protein: 22.3g; Carbs: 7g; Fiber: 1.9g; Sugar: 2.9g - Fat 71% / Protein 25% / Carbs 4%

Tuna Garlic Salad with Jalapeno Coleslaw

Serves: 4 / Preparation time: 14 minutes / Cooking time: 14 minutes

½ lb. tuna fillet	1 medium carrot
2 tablespoons lemon juice	2 cups shredded cabbage
2 tablespoons minced garlic	1 green jalapeno
A pinch of black pepper	3 tablespoons mayonnaise
2 tablespoons butter	1 ½ tablespoons extra virgin olive oil
1 fresh apple	

- Drizzle lemon juice over the tuna fillet then let it rest for approximately 10 minutes.
- In the meantime, cut the apple into small pieces then place in a bowl.
- Quickly peel the carrot and shred it into pieces.
- Next, cup the green jalapeno into slices then combine with apple dices, shredded carrots, shredded cabbage.
- Drizzle extra virgin olive oil over the coleslaw then toss to combine. Set aside.
- After 10 minutes, rub the tuna fillet with minced garlic and pepper then set aside.
- In the meantime, preheat a grill over medium heat then wait until it reaches the desired temperature.
- Once the grill is ready, brush the tuna fillet with butter then place directly on the grill.
- Grill the tuna for approximately 5 minutes each side or until the tuna fillet is cooked through.

- Remove the tuna from the grill then serve with jalapeno coleslaw and mayonnaise.

Per Serving: Net Carbs: 5.9g; Calories: 352; Total Fat: 30.2g; Saturated Fat: 3g
Protein: 14.2g; Carbs: 7.3g; Fiber: 1.4g; Sugar: 2.6g - Fat 77% / Protein 16% / Carbs 7%

Tasty and Cheesy Scallops

Serves: 4 / Preparation time: 5 minutes / Cooking time: 11 minutes

20 fresh scallops	½ cup butter
½ teaspoon salt	½ cup mayonnaise
½ teaspoon pepper	1 cup grated cheddar cheese

- Preheat an Air Fryer to 400°F (204°C) and place a rack in the Air Fryer.
- Remove the shells of the scallops then wash and clean them.
- Place the scallops in a disposable aluminum pan then place the pan on the rack in the Air Fryer.
- Cook the scallops and set the time to 7 minutes.
- Once the scallops are done, remove from the Air Fryer then discard the liquid.
- Next, melt butter in a microwave then combine with mayonnaise. Stir until incorporated.
- Drizzle the butter and mayonnaise mixture over the scallops then sprinkle cheddar cheese on top.
- Return the scallops to the Air Fryer and cook for 4 minutes.
- Once it is done, remove from the Air Fryer then transfer to a serving dish.
- Serve and enjoy.

Per Serving: Net Carbs: 2.2g; Calories: 553; Total Fat: 55.4g; Saturated Fat: 24.1g
Protein: 12.3g; Carbs: 2.3g; Fiber: 0.1g; Sugar: 1.2 g - Fat 90% / Protein 9% / Carbs 1%

Oven Fried Cheesy Tilapia with Avocado [FA] [GF]

Serves: 4 / Preparation time: 5 minutes / Cooking time: 15 minutes

1 lb. tilapia	1-cup fresh chopped basils
3 tablespoons mayonnaise	½ teaspoon salt
¼ cup grated cheddar cheese	½ teaspoon pepper
2 tablespoons lemon juice	2 ripe avocados
3 teaspoons minced garlic	

- Preheat an oven to 350°F (177°C) and line a baking tray with aluminum foil.
- Spread fresh basils on the baking tray then set aside.
- Season the tilapia with lemon juice, minced garlic, salt, and pepper then place on the prepared baking tray.
- Drizzle mayonnaise over the tilapia and sprinkle grated cheddar cheese on top.
- Bake the tilapia for approximately 15 minutes or until cooked through.
- In the meantime, cut the avocados into halves and discard the seeds.
- Peel the avocados then cut into small cubes.
- Once the tilapia is done, remove from the oven and transfer to a serving dish.
- Top the tilapia with avocado cubes then serve.
- Enjoy!

Per Serving: Net Carbs: 5.6g: Calories: 460; Total Fat: 35.4g; Saturated Fat: 11.7g; Protein: 26.3g; Carbs: 12.6g;
Fiber: 7g; Sugar: 1.5g - Fat 70% / Protein 25% / Carbs 5%

Savory Fried Prawn with Red Chili Sauce and Steamed Collard Green

Serves: 4 / Preparation time: 9 minutes / Cooking time: 11 minutes

½ lb. fresh prawns	3 shallots
3 tablespoons minced garlic	¼ cup red chili
2 teaspoons coriander	1 medium red tomatoes
½ cup extra virgin olive oil, to fry	2 cups collard green

- Season the prawn with minced garlic and coriander then let it rest for approximately 10 minutes.
- In the meantime, preheat a steamer over medium heat then steam the collard green until tender. Remove from the steamer and set aside.
- Preheat a frying pan over medium heat then pour extra virgin olive oil into it.
- Once the oil is hot, put the prawns in the frying pan and fry for a few minutes or until the prawns turn into pink.
- Remove the fried prawns from the frying pan and place on a serving dish.
- Stir in red chili, shallots, and red tomatoes to the frying pan then fry for a few minutes or until wilted.
- Transfer the fried chili, shallots, and tomatoes to a food processor then process until smooth.
- To serve, place the steamed collard green and red chili sauce next to the fried prawn and enjoy warm.

Per Serving: Net Carbs: 4.6g; Calories: 353; Total Fat: 28.3g; Saturated Fat: 4g
Protein: 21g; Carbs: 5.8g; Fiber: 1.2g; Sugar: 0.8g - Fat 72% / Protein 23% / Carbs 5%

Original Shrimps with Pecan Sauce [FA] [GF]

Serves: 4 / Preparation time: 3 minutes / Cooking time: 5 minutes

1 lb. fresh jumbo shrimps	1 ½ tablespoons lemon juice
2 teaspoons minced garlic	1 tablespoon grated Parmesan cheese
¼ teaspoon salt	½ cup roasted pecans
2 tablespoons butter	½ cup coconut milk
½ cup chicken broth	2 tablespoons coconut aminos

- Rub the jumbo shrimps with minced garlic and salt then set aside.
- Place butter in an Instant Pot then select "Sauté" setting.
- Stir in seasoned shrimps to the Instant Pot then sauté until pink.
- Pour chicken broth to the Instant Pot then add Parmesan cheese.
- Put the lid on and seal the Instant Pot properly.
- Select "Manual" setting then cook the shrimps for 2 minutes.
- Meanwhile, place roasted pecans together with coconut milk, lemon juice, and coconut aminos in a blender then blend until smooth. Set aside.
- Once it is done, quickly release the Instant Pot then open the lid.
- Transfer the cooked shrimps to a serving dish then drizzle pecan sauce on top.
- Serve and enjoy!

Per Serving: Net Carbs: 4.2g; Calories: 396; Total Fat: 31.9g; Saturated Fat: 8.5g; Protein: 23.1g; Carbs: 7.8g; Fiber: 3.6g; Sugar: 2g - Fat 73% / Protein 23% / Carbs 4%

Steamed Oyster with Lemon Aroma [FA] [GF]

Serves: 4 / Preparation time: 5 minutes / Cooking time: 5 minutes

2 lbs. oyster   ½ cup sliced lemon

½ cup butter

- Cut the butter into cubes then spread in a disposable aluminum pan.
- Add oyster to the pan then sprinkle sliced lemon on top.
- Pour water into the Instant Pot then place a trivet in it.
- Place the disposable aluminum pan on the trivet then close and seal the Instant Pot.
- Select "Manual" setting and cook the oyster on high for 5 minutes.
- Once it is done, naturally release the Instant Pot then open the lid.
- Transfer the cooked oyster to a serving dish and enjoy right away.

Per Serving: Net Carbs: 6g; Calories: 312; Total Fat: 26.6g; Saturated Fat: 15.6g; Protein: 12.3g; Carbs: 6.1g; Fiber: 0.1g; Sugar: 1.4g - Fat 77% / Protein 16% / Carbs 7%

Yellow Squid Curry with Chopped Cabbage

Serves: 4 / Preparation time: 9 minutes / Cooking time: 12 minutes

1 lb. fresh squids   1 bay leaf

2 tablespoons extra virgin olive oil   1 lemon grass

2 teaspoons minced garlic   1-inch galangal

2 teaspoons sliced shallots   1 kaffir lime leaf

½ teaspoon turmeric   1-cup coconut milk

1-teaspoon curry powder   ½ cup chopped cabbage

- Discard the squid ink then wash and rinse the squids.
- Preheat a skillet over medium heat then pour extra virgin olive oil into it.
- Once the oil is hot, stir in minced garlic and sliced shallots then sauté until aromatic and wilted.
- Stir in the squids then season with turmeric, curry powder, bay leaf, lemon grass, galangal, and kaffir lime leaf then sauté until wilted and completely seasoned.
- Pour coconut milk over the squids then bring to boil.
- Once it is boiled, remove from heat and transfer to a serving dish.
- Serve and enjoy.

Per Serving: Net Carbs: 6.9g; Calories: 288; Total Fat: 22.6g; Saturated Fat: 14g
Protein: 14.9g; Carbs: 8.6g; Fiber: 1.7g; Sugar: 2.1g - Fat 71% / Protein 19% / Carbs 10%

Fried Shrimps Garlic

Serves: 2 / Preparation time: 15 minutes / Cooking time: 5 minutes

1 lb. fresh shrimps   3 tablespoons minced garlic

¼ teaspoon salt   1-teaspoon extra virgin olive oil

1-tablespoon coriander   ¼ cup butter

1-½ teaspoons cayenne

1 teaspoon smoked paprika

1 ½ tablespoons Worcestershire sauce

2 teaspoons lemon juice

1-teaspoon ginger

- Peel the shrimps then remove the head.
- Season the shrimp with coriander, minced garlic, and salt. Let the shrimps rest for at least 10 minutes.
- Place butter in a mixing bowl then add cayenne, smoked paprika, Worcestershire sauce, ginger, and lemon juice.
- Using an electric mixer beat the butter until smooth and creamy. Set aside.
- Preheat an Air Fryer to 400°F (204°C) and put a rack in it.
- Place the seasoned shrimps on the rack then cook for 5 minutes.
- Remove the cooked shrimps from the Air Fryer then serve with creamy hot butter.

Per Serving: Net Carbs: 5.8g; Calories: 376; Total Fat: 31.5g; Saturated Fat: 15.7g
Protein: 19.4g; Carbs: 6.8g; Fiber: 1g; Sugar: 1.2g - Fat 75% / Protein 21% / Carbs 4%

Oyster Stew Creamy Kale

Serves: 4 / Preparation time: 9 minutes / Cooking time: 19 minutes

1 lb. oyster

2 tablespoons extra virgin olive oil

2 teaspoons sliced shallots

2 tablespoons chopped celeries

1-cup coconut milk

1-teaspoon thyme

½ teaspoon pepper

2 cups chopped kale

- Place the oyster in a pot then pour water to cover. Bring to boil.
- Once it is boiled, reduce the heat and cook for approximately 10 minutes.
- Strain the oysters then discard the water. Set aside.
- Next, preheat a skillet over medium heat then pour extra virgin olive oil into the skillet.
- Stir in sliced shallots and sauté until wilted and aromatic.
- Pour coconut milk into the skillet then bring to boil.
- Once it is boiled, season with thyme and pepper then stir in chopped kale. Bring to a simmer.
- Transfer to a serving dish then serve.
- Enjoy!

Per Serving: Net Carbs: 5.2g; Calories: 207; Total Fat: 18.9g; Saturated Fat: 10.8g
Protein: 19.4g; Carbs: 6.7g; Fiber: 1.5g; Sugar: 1.9g - Fat 82% / Protein 8% / Carbs 10%

Halibut Fillet with Mushroom Parsley Butter [FA] [GF] [SF]

Serves: 4 / Preparation time: 5 minutes / Cooking time: 13 minutes

1 lb. mackerel fillet

2 tablespoons extra virgin olive oil

¼ teaspoon salt

¼ teaspoon pepper

2 tablespoons butter

½ cup chopped mushrooms

2 tablespoons chopped parsley

- Preheat an oven to 350°F (177°C) and line a baking tray with aluminum foil.
- Place the mackerel fillets on the prepared baking tray then drizzle extra virgin olive oil over the fillet.

- Sprinkle salt and pepper on top then bake for approximately 10 minutes or until the mackerel fillet is cooked through.
- In the meantime, preheat a saucepan over medium heat then place butter in it.
- Once the butter is melted, stir in chopped mushrooms and parsley then sauté until wilted.
- Remove from heat and set aside.
- Once the mackerel fillet is done, remove from the oven and transfer to a serving dish.
- Top the mackerel fillet with mushroom and parsley butter then serve.
- Enjoy!

Per Serving: Net Carbs: 1.8g: Calories: 387; Total Fat: 32.8g; Saturated Fat: 9.2g; Protein: 21.7g; Carbs: 2; Fiber: 021g; Sugar: 0.2g - Fat 76% / Protein 21.4% / Carbs 2%

Calamari Crispy with Lemon Butter

Serves: 8 / Preparation time: 15 minutes / Cooking time: 6 minutes

1 lb. fresh squids	1-cup water
1-teaspoon salt	1-cup butter
1-teaspoon pepper	1-½ tablespoons mustard
2 cups almond flour	2 teaspoons lemon juice

- Peel the outer skin of the squids then discard the ink.
- Cut the squids into rings then rub with salt and pepper.
- Roll the seasoned squids in the almond flour then dip in the water.
- Return the squids to the almond flour then roll until the squids are completely coated with almond flour.
- Preheat an Air Fryer to 400°F (204°C).
- Place the coated squids in the Air Fryer then cook for 6 minutes.
- Once it is done, remove from the Air Fryer then place on a serving dish.
- Place butter in a mixing bowl then add mustard and lemon juice.
- Using a hand mixer mix until smooth and fluffy.
- Serve the fried calamari with the lemon butter.
- Enjoy!

Per Serving: Net Carbs: 4.9g; Calories: 429; Total Fat: 38.7g; Saturated Fat: 15.9g
Protein: 16.3g; Carbs: 8.2g; Fiber: 3.3g; Sugar: 1.2g - Fat 81% / Protein 15% / Carbs 4%

Healthy Pan Seared Salmon with Mushroom and Spinach

Serves: 4 / Preparation time: 4 minutes / Cooking time: 16 minutes

1 lb. salmon fillet	¼ cup chopped tomatoes
3 tablespoons extra virgin olive oil	½ teaspoon pepper
1 cup chopped mushroom	1-tablespoon balsamic vinegar
2 cups chopped spinach	

- Sprinkle pepper over the salmon fillet then set aside.
- Preheat a pan over medium heat then pour olive oil into it.
- Once it is hot, put the salmon in the pan and sear it for approximately 4 minutes then flip it.

- Sear the other side of the salmon and cook until it is completely done and both sides of the salmon are lightly golden brown.
- Remove the cooked salmon from the pan and transfer to a plate.
- Next, stir in mushroom then sauté with the remaining olive oil.
- Once the mushroom is wilted, stir in chopped spinach and tomatoes then toss with balsamic vinegar.
- Transfer the vegetables to a serving dish then put the cooked salmon on top.
- Serve and enjoy.

Per Serving: Net Carbs: 0.9g; Calories: 275; Total Fat: 21.6g; Saturated Fat: 3.3g
Protein: 19.1g; Carbs: 1.6g; Fiber: 0.7g; Sugar: 0.7g - Fat 71% / Protein 27% / Carbs 2%

Scallops in Lemon Creamy Sauce [FA] [GF]

Serves: 4 / Preparation time: 5 minutes / Cooking time: 15 minutes

1 lb. scallops	½ teaspoon pepper
2 tablespoons extra virgin olive oil	1-cup heavy cream
2 tablespoons butter	2 tablespoons lemon juice
3 tablespoons minced garlic	¼ cup chopped parsley
¼ teaspoon salt	

- Preheat a saucepan over medium heat then pour extra virgin olive oil into it.
- Once the olive oil is hot, place scallops in it and fry for approximately 2 minutes each side.
- Remove the scallops from heat and strain the excessive water.
- Place butter in the same saucepan and wait until melted.
- Stir minced garlic into the saucepan then sauté until wilted and aromatic.
- Pour heavy cream into the saucepan then season with salt and pepper.
- After that, add chopped parsley and stir well. Bring to a simmer.
- Return the scallops to the saucepan and cook for a minute or two then transfer to a serving dish.
- Serve and enjoy.

Per Serving: Net Carbs: 5.1g: Calories: 302; Total Fat: 24.6g; Saturated Fat: 11.7g; Protein: 15.5g; Carbs: 5.5g; Fiber: 0.4g; Sugar: 0.3g - Fat 73% / Protein 20% / Carbs 7%

Cod Crispy Popcorn

Serves: 4 / Preparation time: 15 minutes / Cooking time: 10 minutes

1 lb. cod fillet	2 tablespoons coconut milk
½ teaspoon salt	1-tablespoon extra virgin olive oil
½ teaspoon pepper	1-cup mayonnaise
1-cup almond flour	½ teaspoon grated lemon zest
1 egg	¾ teaspoon Worcestershire sauce

- Combine mayonnaise with grated lemon zest and Worcestershire sauce then stir until incorporated.
- Transfer the mayonnaise mixture to a container with a lid then store in the fridge.
- Next, cut the cod fillet into cubes then season with salt and pepper. Set aside.
- Crack the egg then place in a bowl.

- Pour coconut milk into the egg then using a fork stir until incorporated. Set aside.
- After that, cut the cod fillet into cubes then dip in the egg mixture.
- Roll the cod cubes in the almond flour mixture and make sure that all sides of the cod popcorn are completely coated.
- Preheat an Air Fryer to 350°F (177°C) and place a rack in it.
- Arrange the coated cod popcorn on the rack.
- Spray with extra virgin olive oil then cook for 10 minutes.
- In the meantime, add grated lemon zest and Worcestershire sauce to the mayonnaise then stir until combined.
- Once the cod popcorn is done, transfer to a serving dish and serve with mayonnaise.
- Enjoy!

Per Serving: Net Carbs: 2.4g; Calories: 406; Total Fat: 33.8g; Saturated Fat: 6.2g
Protein: 23.3g; Carbs: 3.4g; Fiber: 1g; Sugar: 1.8g - Fat 75% / Protein 23% / Carbs 2%

Spicy Crispy Squids with Onion

Serves: 4 / Preparation time: 4 minutes / Cooking time: 14 minutes

½ lb. fresh squids	¾ cup water
1 big onion	½ cup extra virgin olive oil, to fry
1-cup almond flour	¼ cup chopped red chili
½ teaspoon pepper	2 teaspoons minced garlic
1 egg	

- Cut the squids and onion into rings then set aside.
- Place almond flour in a bowl then season with pepper.
- Crack the egg and add to the almond flour then pour water over the almond flour. Stir until incorporated. Set aside.
- Preheat a frying pan over medium heat then pour olive oil into it.
- Dip the onion ring in the almond flour mixture then fry.
- Once the onion is done, do the same thing to the squids.
- Next, take about 2 tablespoons of olive oil then pour into a pan.
- Stir in minced garlic and chopped red chili then sauté until wilted and aromatic.
- Add fried onion and squid rings to the pan then stir until the rings are completely seasoned.
- Remove from heat and transfer then crispy squids to a serving dish.
- Serve and enjoy warm.

Per Serving: Net Carbs: 6.5g; Calories: 358; Total Fat: 30.9g; Saturated Fat: 4.5g
Protein: 14.6g; Carbs: 8.6g; Fiber: 2.1g; Sugar: 2.6g - Fat 78% / Protein 15% / Carbs 7%

Crispy Coconut Prawns with Lemon Mayo Dip [FA]

Serves: 4 / Preparation time: 10 minutes / Cooking time: 12 minutes

1 lb. fresh prawns	½ teaspoon pepper
½ teaspoon salt	½ cup coconut flour

186

1 cup grated coconut	¼ cup mayonnaise
¼ cup water	2 tablespoons lemon juice
Coconut oil, to fry	1-teaspoon minced garlic

- Place coconut flour in a bowl then season with salt and pepper.
- Pour water over the coconut flour then stir until incorporated.
- Next, discard the prawn's head then dip in the coconut flour mixture.
- Roll the prawns in the grated coconut then set aside.
- After that, preheat a frying pan over medium heat then pour coconut oil into the frying pan.
- Once it is hot, fry the coated prawns for approximately 2 minutes each side or until the prawns are lightly golden brown.
- Remove the fried prawns from the frying pan and strain the excessive oil.
- Arrange the fried prawns on a serving dish then set aside.
- Quickly combine mayonnaise with lemon juice and minced garlic then stir well.
- Drizzle the lemon mayonnaise over the fried prawns then serve immediately.
- Enjoy warm.

Per Serving: Net Carbs: 5.6g: Calories: 326; Total Fat: 25.5g; Saturated Fat: 18.7g; Protein: 16.9g; Carbs: 8.1g; Fiber: 2.5g; Sugar: 2.5g - Fat 70% / Protein 23% / Carbs 7%

Crispy Shrimps Coconuts

Serves: 6 / Preparation time: 15 minutes / Cooking time: 10 minutes

1 lb. fresh shrimps	2 tablespoons butter
1-teaspoon salt	2 teaspoons minced garlic
1-teaspoon pepper	½ cup cilantro
1-cup coconut flour	1-cup coconut milk
2 eggs	2 tablespoons lemon juice
2 cups grated coconuts	

- Peel the fresh shrimps then discard the head.
- Rub the peeled shrimps with salt and pepper then let it sit for 5 minutes.
- Prepare coconut flour, beaten eggs, and grated coconuts in three different bowls in a row.
- Roll the fresh shrimps in the coconut flour then dip in beaten eggs.
- Take the shrimps out of the beaten eggs then roll in the grated coconuts. Using your finger squeeze the shrimps until all sides of the shrimps are completely coated with grated coconuts.
- Preheat an Air Fryer to 400°F (204°C).
- Arrange the shrimps in the Air Fryer then set the time to 10 minutes.
- Once it is done, check the color of the shrimps. If you want them to be more golden brown, cook the shrimps for 2 minutes more.
- Place the crispy fried shrimps in a serving dish then serve.
- Enjoy right away or serve with tomato sauce.

Per Serving: Net Carbs: 4.1g; Calories: 342; Total Fat: 27.1g; Saturated Fat: 20.9g
Protein: 19.5g; Carbs: 8.4g; Fiber: 4.3g; Sugar: 3.4g - Fat 71% / Protein 23% / Carbs 6%

Baked Juicy Salmon with Sautéed Leek and Asparagus

Serves: 4 / Preparation time: 11 minutes / Cooking time: 26 minutes

1 lb. salmon fillet	½ cup chopped leek
6 tablespoons extra virgin olive	½ cup chopped asparagus
2 tablespoons lemon juice	½ teaspoon pepper
2 teaspoons minced garlic	½ teaspoon ginger

- Preheat an oven to 400°F (204°C) and prepare a baking tray. Set aside.
- Drizzle lemon juice over the salmon fillet then brush with extra virgin olive oil.
- Wrap the salmon fillet with aluminum foil then place on the baking tray.
- Place the baking tray in the oven and bake for approximately 10 minutes.
- After 10 minutes, take the baking tray out of the oven and unwrap the aluminum foil.
- Return the salmon back to the oven and bake again for another 10 minutes or until the salmon is lightly golden brown.
- In the meantime, preheat a saucepan over medium heat and pour olive oil into the saucepan.
- Once the oil is hot, stir in minced garlic then sauté until lightly golden brown.
- Next, add chopped leek and asparagus to the saucepan then season with pepper and ginger. Stir occasionally and cook until the vegetables are wilted.
- Transfer the sautéed vegetables to a serving dish then wait until the baked salmon is ready.
- When the salmon is done, take it out of the oven and place on the top of the vegetables.
- Serve and enjoy!

Per Serving: Net Carbs: 2.5g; Calories: 413; Total Fat: 32.4g; Saturated Fat: 5g
Protein: 27.7g; Carbs: 3.2g; Fiber: 0.7g; Sugar: 0.9g - Fat 71% / Protein 27% / Carbs 2%

Green Chili Fish Soup [FA] [GF]

Serves: 8 / Preparation time: 5 minutes / Cooking time: 20 minutes

½ lb. salmon fillet	2 tablespoons sliced shallots
¼ cup chopped green chilies	2 teaspoons sliced garlic
¼ cup chopped tomatoes	½ teaspoon salt
2 bay leaves	1-½ cups coconut milk
1-inch galangal	1-½ cups water
1-teaspoon ginger	

- Cut the salmon fillet into cubes then place in the Instant Pot.
- Add green chilies, chopped tomatoes, bay leaves, galangal, ginger, sliced shallots, sliced garlic, and salt to the Instant Pot then pour water and coconut milk over the fish fillet.
- Put the lid on and seal the Instant Pot properly. Close the steam valve.
- Select "Soup" setting on the Instant Pot and cook the salmon on high. Set the time to 10 minutes.
- Once it is done, naturally release the Instant Pot then open the lid.
- Transfer the salmon soup to a serving bowl then serve immediately.
- Enjoy warm.

Per Serving: Net Carbs: 6.4g; Calories: 406; Total Fat: 32.7g; Saturated Fat: 21.1g; Protein: 22.8g; Carbs: 9.1g; Fiber: 2.7g; Sugar: 4.5g - Fat 72% / Protein 22% / Carbs 6%

Baked Salmon with Green Basil Pesto [FA] [GF]

Serves: 4 / Preparation time: 5 minutes / Cooking time: 20 minutes

2 lbs. salmon fillet	2 teaspoons minced garlic
½ teaspoon salt	¼ cup ground roasted peanuts
½ teaspoon pepper	½ cup grated cheddar cheese
2 tablespoons butter	¼ cup extra virgin olive oil
1 ½ cups fresh basils	

- Place fresh basils, minced garlic, roasted peanuts, and cheddar cheese in a food processor.
- Drizzle olive oil over the basils then process until smooth. Set aside.
- Rub the salmon with salt and pepper then set aside.
- Preheat a grill over medium heat then wait until it is ready.
- Once the grill is ready, place the seasoned salmon on the grill and brush with butter as many as possible.
- Flip and rotate the salmon fillet then grill until both sides of the salmon are lightly golden brown.
- Remove the grilled salmon and place on a serving dish.
- Top with green basil pesto then serve.
- Enjoy immediately.

Per Serving: Net Carbs: 1.1g: Calories: 450; Total Fat: 38.6g; Saturated Fat: 11.1g; Protein: 26.3g; Carbs: 2.1g; Fiber: 1g; Sugar: 0.5g - Fat 77% / Protein 22% / Carbs 1%

Calamari Mayo with Cauliflower Broccoli Salad

Serves: 4 / Preparation time: 16 minutes / Cooking time: 13 minutes

¾ lb. fresh squids	1-cup cauliflower florets
1 egg	¼ cup diced cheddar cheese
¼ teaspoon pepper	2 tablespoons diced onion
1 cup almond flour	¼ cup mayonnaise
½ cup extra virgin olive oil, to fry	¼ cup sour cream
1-cup broccoli florets	1-tablespoon lemon juice

- Preheat a steamer over medium heat then steam broccoli and cauliflower florets until tender. Set aside.
- Remove the squid ink and cut the squids into rings.
- Crack the egg then place in a bowl.
- Season the egg with pepper and stir until incorporated.
- Dip the squids in the beaten egg then roll in the almond flour. Set aside.
- Preheat a frying pan over medium heat then pour extra virgin olive oil into it.
- Once the oil is hot, put the rolled squids into the frying pan and fry for a few minutes or until lightly golden brown.
- Remove the squids from the frying pan and discard the excessive oil.
- Next, combine mayonnaise with sour cream and lemon juice then mix well.

- To serve, place the fried calamari on a serving dish then arrange the steamed broccoli and cauliflower florets on the same serving dish.
- Drizzle mayonnaise mixture over the salad then sprinkle diced cheddar cheese on to.
- Serve and enjoy immediately.

Per Serving: Net Carbs: 6g; Calories: 452; Total Fat: 39.3g; Saturated Fat: 7.5g
Protein: 19.3g; Carbs: 8.2g; Fiber: 2g; Sugar: 2g - Fat 78% / Protein 17% / Carbs 5%

Nutty Shrimps with Chili Sauce

Serves: 4 / Preparation time: 15 minutes / Cooking time: 5 minutes

1 lb. fresh shrimps	¼ teaspoon salt
1 egg white	1-teaspoon pepper
½ cup almond flour	½ cup Greek yogurt
1 cup roasted pecans	2 tablespoons chili sauce
1-teaspoon paprika	

- Peel the fresh shrimps then discard the head. Set aside.
- Season the egg white with salt and paprika then whisk to combine.
- Place roasted pecans in a food processor then season with pepper. Process until smooth and becoming flour.
- Roll the shrimps in the almond flour then dip in the seasoned egg white.
- Next, roll again the shrimps in the pecans mixture then set aside. Repeat with the remaining shrimps and flour.
- Preheat an Air Fryer to 400°F (204°C).
- Arrange the coated shrimps in the Air Fryer then spray with cooking spray.
- Cook the shrimps for 5 minutes then arrange on a serving dish.
- Combine Greek yogurt with chili sauce then mix until incorporated.
- Drizzle the chili yogurt mixture over the shrimps then serve. Enjoy right away.

Per Serving: Net Carbs: 3g; Calories: 288; Total Fat: 23.9g; Saturated Fat: 2.3g
Protein: 16g; Carbs: 6.4g; Fiber: 2.5g; Sugar: 2.5g - Fat 75% / Protein 22% / Carbs 3%

Halibut Cheesy Lemon

Serves: 6 / Preparation time: 5 minutes / Cooking time: 14 minutes

1 lb. halibut fillet	½ cup butter
¼ teaspoon salt	2-½ tablespoons mayonnaise
¼ teaspoon pepper	2-½ tablespoons lemon juice
1-tablespoon extra virgin olive oil	¼ cup chopped onion
¾ cup grated Parmesan cheese	

- Brush the halibut fillet with olive oil then season with salt and pepper.
- Preheat an Air Fryer to 375°F (191°C).
- Once the Air Fryer is ready, place the seasoned halibut fillet in the Air Fryer and cook for 12 minutes.
- Meanwhile, place butter in a mixing bowl then pour lemon juice over the butter.
- Add mayonnaise to the mixing bowl then using an electric mixer beat the butter until smooth and creamy.

- Next, stir in grated Parmesan cheese and chopped onion then mix well.
- After 12 minutes of cooking time, open the drawer then spread the butter mixture over the cooked halibut.
- Cook for 2 minutes then remove from the Air Fryer.
- Transfer the cooked halibut to a serving dish then serve.
- Enjoy right away.

Per Serving: Net Carbs: 1g; Calories: 346; Total Fat: 31.2g; Saturated Fat: 13.6g
Protein: 15.8g; Carbs: 1.1g; Fiber: 0.1g; Sugar: 0.7g - Fat 81% / Protein 18% / Carbs 1%

Lemon Mint Grilled Prawns

Serves: 4 / Preparation time: 16 minutes / Cooking time: 12 minutes

2 lb. fresh prawn	¼ cup extra virgin olive oil
2 tablespoons chopped mint leaves	2 tablespoons lemon juice
¼ teaspoon thyme	¼ cup carrot stick
2 tablespoons chopped parsley	¼ cup chopped lettuce
4 teaspoons minced garlic	½ cup grated cheddar cheese

- Place mint leaves, thyme, chopped parsley, minced garlic, lemon juice, and extra virgin olive oil in a blender then blend until incorporated.
- Drizzle the spice mixture over the prawns then toss until the prawn is completely seasoned.
- Preheat a grill over medium heat then wait until it is ready.
- In the meantime, preheat a steamer and steam the carrot until tender. Set aside.
- Once the grill is ready, place the prawns on it. Grill for a few minutes until the prawns are completely cooked and brush with the spices once in a while.
- When the prawn is done, remove from grill and place on a serving dish.
- Garnish with lettuce and steamed carrots then sprinkle grated cheddar cheese on top.
- Serve and enjoy.

Per Serving: Net Carbs: 1.4g; Calories: 238; Total Fat: 19.6g; Saturated Fat: 5.6g
Protein: 14.3g; Carbs: 1.8g; Fiber: 0.4g; Sugar: 0.3g - Fat 74% / Protein 14% / Carbs 2%

Boiled Halibut in Ginger Broth [FA] [GF]

Serves: 4 / Preparation time: 5 minutes / Cooking time: 13 minutes

¾ lb. halibut fillet	2 tablespoons chopped fresh basil
1-tablespoon extra virgin olive oil	1 teaspoon minced garlic
1-teaspoon ginger	2 cups water
½ teaspoon salt	

- Preheat a skillet over medium heat then pour extra virgin olive oil into it.
- Once the oil is hot, stir in minced garlic then sauté until wilted and aromatic.
- Next, pour water into the skillet then bring to boil.
- Once it is boiled, season the gravy with salt, ginger, and basil then stir well.
- Add halibut fillet to the skillet then cook for about 8 minutes or until the halibut fillet is opaque.

- Remove from heat then transfer the halibut and the gravy in different bowls.
- Serve and enjoy warm.

Per Serving: Net Carbs: 1.6g: Calories: 324; Total Fat: 26.1g; Saturated Fat: 2.3g; Protein: 20.1g; Carbs: 4.4g; Fiber: 2.8g; Sugar: 1.2g - Fat 73% / Protein 26% / Carbs 1%

Salmon Steak with Basil and Cheese Pesto

Serves: 4 / Preparation time: 5 minutes / Cooking time: 10 minutes

1 lb. salmon steak	2 teaspoons minced garlic
1-tablespoon butter	¼ cup roasted pecans
½ teaspoon salt	2 tablespoons grated Parmesan cheese
½ teaspoon pepper	½ cup extra virgin olive oil
2 cups fresh basils	

- Preheat an Air Fryer to 325°F (163°C) and place a rack in the Air Fryer.
- Brush the salmon with butter then season with salt and pepper.
- Cook the salmon and set the time to 8 minutes.
- In the meantime, place fresh basils in a blender then add minced garlic, roasted pecans, and grated Parmesan cheese to the blender.
- Pour olive oil over the basils then blend until smooth and creamy.
- Once the salmon is done, remove from the Air Fryer then place on a serving dish.
- Drizzle the basil pesto on top then serve.
- Enjoy!

Per Serving: Net Carbs: 0.9g; Calories: 514; Total Fat: 48g; Saturated Fat: 8.8g
Protein: 22.2g; Carbs: 1.9g; Fiber: 1g; Sugar: 0.3g - Fat 84% / Protein 15% / Carbs 1%

Tuna Cheese Steak with Asparagus Lemon Salad

Serves: 4 / Preparation time: 12 minutes / Cooking time: 19 minutes

1 lb. tuna fillet	2 tablespoons lemon juice
3 tablespoons extra virgin olive oil	½ teaspoon grated lemon zest
½ teaspoon pepper	¼ cup mayonnaise
½ handful asparagus	½ cup grated cheddar cheese

- Preheat a saucepan over medium heat then pour olive oil into it.
- Sprinkle pepper over the tuna and once the oil is hot, place the tuna in the saucepan.
- Cook the tuna for approximately 4 minutes or until opaque then flip it.
- Continue cooking the tuna for another 4 minutes or until the tuna is lightly golden brown and cooked through.
- Remove the tuna from the saucepan then place on a serving dish.
- Next, cut and trim the asparagus then sauté with the remaining olive oil.
- Once it is done, place the asparagus next to the tuna then set aside.
- Quickly combine mayonnaise with lemon juice and grated lemon zest then stir well.
- Drizzle the lemon mayonnaise over the tuna and asparagus then sprinkle grated cheese on top.

- Serve and enjoy.

Per Serving: Net Carbs: 0.7g; Calories: 656; Total Fat: 59.7g; Saturated Fat: 5.4g
Protein: 29.9g; Carbs: 0.9g; Fiber: 0.2g; Sugar: 0.5g - Fat 82% / Protein 17% / Carbs 1%

Buttery Prawns with Refreshing Kaffir Lime Leaves Aroma [FA] [GF]

Serves: 4 / Preparation time: 5 minutes / Cooking time: 5 minutes

1 lb. fresh prawns	¼ cup diced tomatoes
¼ cup butter	2 teaspoons chopped kaffir lime leaves
2 tablespoons red chili flakes	

- Discard the prawn's head then set aside.
- Preheat a saucepan over low heat and place butter in it.
- Once the butter is melted, add prawns to the saucepan then sauté until just opaque.
- Season the prawns with red chili flakes, diced tomatoes, and kaffir lime leaves and stir for a few minutes.
- Once it is done, remove the cooked prawns from the saucepan and transfer to a serving dish.
- Serve and enjoy.

Per Serving: Net Carbs: 1.9g: Calories: 134; Total Fat: 11.6g; Saturated Fat: 7.3g; Protein: 5.5g; Carbs: 2.4g; Fiber: 0.5g; Sugar: 1.5g - Fat 78% / Protein 16% / Carbs 6%

Carrot and Leek in Spicy Tuna Fritter

Serves: 4 / Preparation time: 16 minutes / Cooking time: 6 minutes

1 lb. tuna fillet	¼ cup grated carrots
2 teaspoons red chili flakes	2 eggs
2 teaspoons minced garlic	½ cup extra virgin olive oil, to fry
½ cup chopped leek	

- Cut the tuna fillet into cubes then place in a food processor.
- Add red chili flakes, minced garlic, and eggs then process until smooth.
- Add chopped leek and grated carrots to the mixture then mix until just combined.
- Shape the tuna mixture into small fritter forms then set aside.
- Next, preheat a frying pan over medium heat then pour olive oil into it.
- Once the oil is hot, put the tuna fritters into the frying pan and fry for approximately 3 minutes.
- Flip the tuna fritters then fry for another 3 minutes or until both sides of the tuna fritters are lightly golden brown.
- Remove the fried tuna fritters from the frying pan and strain the excessive oil.
- Arrange the fried tuna on a serving dish then serve.
- Enjoy warm.

Per Serving: Net Carbs: 2.6g; Calories: 351; Total Fat: 35.2g; Saturated Fat: 4.3g
Protein: 8.4g; Carbs: 3g; Fiber: 0.4g; Sugar: 1g - Fat 90% / Protein 7% / Carbs 3%

Crispy Tilapia with Cilantro Guacamole

Serves: 8 / Preparation time: 10 minutes / Cooking time: 10 minutes

1 lb. tilapia fillet

½ cup almond flour

3 eggs

1 cup grated coconut

2 ripe avocados

2 cloves garlic

1 tablespoon lemon juice

3 tablespoons butter

¼ cup chopped onion

¼ cup cilantro

¼ cup diced tomatoes

¼ teaspoon salt

½ teaspoon pepper

- Melt butter over low heat then set aside.
- Crack the eggs then place in a bowl.
- Add almond flour to the eggs then stir until incorporated.
- Cut the tilapia fillet into slices then dip into the egg and almond mixture.
- Next, roll the tilapia fillet in the grated coconut then set aside.
- Preheat an Air Fryer to 400°F (204°C).
- Place a rack in the Air Fryer then place the coated tilapia on it.
- Cook the tilapia for 10 minutes then remove from the Air Fryer. Arrange on a serving dish.
- Meanwhile, cut the avocados into halves then discard the seeds.
- Scoop out the avocado flesh then using a fork mash the avocados. Don't need to make it smooth.
- Grate the garlic cloves then add to the avocado.
- Pour melted butter and lemon juice into the avocados then add chopped onion, cilantro, and diced tomatoes.
- Season with salt and pepper then toss to combine.
- Serve the crispy tilapia with cilantro guacamole. Enjoy.

Per Serving: Net Carbs: 3.5g; Calories: 348; Total Fat: 27.4g; Saturated Fat: 11.4g
Protein: 19.3g; Carbs: 9.7g; Fiber: 6.2g; Sugar: 1.9g - Fat 72% / Protein 22% / Carbs 6%

Savory Tuna with Creamy Mint Sauce [FA] [GF]

Serves: 6 / Preparation time: 5 minutes / Cooking time: 15 minutes

1 lb. tuna fillet

1-cup low sodium chicken broth

¼ cup coconut milk

¾ teaspoon oregano

1-tablespoon butter

2 tablespoons minced garlic

¼ cup chopped mint leaves

1-cup heavy cream

- Pour chicken broth and coconut milk into the Instant Pot then season with oregano. Stir well.
- Add the tuna fillet to the Instant Pot then put the lid on. Seal the Instant Pot properly and close the steam valve.
- Select "Manual" setting on the Instant Pot and cook the tuna on high for 5 minutes.
- Once the tuna is done, quickly release the Instant Pot then open the lid.
- Take the cooked tuna out of the Instant Pot and place on a serving dish. Pour the liquid into another bowl.
- Place butter in the Instant Pot then select the "Sauté" setting.
- Stir in minced garlic then sauté until aromatic and lightly golden.
- Pour the liquid into the Instant Pot then bring to a simmer for about 5 minutes. Press the "Cancel" button.
- Next, pour heavy cream and add chopped mint leaves to the Instant Pot then mix well.
- Drizzle the sauce over the tuna then serve immediately.

Per Serving: Net Carbs: 2.1g; Calories: 390; Total Fat: 35g; Saturated Fat: 8g; Protein: 17.1g; Carbs: 2.7g; Fiber: 0.6g; Sugar: 0.4g - Fat 81% / Protein 18% / Carbs 1%

Tasty Asparagus Crab Soup

Serves: 4 / Preparation time: 7 minutes / Cooking time: 22 minutes

½ lb. crabmeat	½ cup cauliflower florets
½ lb. chopped asparagus	2 cups water
2 tablespoons extra virgin olive oil	2 tablespoons chopped parsley
½ cup chopped onion	½ teaspoon pepper
2 teaspoons minced garlic	2 eggs

- Preheat a skillet over medium heat then pour extra virgin olive oil into the skillet.
- Once the oil is hot, stir in chopped onion and minced garlic then sauté until wilted and aromatic.
- Pour water into the skillet over the spice and bring to boil.
- Once it is boiled, season the soup with pepper then stir in crabmeat, asparagus, and cauliflower florets.
- Cook the soup for approximately 10 minutes or until the asparagus is tender.
- Crack the eggs over boiled gravy and quickly stir well.
- Transfer the soup to a serving bowl then garnish with chopped parsley.
- Serve and enjoy.

Per Serving: Net Carbs: 2.5g; Calories: 118; Total Fat: 9.5g; Saturated Fat: 1.7g
Protein: 5.3g; Carbs: 3.5g; Fiber: 1g; Sugar: 1.3g - Fat 72% / Protein 20% / Carbs 8%

VEGGIE RECIPES

Cabbage Coconut Salad

Total Time: 15 minutes - Serves: 4

Ingredients:

- 1/3 cup unsweetened desiccated coconut
- ½ medium head cabbage, shredded
- 2 tsp sesame seeds
- ¼ cup tamari sauce
- ¼ cup olive oil
- 1 fresh lemon juice
- ½ tsp cumin
- ½ tsp curry powder
- ½ tsp ginger powder

Directions:

- Add all ingredients into the large mixing bowl and toss well.
- Place salad bowl in refrigerator for 1 hour.
- Serve and enjoy.

Nutritional Value (Amount per Serving): Calories 197; Fat 16.6 g; Carbohydrates 11.4 g; Sugar 7.1 g; Protein 3.5 g; Cholesterol 0 mg;

Delicious Vegan Zoodles

Total Time: 15 minutes - Serves: 4

Ingredients:

- 4 small zucchinis, spiralized into noodles
- 3 tbsp vegetable stock
- 1 cup red pepper, diced
- 1/2 cup onion, diced
- 3/4 cup nutritional yeast
- 1 tbsp garlic powder
- Pepper
- Salt

Directions:

- Add zucchini noodles, red pepper, and onion in a pan with vegetable stock and cook over medium heat for few minutes.
- Add nutritional yeast and garlic powder and cook for few minutes until creamy.
- Season with pepper and salt.
- Stir well and serve.

Nutritional Value (Amount per Serving): Calories 71; Fat 0.9 g; Carbohydrates 12.1 g; Sugar 5.7 g; Protein 5.7 g; Cholesterol 0 mg;

Healthy Breakfast Granola

Total Time: 15 minutes - Serves: 5

Ingredients:

- 1 cup walnuts, diced
- 1 cup unsweetened coconut flakes
- 1 cup sliced almonds
- 2 tbsp coconut oil, melted
- 4 packets Splenda
- 2 tsp cinnamon

Directions:

- Preheat the oven to 375 F/ 190 C.
- Spray a baking tray with cooking spray and set aside.
- Add all ingredients into the medium bowl and toss well.
- Spread bowl mixture on a prepared baking tray and bake in preheated oven for 10 minutes.

- Serve and enjoy.

Nutritional Value (Amount per Serving): Calories 458; Fat 42.5 g; Carbohydrates 13.7 g; Sugar 2.7 g; Protein 11.7 g; Cholesterol 0 mg;

Avocado Cream Soup with Chipotle

Serves: 4 / Preparation time: 4 minutes / Cooking time: 12 minutes

4 ripe avocados

2 cups water

2 cups Greek yogurt

1-teaspoon chipotle

- Cut the avocados into halves then remove the seeds.
- Scoop out the avocado flesh then place in a blender.
- Pour Greek yogurt to the blender then blend until smooth. Set aside.
- Next, pour water into a saucepan then season with chipotle. Bring to boil.
- Once it is boiled, stir in avocado mixture then stir well.
- Transfer the avocado cream soup to a serving bowl then serve immediately.
- Enjoy warm.

Per Serving: Net Carbs: 6.5g; Calories: 477; Total Fat: 41.5g; Saturated Fat: 10.9g
Protein: 5.8g; Carbs: 20g; Fiber: 13.5g; Sugar: 3.8g - Fat 78% / Protein 17% / Carbs 5%

Cauliflower Coconut Rice

Total Time: 20 minutes - Serves: 3
Ingredients:

- 3 cups cauliflower rice
- ½ tsp onion powder
- 1 tsp chili paste
- 2/3 cup coconut milk
- Salt

Directions:

- Add all ingredients to the pan and heat over medium-low heat. Stir to combine.
- Cook for 10 minutes. Stir after every 2 minutes.
- Remove lid and cook until excess liquid absorbed.
- Serve and enjoy.

Nutritional Value (Amount per Serving): Calories 155; Fat 13.1 g; Carbohydrates 9.2 g; Sugar 4.8 g; Protein 3.4 g; Cholesterol 1 mg;

Vegetable Salad

Total Time: 15 minutes - Serves: 6
Ingredients:

- 2 cups cauliflower florets
- 2 cups carrots, chopped
- 2 cups cherry tomatoes, halved
- 2 tbsp shallots, minced
- 1 bell pepper, seeded and chopped
- 1 cucumber, seeded and chopped
- For dressing:
- 2 garlic cloves, minced
- 1/2 cup red wine vinegar
- 1/2 cup olive oil
- Pepper
- Salt

Directions:

- In a small bowl, combine together all dressing ingredients.
- Add all salad ingredients to the large bowl and toss well.
- Pour dressing over salad and toss well.
- Place salad bowl in refrigerator for 4 hours.
- Serve chilled and enjoy.

Nutritional Value (Amount per Serving): Calories 200; Fat 17.1 g; Carbohydrates 12.1 g; Sugar 6.1 g; Protein 2.2 g; Cholesterol 0 mg;

Mexican Cauliflower Rice

Total Time: 25 minutes - Serves: 4
Ingredients:

- 1 medium cauliflower head, cut into florets
- ½ cup tomato sauce
- ¼ tsp black pepper
- 1 tsp chili powder
- 2 garlic cloves, minced
- ½ medium onion, diced
- 1 tbsp coconut oil
- ½ tsp sea salt

Directions:

- Add cauliflower florets into the food processor and process until it looks like rice.
- Heat oil in a pan over medium-high heat.
- Add onion to the pan and sauté for 5 minutes or until softened.
- Add garlic and cook for 1 minute.
- Add cauliflower rice, chili powder, pepper, and salt. Stir well.
- Add tomato sauce and cook for 5 minutes.
- Stir well and serve warm.

Nutritional Value (Amount per Serving): Calories 83; Fat 3.7g; Carbohydrates 11.5 g; Sugar 5.4 g; Protein 3.6 g; Cholesterol 0 mg;

Spicy Broccoli

Total Time: 25 minutes - Serves: 5
Ingredients:

- 2 tbsp fresh ginger, grated
- 2 tsp chili pepper, chopped
- 8 cups broccoli florets
- 1/2 cup olive oil
- 2 fresh lime juice
- 4 garlic cloves, chopped

Directions:

- Add broccoli florets into the steamer and steam for 8 minutes.
- Meanwhile, for dressing in a small bowl, combine together lime juice, oil, ginger, garlic, and chili pepper.
- Add steamed broccoli in a large mixing bowl then pour dressing over broccoli. Toss well.
- Serve and enjoy.

Nutritional Value (Amount per Serving): Calories 239; Fat 20.8 g; Carbohydrates 13.7 g; Sugar 3 g; Protein 4.5 g; Cholesterol 0 mg;

Zucchini Soup

Total Time: 20 minutes - Serves: 8
Ingredients:

- 2 ½ lbs zucchini, peeled and sliced
- 1/3 cup basil leaves
- 4 cups vegetable stock
- 4 garlic cloves, chopped
- 2 tbsp olive oil
- 1 medium onion, diced
- Pepper
- Salt

Directions:

- Heat olive oil in a pan over medium-low heat.
- Add zucchini and onion and sauté until softened. Add garlic and sauté for a minute.
- Add vegetable stock and simmer for 15 minutes.
- Remove from heat. Stir in basil and puree the soup using a blender until smooth and creamy. Season with pepper and salt.
- Stir well and serve.

Nutritional Value (Amount per Serving): Calories 62; Fat 4 g; Carbohydrates 6.8 g; Sugar 3.3 g; Protein 2 g; Cholesterol 0 mg;

Savory Kale Garlic with Crispy Coconut Cubes

Serves: 4 / Preparation time: 6 minutes / Cooking time: 22 minutes

1-cup coconut flour

½ cup water

5 tablespoons minced garlic

1-teaspoon pepper

¼ cup extra virgin olive oil, to sauté and fry

3 cups chopped kale

2 tablespoons coconut aminos

1 teaspoon red chili flakes

- Preheat a steamer over medium heat and wait until it is ready.
- In the meantime, combine coconut flour with water, 2 tablespoons of minced garlic, and ½ teaspoon pepper. Mix well until becoming a soft dough.
- Wrap the dough with aluminum foil then place in the steamer. Steam for about 10 minutes or until set.
- Remove the cooked dough from the steamer and let it cool.
- Once the cooked coconut dough is cool, unwrap it and cut into cubes. Set aside.
- Preheat a frying pan over medium heat then pour olive oil into it.
- Once the oil is hot, put the coconut cubes in the frying pan and fry until lightly golden brown and crispy.
- Remove the crispy coconut cubes from the frying pan then strain the excessive oil. Set aside.
- Next, take 2 tablespoons of olive oil and pour into a skillet.
- Preheat the skillet to medium heat then stir in the remaining minced garlic into it. Sauté until aromatic and lightly golden brown.
- Add chopped kale to the skillet then season with pepper, red chili flakes, and coconut aminos. Stir well and cook until the kale is wilted.
- Once it is done, remove the sautéed kale from the skillet and transfer to a serving dish.
- Serve and enjoy.

Per Serving: Net Carbs: 6.2g; Calories: 152; Total Fat: 13.2g; Saturated Fat: 2.3g
Protein: 2g; Carbs: 8.3g; Fiber: 2.1g; Sugar: 0.9g - Fat 78% / Protein 6% / Carbs 16%

Flavors Cauliflower Chowder

Total Time: 25 minutes - Serves: 4

Ingredients:

- 1 cauliflower head, chopped
- 1 cup coconut milk
- 4 cups vegetable stock
- 2 celery stalk, chopped
- 1 onion, chopped
- 3 garlic cloves, minced
- 1/2 tsp coriander powder
- 1 tsp turmeric
- 1 1/4 tsp ground cumin
- 2 tbsp olive oil
- Pepper
- Salt

Directions:

- Heat olive oil in a large saucepan over medium-high heat.
- Add celery, onion, and garlic and sauté for 5 minutes.
- Add cauliflower and stir well and cook for 5 minutes.
- Add stock, coconut milk, coriander, turmeric, and cumin and stir well. Bring to boil.
- Turn heat to low and simmer for 15 minutes. Season with pepper and salt.
- Serve and enjoy.

Nutritional Value (Amount per Serving): Calories 237; Fat 22.1 g; Carbohydrates 11 g; Sugar 5.4 g; Protein 3.3 g; Cholesterol 0 mg;

Sautéed Mushrooms

Total Time: 15 minutes - Serves: 4
Ingredients:

- 1 lb mushrooms, wash, dry and quartered
- 1 tsp fresh thyme, chopped
- 2 tbsp olive oil
- 2 tsp vinegar
- 2 tbsp dry white wine
- Pepper
- Salt

Directions:

- Heat olive oil in a pan over medium heat.
- Add mushrooms and stir well to coat. Cook mushrooms for 3 minutes.
- Reduce heat to low and add thyme and wine and cook until thyme is fragrant.
- Remove mushrooms from pan and add vinegar, pepper, and salt.
- Pour pan liquid over mushrooms and serve.

Nutritional Value (Amount per Serving): Calories 117; Fat 10.2 g; Carbohydrates 4.1 g; Sugar 2 g; Protein 3.6 g; Cholesterol 8 mg;

Easy Chia Seed Pudding

Total Time: 10 minutes - Serves: 4
Ingredients:

- ¼ tsp cinnamon
- 15 drops liquid stevia
- ½ tsp vanilla extract
- ½ cup chia seeds
- 2 cups unsweetened coconut milk

Directions:

- Add all ingredients into the glass jar and mix well.
- Close jar with lid and place in refrigerator for 4 hours.
- Serve chilled and enjoy.

Nutritional Value (Amount per Serving): Calories 347; Fat 33.2 g; Carbohydrates 9.8 g; Sugar 4.1 g; Protein 5.9 g; Cholesterol 0 mg;

5 Minutes Crispy Spinach

Serves: 4 / Preparation time: 4 minutes / Cooking time: 2 minutes

2 bunches spinach	1-cup water
½ cup almond flour	½ cup extra virgin olive oil, to fry
¼ teaspoon pepper	

- Season the almond flour with pepper then stir well. Set aside.
- Cut the spinach leaves and remove the stem.
- Coat the spinach leaves with almond flour mixture then dip into the water.
- Take the spinach out of the water then coat again with almond flour. Repeat with the remaining spinach and almond flour.
- Preheat a frying pan over medium heat then pour olive oil into it.
- Once the oil is hot, put the coated spinach in the hot oil and fry for approximately 2 minutes each side.
- Remove the fried spinach from the frying pan and strain the oil.
- Serve and enjoy.

Per Serving: Net Carbs: 2.8g; Calories: 299; Total Fat: 30.4g; Saturated Fat: 4.2g
Protein: 5.6g; Carbs: 7g; Fiber: 4.2g; Sugar: 0.8g - Fat 92% / Protein 7% / Carbs 1%

Roasted Cauliflower

Total Time: 20 minutes - Serves: 4
Ingredients:

- 1 large cauliflower head, cut into florets
- 1 lemon zest
- 3 tbsp olive oil
- 2 tsp lemon juice
- ½ tsp Italian seasoning
- ½ tsp garlic powder
- ¼ tsp pepper
- ¼ tsp salt

Directions:

- Preheat the oven to 425 F/ 218 C.
- In a bowl, combine together olive oil, lemon juice, Italian seasoning, garlic powder, lemon zest, pepper, and salt.
- Add cauliflower florets to the bowl and toss well.
- Spread cauliflower florets on baking tray and roast in preheated oven for 15 minutes.
- Serve and enjoy.

Nutritional Value (Amount per Serving): Calories 146; Fat 10.9 g; Carbohydrates 11.6 g; Sugar 5.2 g; Protein 4.3 g; Cholesterol 0 mg;

Refreshing Cucumber Salad

Total Time: 10 minutes - Serves: 4
Ingredients:

- 1/3 cup cucumber basil ranch
- 1 cucumber, chopped
- 3 tomatoes, chopped
- 3 tbsp fresh herbs, chopped
- ½ onion, sliced

Directions:

- Add all ingredients into the large mixing bowl and toss well.
- Serve immediately and enjoy.

Nutritional Value (Amount per Serving): Calories 84; Fat 3.4 g; Carbohydrates 12.5 g; Sugar 6.8 g; Protein 2 g; Cholesterol 0 mg;

Lemon Zucchini Noodles

Total Time: 15 minutes - Serves: 4
Ingredients:

- 4 small zucchini, spiralized into noodles
- 2 garlic cloves
- 2 cups fresh basil leaves
- 2 tsp lemon juice
- 1/3 cup olive oil
- Pepper
- Salt

Directions:

- Add garlic, basil, olive oil, and lemon juice into the blender and blend well. Season with pepper and salt.
- In a large bowl, combine together pesto and zucchini noodles.
- Stir well and serve.

Nutritional Value (Amount per Serving): Calories 169; Fat 17.1 g; Carbohydrates 4.8 g; Sugar 2.2 g; Protein 1.9 g; Cholesterol 0 mg;

Baked Spaghetti Squash with Spicy Almond Sauce

Serves: 4 / Preparation time: 6 minutes / Cooking time: 24 minutes

½ spaghetti squash	1 ½ tablespoons extra virgin olive oil
2 tablespoons sesame oil	¼ teaspoon garlic powder
¼ cup almond butter	1 teaspoon red chili flakes
2 tablespoons coconut aminos	2 tablespoons chopped roasted almonds

- Preheat an oven to 250°F (121°C) and cover a baking tray with aluminum foil.
- Brush the spaghetti squash with sesame oil then place on the prepared baking tray.
- Bake the spaghetti squash for approximately 15 minutes or until tender then remove from the oven and let it cool.
- Using a julienne peeler cut the spaghetti squash into noodle forms then place in a salad bowl. Set aside.
- Next, combine almond butter with coconut aminos, extra virgin olive oil, garlic powder, and red chili flakes then stir until incorporated.
- Drizzle the sauce over the baked spaghetti squash then sprinkle chopped roasted almonds on top.
- Serve and enjoy!

Per Serving: Net Carbs: 2.2g; Calories: 139; Total Fat: 14.2g; Saturated Fat: 1.9g
Protein: 1.2g; Carbs: 3g; Fiber: 0.8g; Sugar: 1.1g - Fat 92% / Protein 2% / Carbs 6%

Roasted Almond Broccoli

Total Time: 25 minutes - Serves: 4
Ingredients:

- 1 1/2 lbs broccoli florets
- 3 tbsp olive oil
- 1 tbsp fresh lemon juice
- 3 tbsp slivered almonds, toasted
- 2 garlic cloves, sliced
- 1/4 tsp pepper

- 1/4 tsp salt

Directions:
- Preheat the oven to 425 F/ 218 C.
- Spray baking dish with cooking spray.
- Add broccoli, pepper, salt, garlic, and oil in large bowl and toss well.
- Spread broccoli on the prepared baking dish and roast in preheated oven for 20 minutes.
- Add lemon juice and almonds over broccoli and toss well.
- Serve and enjoy.

Nutritional Value (Amount per Serving): Calories 177; Fat 13.3 g; Carbohydrates 12.9 g; Sugar 3.2 g; Protein 5.8 g; Cholesterol 0 mg;

Protein Breakfast Shake

Total Time: 10 minutes - Serves: 2
Ingredients:

- 1 cup coconut milk, unsweetened
- 1 scoop protein powder
- 7 oz firm tofu
- 15 drops liquid stevia
- 1 tbsp cocoa powder
- 1 tbsp cocoa nibs
- 1 tbsp chia seeds
- 2 tbsp hemp hearts
- 1/2 oz almonds

Directions:
- Add all ingredients into the blender and blend until you get a thick consistency.
- Serve and enjoy.

Nutritional Value (Amount per Serving): Calories 243; Fat 13 g; Carbohydrates 11 g; Sugar 1.4 g; Protein 21.2 g; Cholesterol 23 mg;

Minty Pumpkin Cheese Bombs

Serves: 4 / Preparation time: 30 minutes / Cooking time: 10 minutes

¾ lb. pumpkin	1-½ tablespoon mustard
¼ cup chopped onion	½ teaspoon salt
¼ cup chopped parsley	½ teaspoon pepper
2 teaspoons chopped mint leaves	¼ lb. mozzarella cheese
¼ cup almond flour	1 egg
2 tablespoons butter	1 cup roasted pecans
1-teaspoon thyme	

- Peel the pumpkin then cut into cubes.
- Place the cubed pumpkin in a food processor then process until smooth.
- Transfer the smooth pumpkin to a bowl then add chopped onion, parsley, mint leaves, and flour.
- Pour melted butter into the bowl then season with thyme, mustard, salt, and pepper. Mix until combined.
- Shape the pumpkin mixture into small balls the fill each ball with Mozzarella cheese.
- Arrange the pumpkin balls on a tray then refrigerate for 15 minutes.
- Meanwhile, place the roasted pecans in a food processor then process until smooth and becoming crumbles. Set aside.
- In a separate bowl, crack the egg then using a fork stir until incorporated.

- Preheat an Air Fryer to 400°F (204°C).
- Take the pumpkin bowl out of the refrigerator then dip in the egg.
- Roll the pumpkin balls in the pecan crumbles then arrange on the Air Fryer's rack.
- Cook the pumpkin balls for 12 minutes then remove from heat.
- Serve and enjoy warm.

Per Serving: Net Carbs: 6g; Calories: 438; Total Fat: 41.3g; Saturated Fat: 13.2g
Protein: 12g; Carbs: 9.9g; Fiber: 3.9g; Sugar: 2.7g - Fat 85% / Protein 11% / Carbs 4%

Celery Salad

Total Time: 10 minutes - Serves: 6
Ingredients:

- 6 cups celery, sliced
- ¼ tsp celery seed
- 1 tbsp lemon juice
- 2 tsp lemon zest, grated
- 1 tbsp parsley, chopped
- 1 tbsp olive oil
- Sea salt

Directions:

- Add all ingredients into the large mixing bowl and toss well.
- Serve immediately and enjoy.

Nutritional Value (Amount per Serving): Calories 38; Fat 2.5 g; Carbohydrates 3.3 g; Sugar 1.5 g; Protein 0.8 g; Cholesterol 0 mg;

Coconut Curry

Total Time: 30 minutes - Serves: 4
Ingredients:

- 1/2 cup coconut cream
- 1/4 medium onion, sliced
- 2 tsp soy sauce
- 1 tsp ginger, minced
- 1 tsp garlic, minced
- 4 tbsp coconut oil
- 2 cups spinach
- 1 cup broccoli florets
- 1 tbsp red curry paste

Directions:

- Heat coconut oil in a saucepan over medium-high heat.
- Add onion in a pan and cook until softened. Add garlic sauté for a minute.
- Turn heat to medium-low and add broccoli and stir well.
- Once broccoli is cooked then add curry paste and stir for 1 minute.
- Add spinach over the top of broccoli and cook until wilted.
- Add ginger, soy sauce, and coconut cream and stir well. Simmer for 10 minutes.
- Stir well and serve.

Nutritional Value (Amount per Serving): Calories 219; Fat 22.1 g; Carbohydrates 5.9 g; Sugar 1.8 g; Protein 2.1 g; Cholesterol 0 mg;

Green Spinach Kale Soup

Total Time: 15 minutes - Serves: 6
Ingredients:

- 2 avocados
- 8 oz spinach
- 8 oz kale
- 1 fresh lime juice
- 1 cup water
- 3 1/3 cup coconut milk
- 3 oz olive oil
- 1/4 tsp pepper
- 1 tsp salt

Directions:
- Heat olive oil in a saucepan over medium heat.
- Add kale and spinach to the saucepan and sauté for 2-3 minutes.
- Remove saucepan from heat. Add coconut milk, spices, avocado, and water. Stir well.
- Puree the soup using an immersion blender until smooth and creamy.
- Add fresh lime juice and stir well.
- Serve and enjoy.

Nutritional Value (Amount per Serving): Calories 233; Fat 20 g; Carbohydrates 12 g; Sugar 0.5 g; Protein 4.2 g; Cholesterol 0 mg;

Spiced Coconut Carrot Fritter

Serves: 4 / Preparation time: 4 minutes / Cooking time: 12 minutes

½ cup coconut flour

2 tablespoons coconut milk

2 tablespoons water

2 tablespoons grated coconut

2 tablespoons shredded carrots

¼ teaspoon coriander

¼ cup olive oil, to fry

- Place coconut flour in a bowl then pour water and coconut milk over the flour.
- Season the flour with coriander then mix until incorporated.
- Add grated coconut and shredded carrots to the mixture then stir until just combined.
- Next, preheat a frying pan over medium heat then pour olive oil into it.
- Once the oil is hot, drop about 2 tablespoons of mixture and fry for approximately 2 minutes.
- Flip the fritter and fry until both sides of the fritter are lightly golden brown.
- Remove the fritter and strain the excessive oil. Repeat with the remaining mixture.
- Once it is done, arrange the fritters on a serving dish and serve.
- Enjoy warm.

Per Serving: Net Carbs: 1g; Calories: 143; Total Fat: 15.5g; Saturated Fat: 4.4g
Protein: 0.5g; Carbs: 2.1g; Fiber: 1.1g; Sugar: 0.7g - Fat 97% / Protein 1% / Carbs 2%

Almond Green Beans

Total Time: 20 minutes - Serves: 4
Ingredients:
- 1 lb fresh green beans, trimmed
- 1/3 cup almonds, sliced
- 4 garlic cloves, sliced
- 2 tbsp olive oil
- 1 tbsp lemon juice
- ½ tsp sea salt

Directions:
- Add green beans, salt, and lemon juice in a mixing bowl. Toss well and set aside.
- Heat oil in a pan over medium heat.
- Add sliced almonds and sauté until lightly browned.
- Add garlic and sauté for 30 seconds.
- Pour almond mixture over green beans and toss well.
- Stir well and serve immediately.

Nutritional Value (Amount per Serving): Calories 146; Fat 11.2 g; Carbohydrates 10.9 g; Sugar 2 g; Protein 4 g; Cholesterol 0 mg;

Cabbage Cucumber Salad

Total Time: 20 minutes - Serves: 8
Ingredients:

- 1/2 cabbage head, chopped
- 2 cucumbers, sliced
- 2 tbsp green onion, chopped
- 2 tbsp fresh dill, chopped
- 3 tbsp olive oil
- 1/2 lemon juice
- Pepper
- Salt

Directions:

- Add cabbage to the large bowl. Season with 1 teaspoon of salt mix well and set aside.
- Add cucumbers, green onions, and fresh dill. Mix well.
- Add lemon juice, pepper, olive oil, and salt. Mix well.
- Place salad bowl in refrigerator for 2 hours.
- Serve chilled and enjoy.

Nutritional Value (Amount per Serving): Calories 71; Fat 5.4 g; Carbohydrates 5.9 g; Sugar 2.8 g; Protein 1.3 g; Cholesterol 0 mg;

Zucchini Muffins

Total Time: 35 minutes - Serves: 8
Ingredients:

- 1 cup almond flour
- 1 zucchini, grated
- 1/4 cup coconut oil, melted
- 15 drops liquid stevia
- 1/2 tsp baking soda
- 1/2 cup coconut flour
- 1/2 cup walnut, chopped
- 1 1/2 tsp cinnamon
- 3/4 cup unsweetened applesauce
- 1/8 tsp salt

Directions:

- Preheat the oven to 325 F/ 162 C.
- Spray muffin tray with cooking spray and set aside.
- In a bowl, combine together grated zucchini, coconut oil, and stevia.
- In another bowl, mix together coconut flour, baking soda, almond flour, walnut, cinnamon, and salt.
- Add zucchini mixture into the coconut flour mixture and mix well.
- Add applesauce and stir until well combined.
- Pour batter into the prepared muffin tray and bake in preheated oven for 25-30 minutes.
- Serve and enjoy.

Nutritional Value (Amount per Serving): Calories 229; Fat 18.9 g; Carbohydrates 12.5 g; Sugar 3.4 g; Protein 5.2 g; Cholesterol 0 mg;

Sautéed Broccoli with Onion and Mushroom

Serves: 4 / Preparation time: 8 minutes / Cooking time: 6 minutes

3 cups broccoli florets

1 cup chopped mushroom

2 tablespoons extra virgin olive oil

½ cup chopped onion

¼ teaspoon pepper

½ teaspoon sesame seeds

- Preheat a skillet over medium heat then pour extra virgin olive oil into it.
- Once the oil is hot, stir in chopped onion and sauté until aromatic and lightly golden brown.
- Next, stir in chopped mushroom and broccoli florets then cook until wilted.
- Season the mushroom and broccoli with pepper then stir well. Cook until the broccoli is done but not too soft.
- Remove the sautéed broccoli and mushroom from heat and transfer to a serving dish.
- Sprinkle sesame seeds on top and serve immediately.
- Enjoy warm.

Per Serving: Net Carbs: 4.3g; Calories: 95; Total Fat: 7.5g; Saturated Fat: 1g
Protein: 2.7g; Carbs: 6.6g; Fiber: 2.3g; Sugar: 2.1g - Fat 71% / Protein 14% / Carbs 15%

Tomato Eggplant Spinach Salad

Total Time: 30 minutes - Serves: 4
Ingredients:

- 1 large eggplant, cut into 3/4 inch slices
- 5 oz spinach
- 1 tbsp sun-dried tomatoes, chopped
- 1 tbsp oregano, chopped
- 1 tbsp parsley, chopped
- 1 tbsp fresh mint, chopped
- 1 tbsp shallot, chopped
- For dressing:
- 1/4 cup olive oil
- 1/2 lemon juice
- 1/2 tsp smoked paprika
- 1 tsp Dijon mustard
- 1 tsp tahini
- 2 garlic cloves, minced
- Pepper
- Salt

Directions:

- Place sliced eggplants into the large bowl and sprinkle with salt and set aside for minutes.
- In a small bowl mix together all dressing ingredients. Set aside.
- Heat grill to medium-high heat.
- In a large bowl, add shallot, sun-dried tomatoes, herbs, and spinach.
- Rinse eggplant slices and pat dry with paper towel.
- Brush eggplant slices with olive oil and grill on medium high heat for 3-4 minutes on each side.
- Let cool the grilled eggplant slices then cut into quarters.
- Add eggplant to the salad bowl and pour dressing over salad. Toss well.
- Serve and enjoy.

Nutritional Value (Amount per Serving): Calories 163; Fat 13 g; Carbohydrates 10 g; Sugar 3 g; Protein 2 g; Cholesterol 0 mg;

Chia Flaxseed Waffles

Total Time: 25 minutes - Serves: 8
Ingredients:

- 2 cups ground golden flaxseed
- 2 tsp cinnamon
- 10 tsp ground chia seed
- 15 tbsp warm water
- 1/3 cup coconut oil, melted
- 1/2 cup water
- 1 tbsp baking powder
- 1 tsp sea salt

Directions:

- Preheat the waffle iron.
- In a small bowl, mix together ground chia seed and warm water.

- In a large bowl, mix together ground flax seed, sea salt, and baking powder. Set aside.
- Add melted coconut oil, chia seed mixture, and water into the blender and blend for 30 seconds.
- Transfer coconut oil mixture into the flax seed mixture and mix well. Add cinnamon and stir well.
- Scoop waffle mixture into the hot waffle iron and cook on each side for 3-5 minutes.
- Serve and enjoy.

Nutritional Value (Amount per Serving): Calories 240; Fat 20.6 g; Carbohydrates 12.9 g; Sugar 0 g; Protein 7 g; Cholesterol 0 mg;

Sage Pecan Cauliflower

Total Time: 40 minutes - Serves: 6
Ingredients:

- 1 large cauliflower head, cut into florets
- 1/2 tsp dried thyme
- 1/2 tsp poultry seasoning
- 1/4 cup olive oil
- 2 garlic clove, minced
- 1/4 cup pecans, chopped
- 2 tbsp parsley, chopped
- 1/2 tsp ground sage
- 1/4 cup celery, chopped
- 1 onion, sliced
- 1/4 tsp black pepper
- 1 tsp sea salt

Directions:

- Preheat the oven to 450 F/ 232 C.
- Spray a baking tray with cooking spray and set aside.
- In a large bowl, mix together cauliflower, thyme, poultry seasoning, olive oil, garlic, celery, sage, onions, pepper, and salt.
- Spread mixture on a baking tray and roast in preheated oven for 15 minutes.
- Add pecans and parsley and stir well. Roast for 10-15 minutes more.
- Serve and enjoy.

Nutritional Value (Amount per Serving): Calories 118; Fat 8.6 g; Carbohydrates 9.9 g; Sugar 4.2 g; Protein 3.1 g; Cholesterol 0 mg;

Savory and Nutritious Fried Cauliflower Rice

Serves: 4 / Preparation time: 6 minutes / Cooking time: 23 minutes

3 cups cauliflower florets

2 tablespoons extra virgin olive oil

½ teaspoon minced garlic

½ teaspoon pepper

2 tablespoons coconut aminos

1 lemon grass

1 cup chopped mushroom

½ cup sliced cabbage

¼ cup shredded carrots

- Place the cauliflower florets in a steamer then steam until soft.
- Remove the steamed cauliflower florets from the steamer and transfer to a food processor. Process until smooth.
- Next, preheat a skillet over medium heat then pour extra virgin olive oil into the skillet.
- Once the oil is hot, stir in minced garlic and sauté until wilted and aromatic.
- Add chopped mushrooms, sliced cabbage, and shredded carrots to the skillet then sauté until wilted.
- After that, stir in cauliflower rice to the skillet then season with pepper, coconut aminos, and lemon grass. Cook until combined.

- Once it is done, transfer the fried cauliflower rice to a serving dish then serve warm.
- Enjoy immediately.

Per Serving: Net Carbs: 4.3g; Calories: 92; Total Fat: 7.2g; Saturated Fat: 1g
Protein: 2.3g; Carbs: 6.8g; Fiber: 2.5g; Sugar: 2.7g - Fat 70% / Protein 12% / Carbs 18%

Apple Avocado Coconut Smoothie

Total Time: 5 minutes - Serves: 2
Ingredients:

- 1 tsp coconut oil
- 1 tbsp collagen powder
- 1 tbsp fresh lime juice
- ½ cup unsweetened coconut milk
- ¼ apple, slice
- 1 avocado

Directions:

- Add all ingredients into the blender and blend until smooth and creamy.
- Serve and enjoy.

Nutritional Value (Amount per Serving): Calories 262; Fat 23.9 g; Carbohydrates 13.6 g; Sugar 3.4 g; Protein 2 g; Cholesterol 0 mg;

Delicious Herb Cauliflower Rice

Total Time: 20 minutes - Serves: 3
Ingredients:

- 10 oz cauliflower rice
- 4 oz mushrooms, sliced
- 8 oz asparagus, cut into 3" pieces
- 1/2 tsp rosemary
- 1/2 tsp cayenne
- 2 tbsp olive oil
- 6 baby carrots, sliced
- 1/2 tsp black pepper
- 1/2 tsp sea salt

Directions:

- Heat olive oil in a pan over medium heat.
- Add vegetables to a pan and sauté for 3-4 minutes.
- Add cauliflower rice and spices and sauté for 10 minutes.
- Serve and enjoy.

Nutritional Value (Amount per Serving): Calories 137; Fat 9.7 g; Carbohydrates 11.5 g; Sugar 5.3 g; Protein 5 g; Cholesterol 0 mg;

Turnip Carrot Salad

Total Time: 50 minutes - Serves: 4
Ingredients:

- 1 turnip, shredded
- 1/4 tsp dill
- 3 cups cabbage, shredded
- 1 carrot, shredded
- 1 green pepper, chopped
- 1 tsp salt

Directions:

- Add cabbage and salt in a bowl. Cover bowl and set aside for 40 minutes.
- Wash and cabbage and dry well.
- Add cabbage in a bowl with remaining ingredients and toss well.
- Serve and enjoy.

Nutritional Value (Amount per Serving): Calories 34; Fat 0.1 g; Carbohydrates 7.9 g; Sugar 4.3 g; Protein 1.3 g; Cholesterol 0 mg;

Garlic Zucchini Squash

Total Time: 20 minutes - Serves: 4

Ingredients:

- 1 small squash, sliced
- 2 tbsp fresh basil, chopped
- 2 tbsp olive oil
- 1 garlic clove, chopped
- 1 large onion, sliced
- 2 fresh tomatoes, cut into wedges
- 1 small zucchini, sliced
- Pepper
- Salt

Directions:

- Heat olive oil in a pan over medium-high heat.
- Add onion, squash, zucchini, and garlic and sauté until lightly brown.
- Add basil and tomatoes and cook for 5 minutes. Season with pepper and salt.
- Simmer over low heat until squash is tender.
- Stir well and serve.

Nutritional Value (Amount per Serving): Calories 97; Fat 7.2 g; Carbohydrates 8.2 g; Sugar 4.4 g; Protein 1.4 g; Cholesterol 0 mg;

Strawberry Chia Matcha Pudding

Total Time: 10 minutes - Serves: 1

Ingredients:

- 5 drops liquid stevia
- 2 strawberries, diced
- 1 ½ tbsp chia seeds
- ¾ cup unsweetened coconut milk
- ½ tsp matcha powder

Directions:

- Add all ingredients except strawberries into the glass jar and mix well.
- Close jar with lid and place in refrigerator for 4 hours.
- Add strawberries into the pudding and mix well.
- Serve and enjoy.

Nutritional Value (Amount per Serving): Calories 93; Fat 6.5 g; Carbohydrates 5.6 g; Sugar 1.2 g; Protein 2.5 g; Cholesterol 0 mg;

Creamy Squash Soup

Total Time: 35 minutes - Serves: 8

Ingredients:

- 3 cups butternut squash, chopped
- 1 ½ cups unsweetened coconut milk
- 1 tbsp coconut oil
- 1 tsp dried onion flakes
- 1 tbsp curry powder
- 4 cups water
- 1 garlic clove
- 1 tsp kosher salt

Directions:

- Add squash, coconut oil, onion flakes, curry powder, water, garlic, and salt into a large saucepan. Bring to boil over high heat.
- Turn heat to medium and simmer for 20 minutes.

- Puree the soup using a blender until smooth. Return soup to the saucepan and stir in coconut milk and cook for 2 minutes.
- Stir well and serve hot.

Nutritional Value (Amount per Serving): Calories 146; Fat 12.6 g; Carbohydrates 9.4 g; Sugar 2.8 g; Protein 1.7 g; Cholesterol 0 mg;

Crispy Broccoli Pop Corn

Serves: 4 / Preparation time: 5 minutes / Cooking time: 6 minutes

2 cups broccoli florets	½ teaspoon salt
2 cups coconut flour	½ teaspoon pepper
4 egg yolks	¼ cup butter

- Soak the broccoli florets in salty water to remove all the insects inside.
- Wash and rinse the broccoli florets then pat them dry.
- Melt butter then let it cool.
- Crack the eggs then place in the same bowl with the melted butter.
- Add coconut flour to the liquid then season with salt and pepper. Mix until incorporated.
- Preheat an Air Fryer to 400°F (204°C).
- Dip a broccoli floret in the coconut flour mixture then place in the Air Fryer. Repeat with the remaining broccoli florets.
- Cook the broccoli florets 6 minutes. You may do this in several batches.
- Once it is done, remove the fried broccoli popcorn from the Air Fryer then place on a serving dish.
- Serve and enjoy immediately.

Per Serving: Net Carbs: 4g; Calories: 202; Total Fat: 17.2g; Saturated Fat: 9.9g
Protein: 5.1g; Carbs: 7.8g; Fiber: 3.8g; Sugar: 1.4g - Fat 77% / Protein 10% / Carbs 13%

Chia Raspberry Pudding Shots

Total Time: 10 minutes - Serves: 4
Ingredients:

- ½ cup raspberries
- 10 drops liquid stevia
- 1 tbsp unsweetened cocoa powder
- ¼ cup unsweetened almond milk
- ½ cup unsweetened coconut milk
- ¼ cup chia seeds

Directions:

- Add all ingredients into the glass jar and stir well to combine.
- Pour pudding mixture into the shot glasses and place in refrigerator for 1 hour.
- Serve chilled and enjoy.

Nutritional Value (Amount per Serving): Calories 117; Fat 10 g; Carbohydrates 5.9 g; Sugar 1.7 g; Protein 2.7 g; Cholesterol 0 mg;

Turnip Salad

Total Time: 10 minutes - Serves: 4
Ingredients:

- 4 white turnips, spiralized
- 1 lemon juice

- 4 dill sprigs, chopped
- 2 tbsp olive oil
- 1 1/2 tsp salt

Directions:

- Season spiralized turnip with salt and gently massage with hands.
- Add lemon juice and dill. Season with pepper and salt.
- Drizzle with olive oil and combine everything well.
- Serve immediately and enjoy.

Nutritional Value (Amount per Serving): Calories 49; Fat 1.1 g; Carbohydrates 9 g; Sugar 5.2 g; Protein 1.4 g; Cholesterol 0 mg;

Avocado Breakfast Smoothie

Total Time: 5 minutes - Serves: 2
Ingredients:

- 5 drops liquid stevia
- ¼ cup ice cubes
- ½ avocado
- 1 tsp vanilla extract
- 1 cup unsweetened coconut milk

Directions:

- Add all ingredients into the blender and blend until smooth and creamy.
- Serve immediately and enjoy.

Nutritional Value (Amount per Serving): Calories 131; Fat 11.8 g; Carbohydrates 5.6 g; Sugar 0.5 g; Protein 1 g; Cholesterol 0 mg;

Grain-free Overnight Oats

Total Time: 10 minutes - Serves: 1
Ingredients:

- 2/3 cup unsweetened coconut milk
- 2 tsp chia seeds
- 2 tbsp vanilla protein powder
- ½ tbsp coconut flour
- 3 tbsp hemp hearts

Directions:

- Add all ingredients into the glass jar and stir to combine.
- Close jar with lid and place in refrigerator for overnight.
- Top with fresh berries and serve.

Nutritional Value (Amount per Serving): Calories 378; Fat 22.5 g; Carbohydrates 15 g; Sugar 1.5 g; Protein 27 g; Cholesterol 0 mg;

Avocado Cabbage Salad

Total Time: 20 minutes - Serves: 4
Ingredients:

- 2 avocados, diced
- 4 cups cabbage, shredded
- 3 tbsp fresh parsley, chopped
- 2 tbsp apple cider vinegar
- 4 tbsp olive oil
- 1 cup cherry tomatoes, halved
- 1/2 tsp pepper
- 1 1/2 tsp sea salt

Directions:

- Add cabbage, avocados, and tomatoes to a medium bowl and mix well.

- In a small bowl, whisk together oil, parsley, vinegar, pepper, and salt.
- Pour dressing over vegetables and mix well.
- Serve and enjoy.

Nutritional Value (Amount per Serving): Calories 253; Fat 21.6 g; Carbohydrates 14 g; Sugar 4 g; Protein 3.5 g; Cholesterol 0 mg;

Almond Pecan Porridge with Cinnamon

Serves: 4 / Preparation time: 4 minutes / Cooking time: 16 minutes

2 cups unsweetened almond milk	2 tablespoons hemp seeds
½ cup almond butter	½ cup chopped pecans
2 tablespoons extra virgin olive oil	1-teaspoon cinnamon

- Preheat an oven to 250°F (121°C)) and line a baking tray with parchment paper.
- Toss the pecans with extra virgin olive then spread over the prepared baking tray.
- Bake the pecans until tender then remove from the oven. Let it cool.
- Once the toasted pecans are cool, transfer to a food processor then process until becoming crumbles. Set aside.
- Preheat almond milk over medium heat then add almond butter to it.
- Wait until the butter is melted then transfer the mixture to a serving bowl.
- Add pecans crumbles to the bowl then sprinkle hemp seeds and cinnamon on top.
- Serve and enjoy immediately.

Per Serving: Net Carbs: 4g; Calories: 200; Total Fat: 17.5g; Saturated Fat: 1.8g
Protein: 6.8g; Carbs: 5.9g; Fiber: 1.9g; Sugar: 0.7g - Fat 79% / Protein 13% / Carbs 8%

Tomato Pumpkin Soup

Total Time: 25 minutes - Serves: 4
Ingredients:

- 2 cups pumpkin, diced
- 1/2 cup tomato, chopped
- 1/2 cup onion, chopped
- 1 1/2 tsp curry powder
- 1/2 tsp paprika
- 2 cups vegetable stock
- 1 tsp olive oil
- 1/2 tsp garlic, minced

Directions:

- In a saucepan, add oil, garlic, and onion and sauté for 3 minutes over medium heat.
- Add remaining ingredients into the saucepan and bring to boil.
- Reduce heat and cover and simmer for 10 minutes.
- Puree the soup using a blender until smooth.
- Stir well and serve warm.

Nutritional Value (Amount per Serving): Calories 70; Fat 2.7 g; Carbohydrates 13.8 g; Sugar 6.3 g; Protein 1.9 g; Cholesterol 0 mg;

Spinach Tomato Stir Fry

Total Time: 25 minutes - Serves: 2
Ingredients:

- 1/2 cup cherry tomatoes, cut in half
- 1/2 onion, sliced
- 4 cups spinach
- 1 garlic clove, diced
- 1/2 tsp lemon zest
- 2 tsp olive oil
- 6 button mushrooms, sliced
- Pepper
- Salt

Directions:

- Heat olive oil in a pan over medium heat.
- Add mushrooms and sauté for 3-4 minutes or until lightly browned.
- Remove mushrooms to a plate and set aside.
- Add onion and sauté for 2-3 minutes or until softened.
- Add tomatoes, garlic and lemon zest, and season with pepper and salt. Cook for 2-3 minutes and lightly smashed tomatoes with a spatula.
- Now add mushrooms and spinach and stir well and cook until spinach is wilted.
- Season with salt and drizzle with lemon juice.
- Serve and enjoy.

Nutritional Value (Amount per Serving): Calories 104; Fat 7.1 g; Carbohydrates 8.9 g; Sugar 3.6 g; Protein 4.3 g; Cholesterol 5 mg;

Flax Almond Muffins

Total Time: 45 minutes - Serves: 6
Ingredients:

- 1 tsp cinnamon
- 2 tbsp coconut flour
- 20 drops liquid stevia
- 1/4 cup water
- 1/4 tsp vanilla extract
- 1/4 tsp baking soda
- 1/2 tsp baking powder
- 1/4 cup almond flour
- 1/2 cup ground flax
- 2 tbsp ground chia

Directions:

- Preheat the oven to 350 F/ 176 C.
- Spray muffin tray with cooking spray and set aside.
- In a small bowl, add 6 tablespoons of water and ground chia. Mix well and set aside.
- In a mixing bowl, add ground flax, baking soda, baking powder, cinnamon, coconut flour, and almond flour and mix well.
- Add chia seed mixture, vanilla, water, and liquid stevia and stir well to combine.
- Pour mixture into the prepared muffin tray and bake in preheated oven for 35 minutes.
- Serve and enjoy.

Nutritional Value (Amount per Serving): Calories 92; Fat 6.3 g; Carbohydrates 6.9 g; Sugar 0.4 g; Protein 3.7 g; Cholesterol 0 mg;

Cheesy Cauliflower Croquettes

Serves: 4 / Preparation time: 10 minutes / Cooking time: 14 minutes

2 cups cauliflower florets	½ teaspoon salt
2 teaspoons minced garlic	½ teaspoon pepper
½ cup chopped onion	2 tablespoons butter
¾ teaspoon mustard	¾ cup grated cheddar cheese

- Place butter in a microwave-safe bowl then melt the butter. Let it cool.
- Place cauliflower florets in a food processor then process until smooth and becoming crumbles.

- Transfer the cauliflower crumbles to a bowl then add chopped onion and cheese.
- Season with minced garlic, mustard, salt, and pepper then pour melted butter over the mixture.
- Shape the cauliflower mixture into medium balls then arrange in the Air Fryer.
- Preheat an Air Fryer to 400°F (204°C) and cook the cauliflower croquettes for 14 minutes.
- If you want them to be more golden brown, cook the cauliflower croquettes for another 2 minutes.
- Serve and enjoy with homemade tomato sauce.

Per Serving: Net Carbs: 3.3g; Calories: 160; Total Fat: 13g; Saturated Fat: 8.1g
Protein: 6.8g; Carbs: 5.1g; Fiber: 1.8g; Sugar: 2g - Fat 73% / Protein 17% / Carbs 10%

Brussels sprouts Salad

Total Time: 20 minutes - Serves: 6
Ingredients:

- 1 ½ lbs Brussels sprouts, trimmed
- ¼ cup toasted hazelnuts, chopped
- 2 tsp Dijon mustard
- 1 ½ tbsp lemon juice
- 2 tbsp olive oil
- Pepper
- Salt

Directions:

- In a small bowl, whisk together oil, mustard, lemon juice, pepper, and salt.
- In a large bowl, combine together Brussels sprouts and hazelnuts.
- Pour dressing over salad and toss well.
- Serve immediately and enjoy.

Nutritional Value (Amount per Serving): Calories 111; Fat 7.1 g; Carbohydrates 11 g; Sugar 2.7 g; Protein 4.4 g; Cholesterol 0 mg;

Baked Cauliflower

Total Time: 55 minutes - Serves: 2
Ingredients:

- 1/2 cauliflower head, cut into florets
- 2 tbsp olive oil
- For seasoning:
- 1/2 tsp garlic powder
- 1/2 tsp ground cumin
- 1/2 tsp black pepper
- 1/2 tsp white pepper
- 1 tsp onion powder
- 1/4 tsp dried oregano
- 1/4 tsp dried basil
- 1/4 tsp dried thyme
- 1 tbsp ground cayenne pepper
- 2 tbsp ground paprika
- 2 tsp salt

Directions:

- Preheat the oven to 400 F/ 200 C.
- Spray a baking tray with cooking spray and set aside.
- In a large bowl, mix together all seasoning ingredients.
- Add oil and stir well. Add cauliflower to the bowl seasoning mixture and stir well to coat.
- Spread the cauliflower florets on a baking tray and bake in preheated oven for 45 minutes.
- Serve and enjoy.

Nutritional Value (Amount per Serving): Calories 177; Fat 15.6 g; Carbohydrates 11.5 g; Sugar 3.2 g; Protein 3.1 g; Cholesterol 0 mg;

Tasty Vegetables Soup in Coconut Gravy

Serves: 4 / Preparation time: 4 minutes / Cooking time: 11 minutes

2 cups chopped spinach	1 teaspoon minced garlic
1 cup chopped cabbage	1-teaspoon cayenne pepper
1 medium carrot	½ teaspoon red chili flakes
¼ cup cooked kidney beans	¾ cup coconut milk
2 tablespoons chopped celeries	1-cup water

- Peel the carrot then cut into slices. Set aside.
- Pour water into a pot then season with minced garlic, cayenne pepper, and red chili flakes then bring to boil.
- Once it is boiled, add kidney beans, chopped cabbage, and carrot to the soup.
- Pour coconut milk into the soup then bring to a simmer.
- Next, stir in chopped spinach to the soup and cook until the spinach is just wilted.
- Transfer the soup to a serving bowl then serve warm.
- Enjoy immediately.

Per Serving: Net Carbs: 5.2g; Calories: 137; Total Fat: 11g; Saturated Fat: 9.5g
Protein: 2.7g; Carbs: 9.6g; Fiber: 3.2g; Sugar: 4g - Fat 72% / Protein 18% / Carbs 10%

Cinnamon Noatmeal

Total Time: 10 minutes - Serves: 2
Ingredients:

- ¾ cup hot water
- 2 tbsp sugar-free maple syrup
- ½ tsp ground cinnamon
- 2 tbsp ground flax seeds
- 3 tbsp vegan vanilla protein powder
- 3 tbsp hulled hemp seeds

Directions:

- Add all ingredients into the bowl and stir until well combined.
- Serve and enjoy.

Nutritional Value (Amount per Serving): Calories 220; Fat 12.5 g; Carbohydrates 9.5 g; Sugar 0.1 g; Protein 17.6 g; Cholesterol 0 mg;

Classic Cabbage Slaw

Total Time: 20 minutesServes: 3
Ingredients:

- 4 cups green cabbage, shredded
- 2 garlic cloves
- 1 tbsp sesame oil
- 2 tbsp tamari
- 1 tsp vinegar
- 1 tsp chili paste
- ½ cup macadamia nuts, chopped

Directions:

- Toss shredded green cabbage in a pan with chili paste, sesame oil, vinegar, and tamari on medium-low heat.
- Add garlic and cook for 5 minutes or until cabbage is softened.
- Stir everything well. Add macadamia nuts and cook for 5 minutes.
- Stir well and serve.

Nutritional Value (Amount per Serving): Calories 240; Fat 21.8 g; Carbohydrates 10.5 g; Sugar 4.7 g; Protein 4.5 g; Cholesterol 1 mg;

Coconut Creamy Pumpkin Porridge

Serves: 4 / Preparation time: 6 minutes / Cooking time: 14 minutes

3 cups chopped pumpkin	½ teaspoon garlic
2 cups water	½ teaspoon thyme
½ cup coconut milk	2 tablespoons chopped parsley
¼ cup extra virgin olive oil	2 tablespoons coconut flakes
¼ teaspoon pepper	¼ cup chopped roasted almonds

- Preheat an oven to 250°F (121°C) and line a baking tray with aluminum foil.
- Toss the pumpkin cubes with extra virgin olive oil then spread on the prepared baking tray.
- Bake the pumpkin until tender then remove from the oven. Set aside.
- Pour water into a pot then season with pepper, garlic, and thyme. Bring to boil.
- Once it is boiled, add baked pumpkin to the pot and pour coconut milk over the pumpkin. Bring to a simmer.
- Once it is done, remove the cooked pumpkin and the gravy from heat then transfer to a blender. Blend until smooth and becoming porridge.
- Pour the creamy pumpkin to a serving bowl then sprinkle coconut flakes and roasted almonds on top.
- Garnish with fresh parsley then serve immediately.
- Enjoy warm.

Per Serving: Net Carbs: 7.2g; Calories: 265; Total Fat: 25.9g; Saturated Fat: 9.4g
Protein: 3.3g; Carbs: 9.5g; Fiber: 2.3g; Sugar: 2.7g - Fat 88% / Protein 2% / Carbs 10%

Healthy Chia-Almond Pudding

Total Time: 10 minutes - Serves: 2
Ingredients:

- ½ tsp vanilla extract
- ¼ tsp almond extract
- 2 tbsp ground almonds
- 1 ½ cups unsweetened almond milk
- ¼ cup chia seeds

Directions:

- Add chia seeds in almond milk and soak for 1 hour.
- Add chia seed and almond milk into the blender.
- Add remaining ingredients to the blender and blend until smooth and creamy.
- Serve and enjoy.

Nutritional Value (Amount per Serving): Calories 138; Fat 10.2 g; Carbohydrates 6 g; Sugar 0.5 g; Protein 5.1 g; Cholesterol 0 mg;

Perfect Brussels sprout and Cheese

Serves: 2 / Preparation time: 3 minutes / Cooking time: 20 minutes

¾ cup Brussels sprouts	1-tablespoon extra virgin olive oil

¼ teaspoon salt   ¼ cup grated Mozzarella cheese

- Cut the Brussels sprouts into halves then place in a bowl.
- Drizzle extra virgin olive oil over the Brussels sprouts then sprinkle salt on top. Toss to combine.
- Preheat an Air Fryer to 375°F (191°C).
- Transfer the seasoned Brussels sprouts to the Air Fryer then cook for 15 minutes.
- After 15 minutes, open the Air Fryer and sprinkle grated Mozzarella cheese over the cooked Brussels sprouts.
- Cook the Brussels sprouts in the Air Fryer for 5 minutes or until the Mozzarella cheese is melted.
- Once it is done, remove from the Air Fryer then transfer to a serving dish.
- Serve and enjoy with tomato sauce if you like.

Per Serving: Net Carbs: 3.3g; Calories: 224; Total Fat: 18.1g; Saturated Fat: 6.8g
Protein: 10.1g; Carbs: 4.5g; Fiber: 1.2g; Sugar: 0.7g - Fat 73% / Protein 18% / Carbs 9%

Chia Cinnamon Smoothie

Total Time: 5 minutes - Serves: 1
Ingredients:

- 2 scoops vanilla protein powder
- 1 tbsp chia seeds
- ½ tsp cinnamon
- 1 tbsp coconut oil
- ½ cup water
- ½ cup unsweetened coconut milk

Directions:

- Add all ingredients into the blender and blend until smooth and creamy.
- Serve immediately and enjoy.

Nutritional Value (Amount per Serving): Calories 397; Fat 23.9 g; Carbohydrates 13.4 g; Sugar 0 g; Protein 31.6 g; Cholesterol 0 mg;

Avocado Almond Cabbage Salad

Total Time: 15 minutes - Serves: 3
Ingredients:

- 3 cups savoy cabbage, shredded
- ½ cup blanched almonds
- 1 avocado, chopped
- ¼ tsp pepper
- ¼ tsp sea salt
- For dressing:
- 1 tsp coconut aminos
- ½ tsp Dijon mustard
- 1 tbsp lemon juice
- 3 tbsp olive oil
- Pepper
- Salt

Directions:

- In a small bowl, mix together all dressing ingredients and set aside.
- Add all salad ingredients to the large bowl and mix well.
- Pour dressing over salad and toss well.
- Serve immediately and enjoy.

Nutritional Value (Amount per Serving): Calories 317; Fat 14.1 g; Carbohydrates 39.8 g; Sugar 9.3 g; Protein 11.6 g; Cholesterol 0 mg;

Cinnamon Muffins

Total Time: 25 minutes - Serves: 20
Ingredients:

- ½ cup coconut oil, melted
- ½ cup pumpkin puree
- ½ cup almond butter
- 1 tbsp cinnamon
- 1 tsp baking powder
- 2 scoops vanilla protein powder
- ½ cup almond flour

Directions:

- Preheat the oven to 180 C/ 350 F.
- Spray muffin tray with cooking spray and set aside.
- Add all dry ingredients into the large bowl and mix well.
- Add wet ingredients and mix until well combined. Pour batter into the prepared muffin tray and bake in preheated oven for 15 minutes.
- Serve and enjoy.

Nutritional Value (Amount per Serving): Calories 80; Fat 7.1 g; Carbohydrates 1.6 g; Sugar 0.4 g; Protein 3.5 g; Cholesterol 0 mg;

Healthy Spinach Green Smoothie

Total Time: 5 minutes - Serves: 1
Ingredients:

- 1 cup ice cube
- 2/3 cup water
- ½ cup unsweetened almond milk
- 5 drops liquid stevia
- ½ tsp matcha powder
- 1 tsp vanilla extract
- 1 tbsp MCT oil
- ½ avocado
- 2/3 cup spinach

Directions:

- Add all ingredients into the blender and blend until smooth and creamy.
- Serve immediately and enjoy.

Nutritional Value (Amount per Serving): Calories 167; Fat 18.3 g; Carbohydrates 3.8 g; Sugar 0.6 g; Protein 1.6 g; Cholesterol 0 mg;

Green Veggie Salad with Brown Cashew Sauce

Serves: 4 / Preparation time: 5 minutes / Cooking time: 7 minutes

2 cups chopped spinach

½ cup chopped long beans

1 cup chopped cabbage

½ cup beans sprouts

¼ cup shredded carrots

2 tablespoons extra virgin olive oil

1-teaspoon minced garlic

¼ cup roasted cashews

½ cup coconut milk

2 teaspoons red chili flakes

2 tablespoons coconut aminos

- Preheat a steamer over medium heat then alternately steam the vegetables.

- Remove the steamed vegetables then arrange on a serving dish. Set aside.

- Place the roasted cashews in a blender then pour coconut milk into the blender. Blend until smooth then set aside.

- Preheat a skillet over medium heat then pour olive oil into it.

- Stir in minced garlic then sauté until lightly golden brown and aromatic.

- Pour cashews and coconut milk mixture into the skillet then season with red chili flakes. Bring to a simmer.
- Once it is done, pour the cashews sauce over the steamed vegetables then drizzle coconut aminos on top.
- Serve and enjoy immediately.

Per Serving: Net Carbs: 6.6g; Calories: 172; Total Fat: 15.2g; Saturated Fat: 7.5g
Protein: 2.8g; Carbs: 8.8g; Fiber: 2.2g; Sugar: 3.7g - Fat 80% / Protein 5% / Carbs 15%

Asparagus Mash

Total Time: 20 minutesServes: 2
Ingredients:

- 10 asparagus shoots, chopped
- 1 tsp lemon juice
- 2 tbsp fresh parsley
- 2 tbsp coconut cream
- 1 small onion, diced
- 1 tbsp coconut oil
- Pepper
- Salt

Directions:

- Sauté onion in coconut oil until onion is softened.
- Blanch chopped asparagus in hot water for 2 minutes and drain immediately.
- Add sautéed onion, lemon juice, parsley, coconut cream, asparagus, pepper, and salt into the blender and blend until smooth.
- Serve warm and enjoy.

Nutritional Value (Amount per Serving): Calories 125; Fat 10.6 g; Carbohydrates 7.5 g; Sugar 3.6 g; Protein 2.6 g; Cholesterol 0 mg;

Cheesy Mushroom Slices

Serves: 8 / Preparation time: 30 minutes / Cooking time: 12 minutes

2 cups chopped mushrooms	2 tablespoons butter
2 eggs	½ teaspoon pepper
¾ cup almond flour	¼ teaspoon salt
½ cup grated cheddar cheese	

- Place butter in a microwave-safe bowl then melt the butter.
- Place chopped mushrooms in a food processor then add eggs, almond flour, and cheddar cheese.
- Season with salt and pepper then pour melted butter into the food processor. Process until mixed.
- Transfer to a silicone loaf pan then spread evenly.
- Preheat an Air Fryer to 375°F (191°C).
- Place the loaf pan on the Air Fryer's rack then cook for 15 minutes.
- Once it is done, remove from the Air Fryer then let it cool.
- Cut the mushroom loaf into slices then serve.
- Enjoy!

Per Serving: Net Carbs: 3.5g; Calories: 365; Total Fat: 34.6g; Saturated Fat: 21.1g
Protein: 10.4g; Carbs: 4.4g; Fiber: 0.9g; Sugar: 0.6g - Fat 85% / Protein 11% / Carbs 4%

Creamy Garlic Onion Soup

Total Time: 45 minutes - Serves: 4

Ingredients:

- 1 onion, sliced
- 4 cups vegetable stock
- 1 1/2 tbsp olive oil
- 1 shallot, sliced
- 2 garlic clove, chopped
- 1 leek, sliced
- Salt

Directions:

- Add stock and olive oil in a saucepan and bring to boil.
- Add remaining ingredients and stir well.
- Cover and simmer for 25 minutes.
- Puree the soup using an immersion blender until smooth.
- Stir well and serve warm.

Nutritional Value (Amount per Serving): Calories 90; Fat 7.4 g; Carbohydrates 10.1 g; Sugar 4.1 g; Protein 1 g; Cholesterol 0 mg;

Super Simple Vegetables Salad

Serves: 4 / Preparation time: 4 minutes / Cooking time: 7 minutes

¾ cup chopped red tomatoes

1 cucumber

½ cup chopped green bell pepper

½ cup chopped onion

¼ cup pitted Kalamata olives

¼ cup extra virgin olive oil

2 tablespoons red vinegar

¼ cup mayonnaise

½ teaspoon oregano

- Cut the cucumber into thin slices then place in a salad bowl.
- Next, add chopped red tomatoes, chopped green bell pepper, chopped onion, and kalamata olives to the salad bowl then drizzle extra virgin olive oil and red vinegar over the vegetables. Toss to combine.
- Once it is done, transfer the salad to a serving dish then drizzle mayonnaise and sprinkle oregano on top.
- Serve and enjoy!

Per Serving: Net Carbs: 6.3g; Calories: 300; Total Fat: 29.6g; Saturated Fat: 12.8g
Protein: 3.3g; Carbs: 8.3g; Fiber: 2g; Sugar: 2.2g - Fat 91% / Protein 1% / Carbs 8%

Avocado Mint Soup

Total Time: 10 minutes - Serves: 2
Ingredients:

- 1 medium avocado, peeled, pitted, and cut into pieces
- 1 cup coconut milk
- 2 romaine lettuce leaves
- 20 fresh mint leaves
- 1 tbsp fresh lime juice
- 1/8 tsp salt

Directions:

- Add all ingredients into the blender and blend until smooth. Soup should be thick not as a puree.
- Pour into the serving bowls and place in the refrigerator for 10 minutes.
- Stir well and serve chilled.

Nutritional Value (Amount per Serving): Calories 268; Fat 25.6 g; Carbohydrates 10.2 g; Sugar 0.6 g; Protein 2.7 g; Cholesterol 0 mg;

Spinach in Cheese Envelopes

Serves: 8 / Preparation time: 30 minutes / Cooking time: 12 minutes

3-cups cream cheese

1-½ cup coconut flour

3 egg yolks

2 eggs

½ cup cheddar cheese

2 cups steamed spinach

¼ teaspoon salt

½ teaspoon pepper

¼ cup chopped onion

- Place cream cheese in a mixing bowl then whisk until soft and fluffy.
- Add egg yolks to the mixing bowl then continue whisking until incorporated.
- Stir in coconut flour to the cheese mixture then mix until becoming a soft dough.
- Place the dough on a flat surface then roll until thin.
- Cut the thin dough into 8 squares then set aside.
- Crack the eggs then place in a bowl.
- Season with salt, pepper, and grated cheese then mix well.
- Add chopped spinach and onion to the egg mixture then stir until combined.
- Put spinach filling on a square dough then fold until becoming an envelope. Repeat with the remaining spinach filling and dough. Glue with water.
- Preheat an Air Fryer to 425°F (218°C).
- Arrange the spinach envelopes in the Air Fryer then cook for 12 minutes or until lightly golden brown.
- Remove from the Air Fryer then serve warm. Enjoy!

Per Serving: Net Carbs: 3.5g; Calories: 365; Total Fat: 34.6g; Saturated Fat: 21.1g
Protein: 10.4g; Carbs: 4.4g; Fiber: 0.9g; Sugar: 0.6g - Fat 85% / Protein 11% / Carbs 4%

Mustard Green Beans

Total Time: 20 minutes - Serves: 4
Ingredients:

- 1 lb green beans, washed and trimmed
- 1 tsp whole grain mustard
- 1 tbsp olive oil

- 2 tbsp apple cider vinegar
- 1/4 cup onion, chopped
- 1/8 tsp pepper
- 1/4 tsp salt

Directions:

- Steam green beans in microwave until tender.
- Meanwhile, in a pan heat olive oil over medium heat.
- Add onion in a pan sauté until softened.
- Add water, apple cider vinegar, and mustard in the pan and stir well.
- Add green beans and stir to coat and heat through. Season green beans with pepper and salt.
- Serve and enjoy.

Nutritional Value (Amount per Serving): Calories 71; Fat 3.7 g; Carbohydrates 8.9 g; Sugar 1.9 g; Protein 2.1 g; Cholesterol 0 mg;

Ginger Avocado Kale Salad

Total Time: 15 minutes - Serves: 4
Ingredients:

- 1 avocado, peeled and sliced

- 1 tbsp ginger, grated
- 1/2 lb kale, chopped

- 1/4 cup parsley, chopped
- 2 fresh scallions, chopped

Directions:
- Add all ingredients into the mixing bowl and toss well.
- Serve and enjoy.

Nutritional Value (Amount per Serving): Calories 139; Fat 9.9 g; Carbohydrates 12 g; Sugar 0.5 g; Protein 3 g; Cholesterol 0 mg;

Sautéed Brussels sprouts

Total Time: 25 minutes - Serves: 6

Ingredients:
- 2 lbs Brussels sprouts, remove stems and shred Brussels sprouts
- 2 oz onion, minced
- 3 garlic cloves, minced
- 1 1/2 tbsp olive oil
- Pepper
- Salt

Directions:
- Heat olive oil in a pan over medium heat.
- Add onion and garlic and sauté for 5 minutes.
- Add Brussels sprouts and sauté over medium-high heat for 5-7 minutes. Season with pepper and salt.
- Serve and enjoy.

Nutritional Value (Amount per Serving): Calories 76; Fat 3 g; Carbohydrates 11 g; Sugar 2.8 g; Protein 4 g; Cholesterol 0 mg;

Carrot Omelet with Avocado Topping

Serves: 4 / Preparation time: 6 minutes / Cooking time: 8 minutes

½ cup grated carrots

½ cup chopped spinach

3 tablespoons coconut flour

½ cup coconut milk

3 tablespoons extra virgin olive oil

2 ripe avocados

½ teaspoon cinnamon

- Cut the avocados into halves then remove the seeds.
- After that, scoop out the avocado flesh then mash until smooth. Set aside.
- Combine coconut flour with coconut milk then stir until incorporated and smooth.
- Add grated carrot and chopped spinach to the mixture then stir until combined.
- Next, preheat a pan over medium heat then pour extra virgin olive oil into the pan.
- Once the oil is hot, pour coconut mixture to the pan then fry until both sides are lightly golden and the omelets cooked trough.
- Place the carrots omelets on a serving dish then top with the avocado topping.
- Sprinkle cinnamon over the avocado then serve.
- Enjoy!

Per Serving: Net Carbs: 6.3g; Calories: 416; Total Fat: 38.8g; Saturated Fat: 13.5g
Protein: 4.3g; Carbs: 18g; Fiber: 11.7g; Sugar: 3g - Fat 84% / Protein 10% / Carbs 6%

Cauliflower Rice Pilaf

Total Time: 25 minutes - Serves: 4

Ingredients:

- 1 lb cauliflower, cut into florets
- 1/4 cup slivered almonds
- 2 oz onion, chopped
- 1 tbsp olive oil
- 1 tbsp parsley, chopped
- 1 garlic clove, minced
- Pepper
- Salt

Directions:

- Add cauliflower florets into the food processor and process until it looks like rice.
- Heat olive oil in a pan over medium heat.
- Add garlic and onion and sauté until onion is softened.
- Add almonds and cook for a minute. Add cauliflower rice and cook until softened.
- Remove pan from heat. Season with pepper and salt.
- Garnish with chopped parsley and serve.

Nutritional Value (Amount per Serving): Calories 100; Fat 6.6 g; Carbohydrates 8.9 g; Sugar 3.6 g; Protein 3.8 g; Cholesterol 0 mg;

Eggplant Salad

Total Time: 45 minutes - Serves: 6

Ingredients:

- 1 lb eggplant, cut into slices
- 1/4 cup olive oil
- 1 tbsp fresh lemon juice
- 1 tbsp parsley, chopped
- 1 tbsp cilantro, chopped
- 1/2 tsp paprika
- 1 tsp ground cumin
- 1 garlic cloves, grated
- 1/2 tsp salt

Directions:

- Preheat the oven to 400 F/ 204 C.
- Coat eggplant slices with 2 tbsp oil.
- Place eggplant slices onto a baking tray and bake in preheated oven for 25 minutes.
- In a bowl, mix together all remaining ingredients and pour over eggplant slices.
- Stir well and serve.

Nutritional Value (Amount per Serving): Calories 94; Fat 8.7 g; Carbohydrates 5 g; Sugar 2.4 g; Protein 0.9 g; Cholesterol 0 mg;

Spicy Eggplant in Coconut Gravy

Serves: 4 / Preparation time: 4 minutes / Cooking time: 14 minutes

2 cups chopped eggplants	1-inch galangal
2 tablespoons extra virgin olive oil	2 lemon grasses
2 cloves garlic	2 bay leaves
2 shallots	1 kaffir lime leaf
¼ cup red chili flakes	1-cup coconut milk

- Place garlic, shallots, and red chili flakes in a food processor then process until smooth.
- Next, preheat a skillet over medium heat then pour olive oil into it.
- Once the oil is hot, stir in the spice mixture then sauté until aromatic.

- Add chopped eggplants to the skillet then season with galangal, lemon grasses, bay leaves, and kaffir lime leaves.
- Pour coconut milk over the eggplants then bring to a simmer.
- Once it is done, transfer the cooked eggplants together with the gravy to a serving dish.
- Serve and enjoy!

Per Serving: Net Carbs: 5.8 g; Calories: 221; Total Fat: 21.5g; Saturated Fat: 13.7g
Protein: 1.9g; Carbs: 8.4g; Fiber: 2.6 g; Sugar: 3.5g - Fat 88% / Protein 2% / Carbs 10%

Chocolate Strawberry Milkshake

Total Time: 5 minutes - Serves: 2
Ingredients:

- 1 cup ice cubes
- ¼ cup unsweetened cocoa powder
- 2 scoops vegan protein powder
- 1 cup strawberries
- 2 cups unsweetened coconut milk

Directions:

- Add all ingredients into the blender and blend until smooth and creamy.
- Serve immediately and enjoy.

Nutritional Value (Amount per Serving): Calories 221; Fat 5.7 g; Carbohydrates 15 g; Sugar 6.8 g; Protein 27.7 g; Cholesterol 0 mg;

Avocado Tofu Scramble

Total Time: 15 minute - Serves: 1
Ingredients:

- 1 tbsp fresh parsley, chopped
- ½ medium avocado
- ½ block firm tofu, drained and crumbled
- ½ cup bell pepper, chopped
- ½ cup onion, chopped
- 1 tsp olive oil
- 1 tbsp water
- ¼ tsp cumin
- ¼ tsp garlic powder
- ¼ tsp paprika
- ¼ tsp turmeric
- 1 tbsp nutritional yeast
- Pepper
- Salt

Directions:

- In a small bowl, mix together nutritional yeast, water, and spices. Set aside.
- Heat olive oil to the pan over medium heat.
- Add onion and bell pepper and sauté for 5 minutes.
- Add crumbled tofu and nutritional yeast to the pan and sauté for 2 minutes.
- Top with parsley and avocado.
- Serve and enjoy.

Nutritional Value (Amount per Serving): Calories 164; Fat 9.7 g; Carbohydrates 15 g; Sugar 6 g; Protein 7.4 g; Cholesterol 0 mg;

Spinach with Coconut Milk

Total Time: 25 minutes - Serves: 6
Ingredients:

- 16 oz spinach
- 2 tsp curry powder
- 13.5 oz coconut milk
- 1 tsp lemon zest
- ½ tsp salt

Directions:

- Add spinach in pan and heat over medium heat. Once it is hot then add curry paste and few tablespoons of coconut milk. Stir well.
- Add remaining coconut milk, lemon zest, and salt and cook until thickened.
- Serve and enjoy.

Nutritional Value (Amount per Serving): Calories 167; Fat 15.6 g; Carbohydrates 6.7 g; Sugar 2.5 g; Protein 3.7 g; Cholesterol 0 mg;

Cauliflower Zucchini Fritters

Total Time: 15 minutes - Serves: 4
Ingredients:

- 3 cups cauliflower florets
- ¼ tsp black pepper
- ¼ cup coconut flour
- 2 medium zucchini, grated and squeezed
- 1 tbsp coconut oil
- ½ tsp sea salt

Directions:

- Steam cauliflower florets for 5 minutes.
- Add cauliflower into the food processor and process until it looks like rice.
- Add all ingredients except coconut oil to the large bowl and mix until well combined.
- Make small round patties from the mixture and set aside.
- Heat coconut oil in a pan over medium heat.
- Place patties on pan and cook for 3-4 minutes on each side.
- Serve and enjoy.

Nutritional Value (Amount per Serving): Calories 68; Fat 3.8 g; Carbohydrates 7.8 g; Sugar 3.6 g; Protein 2.8 g; Cholesterol 0 mg;

Vegetable Tofu Scramble

Total Time: 20 minutes - Serves: 2
Ingredients:

- 1 block firm tofu, drained and crumbled
- ½ tsp turmeric
- ¼ tsp garlic powder
- 1 cup spinach
- 1 red pepper, chopped
- 10 oz mushrooms, chopped
- ½ onion, chopped
- 1 tbsp olive oil
- Pepper
- Salt

Directions:

- Heat olive oil in a large pan over medium heat.
- Add onion, pepper, and mushrooms and sauté until cooked.
- Add crumbled tofu, spices, and spinach. Stir well and cook for 3-5 minutes.
- Serve and enjoy.

Nutritional Value (Amount per Serving): Calories 159; Fat 9.6 g; Carbohydrates 13.7 g; Sugar 7 g; Protein 9.6 g; Cholesterol 0 mg;

Coconut Blackberry Breakfast Bowl

Total Time: 10 minutes - Serves: 2

Ingredients:

- 2 tbsp chia seeds
- ¼ cup coconut flakes
- 1 cup spinach
- ¼ cup water

- 3 tbsp ground flaxseed
- 1 cup unsweetened coconut milk
- 1 cup blackberries

Directions:

- Add blackberries, flaxseed, spinach, and coconut milk into the blender and blend until smooth.
- Fry coconut flakes in pan for 1-2 minutes.
- Pour berry mixture into the serving bowls and sprinkle coconut flakes and chia seeds on top.
- Serve immediately and enjoy.

Nutritional Value (Amount per Serving): Calories 182; Fat 11.4 g; Carbohydrates 14.5 g; Sugar 4.3 g; Protein 5.3 g; Cholesterol 0 mg;

Keto Porridge

Total Time: 10 minutes - Serves: 1
Ingredients:

- ½ tsp vanilla extract
- ¼ tsp granulated stevia
- 1 tbsp chia seeds
- 1 tbsp flaxseed meal
- 2 tbsp unsweetened shredded coconut

- 2 tbsp almond flour
- 2 tbsp hemp hearts
- ½ cup water
- Pinch of salt

Directions:

- Add all ingredients except vanilla extract to a saucepan and heat over low heat until thickened.
- Stir well and serve warm.

Nutritional Value (Amount per Serving): Calories 370; Fat 30.2 g; Carbohydrates 12.8 g; Sugar 1.9 g; Protein 13.5 g; Cholesterol 0 mg;

Zucchini Parmesan Bites

Serves: 4 / Preparation time: 15 minutes / Cooking time: 10 minutes

4 medium zucchinis	2 tablespoons butter
1 cup grated coconuts	½ cup grated Parmesan cheese
1-tablespoon Italian seasoning	1 egg

- Melt butter in a microwave then let it cool.
- Peel the zucchinis then cut into halves.
- Discard the seeds then grate the zucchinis. Place in a bowl.
- Add grated coconuts, Italian seasoning, melted butter, egg, and Parmesan cheese to the bowl. Mix well.
- Shape the zucchini mixture into small balls forms then set aside.
- Preheat an Air Fryer to 400°F (204°C).
- Place a rack in the Air Fryer then arrange the zucchini balls on it.
- Cook the zucchini balls for 10 minutes then remove from heat.
- Serve and enjoy.

Per Serving: Net Carbs: 6.6g; Calories: 225; Total Fat: 17.9g; Saturated Fat: 12.1g
Protein: 9g; Carbs: 10.6g; Fiber: 4g; Sugar: 5g - Fat 71% / Protein 16% / Carbs 13%

Herb Spaghetti Squash

Total Time: minutes - Serves: 4

Ingredients:

- 4 cups spaghetti squash, cooked
- ½ tsp pepper
- ½ tsp sage
- 1 tsp dried parsley
- 1 tsp dried thyme
- 1 tsp dried rosemary
- 1 tsp garlic powder
- 2 tbsp olive oil
- 1 tsp salt

Directions:

- Preheat the oven to 350 F/ 180 C.
- Add all ingredients into the mixing bowl and mix well to combine.
- Transfer bowl mixture to the oven safe dish and cook in preheated oven for 15 minutes.
- Stir well and serve.

Nutritional Value (Amount per Serving): Calories 96; Fat 7.7 g; Carbohydrates 8.1 g; Sugar 0.2 g; Protein 0.9 g; Cholesterol 0 mg;

Basil Tomato Soup

Total Time: 20 minutes - Serves: 6

Ingredients:

- 28 oz can tomatoes
- ¼ cup basil pesto
- ¼ tsp dried basil leaves
- 1 tsp apple cider vinegar
- 2 tbsp erythritol
- ¼ tsp garlic powder
- ½ tsp onion powder
- 2 cups water
- 1 ½ tsp kosher salt

Directions:

- Add tomatoes, garlic powder, onion powder, water, and salt in a saucepan.
- Bring to boil over medium heat. Reduce heat and simmer for 2 minutes.
- Remove saucepan from heat and puree the soup using a blender until smooth.
- Stir in pesto, dried basil, vinegar, and erythritol.
- Stir well and serve warm.

Nutritional Value (Amount per Serving): Calories 30; Fat 0 g; Carbohydrates 12.1 g; Sugar 9.6 g; Protein 1.3 g; Cholesterol 0 mg;

Fresh Berries with Cream

Total Time: 10 minutes - Serves: 1

Ingredients:

- 1/2 cup coconut cream
- 1 oz strawberries
- 1 oz raspberries
- 1/4 tsp vanilla extract

Directions:

- Add all ingredients into the blender and blend until smooth.
- Pour in serving bowl and top with fresh berries.
- Serve and enjoy.

Nutritional Value (Amount per Serving): Calories 303; Fat 28.9 g; Carbohydrates 12 g; Sugar 6.8 g; Protein 3.3 g; Cholesterol 0 mg;

Almond Hemp Heart Porridge

Total Time: 10 minutes - Serves: 2

Ingredients:

- ¼ cup almond flour
- ½ tsp cinnamon
- ¾ tsp vanilla extract
- 5 drops stevia
- 1 tbsp chia seeds

- 2 tbsp ground flax seed
- ½ cup hemp hearts
- 1 cup unsweetened coconut milk

Directions:

- Add all ingredients except almond flour to a saucepan. Stir to combine.
- Heat over medium heat until just starts to lightly boil.
- Once start bubbling then stir well and cook for 1 minute more.
- Remove from heat and stir in almond flour.
- Serve immediately and enjoy.

Nutritional Value (Amount per Serving): Calories 329; Fat 24.4 g; Carbohydrates 9.2 g; Sugar 1.8 g; Protein 16.2 g; Cholesterol 0 mg;

Breakfast Granola

Total Time: 30 minute - Serves: 15
Ingredients:

- 1 tsp ground ginger
- 1 tsp ground cinnamon
- ¼ cups coconut oil, melted
- 1 cup walnuts, chopped

- 2/3 cup pumpkin seeds
- 2/3 cup sunflower seeds
- ½ cup flaxseeds
- 3 cups desiccated coconut

Directions:

- Add all ingredients into the large bowl and toss well.
- Spread granola mixture on a baking tray and bake at 350 F/ 180 C for 20 minutes. Turn granola mixture with a spoon after every 3 minutes.
- Allow to cool completely and serve.

Nutritional Value (Amount per Serving): Calories 208; Fat 17 g; Carbohydrates 11.4 g; Sugar 5.8 g; Protein 4.1 g; Cholesterol 0 mg;

Mushroom Black Pepper in Cabbage Blanket

Serves: 4 / Preparation time: 11 minutes / Cooking time: 22 minutes

2 cups mushroom

3 tablespoons extra virgin olive oil

1 teaspoon minced garlic

½ cup sliced onion

3 tablespoons coconut aminos

2 teaspoons cayenne pepper

¾ cup coconut milk

¼ teaspoon black pepper

¼ lb. cabbage

- Cut the mushroom s into small pieces then set aside.
- Preheat a skillet over medium heat then pour extra virgin olive oil into it.
- Once the olive oil is hot, stir in minced garlic and sliced onion to the skillet then sauté until aromatic and lightly golden brown.
- Next, add mushrooms to the skillet then season with black pepper.
- Pour coconut milk over the mushrooms then cook until the coconut milk is completely absorbed into the mushrooms.
- In the meantime, place the cabbage in the steamer then steam until wilted.

- Remove the steamed cabbage from the steamer and let it cool.

- Next, return back to the mushroom.

- Once the coconut milk is completely absorbed into the mushroom, season with cayenne pepper and coconut aminos then stir well. Remove from heat and let it cool.

- Place a sheet of steamed cabbage on a flat surface then put the cooked mushroom on it.

- Wrap the mushrooms with steamed cabbage and roll it tightly. Repeat with the remaining steamed cabbage and mushrooms.

- Serve and enjoy.

Per Serving: Net Carbs: 7.3g; Calories: 282; Total Fat: 27.3g; Saturated Fat: 11.9g
Protein: 3.2g; Carbs: 9.8g; Fiber: 2.5g; Sugar: 3.8g - Fat 73% / Protein 7% / Carbs 10%

Cinnamon Coconut Pancake

Total Time: 15 minutes - Serves: 1
Ingredients:

- 1/2 cup almond milk
- 1/4 cup coconut flour
- 2 tbsp egg replacer
- 8 tbsp water
- 1 packet stevia
- 1/8 tsp cinnamon
- 1/2 tsp baking powder
- 1 tsp vanilla extract
- 1/8 tsp salt

Directions:

- In a small bowl, mix together egg replacer and 8 tablespoons of water.
- Add all ingredients into the mixing bowl and stir until combined.
- Spray pan with cooking spray and heat over medium heat.
- Pour the desired amount of batter onto hot pan and cook until lightly golden brown.
- Flip pancake and cook for a few minutes more.
- Serve and enjoy.

Nutritional Value (Amount per Serving): Calories 110; Fat 4.3 g; Carbohydrates 10.9 g; Sugar 2.8 g; Protein 7 g; Cholesterol 0 mg;

Avocado Chocó Cinnamon Smoothie

Total Time: 5 minutes - Serves: 1
Ingredients:

- ½ tsp coconut oil
- 5 drops liquid stevia
- ¼ tsp vanilla extract
- 1 tsp ground cinnamon
- 2 tsp unsweetened cocoa powder
- ½ avocado
- ¾ cup unsweetened coconut milk

Directions:

- Add all ingredients into the blender and blend until smooth and creamy.
- Serve immediately and enjoy.

Nutritional Value (Amount per Serving): Calories 95; Fat 8.3 g; Carbohydrates 5.1 g; Sugar 0.2 g; Protein 1.2 g; Cholesterol 0 mg;

Roasted Asparagus with Creamy Cashew Topping

Serves: 4 / Preparation time: 6 minutes / Cooking time: 14 minutes

½ lb. asparagus	1-tablespoon sesame oil
2 tablespoons extra virgin olive oil	¼ cup coconut milk
½ teaspoon black pepper	2 tablespoons lemon juice
¼ cup butter	2 teaspoons minced garlic
¼ cup roasted cashews	2 tablespoons coconut aminos

- Preheat an oven to 425°F (218°C) and line a baking tray with parchment paper. Set aside.
- Cut and trim the end of the asparagus then drizzle olive oil over the asparagus.
- Rub the asparagus with black pepper then spread over the prepared baking tray.
- Once the oven is ready, place the baking tray in the oven and bake the asparagus for approximately 15 minutes or until tender.
- In the meantime, place roasted cashew, butter, minced garlic, and coconut aminos in a food processor then pour sesame oil, coconut milk, and lemon juice over the cashews. Process until smooth then set aside.
- When the roasted asparagus is done, take it out of the oven and transfer to a serving dish.
- Drizzle cashew sauce over the roasted asparagus then serve warm.
- Enjoy!

Per Serving: Net Carbs: 6.3g; Calories: 300; Total Fat: 29.6g; Saturated Fat: 12.8g
Protein: 3.3g; Carbs: 8.3g; Fiber: 2g; Sugar: 2.2g - Fat 88% / Protein 4% / Carbs 8%

Delicious Cabbage Steaks

Total Time: 1 hour 10 minutes - Serves: 6
Ingredients:

- 1 medium cabbage head, slice 1" thick
- 2 tbsp olive oil
- 1 tbsp garlic, minced
- Pepper
- Salt

Directions:

- In a small bowl, mix together garlic and olive oil.
- Brush garlic and olive oil mixture onto both sides of sliced cabbage.
- Season cabbage slices with pepper and salt.
- Place cabbage slices onto a baking tray and bake at 350 F/ 180 C for 1 hour. Turn after 30 minutes.
- Serve and enjoy.

Nutritional Value (Amount per Serving): Calories 72; Fat 4.8 g; Carbohydrates 7.4 g; Sugar 3.8 g; Protein 1.6 g; Cholesterol 0 mg;

Fresh Green in Red Curry Gravy

Serves: 4 / Preparation time: 4 minutes / Cooking time: 16 minutes

2 cups broccoli florets	2 tablespoons extra virgin olive oil
1 cup chopped spinach	¼ cup chopped onion
1 cup chopped kale	2 teaspoons minced garlic
2 tablespoons chopped celeries	1-teaspoon ginger

1-teaspoon red curry paste   ½ cup water

¾ cup coconut milk

- Preheat a skillet over medium heat then pour extra virgin olive oil into it.

- Once the oil is hot, stir in chopped onion and minced garlic then sauté until lightly golden brown and aromatic.

- Next, pour water into the skillet then season with ginger and red curry paste. Bring to boil.

- Once it is boiled, stir in broccoli florets, chopped spinach, and chopped kale to the skillet then pour coconut milk over the vegetables. Bring to a simmer.

- Once it is done, remove the vegetable curry from heat and transfer to a serving bowl.

- Serve and enjoy warm.

Per Serving: Net Carbs: 6.4g; Calories: 201; Total Fat: 18.4g; Saturated Fat: 10.6g
Protein: 3.3g; Carbs: 9.3g; Fiber: 2.9g; Sugar: 2.7g - Fat 82% / Protein 5% / Carbs 13%

Cauliflower Radish Salad

Total Time: 15 minutes - Serves: 4
Ingredients:

- 12 radishes, trimmed and chopped
- 1 tsp dried dill
- 1 tsp Dijon mustard
- 1 tbsp cider vinegar
- 1 tbsp olive oil

- 1 cup parsley, chopped
- ½ medium cauliflower head, trimmed and chopped
- ½ tsp black pepper
- ¼ tsp sea salt

Directions:

- In a mixing bowl, combine together cauliflower, parsley, and radishes.
- In a small bowl, whisk together olive oil, dill, mustard, vinegar, pepper, and salt.
- Pour dressing over salad and toss well.
- Serve immediately and enjoy.

Nutritional Value (Amount per Serving): Calories 58; Fat 3.8 g; Carbohydrates 5.6 g; Sugar 2.1 g; Protein 2.1 g; Cholesterol 0 mg;

Cauliflower Couscous

Total Time: 25 minutes - Serves: 4
Ingredients:

- 1 head cauliflower, cut into florets
- 14 black olives
- 1 garlic cloves, chopped
- 14 oz can artichokes

- 2 tbsp olive oil
- 1/4 cup parsley, chopped
- 1 lemon juice
- 1/2 tsp pepper
- 1/2 tsp salt

Directions:

- Preheat the oven to 400 F/ 200 C.
- Add cauliflower florets into the food processor and process until it looks like rice.
- Spread cauliflower rice on a baking tray and drizzle with olive oil. Bake in preheated oven for 12 minutes.
- In a bowl, mix together garlic, lemon juice, artichokes, parsley, and olives.
- Add cauliflower to the bowl and stir well. Season with pepper and salt.

* Serve and enjoy.

Nutritional Value (Amount per Serving): Calories 116; Fat 8.8 g; Carbohydrates 8.4 g; Sugar 3.3 g; Protein 3.3 g; Cholesterol 0 mg;

Cauliflower Florets in Curly Egg

Serves: 2 / Preparation time: 3 minutes / Cooking time: 20 minutes

2 cups cauliflower florets	3 eggs
3 teaspoons minced garlic	½ teaspoon pepper
½ teaspoon salt	¼ cup grated Mozzarella cheese
½ teaspoon coriander	2 tablespoons tomato puree

2 cups water

* Place minced garlic, salt, and coriander in a container then pour water into it. Stir until the seasoning is completely dissolved.
* Add the cauliflower florets to the brine then submerge for at least 30 minutes.
* After 30 minutes, remove the cauliflower florets from the brine then wash and rinse them. Pat them dry.
* Preheat an Air Fryer to 400°F (204°C).
* Crack the eggs then place in a bowl.
* Season with pepper then whisk until incorporated.
* Dip a cauliflower floret in the egg then place in the air fryer. Repeat with the remaining cauliflower florets and egg.
* Cook the cauliflower florets for 12 minutes or until lightly golden and the egg is curly.
* Sprinkle grated Mozzarella cheese then drizzle tomato puree on top.
* Cook the cauliflower florets again for another 5 minutes then remove from the Air Fryer.
* Transfer to a serving dish then serve. Enjoy warm.

Per Serving: Net Carbs: 3.9g; Calories: 276; Total Fat: 21.8g; Saturated Fat: 9.6g
Protein: 13.8g; Carbs: 5.4g; Fiber: 1.5g; Sugar: 1.5g - Fat 71% / Protein 20% / Carbs 9%

Roasted Squash

Total Time: 1 hour 10 minutes - Serves: 3
Ingredients:

* 2 lbs summer squash, cut into 1-inch pieces
* 1/8 tsp pepper
* 1/8 tsp garlic powder
* 3 tbsp olive oil
* 1 large lemon juice
* 1/8 tsp paprika
* Pepper
* Salt

Directions:

* Preheat the oven to 400 F/ 204 C.
* Spray a baking tray with cooking spray.
* Place squash pieces onto the prepared baking tray and drizzle with olive oil.
* Season with paprika, pepper, and garlic powder.
* Squeeze lemon juice over the squash and bake in preheated oven for 50-60 minutes.
* Serve hot and enjoy.

Nutritional Value (Amount per Serving): Calories 182; Fat 15 g; Carbohydrates 12.3 g; Sugar 11 g; Protein 3.2 g; Cholesterol 0 mg;

Fried Okra

Total Time: 20 minutes - Serves: 4
Ingredients:

- 1 lb fresh okra, cut into ¼"
  slices
- 1/3 cup almond meal
- Pepper
- Salt
- Oil for frying

Directions:

- Heat oil in large pan over medium-high heat.
- In a bowl, mix together sliced okra, almond meal, pepper, and salt until well coated.
- Once the oil is hot then add okra to the hot oil and cook until lightly browned.
- Remove fried okra from pan and allow to drain on paper towels.
- Serve and enjoy.

Nutritional Value (Amount per Serving): Calories 91; Fat 4.2 g; Carbohydrates 10.2 g; Sugar 10.2 g; Protein 3.9 g; Cholesterol 0 mg;

Tomato Avocado Cucumber Salad

Total Time: 10 minutes - Serves: 4
Ingredients:

- 1 cucumber, sliced
- 2 avocado, chopped
- ½ onion, sliced
- 2 tomatoes, chopped
- 1 bell pepper, chopped
- For dressing:
- 2 tbsp cilantro
- ¼ tsp garlic powder
- 2 tbsp olive oil
- 1 tbsp lemon juice
- ½ tsp black pepper
- ½ tsp salt

Directions:

- In a small bowl, mix together all dressing ingredients and set aside.
- Add all salad ingredients into the large mixing bowl and mix well.
- Pour dressing over salad and toss well.
- Serve immediately and enjoy.

Nutritional Value (Amount per Serving): Calories 130; Fat 9.8 g; Carbohydrates 10.6 g; Sugar 5.1 g; Protein 2.1 g; Cholesterol 0 mg;

Light Sour Soup with Kabocha

Serves: 4 / Preparation time: 8 minutes / Cooking time: 6 minutes

1 cup chopped Kabocha

½ cup chopped long beans

¼ cup chopped carrots

¾ cup chopped cabbage

½ cup pecans

1-tablespoon extra virgin olive oil

½ teaspoon minced garlic

1-teaspoon sliced shallot

1-teaspoon red chili flakes

¼ cup chopped green tomatoes

3 cups water

- Pour water into a pot then bring to boil.
- Once it is boiled, add pecans to the pot then cook the pecans until tender.

- Remove the pecans from the pot and strain the water. Set aside.

- Next, preheat a pot over medium heat then pour olive oil into the pot.

- Once the oil is hot, stir in minced garlic and sliced shallots then sauté until aromatic and lightly golden.

- Pour water into the pot then season with red chili flakes. Bring to boil.

- Once it is boiled, reduce the heat and add kabocha, long beans, carrots, cabbages, pecans, and chopped green tomatoes to the pot. Cook for approximately 3 minutes or until the vegetables are tender.

- Transfer the soup to a serving bowl then serve immediately.

- Enjoy warm.

Per Serving: Net Carbs: 5.4g; Calories: 104; Total Fat: 8.3g; Saturated Fat: 0.9g
Protein: 1.6g; Carbs: 7g; Fiber: 1.6g; Sugar: 2.7g - Fat 72% / Protein 8% / Carbs 20%

Creamy Celery Soup

Total Time: 40 minutes - Serves: 4
Ingredients:

- 6 cups celery
- ½ tsp dill
- 2 cups water
- 1 cup coconut milk
- 1 onion, chopped
- Pinch of salt

Directions:

- Add all ingredients into the instant pot and stir well.
- Cover instant pot with lid and select soup setting.
- Release pressure using quick release method than open the lid.
- Puree the soup using an immersion blender until smooth and creamy.
- Stir well and serve warm.

Nutritional Value (Amount per Serving): Calories 174; Fat 14.6 g; Carbohydrates 10.5 g; Sugar 5.2 g; Protein 2.8 g; Cholesterol 0 mg;

Tomato Asparagus Salad

Total Time: 20 minutes - Serves: 4
Ingredients:

- 1/2 lb asparagus, trimmed and cut into pieces
- 8 oz cherry tomatoes, halved
- For dressing:
- 1/4 tsp garlic and herb seasoning blend
- 1 tbsp vinegar
- 1 tbsp shallot, minced
- 1 garlic clove, minced
- 1 tbsp water
- 2 tbsp olive oil

Directions:

- Add 1 tablespoon of water and asparagus in a heatproof bowl and cover with cling film and microwave for 2 minutes.
- Remove asparagus from bowl and place into ice water until cool.
- Add asparagus and tomatoes into a medium bowl.
- In a small bowl, mix together all remaining ingredients and pour over vegetables.
- Toss vegetables well and serve.

Nutritional Value (Amount per Serving): Calories 85; Fat 7.2 g; Carbohydrates 5.1 g; Sugar 2.6 g; Protein 1.9 g; Cholesterol 0 mg;

Fried Green Beans Rosemary

Serves: 2 / Preparation time: 3 minutes / Cooking time: 5 minutes

¾ cup chopped green beans

3 teaspoons minced garlic

2 tablespoons rosemary

½ teaspoon salt

1-tablespoon butter

- Preheat an Air Fryer to 390°F (200°C).
- Place the chopped green beans in the Air Fryer then brush with butter.
- Sprinkle salt, minced garlic, and rosemary over the green beans then cook for 5 minutes.
- Once the green beans are done, remove from the Air Fryer then place on a serving dish.
- Serve and enjoy warm.

Per Serving: Net Carbs: 2.5g; Calories: 72; Total Fat: 6.3g; Saturated Fat: 3.9g
Protein: 0.7g; Carbs: 4.5g; Fiber: 2g; Sugar: 0.2g - Fat 79% / Protein 7% / Carbs 14%

Spicy Jalapeno Brussels sprouts

Total Time: 15 minutes - Serves: 4
Ingredients:

- 1 lb Brussels sprouts
- 1 medium onion, chopped
- 1 tbsp olive oil

- 1 jalapeno pepper, seeded and chopped
- Pepper
- Salt

Directions:

- Heat olive oil in a pan over medium heat.
- Add onion and jalapeno in the pan and sauté until softened.
- Add Brussels sprouts and stir until golden brown, about 10 minutes.
- Season with pepper and salt.
- Serve and enjoy.

Nutritional Value (Amount per Serving): Calories 91; Fat 3.9 g; Carbohydrates 13.1 g; Sugar 3.7 g; Protein 4.2 g; Cholesterol 0 mg;

Asian Cucumber Salad

Total Time: 10 minutes - Serves: 6
Ingredients:

- 4 cups cucumbers, sliced
- ¼ tsp red pepper flakes
- ½ tsp sesame oil
- 1 tsp sesame seeds

- ¼ cup rice wine vinegar
- ¼ cup red pepper, diced
- ¼ cup onion, sliced
- ½ tsp sea salt

Directions:

- Add all ingredients into the mixing bowl and toss well.
- Serve immediately and enjoy.

Nutritional Value (Amount per Serving): Calories 27; Fat 0.7 g; Carbohydrates 3.5 g; Sugar 1.6 g; Protein 0.7 g; Cholesterol 0 mg;

Scrumptious Zucchini Noodles with Avocado Pecans Sauce

Serves: 4 / Preparation time: 4 minutes / Cooking time: 14 minutes

4 medium zucchinis	½ cup roasted pecans
2 tablespoons extra virgin olive oil	2 teaspoons minced garlic
1 fresh avocado	2 tablespoons lemon juice
1-cup fresh basil leaves	¼ cup water

- Cut the avocado into halves then remove the seed.
- Scoop out the avocado flesh then place in a blender.
- Add fresh basil leaves and roasted pecans to the blender then season with minced garlic and lemon juice.
- Pour water into the blender then blend until smooth. Set aside.
- Peel the zucchinis then cut into halves lengthwise.
- Using a julienne peeler cut the zucchini into noodles form then set aside.
- Next, preheat a skillet over medium heat then pour olive oil into it.
- Once the oil is hot, stir in the zucchini noodles and mix well.
- Sauté the zucchini until wilted then remove from heat. Transfer to a salad bowl.
- Drizzle avocado pecans sauce over the zucchini noodles then toss to combine.
- Serve and enjoy.

Per Serving: Net Carbs: 6.2g; Calories: 249; Total Fat: 22.5g; Saturated Fat: 3.6g
Protein: 4.3g; Carbs: 12.6g; Fiber: 6.4g; Sugar: 4.1g - Fat 81% / Protein 9% / Carbs 10%

Almond Coconut Porridge

Total Time: 10 minutes - Serves: 2
Ingredients:

- ¾ cup unsweetened almond milk
- ½ tsp vanilla extract
- 1 ½ tbsp ground flaxseed
- 3 tbsp ground almonds
- 6 tbsp unsweetened shredded coconut
- Pinch of sea salt

Directions:

- Add almond milk in microwave safe bowl and microwave for 2 minutes.
- Add remaining ingredients and stir well and cook for 1 minute.
- Top with fresh berries and serve.

Nutritional Value (Amount per Serving): Calories 197; Fat 17.4 g; Carbohydrates 8.3 g; Sugar 0.6 g; Protein 4.2 g; Cholesterol 0 mg;

Healthy Veggie Rolls with Dill Sauce

Serves: 4 / Preparation time: 4 minutes / Cooking time: 12 minutes

4 fresh collard green leaves	¼ cup cherry tomatoes
1 cucumber	½ cup almond yogurt
½ red bell pepper	¾ teaspoon garlic powder
¼ cup diced onion	½ teaspoon vinegar
1 tablespoon sliced olives	2 tablespoons extra virgin olive oil

5 sprigs fresh dill   ¼ teaspoon pepper

- Combine almond yogurt with garlic powder, vinegar, olive oil, fresh dill, and pepper in a blender then blend until smooth. Set aside.
- Peel the cucumber and remove the seeds.
- Using a julienne peeler cut the cucumber into noodle forms then set aside. Do the same thing with the bell pepper.
- Arrange collard green leaves on a flat surface then spread the almond yogurt mixture over the leaves.
- After that, arrange cucumber noodles and bell pepper noodles on the leaves then sprinkle diced onion, sliced olives, and cherry tomatoes on top.
- Carefully roll the leaves then cut into halves.
- Arrange the rolls on a serving dish then serve. Enjoy!

Per Serving: Net Carbs: 6.9g; Calories: 111; Total Fat: 8.6g; Saturated Fat: 1.1g
Protein: 1.9g; Carbs: 8.8g; Fiber: 1.9g; Sugar: 3.8g - Fat 70% / Protein 5% / Carbs 25%

Mushroom Asparagus

Total Time: 10 minutes - Serves: 4
Ingredients:

- 1 lb asparagus, trimmed and cut into pieces
- 1/4 cup water
- 12 mushrooms, sliced
- 3 tbsp olive oil
- Pepper
- Salt

Directions:

- Heat oil in a large pan over medium heat.
- Add mushroom and salt and sauté for 1 minute or until mushroom is golden brown.
- Remove mushrooms to plate and add asparagus season with pepper and salt.
- Cook asparagus for 2 minutes or until softened.
- Remove from heat and mix with mushrooms.
- Serve and enjoy.

Nutritional Value (Amount per Serving): Calories 124; Fat 10.8 g; Carbohydrates 6.2 g; Sugar 3.1 g; Protein 4.2 g; Cholesterol 0 mg;

Baked Asparagus

Total Time: 25 minutes - Serves: 4
Ingredients:

- 40 asparagus spears
- 2 tbsp vegetable seasoning
- 2 tbsp garlic powder
- 2 tbsp salt

Directions:

- Preheat the oven to 450 F/ 232 C.
- Arrange all asparagus spears on baking tray and season with vegetable seasoning, garlic powder, and salt.
- Place in preheated oven and bake for 20 minutes.
- Serve warm and enjoy.

Nutritional Value (Amount per Serving): Calories 75; Fat 0.9 g; Carbohydrates 13.5 g; Sugar 5.5 g; Protein 6.7 g; Cholesterol 0 mg;

Delicious Tofu Fries

Total Time: 50 minutes - Serves: 4
Ingredients:

- 15 oz firm tofu, drained, pressed and cut into long strips
- ¼ tsp garlic powder
- ¼ tsp onion powder
- ¼ tsp cayenne pepper
- ¼ tsp paprika
- ½ tsp oregano
- ½ tsp basil
- 2 tbsp olive oil
- Pepper
- Salt

Directions:

- Preheat the oven to 190 C/ 375 F.
- Add all ingredients into the large mixing bowl and toss well.
- Place marinated tofu strips on a baking tray and bake in preheated oven for 20 minutes.
- Turn tofu strips to other side and bake for another 20 minutes.
- Serve and enjoy.

Nutritional Value (Amount per Serving): Calories 137; Fat 11.5 g; Carbohydrates 2.3 g; Sugar 0.8 g; Protein 8.8 g; Cholesterol 0 mg;

Lemon Garlic Mushrooms

Total Time: 25 minutes - Serves: 4
Ingredients:

- 3 oz enoki mushrooms
- 1 tbsp olive oil
- 1 tsp lemon zest, chopped
- 2 tbsp lemon juice
- 3 garlic cloves, sliced
- 6 oyster mushrooms, halved
- 5 oz cremini mushrooms, sliced
- 1/2 red chili, sliced
- 1/2 onion, sliced
- 1 tsp sea salt

Directions:

- Heat olive oil in a pan over high heat.
- Add shallots, enoki mushrooms, oyster mushrooms, cremini mushrooms, and chili.
- Stir well and cook over medium-high heat for 10 minutes.
- Add lemon zest and stir well. Season with lemon juice and salt and cook for 3-4 minutes.
- Serve and enjoy.

Nutritional Value (Amount per Serving): Calories 87; Fat 5.6 g; Carbohydrates 7.5 g; Sugar 1.8 g; Protein 3 g; Cholesterol 8 mg;

DESSERT RECIPES

Quick Chocó Brownie

Total Time: 10 minutes - Serves: 1
Ingredients:

- 1/4 cup almond milk
- 1 tbsp cocoa powder
- 1 scoop chocolate protein powder
- 1/2 tsp baking powder

Directions:

- In a microwave-safe mug blend together baking powder, protein powder, and cocoa.
- Add almond milk in a mug and stir well.
- Place mug in microwave and microwave for 30 seconds.
- Serve and enjoy.

Nutritional Value (Amount per Serving): Calories 207; Fat 15.8 g; Carbohydrates 9.5 g; Sugar 3.1 g; Protein 12.4 g; Cholesterol 20 mg;

Avocado Chocolate Creamy Pudding

Serves: 4 / Preparation time: 9 minutes / Cooking time: 13 minutes

2 ripe avocados

2-½ tablespoons cocoa powder

½ teaspoon cinnamon

2 tablespoons coconut milk

- Cut the avocados into halves then discard the seeds.
- Scoop out the avocado flesh then place in a food processor.
- Add cocoa powder to the food processor then pour coconut milk into the food processor. Process until smooth.
- Divide the mixture into 4 and put into the serving pots.
- Once it is done, sprinkle cinnamon on top then serve.
- Enjoy!

Per Serving: Net Carbs: 6.7g; Calories: 236; Total Fat: 20.7g; Saturated Fat: 3.1g
Protein: 12.1g; Carbs: 11.6g; Fiber: 4.9g; Sugar: 4.1g - Fat 85% / Protein 10% / Carbs 5%

Chocolate Fudge

Total Time: 10 minutes - Serves: 12
Ingredients:

- 4 oz unsweetened dark chocolate
- 3/4 cup coconut butter

- 15 drops liquid stevia
- 1 tsp vanilla extract

Directions:

- Melt coconut butter and dark chocolate.
- Add ingredients to the large bowl and combine well.
- Pour mixture into a silicone loaf pan and place in refrigerator until set.
- Cut into pieces and serve.

Nutritional Value (Amount per Serving): Calories 157; Fat 14.1 g; Carbohydrates 6.1 g; Sugar 1 g; Protein 2.3 g; Cholesterol 0 mg;

Strawberry Almond Pie

Serves: 4 / Preparation time: 10 minutes / Cooking time: 12 minutes

½ cup almond flour

¼ cup butter

1 egg yolk

1-cup fresh strawberries

¼ cup coconut cream

1 egg

- Place butter and egg yolk in a mixing bowl then using an electric mixer beat until smooth.
- Add almond flour to the butter then using a wooden spatula mix until becoming dough.
- Place the dough 4 silicon pie pans then set aside.

- Next, place fresh strawberries in a blender then pour coconut cream into the blender.
- Add egg to the blender then blend until smooth.
- Pour the strawberry filling into the piecrust then spread evenly.
- Preheat an Air Fryer to 350°F (177°C).
- Arrange the pie pans in the Air Fryer then cook for 12 minutes.
- Once it is done, remove from the Air Fryer then let them cool.
- Serve and enjoy.

Per Serving: Net Carbs: 3.2g; Calories: 197; Total Fat: 19.2g; Saturated Fat: 11.3g
Protein: 3.5g; Carbs: 4.6g; Fiber: 1.4g; Sugar: 2.5g - Fat 88% / Protein 7% / Carbs 3.2%

Lemon Mousse

Total Time: 10 minutes - Serves: 2
Ingredients:

- 14 oz coconut milk
- 12 drops liquid stevia
- 1/2 tsp lemon extract
- 1/4 tsp turmeric

Directions:

- Place coconut milk can in the refrigerator for overnight. Scoop out thick cream into a mixing bowl.
- Add remaining ingredients to the bowl and whip using a hand mixer until smooth.
- Transfer mousse mixture to a zip-lock bag and pipe into small serving glasses. Place in refrigerator.
- Serve chilled and enjoy.

Nutritional Value (Amount per Serving): Calories 444; Fat 45.7 g; Carbohydrates 10 g; Sugar 6 g; Protein 4.4 g; Cholesterol 0 mg;

Almond Savory Cookies

Serves: 4 / Preparation time: 19 minutes / Cooking time: 11 minutes

1 cup almond flour

2 eggs

¼ cup almond butter

½ cup chopped roasted almonds

2 tablespoons extra virgin olive oil

- Preheat an oven to 350°F (177°C) and line a small baking tray with parchment paper. Set aside.
- Place almond butter and eggs in a mixing bowl then using an electric mixer beat until smooth and fluffy.
- Pour extra virgin olive oil into the batter then stir well. Remove the electric mixer.
- Add almond flour to the batter then using a wooden spatula mix until combined.
- Take a small scoop of batter then drop on the prepared baking tray. Repeat with the remaining batter.
- Sprinkle chopped roasted almonds on top then bake for approximately 10 minutes or until set and the top of the cookies is lightly golden brown.
- Once it is done, remove the cookies from the oven and transfer to a cooling rack.
- When the cookies are cool, arrange them in a jar with a lid then serve.
- Enjoy.

Per Serving: Net Carbs: 2.1g; Calories: 206; Total Fat: 19.5g; Saturated Fat: 2.5g
Protein: 7g; Carbs: 4.2g; Fiber: 2.1g; Sugar: 0.9g - Fat 85% / Protein 11% / Carbs 4%

Coconut Peanut Butter Fudge

Total Time: 1 hour 15 minutes - Serves: 20
Ingredients:

- 12 oz smooth peanut butter
- 3 tbsp coconut oil
- 4 tbsp coconut cream
- 15 drops liquid stevia
- Pinch of salt

Directions:

- Line baking tray with parchment paper.
- Melt coconut oil in a saucepan over low heat.
- Add peanut butter, coconut cream, stevia, and salt in a saucepan. Stir well.
- Pour fudge mixture into the prepared baking tray and place in refrigerator for 1 hour.
- Cut into pieces and serve.

Nutritional Value (Amount per Serving): Calories 125; Fat 11.3 g; Carbohydrates 3.5 g; Sugar 1.7 g; Protein 4.3 g; Cholesterol 0 mg;

Cinnamon Chocolate Churros

Serves: 6 / Preparation time: 10 minutes / Cooking time: 8 minutes

¼ cup butter

½ cup warm water

½ cup almond flour

2 eggs

2 ½ teaspoons cinnamon

¼ cup semi-sweet chocolate chips

2 tablespoons almond milk

- Place water and butter in a saucepan then bring to boil.
- Once it is boiled, add almond flour to the saucepan then stir until becoming a soft dough.
- Wait until the dough is soft then add eggs to the dough.
- Using an electric mixer mix until fluffy.
- Transfer the fluffy dough to a piping bag then set aside.
- Preheat an Air Fryer to 380°F (193°C).
- Pipe several pieces of 3-inch-long dough in the Air Fryer then cook for 10 minutes.
- Remove the churros from the Air Fryer then repeat with the remaining dough.
- Meanwhile, place semi-sweet chocolate chips in a microwave-safe bowl. Melt the butter in the microwave.
- Pour almond milk into the melted chocolate then stir until incorporated.
- Arrange the churros on a serving dish then drizzle melted chocolate over the churros.
- Sprinkle cinnamon on top then serve.
- Enjoy.

Per Serving: Net Carbs: 3.4g; Calories: 194; Total Fat: 18.3g; Saturated Fat: 10.2g
Protein: 4.1g; Carbs: 5g; Fiber: 1.6g; Sugar: 2.8g - Fat 85% / Protein 8% / Carbs 7%

Chocó Chia Pudding

Total Time: 10 minutes - Serves: 6
Ingredients:

- 2 1/2 cups coconut milk
- 2 scoops stevia extract powder
- 6 tbsp cocoa powder
- 1/2 cup chia seeds
- 1/2 tsp vanilla extract

- 1/8 cup xylitol
- 1/8 tsp salt

Directions:
- Add all ingredients into the blender and blend until smooth.
- Pour mixture into the glass container and place in refrigerator.
- Serve chilled and enjoy.

Nutritional Value (Amount per Serving): Calories 259; Fat 25.4 g; Carbohydrates 10.2 g; Sugar 3.5 g; Protein 3.8 g; Cholesterol 0 mg;

Cheesy Pumpkin Balls

Serves: 4 / Preparation time: 12 minutes / Cooking time: 22 minutes

1-cup cream cheese

½ cup pumpkin puree

¾ cup almond butter

1-cup coconut flour

½ teaspoon pumpkin spice

¼ teaspoon ground clove

¼ teaspoon nutmeg

1-tablespoon extra virgin olive oil

- Preheat an oven to 350°F (177°C) and line a baking tray with parchment paper.
- Place cream cheese in a mixing bowl then using an electric mixer beat until soft.
- Add almond butter together with pumpkin spice, ground clove, and nutmeg to the mixing bowl then beat until fluffy.
- Stir in pumpkin puree to the mixture then mix until incorporated. Remove the electric mixer.
- After that, add coconut flour to the mixture then using a wooden spatula mix until becoming dough.
- Shape the dough into small balls then arrange on the prepared baking tray.
- Brush the top of the balls with extra virgin olive oil then bake for approximately 20 minutes or until done and cooked through.
- Once it is done, remove the balls from the oven and place on the cooling rack.
- When the cookies are cool, transfer to a serving dish then serve.
- Enjoy!

Per Serving: Net Carbs: 4.4g; Calories: 278; Total Fat: 26g; Saturated Fat: 13.9g
Protein: 5.9g; Carbs: 6.6g; Fiber: 2.4g; Sugar: 1.5g - Fat 85% / Protein 9% / Carbs 6%

Lemon Chocolate Cookies

Serves: 4 / Preparation time: 15 minutes / Cooking time: 5 minutes

1 cup almond flour

6 tablespoons butter

4 tablespoons Stevia

1 egg yolk

½ cup semi-sweet chocolate chips

- Place butter and stevia in a mixing bowl then using an electric mixer beat until fluffy.
- Add egg yolk to the bowl then continue beating until incorporated.
- Stir almond flour into the mixture then using a wooden spatula mix until becoming dough.
- Add chocolate chips to the dough then mix until just combined.
- Preheat an Air Fryer to 180°F (82°C).
- Shape the dough into small ball forms then arrange in the Air Fryer.

- Press the cookie balls until becoming coin forms then cook in the Air Fryer for 5 minutes.
- Once it is done, remove from the Air Fryer then place on a cooling rack. Let them cool.
- Serve and enjoy.

Per Serving: Net Carbs: 5.4g; Calories: 246; Total Fat: 23.9g; Saturated Fat: 12.6g
Protein: 2.9g; Carbs: 6.7g; Fiber: 1.3g; Sugar: 4.8g - Fat 87% / Protein 5% / Carbs 8%

Very Berry Nutty Crumbles

Serves: 4 / Preparation time: 12 minutes / Cooking time: 16 minutes

1-tablespoon extra virgin olive oil

1 cup chopped almonds

1-cup fresh strawberries

½ cup chopped pecans

½ cup fresh blueberries

2 tablespoons almond butter

¼ cup fresh blackberries

1 ½ teaspoon cinnamon

¼ cup fresh raspberries

- Preheat an oven to 400°F (204°C) and prepare a casserole dish.
- Preheat a skillet over medium heat then pour olive oil into it.
- Stir in strawberries, blueberries, blackberries, and raspberries then cook until softened.
- Transfer the softened berries to the prepared casserole dish then spread evenly.
- Place chopped almonds and pecans into a food processor then add butter to the food processor. Process until smooth.
- Put the nut mixture into a plastic then pipe over the berries.
- Sprinkle cinnamon on top then place in the oven. Bake for 10 minutes or until crispy on top.
- Once it is done, remove the casserole dish from the oven and let it cool.
- Serve and enjoy.

Per Serving: Net Carbs: 6.9g; Calories: 264; Total Fat: 22.5g; Saturated Fat: 4.8g
Protein: 8.1g; Carbs: 11.4g; Fiber: 4.5g; Sugar: 5.2g - Fat 77% / Protein 13% / Carbs 10%

Avocado Pudding

Total Time: 10 minutes - Serves: 8
Ingredients:

- 2 ripe avocados, peeled, pitted and cut into pieces
- 1 tbsp fresh lime juice
- 14 oz can coconut milk
- 80 drops of liquid stevia
- 2 tsp vanilla extract

Directions:

- Add all ingredients into the blender and blend until smooth.
- Serve and enjoy.

Nutritional Value (Amount per Serving): Calories 317; Fat 30.1 g; Carbohydrates 9.3 g; Sugar 0.4 g; Protein 3.4 g; Cholesterol 0 mg;

Delicious Vanilla Mug Cake

Serves: 1 / Preparation time: 15 minutes / Cooking time: 15 minutes

3 tablespoons coconut flour

2 tablespoons stevia

1 egg

1-½ tablespoons butter

1-½ tablespoons sour cream

½ teaspoon cinnamon

¼ teaspoon vanilla

- Place butter in an Air Fryer-safe mug then melt the microwave.
- Add stevia, egg, coconut flour, sour cream, cinnamon, and vanilla to the mug then stir until smooth. Remove as many lumps as possible.
- Preheat an Air Fryer to 375°F (191°C).
- Place the mug cake in the Air Fryer then cook for 10 minutes.
- After 10 minutes, increase the temperature to 400°F (204°C) and cook for another 5 minutes.
- Once it is done, remove from the Air Fryer then enjoy warm.

Per Serving: Net Carbs: 1.2g; Calories: 228; Total Fat: 21.2g; Saturated Fat: 10.4g
Protein: 7.3g; Carbs: 3.1g; Fiber: 1.2g; Sugar: 0.7g - Fat 83% / Protein 13% / Carbs 4%

Cheesy Pumpkin Puree

Serves: 4 / Preparation time: 4 minutes / Cooking time: 12 minutes

1-cup pumpkin puree

1 cup almond butter

2 tablespoons almond flour

¼ cup coconut milk

2 tablespoons chopped roasted pecans

½ cup grated cheddar cheese

- Preheat an oven to 250°F (121°C) and line a baking tray with parchment paper.
- Spread the almond flour over the baking tray then roast for 5 minutes.
- Remove the almond flour from the oven and let it cool.
- Combine pumpkin puree, almond butter, and almond flour in a bowl then mix well.
- Pour coconut milk over the mixture then stir until incorporated.
- After that, add chopped roasted pecans to the mixture then mix until just combined.
- Divide the mixture into 4 cups then sprinkle grated cheddar cheese on top.
- Refrigerate the dessert for at least an hour before serving then enjoy cold!

Per Serving: Net Carbs: 3.1g; Calories: 140; Total Fat: 11.6g; Saturated Fat: 6.4g
Protein: 5.5g; Carbs: 4.8g; Fiber: 1.7g; Sugar: 1.8g - Fat 75% / Protein 16% / Carbs 9%

Almond Coconut Cheesecake

Serves: 8 / Preparation time: 10 minutes / Cooking time: 8 minutes

¾ cup almond flour

¾ cup coconut flour

½ cup grated coconut

¾ cup butter

3 cups cream cheese

1-cup sour cream

5 tablespoons Stevia

4 eggs

1 teaspoon lemon zest

- Prepare a spring-form pan that fits the Air Fryer.

- Melt butter in a microwave then combine with almond flour, coconut flour, and grated coconut. Mix until becoming dough.
- Place the dough in the prepared spring-form pan then spread evenly.
- Press to the bottom of the spring-form pan then store in the fridge.
- Meanwhile, place cream cheese in a mixing bowl then using an electric mixer beat the cream cheese until soft and fluffy.
- Add sour cream, stevia, eggs, and lemon zest to the bowl then beat again until incorporated and fluffy.
- Remove the spring-form pan from the fridge then pour the filling over the base. Spread evenly.
- Preheat an Air Fryer to 180°F (82°C).
- Place the spring-form pan in the Air Fryer then cook for 15 minutes.
- Remove the cheesecake from the Air Fryer then let it cool.
- Once the cheesecake is cool, store in the fridge for at least 6 hours.
- Serve and enjoy cold.

Per Serving: Net Carbs: 3.5g; Calories: 463; Total Fat: 46.8g; Saturated Fat: 28.8g
Protein: 8.3g; Carbs: 4.7g; Fiber: 1.2g; Sugar: 0.8g - Fat 91% / Protein 7% / Carbs 2%

Crispy Broccoli Bites with Cheese

Serves: 4 / Preparation time: 12 minutes / Cooking time: 13 minutes

1 ½ cups broccoli florets

¾ cup almond flour

½ cup grated cheese

2 eggs

½ teaspoon pepper

½ cup extra virgin olive oil, to fry

¼ cup mayonnaise

- Place broccoli florets in a food processor then process until smooth.
- Add almond flour, grated cheese, and eggs to the food processor then season with pepper. Process until becoming dough.
- Take about a tablespoon of dough then shape into small ball form. Repeat with the remaining dough.
- Next, preheat a frying pan over medium heat then pour olive oil into it.
- Once the oil is hot, put the broccoli bites into the frying pan and fry until all sides of the balls are lightly golden brown.
- Remove the broccoli bites from the frying pan and strain the excessive oil.
- Arrange the fried broccoli bites on a serving dish then serve with mayonnaise.
- Enjoy!

Per Serving: Net Carbs: 5.9g; Calories: 404; Total Fat: 39.7g; Saturated Fat: 8.2g
Protein: 8.5g; Carbs: 7.4g; Fiber: 1.5g; Sugar: 2g - Fat 88% / Protein 6% / Carbs 6%

Cinnamon Pumpkin Muffins

Serves: 4 / Preparation time: 10 minutes / Cooking time: 6 minutes

½ cup almond flour

1 ½ tablespoons cinnamon

¼ cup butter

½ cup pumpkin puree

¼ cup almond oil

- Melt butter over low heat then combine with almond oil and pumpkin puree. Stir until incorporated.

- In another bowl, combine almond flour and cinnamon then mix well.
- Pour the liquid mixture into the dry mixture then stir until smooth and combine.
- Divide the batter into 4-muffin cups then set aside.
- Preheat an Air Fryer to 350°F (177°C).
- Arrange the muffin in the preheated Air Fryer then set the time to 6 minutes. Cook the muffins.
- Once it is done, remove the muffins out of the Air Fryer then let them cool.
- Serve and enjoy.

Per Serving: Net Carbs: 2.7g; Calories: 259; Total Fat: 27g; Saturated Fat: 8.6g
Protein: 1.3g; Carbs: 5.3g; Fiber: 2.6g; Sugar: 1.2g - Fat 94% / Protein 2% / Carbs 4%

Smooth Chocolate Mousse

Total Time: 10 minutes - Serves: 2
Ingredients:

- 1/2 tsp cinnamon
- 3 tbsp unsweetened cocoa powder
- 1 cup creamed coconut milk
- 10 drops liquid stevia

Directions:

- Place coconut milk can in the refrigerator for overnight; it should get thick and the solids separate from water.
- Transfer thick part into the large mixing bowl without water.
- Add remaining ingredients to the bowl and whip with electric mixer until smooth.
- Serve and enjoy.

Nutritional Value (Amount per Serving): Calories 296; Fat 29.7 g; Carbohydrates 11.5 g; Sugar 4.2 g; Protein 4.4 g; Cholesterol 0 mg;

Avocado Cinnamon Walnuts Cups

Serves: 4 / Preparation time: 10 minutes / Cooking time: 15 minutes

2 ripe avocados

¼ cup chopped roasted walnuts

2 tablespoons butter

½ teaspoon cinnamon

- Cut the avocados into halves then discard the seeds. Set aside.
- Combine butter with walnuts and cinnamon then fill the avocado hole with the butter mixture.
- Preheat an Air Fryer to 350°F (177°C).
- Place a rack in the Air Fryer then arrange the filled avocados on it.
- Cook the avocados for 15 minutes then remove from the Air Fryer.
- Let the Avocados cool for a few minutes then serve.
- Enjoy!

Per Serving: Net Carbs: 2.2g; Calories: 279; Total Fat: 27.5g; Saturated Fat: 8g
Protein: 2.4g; Carbs: 9.3g; Fiber: 7.1g; Sugar: 0.6g - Fat 89% / Protein 3% / Carbs 8%

Almond Cheesy Cookie Dough

Serves: 4 / Preparation time: 14 minutes / Cooking time: 4 minutes

1 cup almond flour

½ cup almond butter

1 tablespoon flax seed

2 tablespoons water

1-cup cheese cream

- Preheat an oven to 225°F (107°C) and line a baking tray with parchment paper.
- Spread almond flour over the baking tray then toast for a few minutes until just lightly golden.
- In the meantime, combine flax seeds with 2 tablespoons of water then stir well. Set aside.
- Once the almond flour is done, remove from the oven and let it cool.
- Next, place almond butter and cheese cream in a mixing bowl then using an electric mixer beat until smooth and fluffy.
- Add flax seed mixture to the bowl batter then mix well. Remove the electric mixer.
- After that, stir in toasted almond flour to the batter then using a wooden spatula mix until becoming dough.
- Shape the dough into small balls form then arrange on a baking tray.
- Refrigerate the balls for at least 2 hours or until set.
- Enjoy as dessert whenever you want.

Per Serving: Net Carbs: 2.5g; Calories: 264; Total Fat: 25.4g; Saturated Fat: 13.2g
Protein: 6.6g; Carbs: 3.9g; Fiber: 1.4g; Sugar: 0.5g - Fat 87% / Protein 9% / Carbs 4%

Avocado Sticks with Garlic Butter

Serves: 6 / Preparation time: 10 minutes / Cooking time: 8 minutes

2 avocados	¼ teaspoon salt
1-cup almond flour	1-cup butter
2 teaspoons black pepper	2 teaspoons minced garlic
4 egg yolks	¼ cup chopped parsley
1-½ tablespoons water	1-tablespoon lemon juice

- Place butter in a mixing bowl then add minced garlic, chopped parsley, and lemon juice to the bowl.
- Using an electric mixer mix until smooth and fluffy.
- Transfer the garlic butter to a container with a lid then store in the fridge.
- Peel the avocados then cut into wedges. Set aside.
- Place the egg yolks in a bowl then pour water into it.
- Season with salt and black pepper then stir until incorporated.
- Take an avocado wedge then roll in the almond flour.
- Dip in the egg mixture then return back to the almond flour. Roll until the avocado wedge is completely coated. Repeat with the remaining avocado wedges.
- Preheat an Air Fryer to 400°F (204°C).
- Arrange the coated avocado wedges in the Air Fryer basket then cook for 8 minutes or until golden.
- Remove from the Air Fryer then arrange on a serving dish.
- Serve with garlic butter then enjoy right away.

Per Serving: Net Carbs: 2.9g; Calories: 340; Total Fat: 33.8g; Saturated Fat: 13.8g
Protein: 4.5g; Carbs: 8.2g; Fiber: 5.3g; Sugar: 0.7g - Fat 90% / Protein 5% / Carbs 5%

Raspberry Chia Pudding

Total Time: 3 hours 10 minutes - Serves: 2
Ingredients:

- 4 tbsp chia seeds
- 1 cup coconut milk

- 1/2 cup raspberries

Directions:

- Add raspberry and coconut milk in a blender and blend until smooth.
- Pour mixture into the Mason jar.
- Add chia seeds in a jar and stir well.
- Close jar tightly with lid and shake well.
- Place in refrigerator for 3 hours.
- Serve chilled and enjoy.

Nutritional Value (Amount per Serving): Calories 361; Fat 33.4 g; Carbohydrates 13.3 g; Sugar 5.4 g; Protein 6.2 g; Cholesterol 0 mg;

Coconut Lemon Cake

Serves: 4 / Preparation time: 11 minutes / Cooking time: 19 minutes

1-cup coconut flour	¼ cup lemon juice
¼ cup almond flour	1-teaspoon grated lemon zest
¼ cup extra virgin olive oil	¼ cup coconut flakes
4 eggs	

- Preheat an oven to 350°F (177°C) and line a small baking pan with parchment paper. Set aside.
- Place coconut flour, almond flour, and grated lemon zest in a mixing bowl then add the eggs to the bowl.
- Using an electric mixer mix until smooth and fluffy.
- Next, pour lemon juice to the bowl then beat until incorporated.
- Remove the electric mixer then add coconut flakes to the bowl. Using a wooden spatula mix until just combined.
- Transfer the batter to the prepared baking pan and spread evenly.
- Place the baking pan in the oven and bake for approximately 15 minutes or until a toothpick that is inserted to the cake comes out clean.
- Once it is done, remove the cake from the oven and let it cool for a few minutes.
- Take the cake out of the baking pan and cut into slices.
- Arrange the sliced cakes on a serving dish and serve.
- Enjoy.

Per Serving: Net Carbs: 1.9g; Calories: 230; Total Fat: 21.5g; Saturated Fat: 5.5g
Protein: 6.7g; Carbs: 3.9g; Fiber: 2g; Sugar: 1.3g - Fat 84% / Protein 13% / Carbs 3%

Super Cheesy Soufflé

Serves: 4 / Preparation time: 10 minutes / Cooking time: 6 minutes

1-cup cream cheese	¼ cup grated Parmesan cheese
4 eggs	3 tablespoons almond flour
½ cup heavy cream	1-cup cheddar cheese cubes
2 tablespoons butter, melted	

- Crack the eggs then place the egg yolks and egg whites in separate bowls.
- Add cream cheese and heavy cream to the egg yolks then using an electric mixer beat until smooth and fluffy.
- Stir in almond flour, melted butter, and Parmesan cheese to the cheese mixture then using a wooden spatula mix until combined.
- Using an electric mixer beat the egg whites until soft peak.
- Add the beaten egg whites to the cheese mixture then mix until incorporated.
- After that, add cheese cubes to the mixture then stir until just combined.
- Divide the cheesecake mixture into 2 ramekins then spread evenly.
- Preheat an Air Fryer to 325°F (163°C).
- Place a rack in the Air Fryer then arrange the ramekins on it.
- Cook the soufflés for 15 minutes then remove from the Air Fryer.
- Let the soufflés cool and enjoy cold.

Per Serving: Net Carbs: 2.1g; Calories: 351; Total Fat: 32.2g; Saturated Fat: 19.4g
Protein: 14.6g; Carbs: 2.1g; Fiber: 0g; Sugar: 0.4g - Fat 83% / Protein 17% / Carbs 2.1%

Simple Almond Butter Fudge

Total Time: 15 minutes - Serves: 8
Ingredients:

- 1/2 cup almond butter
- 15 drops liquid stevia
- 2 1/2 tbsp coconut oil

Directions:

- Combine together almond butter and coconut oil in a saucepan. Gently warm until melted.
- Add stevia and stir well.
- Pour mixture into the candy container and place in refrigerator until set.
- Serve and enjoy.

Nutritional Value (Amount per Serving): Calories 43; Fat 4.8 g; Carbohydrates 0.2 g; Protein 0.2 g; Sugars 0 g; Cholesterol 0 mg;

Sweet Date in Savory White Pond

Serves: 4 / Preparation time: 12 minutes / Cooking time: 14 minutes

1-cup coconut flour

1-tablespoon chopped date

1-cup coconut milk

- Preheat a steamer over medium heat then wait until it is ready.
- Prepare 4 aluminum muffin cups then set aside.
- Next, combine coconut flour with coconut milk then stir until smooth and incorporated.
- After that, divide the mixture into 4 prepared aluminum muffin cups then sprinkle chopped date on top.
- Arrange the muffin cups in the steamer and steam for approximately 15 minutes or until set.
- Once it is done, remove from the steamer and arrange on a serving dish.
- Serve and enjoy.

Per Serving: Net Carbs: 3.8g; Calories: 151; Total Fat: 14.6g; Saturated Fat: 12.9g
Protein: 1.7g; Carbs: 5.9g; Fiber: 2.1g; Sugar: 3.5g - Fat 87% / Protein 3% / Carbs 10%

Nutty Coconut Bars

Serves: 8 / Preparation time: 10 minutes / Cooking time: 10 minutes

¼ cup coconut oil	2 tablespoons chopped roasted almonds
½ cup butter	2 tablespoons chopped roasted walnuts
½ cup coconut flour	2 tablespoons chopped roasted pecans
½ cup grated coconut	½ teaspoon cinnamon

- Preheat an Air Fryer to 350°F (177°C).
- Combine the entire ingredients in a bowl then stir until incorporated.
- Transfer the mixture to the Air Fryer pan then spread evenly.
- Cook for 10 minutes then turn the Air Fryer off.
- Remove from the Air Fryer then cut into bars.
- Let the bars cool then enjoy.

Per Serving: Net Carbs: 1.1g; Calories: 253; Total Fat: 27.3g; Saturated Fat: 15.4g
Protein: 1.9g; Carbs: 2.9g; Fiber: 1.8g; Sugar: 0.8g - Fat 97% / Protein 2% / Carbs 1%

Almond Butter Brownies

Total Time: 30 minutes - Serves: 4
Ingredients:

- 1 scoop protein powder
- 2 tbsp cocoa powder
- 1/2 cup almond butter, melted
- 1 cup bananas, overripe

Directions:

- Preheat the oven to 350 F/ 176 C.
- Spray brownie tray with cooking spray.
- Add all ingredients into the blender and blend until smooth.
- Pour batter into the prepared dish and bake in preheated oven for 20 minutes.
- Serve and enjoy.

Nutritional Value (Amount per Serving): Calories 82; Fat 2.1 g; Carbohydrates 11.4 g; Protein 6.9 g; Sugars 5 g; Cholesterol 16 mg;

Strawberry Cheesy Pie

Serves: 4 / Preparation time: 12 minutes / Cooking time: 16 minutes

¾ cup almond flour	½ cup fresh strawberries
¼ cup almond butter	2 tablespoons goat cheese
1 egg	½ cup almond yogurt

- Preheat an oven to 350°F (177°C) and coat a pie pan with cooking spray. Set aside.
- Next, place almond butter and egg in a mixing bowl then using an electric mixer beat until just combined. Remove the electric mixer.
- Add almond flour to the mixture then using a wooden spatula mix until becoming dough.
- Place the dough in the prepared pie pan then press on the bottom and sides.
- Once the oven is ready, place the pie in the oven and bake for approximately 10 minutes or until the top of the pie is lightly golden brown. Remove from oven and let it cool.
- Place fresh strawberries in the food processor then process until smooth. Set aside.

- After that, combine the goat cheese with almond yogurt and stir until combined.
- Once the pie is cool, spread strawberries over the pie and top with the goat cheese mixture.
- Store the pie in the refrigerator for at least 2 hours before serving.
- Enjoy cold!

Per Serving: Net Carbs: 6.7g; Calories: 236; Total Fat: 20.7g; Saturated Fat: 3.1g
Protein: 12.1g; Carbs: 11.6g; Fiber: 4.9g; Sugar: 4.1g - Fat 79% / Protein 11% / Carbs 10%

HOW TO USE RECIPE TAGS IN THIS COOKBOOK

Look for the following tags next to recipe titles to help you choose meals that are appropriate for your schedule, budget, and dietary needs.

[FA] Fast (less than 30 mins total prep time + cooking time)

[F] Frugal (whole meal costs $5 or less)

[GF] Gluten Free

[SF] Sugar Free

The "Dirty Dozen" And "Clean 15"

The Environmental Working Group (EWG) publishes annual lists of produce containing the highest and lowest levels of pesticide residue. The lists are based on analyzing data from the USDA Pesticide Data Program report.

The EWG found that a majority (70%) of the 48 different kinds of produce tested contained some residue of at least one type of pesticide. Overall they found 178 different kinds of pesticides. This pesticide residue can remain on produce despite washing and peeling. Every kind of pesticide is toxic for people and ingesting them can cause damage to the immune system, reproductive system, nervous system, cancer, and more. Pregnant women may harm the health and development of the unborn baby as a result of consuming pesticide residue.

Keep these facts in mind when you are selecting produce and deciding whether to buy organic.

THE DIRTY DOZEN

- Celery
- Pears
- Spinach
- Strawberries
- Apples
- Nectarines
- Peaches
- Grapes
- Cherries
- Sweet bell peppers
- Tomatoes
- Potatoes

THE CLEAN 15

- Eggplant
- Cauliflower
- Sweet corn
- Pineapples
- Avocados
- Onions
- Cabbage
- Frozen sweet peas
- Asparagus
- Papayas
- Mangoes
- Honeydew
- Cantaloupe
- Kiwi
- Grapefruit

Measurement Conversion Tables

Volume Equivalents (Dry)

US Standard	Metric (Approx.)
¼ teaspoon	1 ml
½ teaspoon	2 ml
1 teaspoon	5 ml
1 tablespoon	15 ml
¼ cup	59 ml
½ cup	118 ml
1 cup	235 ml

Weight Equivalents

US Standard	Metric (Approx.)
½ ounce	15 g
1 ounce	30 g
2 ounces	60 g
4 ounces	115 g
8 ounces	225 g
12 ounces	340 g
16 oz or 1 lb	455 g

Volume Equivalents (Liquid)

US Standard	US Standard (ounces)	Metric (Approx.)
2 tablespoons	1 fl oz	30 ml
¼ cup	2 fl oz	60 ml
½ cup	4 fl oz	120 ml
1 cup	8 fl oz	240 ml
1 ½ cups	12 fl oz	355 ml
2 cups or 1 pint	16 fl oz	475 ml
4 cups or 1 quart	32 fl oz	1 L
1 gallon	128 fl oz	4 L

Oven Temperatures

Fahrenheit (F)	Celsius (C) (Approx)
250°F	120°C
300°F	150°C
325°F	165°C
350°F	180°C
375°F	190°C
400°F	200°C
425°F	220°C
450°F	230°C

Made in the USA
Lexington, KY
29 March 2019